NEW ESSAYS ON DIDEROT

The great eighteenth-cen̶̶̶̶̶̶̶̶̶̶̶̶̶̶̶̶̶̶̶̶ ̶̶̶̶̶̶̶̶̶̶̶̶Denis Diderot (1713–84) once compared himself to a weathervane, by which he meant that his mind was in constant motion. In an extraordinarily diverse career he produced novels, plays, art criticism, works of philosophy and poetics; he also reflected on music and opera. Perhaps most famously, he ensured the publication of the *Encyclopédie*, which has often been credited with hastening the onset of the French Revolution. Known as one of the three greatest *philosophes* of the Enlightenment, Diderot rejected the Christian ideas in which he had been raised. Instead, he became an atheist and a determinist. His radical questioning of received ideas and established religion led to a brief imprisonment; for that reason, no doubt, some of his subsequent works were written for posterity. This collection of essays celebrates the life and work of this extraordinary figure as we approach the tercentenary of his birth.

JAMES FOWLER teaches French at the University of Kent. He has written extensively on the eighteenth-century French novel and French philosophy. His publications include *Voicing Desire: Family and Sexuality in Diderot's Narrative* (2000) and *The Libertine's Nemesis: The Prude in 'Clarissa' and the 'roman libertin'* (2011).

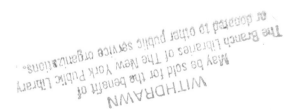

NEW ESSAYS ON DIDEROT

EDITED BY

JAMES FOWLER

CAMBRIDGE
UNIVERSITY PRESS

CAMBRIDGE
UNIVERSITY PRESS

University Printing House, Cambridge CB2 8BS, United Kingdom

Published in the United States of America by Cambridge University Press, New York

Cambridge University Press is part of the University of Cambridge.

It furthers the University's mission by disseminating knowledge in the pursuit of education, learning and research at the highest international levels of excellence.

www.cambridge.org
Information on this title: www.cambridge.org/9781107649606

© Cambridge University Press 2011

First published 2011
First paperback edition 2014

A catalogue record for this publication is available from the British Library

Library of Congress Cataloguing in Publication data
New essays on Diderot / edited by James Fowler.
p. cm
Includes bibliographical references and index.
ISBN 978-0-521-76956-3 (hardback)
1. Diderot, Denis, 1713–1784.   I. Fowler, James (James E.), 1961–   II. Title.
PQ1979.N49   2011
848'.509–dc22
2010044823

ISBN 978-0-521-76956-3 Hardback
ISBN 978-1-107-64960-6 Paperback

In memory of John Lough

Contents

Notes on contributors

TOM BALDWIN teaches French at the University of Kent. His interests include aesthetics and ekphrasis from the eighteenth century to the present. He is author of *The Material Object in the Work of Marcel Proust* (2005) and co-editor, with James Fowler and Shane Weller, of *The Flesh in the Text* (2007). He has recently completed a study entitled *The Picture as Spectre in Diderot, Proust, and Deleuze* (2011).

JOSEPH BREINES studied for his Ph.D. in French Literature at Yale University. His topic was the French novel and philosophy (Diderot, Zola, Sartre). He currently teaches at Boston College. He has published on Diderot and Zola.

DANIEL BREWER teaches in the Department of French and Italian at the University of Minnesota. He is a co-editor of *L'Esprit Créateur*. His extensive publications include *The Discourse of the Enlightenment in Eighteenth-Century France: Diderot and the Art of Philosophizing* (1993) and *The Enlightenment Past: Reconstructing Eighteenth-Century Thought* (2008). He is currently working on a book-length study of the intersection of sentiment and ethics in eighteenth-century French culture.

DEREK CONNON is Professor of French at the College of Arts and Humanities of Swansea University. His varied research interests are originally rooted in eighteenth-century French theatre, especially Diderot's plays and dramatic theory. His many publications include *Innovation and Renewal: A Study of the Theatrical Works of Diderot* (1989) and *Diderot's Endgames* (2002).

ANDREW CURRAN is Professor at the Romance Languages and Literatures Department of Wesleyan University. He has wide-ranging interests in the field of eighteenth-century literature, culture and thought and his publications include *Sublime Disorder: Physical Monstrosity in Diderot's Universe* (2001). His new book, *The Anatomy of Blackness: Science and Slavery in an Age of Enlightenment*, is forthcoming.

MARK DARLOW is Senior Lecturer in French at the University of Cambridge, and Fellow of Christ's College. He has published *Nicolas-Étienne Framery and Lyric Theatre in Eighteenth-Century France* (2003), edited *Revolutionary Culture: Continuity and Change* (2006), and co-edited *The Discursive Culture: Action and Reaction, Text and Intertext* (2007). His study of the Paris Opéra in the Revolution is forthcoming, and he is currently co-editor of Laya's *L'Ami des lois*. He also has a book-length project underway on the concept of chiaroscuro in eighteenth-century theatre, spoken and lyric.

ANNE DENEYS-TUNNEY is Professor of French at New York University, Chercheur associé at the CNRS, Paris, and Directrice d'Études Associée at the Maison des Sciences de l'Homme, Paris. She has written extensively on seventeenth- and eighteenth-century French writers and philosophers, including Marivaux, Rousseau, Laclos, Diderot and the Idéologues Volney and Destutt de Tracy, and on Epicureanism during the Enlightenment. Her publications include *Écritures du corps, de Descartes à Laclos* (1992) and *Un autre Jean-Jacques Rousseau, le paradoxe de la technique* (2010). She is co-editor, with Pierre-François Moreau, of *L'Épicurisme des Lumières* (2003), and, with Hélène Cussac and Catriona Seth, of *Les Discours du corps au XVIIIe siècle* (2009).

BÉATRICE DIDIER is Professor Emerita at the École Normale Supérieure, Paris. Her extremely wide-ranging research interests extend to French literature of the eighteenth and nineteenth centuries and the relationship between literature and music. She has written many books, including *La Musique des Lumières* (1985), *Alphabet et raison: le paradoxe des dictionnaires au XVIIIe siècle* (1996) and *Diderot dramaturge du vivant* (2001).

JAMES FOWLER teaches French at the University of Kent. He has written extensively on the eighteenth-century French novel and French philosophy, especially on Crébillon *fils*, Diderot, Laclos and the marquis de Sade. His publications include *Voicing Desire: Family and Sexuality in Diderot's Narrative* (2000) and *The Libertine's Nemesis: The Prude in 'Clarissa' and the 'roman libertin'* (2011). He is currently working on the ways in which French writers and thinkers of the eighteenth century reacted to Richardson's novels. He is co-editor, with Tom Baldwin and Shane Weller, of *The Flesh in the Text* (2007).

ANGELICA GOODDEN is University Lecturer in French and Fellow of St Hilda's College, Oxford. Her main research interests are in eighteenth- and nineteenth-century French literature (especially Diderot, Rousseau and a range of women writers) and culture, particularly painting. She is currently working on Rousseau and the problem of writing. Her publications include *Diderot and the Body* (2002), *The Backward Look: Memory and the Writing of Self in France 1580–1920* (2000), *The Complete Lover: Eros, Nature and Artifice in the Eighteenth-Century French Novel* (1989) and *'Actio' and Persuasion: Dramatic Performance in Eighteenth-Century France* (1986).

RUSSELL GOULBOURNE is Professor of Early Modern French Literature in the School of Modern Languages and Cultures at the University of Leeds. He has published widely on a broad range of subjects and French authors drawn from the seventeenth and eighteenth centuries, and is interested in the reception of classical antiquity in France throughout this period. His publications include *Voltaire Comic Dramatist* (2006) and numerous critical editions of Voltaire's works for the ongoing edition of the *Œuvres complètes*.

MARIAN HOBSON is Professorial Research Fellow at Queen Mary University of London. A Fellow of the British Academy, she has published extensively on eighteenth-century French art, literature and philosophy, and on Jacques Derrida (*Jacques Derrida: Opening Lines*, 1998). She is author of *The Object of Art: The Theory of Illusion in Eighteenth-Century France* (1982); with Simon Harvey she has co-edited a new edition of Diderot's *Lettre sur les aveugles* and *Lettre sur les sourds et muets* (2000); and she is producing a new edition of Diderot's *Le Neveu de Rameau*. *Diderot and Rousseau: Networks of Enlightenment*, a selection of her articles, edited with an introduction by Kate Tunstall and Caroline Warman, is to be published in 2011.

PIERRE SAINT-AMAND holds the Francis Wayland Chair at the Department of French Studies, Brown University. He has published extensively on various aspects of Enlightenment thought and the French eighteenth-century novel, including the *roman du libertinage*. His numerous books include: *Diderot. Le labyrinthe de la relation* (1984); *The Libertine's Progress: Seduction in the Eighteenth-Century French Novel*, trans. Jennifer C. Gage (1994); and *The Laws of Hostility: Politics, Violence, and the Enlightenment*, trans. Jennifer C. Gage (1996). He has recently completed a study entitled *The Pursuit of Laziness: An Idle Interpretation of the Enlightenment*, trans. Jennifer C. Gage.

CAROL L. SHERMAN is Professor Emerita at the Department of Romance Languages and Literatures of the University of North Carolina at Chapel

Hill. Her many publications on eighteenth-century literature include *Diderot and the Art of Dialogue* (1976), *Reading Voltaire's Contes: A Semiotics of Philosophical Narration* (1985) and *The Family Crucible in Eighteenth-Century Literature* (2005).

ANTHONY STRUGNELL is Emeritus Reader in the Department of Modern Languages at the University of Hull and director of a critical edition of Raynal's *Histoire des deux Indes* for the Centre International d'Étude du XVIIIe Siècle, the first volume of which, together with the Atlas, has just appeared. He has written extensively on eighteenth-century French literature and thought, with particular emphasis on Diderot's collaboration on the *Histoire*. His publications include *Diderot's Politics: A Study of the Evolution of Diderot's Political Thought after the 'Encyclopédie'* (1973). He co-edited, with Peter France, the bicentennial tribute *Diderot: Les Dernières Années, 1770–84* (1985), and, with Frédéric Ogée, *Diderot and European Culture* (2006).

KATE E. TUNSTALL, University Lecturer in French and Fellow of Worcester College, University of Oxford, has published widely on eighteenth-century and Enlightenment writing, as well as on the relations between literature and the visual. She is also Programme Director of the Besterman Centre for the Enlightenment. With Caroline Warman and Thierry Belleguic, she organised the major conference 'Celebrating Diderot Studies', held in 2009 at the Maison Française, Oxford. Her book *Blindness and Enlightenment. Diderot's 'Lettre sur les aveugles'. An Essay with a New Translation* is forthcoming.

Acknowledgements

The collective thanks of the contributors, and especially the editor, are due to Linda Bree and her team at Cambridge University Press. Julian Preece, Peter Read and Laurence Goldstein provided warm encouragement. Philip Robinson and Mark Darlow offered expert musicological advice on my translation of Chapter 15. Ana de Medeiros provided judicious comments on Chapter 9, and a great deal of moral support. Finally, Milly helped me to structure my work schedule. From the outset, the contributors have displayed a spirit of cooperation that has ensured the steady progress of the volume.

Abbreviations

Corr.	Denis Diderot, *Correspondance*, ed. Georges Roth and Jean Varloot, 16 vols. (Paris: Éditions de Minuit, 1955–70)
DPV	Denis Diderot, *Œuvres complètes*, ed. Herbert Dieckmann, Jacques Proust and Jean Varloot (Paris: Hermann, 1975–)
Encyclopédie	*Encyclopédie, ou Dictionnaire raisonné des sciences, des arts et des métiers, par une société de gens de lettres*, 17 vols. text and 11 vols. plates (Paris: Briasson/David/Le Breton/ Durand, 1751–72)
LEW	Diderot, *Œuvres complètes*, ed. Roger Lewinter, 15 vols. (Paris: Le Club Français du Livre, 1969–73)
SVEC	*Studies on Voltaire and the Eighteenth Century*

Introduction

James Fowler

Strictly speaking, there is only one kind of cause: the physical kind.

Diderot, Lettre à Landois

In the Louvre hangs an attractive portrait of Diderot by Michel Van Loo. But how closely does it resemble the sitter? The *philosophe* writes amusingly that it is 'too young, the head too small, as pretty as a woman, coquettish, smiling, dainty'. The problem, Diderot suggests, lay largely with himself: 'whether it is because there are too many things blended together [in my face] or because the painter's eye sees it changing every instant (for the impressions of my soul succeed each other with great rapidity and they all paint themselves on my face), the artist's task becomes much more difficult than he thought it was'.[1] In a word, it is very hard to take the likeness of such a face. Yet this is the metaphorical task collectively assumed by the contributors to these *New Essays*. The founding aim of this project was to capture the most characteristic aspects of this thinker who is extraordinarily mobile, but repeatedly returns to certain beliefs and concerns.

This Introduction is designed to provide thematic 'entry points' into the chapters, which in turn open up perspectives on the oeuvre. To organise the whole, it was decided that the following headings would be used: Diderot the *philosophe*; the novels; the dialogues; the plays and dramatic theory; music, performance and aesthetics. It will be useful to say a few words on each of these in turn.

DIDEROT THE *PHILOSOPHE*

In the eighteenth century the word 'philosophe' connoted a man of ideas but also a man of action, a would-be agent of social and political change, a champion of progress. In a post-Lockean, post-Cartesian world a number of Enlightenment philosophers embraced the exciting new possibility that nothing exists in the universe except matter. In fact it is more accurate to say that it was an exciting old possibility, argued for by the Roman philosopher–poet Lucretius (himself a follower of Epicurus), whose *De rerum natura* (*On the Nature of Things*) had already had an influence in Renaissance thinking. According to Lucretius, we should not worry about the existence of the gods. To know the universe, we should understand that there is no immaterial soul and no afterlife; there are only indivisible particles of matter or 'atoms' ceaselessly combining, separating and recombining. Renewed in various ways by eighteenth-century thinkers including Diderot and d'Holbach (the *philosophe*'s friend and frequent host), this tradition opposes that other form of monism, Berkeley's idealism.[2]

We can broadly characterise Diderot's philosophical development as follows: rejecting the Christianity in which he had been raised, he moved through a version of deism into monist-materialist determinism. A key text is the *Lettre à Landois* (*Letter to Landois*) of 1756, where the *philosophe* writes: 'Look carefully, and you will see that the word "liberty" is empty of meaning; that there are not, that there cannot be, free beings; that we are only what we are allowed to be by the general order, our organisation, our upbringing and the chain of events.'[3] But he struggles with the ramifications of this axiom. Of atheistic determinism he writes (probably in 1769): 'Oh what a fine system for ingrates! It makes me wild to be entangled in a devil of a philosophy that forces the assent of my mind but which my heart cannot help denying.'[4] For Diderot worries that determinism calls the ideas of vice and virtue into question (a problem he tries to solve in the *Letter to Landois* and elsewhere). After all, what sense does it make to apportion blame or praise if no one ever truly makes a moral choice, but simply acts out of necessity? Moreover, determinism may seem to threaten to erode any optimism that, through the efforts of reformers, a better world can be brought into existence. For if everything happens because it must, there is no reason to believe that the world will improve – except thanks to blind necessity, which might instead, for all we know, cause it to worsen. Sade was to embrace the darkest implications of monist materialism, arguing that the eternal flux of matter (mysteriously guided by the aims of 'Nature') justifies violence at the service of selfishness, hedonism and the survival of the fittest. The conclusion drawn by the marquis's major libertine characters is that we should withdraw all positive connotations from 'virtue' and attach them instead to 'vice'. But it would be a distortion to present Diderot as a precursor of Sade. Admittedly in *Le Rêve de d'Alembert* (*D'Alembert's Dream*) the eponymous dreamer, under the influence of a character named 'Diderot', voices the opinion that the universe is a constant, aimless flux that has produced humanity as one of an endless series of ephemeral phenomena.[5] Now, although we must beware of the author's notorious playfulness (in various texts, 'Diderot' appears but is not necessarily Diderot's 'mouthpiece'), it is safe to assert that this position represents the mature author's settled belief.[6] Nevertheless, he clings doggedly to notions of justice and progress.[7] And to reconcile these with determinism, he experiments with concepts such as modifiability and the general good. For instance, he suggests that though we lack free will it so happens that vice is self-punishing. This entails the consequence that if we are sufficiently enlightened we will pursue virtue for the sake of our own happiness (and so selfishness and unselfishness, individual and collective interests, become indistinguishable, to the benefit of all). This idea is already tried out in the *Lettre à Landois*.[8]

But such attempts to reconcile the blind forces of determinism with ideas of virtue and progress fail to put Diderot's philosophical anxiety to rest. Years later he dramatises his dilemma in *Jacques le fataliste* (*Jacques the Fatalist*); to the amusement of his master, the fatalistic/deterministic Jacques cannot hit on any form of (non-verbal) behaviour that might distinguish him from believers in free will (short of falling into the utmost absurdity). The master, meanwhile, continues to believe he is free simply because he *feels* he is free, as he goes about the business of everyday life.[9] This raises the question: when they contradict each other, which are we to believe – abstract truth or lived experience? Jacques or the master? In *De l'interprétation de la nature* (*The Interpretation of Nature*), Diderot expresses the belief that the science practised by mathematicians such as d'Alembert was moribund. His reasoning is that the kind of truths which it discovers can have no application in the real world: 'The region of mathematics is an abstract world, where what counts as rigorous truth absolutely loses this advantage when it is brought into our world.'[10] And he makes it clear that he is also talking about abstract philosophical truths ('la métaphysique') – a heading under which we can surely place determinism.[11] This also explains, perhaps, why Diderot never managed to write a treatise on virtue, though he wanted to: he must have felt he could not match universal principles to the ethical complexities of real life in any systematic way.[12] He was content instead to inhabit the paradox of the deterministic reformer, disbelieving in free will but campaigning tirelessly for greater freedom (freedom of thought and expression, freedom from indoctrination and oppression). Doubtless he thought of himself (to use Jacques's phrase) as 'happily born',[13] which is to say believed that he had no choice but to work towards the general good. Meanwhile, his conviction that humanity was made up of material (but modifiable) beings existing in a material world can be traced through his thinking in areas as diverse as morality, aesthetics, music, politics, poetics and theories of language and representation. He never ceased to pursue those elusive connections between his 'devil of a philosophy', so convincing in the abstract, and the very real world in which he lived.

Chapters 1–6 of the present volume explore various aspects of Diderot the *philosophe* (understood in one or both senses). It seems certain that Diderot's interest in determinism was intensified by reading Lucretius. Speaking more generally, it is impossible to understand his thought without understanding its debt to antiquity. In Chapter 1, Russell Goulbourne guides the reader through the most important of the classical influences on Diderot. But at the same time, he shows that the *philosophe's* passion for the ancients is at the heart of his modernity. In Chapter 2 Marian Hobson attends to the main directions of Diderot's thought as they are adumbrated in the earlier philosophical writings, and exposes several key points of divergence from Rousseau.

Diderot's desire to be a *philosophe* found an extraordinarily fortuitous outlet in the *Encyclopédie*, which he edited from 1747 to 1772 (often in the face of powerful opposition). One of Diderot's ambitions for this massive undertaking was that it should record the arts, sciences and trade technologies of modern Europe, for the benefit of his contemporaries and posterity alike. But he also aimed to use the project to 'change the general way of thinking',[14] which extended to questioning many aspects of the *ancien régime*.[15] To help counter the threat of censorship, he famously used an ingenious system of cross-references that invite the reader to draw amusing and often subversive comparisons between articles. In Chapter 3 Daniel Brewer provides an account of the *Encyclopédie's* radical programme and its rhetorical strategies, and emphasises that Diderot saw the effective use of language as central to the undertaking's success. He also points to the enduring effect of what he describes as the *Encyclopédie's* 'meta-critical function'.

It has often been noted that Diderot's thinking thrived on dialogue. He had many philosophical interlocutors over the years; in his later career, these included Catherine the Great of Russia, for whom he optimistically wrote texts suggesting a range of social and political reforms. But doubtless the most significant of all his interlocutors was Rousseau. A deep friendship sprang up between these two great thinkers before either had achieved real fame; but it would not survive when their social and intellectual tendencies were to pull them in divergent directions. In 1749–50, encouraged by Diderot, Rousseau wrote the epoch-making First Discourse, which contained an eloquent denunciation of intellectual and technical progress in the modern age. This jarred significantly with the ideals of the *Encyclopédie* in ways that were to become increasingly clear. In subsequent writings,

Rousseau used the concept of nature to question many of the values and ideas promoted by the *philosophes*. In Chapter 4 Angelica Goodden explores the ramifications of the complex, ambivalent relationship between Rousseau and Diderot. In doing so, she exposes the main divergences but also some persistent affinities.

Diderot's desire for political reform is expressed in many texts besides the *Encyclopédie*. Of particular significance is Raynal's *Histoire des deux Indes* (*A History of the Two Indies*), published in 1770–80. Diderot wrote many anonymous contributions for the *Histoire*, and brought to the project his cherished philosophical ideas and social concerns. In important ways he can be described as an early anti-colonialist. But as we look back to the Enlightenment, there is a risk that we misunderstand the historical and cultural horizons (which is probably to say the necessary outer limits) of the *philosophe*'s 'anti-colonialism'. Anthony Strugnell explores this issue in Chapter 5, with reference to the *Histoire* and other key texts.

Finally, the letters to 'Sophie' Volland allow us to observe Diderot moving between philosophical and amorous discourse, and to access his private thoughts on everyday events. This correspondence lasted from 1755 to the year of Diderot's death (1784) – but unfortunately not all the letters have survived. Pierre Saint-Amand explores the beautiful poignancy of the 'sweet bond' ('liaison douce') between Diderot and his mistress (Chapter 6). He also shows that the *philosophe* reflected in his correspondence on the material conditions governing the writing, sending and receiving of letters, and on the variations which love brings to our experience of time (time for philosophy, time for leisure and time claimed by the irksome business of everyday life).

NOVELS

As we read Diderot's first, licentious novel (often decried but often reprinted) we still hear a *philosophe*'s voice. In Chapter 7 Anne Deneys-Tunney shows how *Les Bijoux indiscrets* (*The Indiscreet Jewels*) engages with the major philosophical issues of the time, and does so in parodic fashion. The 'indiscreet jewels' of the title are female genitals to which a magic ring grants the power to speak about 'what they know'. This central conceit, Deneys-Tunney suggests, is used to suggest that Enlightenment discoveries about the empirical world are severely hindered by problems of 'translation'. For the modern philosopher may discover that it is difficult to decode new (or newly exposed) truths concerning sexuality and the body in his own terms. After all, the terminology inherited from philosophical tradition is not (yet?) adapted to express such truths.

Perhaps because *Les Bijoux indiscrets* was among the works that contributed to Diderot's imprisonment in the chateau of Vincennes (July–November 1749), the three fictions or novels that are best known to modern readers remained unpublished during his lifetime.[16] Of these, *Jacques le fataliste* explores the issues of fatalism and determinism while raising questions concerning the theory and practice of story-telling. In Chapter 8 Joseph Breines succinctly conveys the radical nature of this novel, or, as some prefer, this 'anti-novel'. Moreover, Breines suggests that *Jacques* involves a 'twist' on materialism, in that it explores a tension between two ideas: Jacques's conviction that at any given point in our lives we are but a 'single cause' that can have a 'single effect', and the radically opposed idea that identity is so unfixed that we can seem to be ourselves and another (as Diderot finds himself in Sterne). As for *La Religieuse*, the subject of the unhappy nun was central to Diderot's thinking about religion. (Tragically, one of his sisters went mad and died in a convent before reaching the age of thirty.) The determinist in him was fascinated by the effects of the 'unnatural' convent environment on individual behaviour; the reformer in him wanted to prevent young people being imprisoned in a system which he saw as a cause of individual suffering and a 'tomb of future generations'. *La Religieuse* has often been called a 'Richardsonian' novel. Does this mean, as has been claimed, that it is anti-conventual without being anti-Christian? In Chapter 9 I show that within this 'satire of convents' the atheistic Diderot offers a subtle but sustained critique of Christianity as such.

DIALOGUES

Some of Diderot's fictions can best be classified as framed dialogues or 'dialogues narrés'. In 1769, Diderot wrote *Le Rêve de d'Alembert*, formed of three dialogues. The key motifs he uses – the 'sensitive harpsichord', the swarm of bees and the spider – have seemed to many readers to build a powerful and eloquent case for materialism. In Chapter 10 Kate E. Tunstall shows how in spite of this, the foregrounding of dreaming in *Le Rêve* places materialism in tension with radically sceptical and even with idealist traditions. It may be, then, that *Le Rêve* is one of Diderot's many heuristic (as opposed to dogmatic) texts. One thinks for instance of *Le Neveu de Rameau*, where 'Diderot' clashes with the nephew on various points of philosophy, but neither interlocutor wins an outright victory.

In the early 1770s Diderot wrote a triptych of short fictions in dialogue form. The third of these is the *Supplément au Voyage de Bougainville* (*Supplement to Bougainville's 'Voyage around the World'*). In this text, two friends discuss unpublished extracts (written of course by Diderot) from Bougainville's famous *Voyage*; these mainly concern the explorer's trip to Tahiti. Through the *Supplément*, which may be read as a riposte to Rousseau's Second Discourse, Diderot investigates the interconnected themes of nature and civilisation, love, marriage, fidelity, social organisation, race and colonialism. In Chapter 11 Andrew Curran shows how the *Supplément* engages with Enlightenment notions of 'natural man', 'varieties' and race. He emphasises that, for Diderot, the Tahitians 'represent but one logic of the human'. Connections are also made with Diderot's contributions to the *Histoire des deux Indes*.

PLAYS AND DRAMATIC THEORY

As many eighteenth-century theatregoers and playwrights continued to be in thrall to neoclassicism, Diderot became the champion of a relatively new type of drama. The key texts are his plays *Le Fils naturel* (*The Natural Son*) and *Le Père de famille* (*The Father*) of 1757–8, and the theoretical discussions attached to each. The type of play recommended by Diderot became known as the *drame*. In the narrative framework that accompanies the earlier play, 'Diderot' converses with Dorval (the fictional author and hero of the supposedly autobiographical *Fils naturel*). In a dramaturgy that was to prove influential for the next 150 years, Dorval argues that henceforth playwrights should portray contemporary middle-class life, and do so using a serious tone; he insists that gesture, tableaux and broken speech can be at least as expressive as the traditional resources of comedy and tragedy. He also sets out innovative ideas concerning opera. But in spite of the programmatic implications of the *Entretiens sur le Fils naturel* (*Conversations on 'The Natural Son'*), Diderot did not confine himself to writing *drames*. Late in his career (1781) he penned a comedy, the intriguingly entitled *Est-il bon? Est-il méchant?* (*Is he Good? Is he Bad?*). This play's hero (Hardouin) is far from preaching any moral absolutes; instead, he experiments (some would say deviously) with the principle that the end justifies the means. The play's treatment of morality thus recalls the *dialogues narrés*, in which Diderot suggests that to pursue the general good through the messy business of everyday life is problematic but ultimately worthwhile. Diderot's interest in theatre and acting is also reflected in the *Paradoxe sur le comédien* (*Paradox on the Actor*) of 1773.

In the eighteenth century there was a backlash against Diderot's *drames* of the 1750s. One reason was their moralising tone. Diderot hoped his plays would teach the audience to admire secular virtue as he conceived it.

Such earnestness was (and of course is) open to ridicule when viewed through cynical eyes. But doubtless the *drames* also aroused such strong reactions because they had political undertones: they confidently expressed certain values and beliefs that were distinct from those of the ruling classes.[17] In Chapter 12 Carol L. Sherman shows the legacy of Diderot's *drames* in the context of Revolutionary France by focusing on Olympe de Gouges, who was concerned with the place of women within the family and that of the family within the state. In her plays, influenced by Diderot's ideas, she gives daring expression to a range of progressive themes. In Chapter 13, Derek Connon explores a late shift in Diderot's attitude to the *drame* which he had done so much to promote. Indeed, by examining the presence of Destouches and other playwrights in *Est-il bon? Est-il méchant?*, Connon shows that it is 'a play by a writer who, despite his aims to make theatre a didactic school for virtue, could not resist the lure of the comic'.

MUSIC, PERFORMANCE, AESTHETICS

In 1752 Rousseau wrote an opera, *Le Devin du village* (*The Village Soothsayer*), which brought him great renown. Diderot wrote no operas, but he developed radical ideas about the genre and about music performance in general. Having raised an exceptionally moderate voice in the Querelle des Bouffons (1752–4), in which Parisians excitedly debated whether Italian or French opera was superior, he went on to develop his ideas over a number of years. His most famous dialogue of all, *Le Neveu de Rameau*, investigates the mysteries of musical genius, and, more generally, asks whether it is possible to discover intrinsic or necessary connections linking the good, the true and the beautiful (a possibility radically challenged by the nephew). In Chapter 14 Mark Darlow examines Diderot's key writings on music, including *Le Neveu*, from the perspective of the singing and speaking voice. The discussion is organised according to the following themes: the voice as index of individuality; the respective approaches to voice of the Italian and French parties during the Querelle des Bouffons; and 'the implications for development of musical theatre ... of Diderot's consistent call for variety' (where Rousseau called for unity). In Chapter 15, Béatrice Didier reconstructs Diderot's aesthetics of the libretto. This is largely elaborated in the *Entretiens sur le Fils naturel*, in which (as noted above) Dorval proposes a range of new possibilities for opera. Didier links this aesthetics with the preceding Querelle des Bouffons, and also makes connections with the development of opera since Diderot's time.

One of Diderot's most important contributions to the realm of aesthetics is his art criticism. Diderot wrote the article 'Beau' for volume II of the *Encyclopédie*, published in 1752; here he proposes that the experience of beauty depends on the perception of 'relationships'. But his ideas on art evolved considerably after 1759, when he began to report on the annual/biennial exhibitions at the Louvre, known as the *Salons*, for the *Correspondance littéraire*. Just as he toured *ateliers* for the purposes of editing the *Encyclopédie*, Diderot became intimately acquainted over the years with artists: their techniques, their imagination and in certain cases their genius. (Those whom he saw as true artists rather than mere masters of technique included, for various reasons, Chardin, Greuze, Vernet and Falconet.) What could have been hackwork opened up radically new possibilities in art criticism.

The initial impulse behind the writing of the *Salons* (delegated to Diderot by Grimm) presupposes the possibility of effective ekphrasis – the verbal representation of a visual representation (typically a painting). We must remember that Grimm's/Diderot's readers would be unlikely to see the *Salon* exhibits in person (short of buying them); and the *Correspondance* was not accompanied by drawings or engravings. A lesser writer would perhaps have described the artworks on display at the Louvre without questioning whether (his) language was transparent on reality. But Diderot became fascinated by the theoretical problems raised by the practice of ekphrasis. Is ekphrasis truly possible? How effective is it? What aspects of the original (itself a 'copy' according to eighteenth-century notions of art) might be lost or gained in the writing and reading of a verbal description? Is ekphrasis capable of supplanting what it describes? The famous 'Promenade Vernet' in the 1767 *Salon*, in which Diderot imagines a 'walk' which he then reveals to be (also) the evocation of a series of paintings, foregrounds these questions in an especially intriguing fashion. Tom Baldwin offers an overview of these issues. He shows how readers have reacted to Diderot's ekphrastic (or seemingly ekphrastic) practices in widely different ways, and guides us towards a nuanced understanding of Diderot's art criticism.[18]

Diderot wrote to the sculptor Falconet: 'Posterity is the philosopher's equivalent of the religious man's afterlife.'[19] He had faith that we 'moderns' would render justice to those aspects of his thought and writing that were too radical for his age. As we approach the tricentenary of his birth (2013), it is clear that his faith was not misplaced. Denis Diderot, son of a cutler from Langres, now ranks as one of the three greatest writers of the French Enlightenment. The materialist has obtained his afterlife.

NOTES

1. See DPV, vol. xvi, pp. 82–3. All translations contained in this Introduction are mine; I also translated Chapters 6, 7 and 15. I wish to record my thanks to Philip Robinson and Mark Darlow, who kindly agreed to read a first draft of Chapter 15 and offered extremely useful advice.

2. George Berkeley (1685–1753), bishop of Cloyne from 1734, attempted to refute materialism by denying the existence of matter. See Thomas Mautner (ed.), *The Penguin Dictionary of Philosophy* (London; Penguin, 2000), pp. 66–7.

3. See DPV, vol. ix, pp. 256–7.

4. See *Corr.*, vol. ix, p. 154.

5. See DPV, vol. xvii, pp. 135–6.

6. In *Le Rêve*, 'Diderot' famously states: 'in all matters, our true opinion is not the one in which we have never wavered, but the one to which we have most frequently returned'. See ibid., p. 113.

7. There is an important humanist tendency in Diderot's writing: unlike some determinists, he refuses to see humankind as just another animal species. One of his most memorable statements of all is to be found in the *Réfutation d'Helvétius* (*Refutation of Helvétius*), written between 1773 and 1777: 'I am human, and I must deal in human causes' ('Je suis homme, et il me faut des causes propres à l'homme'). See DPV, vol. xxiv, p. 523.

8. See DPV, vol. ix, p. 256.

9. See DPV, vol. xxiii, p. 270.

10. See DPV, vol. ix, p. 30.

11. See ibid., p. 29.

12. See Arthur M. Wilson, *Diderot* (New York: Oxford University Press, 1972), p. 667.

13. See DPV, vol. xxiii, p. 189.

14. See DPV, vol. vii, p. 222.

15. A survey of enduring importance is John Lough, *The 'Encyclopédie'* (London: Longman, 1971).

16. Their titles are: *Jacques le fataliste*, *La Religieuse* (*The Nun*) and *Le Neveu de Rameau* (*Rameau's Nephew*). A case might be made for categorising *Le Neveu* either as an unusual kind of novel or as a framed dialogue. But as it constitutes Diderot's most famous contribution to eighteenth-century thinking on music, for the purposes of the present volume it is discussed in Chapters 14 and 15. *Jacques* and *La Religieuse* circulated before Diderot's death in the *Correspondance littéraire* (*Literary Correspondence*), a manuscript journal edited by Diderot's close friend Friedrich Melchior Grimm until 1773 (when Jakob Heinrich Meister took over), which was distributed to a small number of extremely select readers, principally crowned heads of Europe.

17. See Wilson, *Diderot*, p. 269.

18. Diderot's reflections on art are not confined to the article 'Beau' and the pages of the *Salons*. These texts should especially be read in conjunction with the *Essais sur la peinture* of 1766 (DPV, vol. xiv, pp. 333–411).

19. See DPV, vol. xv, p. 33.

PART I

Diderot the philosophe

CHAPTER I

Diderot and the ancients

Russell Goulbourne

Diderot seems in many ways to be the most forward-looking, the most 'modern', of the eighteenth-century French *philosophes*. Even his attitude to his works, just as much as the content and form of them, suggests this: although he composed many of what we now regard as his most important works without thought of conventional publication in his lifetime, he nevertheless did so with a keen eye on posterity. He fervently hoped that the future would be as interested in him as he was in it, as he suggests in a letter to the sculptor Étienne-Maurice Falconet in December 1765: 'En vérité, cette postérité serait une ingrate si elle m'oubliait tout à fait, moi qui me suis tant souvenu d'elle.'[1] ('Indeed, posterity would truly be ungrateful if it forgot me completely, given that I have been thinking about it so much.') But this is only part of the story. For Diderot was just as concerned with the past as he was with the future. Pursuing his epistolary debate with Falconet about posterity, he notes in a letter of February 1766: 'Plus l'homme remonte en arrière, plus il s'élance en avant, plus il est grand.'[2] ('The further a man turns back, the more he launches forward, the greater he is.') Diderot looks back in order to move forward. In particular he looks back to antiquity and finds in it the springboard for his daring intellectual adventure. Indeed, it is no exaggeration to say that it is impossible to understand Diderot the *philosophe* without understanding his debt to antiquity.[3]

Diderot's far-reaching interest in antiquity dates back to his childhood. From the age of ten, he was educated in Langres by the Jesuits, before he moved to Paris in 1728, aged fifteen, where he continued his education at the Jesuit Collège Louis-le-Grand and the Jansenist Collège d'Harcourt. At these he received an excellent classical education, particularly in Latin. He even pursued his studies once he had left school: in 1735, he entered the office of a solicitor, Clément de Ris, in order to study law, but, according to his daughter, during the two years he worked there, he devoted every spare moment he had to studying Latin and Greek.[4] Diderot's recollection in his *Plan d'une université pour le gouvernement de Russie* (*Plan of a University for the Government of Russia*) of his formative reading of, and subsequent familiarity with, the ancients is revealing of his catholic, unorthodox tastes: 'Plusieurs années de suite, j'ai été aussi religieux à lire un chant d'Homère, avant que de me coucher, que l'est un bon prêtre à réciter son bréviaire. J'ai sucé de bonne heure le lait d'Homère, de Virgile, d'Horace, de Térence, d'Anacréon, de Platon, d'Euripide, coupé avec celui de Moïse et des prophètes.'[5] ('For many years I read a canto of Homer before bedtime as religiously as a good priest says his prayers. I was suckled from a young age on the milk of Homer, Virgil, Horace, Terence, Anacreon, Plato and Euripides, diluted with that of Moses and the prophets.')

Diderot's classical education laid the intellectual foundations for the future atheist *philosophe*. Indeed, it is precisely this unorthodox approach that will characterise Diderot's debt to antiquity in all aspects of his thought – aesthetic, philosophical and political.

ART, AESTHETICS AND ANTIQUITY

To begin with his aesthetic thought, it is clear that Diderot found in the ancients, not models for modern artists – painters, sculptors, poets and dramatists alike – literally to imitate, but rather models of how to approach their subject-matter, as he suggests in his discussion of sculpture in the *Salon de 1765*:

Celui qui dédaigne l'antique risque de n'être jamais que petit, faible et mesquin de dessin, de caractère, de draperie et d'expression. Celui qui aura négligé la nature pour l'antique, risquera d'être froid, sans vie, sans aucune de ces vérités cachées ou secrètes, qu'on n'aperçoit que dans la nature elle-même. Il me semble qu'il faudrait étudier l'antique pour apprendre à voir la nature.[6]

(Anyone who scorns nature in favour of the antique risks never producing anything that is not small, weak and paltry in its outline, character, drapery and expression. Anyone who neglects nature in favour of the antique risks being cold, lifeless and devoid of the hidden, secret truths which can only be perceived in nature itself. It seems to me that we have to study the antique in order to learn how to see nature.)

There is no contradiction between *la nature* and *l'antique* for Diderot. Rather, his call for a return to nature in art is a call to his contemporaries to rediscover originality by following ancient examples, by working in the way the ancients did.

Diderot sounded this call particularly loudly in his writings on the theatre. Ancient theatre provided Diderot with models of how to write powerful, emotional drama – plays whose power is intended to derive precisely from their proximity to nature.[7] Diderot challenges contemporary notions of *bienséance*, or dramatic decency, by championing ancient drama, deploying a suitably paradoxical argument in his *Paradoxe sur le comédien* (*The Paradox of the Actor*): 'La vraie tragédie est encore à trouver, et . . . avec tous leurs défauts, les Anciens en étaient peut-être plus voisins que nous.'[8] ('True tragedy remains to be found, and . . . despite all their failings, perhaps the Ancients were closer to it than we are.') If French tragedy had reached its high-water mark with Racine in the seventeenth century, Diderot envisages revitalising it by calling on eighteenth-century dramatists to write the kind of primitive, visceral tragedy he so admires in the ancient Greek dramatists in particular.[9]

Diderot's critique of contemporary dramatic aesthetics also leads him to formulate a vision for a new genre mid-way between tragedy and comedy – serious plays in prose about ordinary people – known as the *drame bourgeois*. Here, too, ancient models support Diderot's modern argument, as the character Dorval suggests in the second of the *Entretiens sur Le Fils naturel* (*Conversations on 'The Natural Son'*) published with Diderot's first *drame*, *Le Fils naturel* (*The Natural Son*): 'J'ai un peu étudié le système dramatique des Anciens. J'espère vous en entretenir un jour, vous exposer sans partialité sa nature, ses défauts et ses avantages, et vous montrer que ceux qui l'ont attaqué ne l'avaient pas considéré d'assez près.'[10] ('I have studied the Ancients' dramatic system a little. I hope to talk to you about it one day, to give you an unbiased account of its nature, its weaknesses and its strengths, and to show you that those who have attacked it have not considered it carefully enough.') This system involved both theory and practice. In ancient poetic theory, notably Horace's *Ars poetica*, Diderot finds arguments in support of his innovative ideas about representing ordinary people in their social conditions, hence the Horatian epigraph to his second *drame*, *Le Père de famille* (*The Father*): 'Aetatis cuiusque notandi sunt tibi mores, / Mobilibusque decor naturis dandus et annis.'[11] ('You must note the manners of each age and give a befitting tone to shifting natures and their years.') And in ancient dramatists as diverse as Aeschylus, Euripides, Sophocles and Terence, Diderot finds inspiring examples of 'realistic', true-to-life subjects, such as a new-born child on stage in Terence's *Andria* and a woman in labour in his *Hecyra*, which he discusses in Chapter 18 of *De la poésie dramatique* (*Discourse on Dramatic Poetry*), published with *Le Père de famille*;[12] and these subjects are treated in a powerfully 'realistic' way: there is nothing superfluous in Terence's dramaturgy, Diderot argues in Chapter 17 of *De la poésie dramatique*,[13] and his plays, as he puts it in his *Sur Térence* (*On Terence*), are mercifully free of 'toutes ces galanteries misérables et froides qui défigurent la plupart de nos pièces' ('all these wretched, cold declarations of love which mar most of our plays').[14] Moreover, the style of performance in ancient theatre was exemplary: with his privileging of the visual over the verbal and his concept of the dramatic *tableau*, Diderot sets out to revive ancient pantomime and recover the powerfully expressive quality of drama, as Dorval makes clear in the second of the *Entretiens*: 'Nous parlons trop dans nos drames, et, conséquemment, nos acteurs n'y jouent pas assez. Nous avons perdu un art, dont les Anciens connaissent bien les ressources.'[15] ('We talk too much in our plays, and, as a result, our actors do not act enough. We have lost an art, the riches of which the Ancients knew well.') Ultimately, Dorval explains, imitating the ancients' way of writing enables the budding French dramatist to write plays that are close to nature: 'Je ne me lasserai point de crier à nos Français: La Vérité! La Nature! Les Anciens! Sophocle! Philoctète! ... Des habits vrais, des discours vrais, une intrigue simple et naturelle.'[16] ('I shall not tire of exclaiming to the French: Truth! Nature! The ancients! Sophocles! Philoctetes! ... Real clothes, real speech, a simple and natural plot.') Diderot's vision for modern theatre is firmly grounded in a re-evaluation of ancient theatre.

THINKING THROUGH/WITH THE ANCIENTS

The 'antiquity' of Diderot's modernity is also evident in his philosophical thought. In some of the ancients Diderot finds models of critical and sceptical thought – modes of intellectual enquiry that are conducive to the pursuit of new knowledge and the telling of useful truths in the present day. In so doing, he is, of course, being highly selective. Like Descartes before him, Diderot is no admirer of Aristotelian logic, for instance, as he makes clear in his *Plan d'une université*: 'Sous le nom de logique, on se remplit la tête des subtilités d'Aristote et de sa très sublime et très inutile théorie du syllogisme.'[17] ('In what is called logic, students' heads are filled with Aristotle's subtleties and his very sublime and very useless theory of the syllogism.') Nor, perhaps more surprisingly, does he attach much value to ancient Pyrrhonism, accusing Pyrrho himself of simply having played a gratuitous and sterile game with ideas and caricaturing him in the *Promenade du sceptique* (*The Sceptic's Walk*) as someone who 'soutenait indifféremment le pour et le contre, établissait une opinion, la détruisait, vous caressait d'une main, vous souffletait de l'autre' ('argued indifferently for and against, established an opinion and then destroyed it, caressed you with one hand and slapped you with the other').[18] Diderot posits a crucial distinction between scepticism in general and Pyrrhonism in particular, as he does in the *Pensées philosophiques* (*Philosophical Thoughts*): 'Qu'est-ce qu'un sceptique? C'est un philosophe qui a douté de tout ce qu'il croit, et qui croit ce qu'un usage légitime de sa raison et de ses sens lui a démontré vrai. Voulez-vous quelque chose de plus précis? Rendez sincère le pyrrhonien, et vous aurez le sceptique.'[19] ('What is a sceptic? A philosopher who has doubted everything he believes and who believes that which a proper use of his reason and his senses has shown him to be true. Do you want a more precise definition? Make the Pyrrhonian sincere and you'll have a sceptic.') This kind of scepticism is, he argues, 'le premier pas vers la vérité' ('the first step towards truth'),[20] and he finds in the ancient eclectics an example of that very pursuit of truth.

In 1755, Diderot wrote his important article 'Éclectisme' ('Eclecticism') for the *Encyclopédie*. The article is ostensibly about the ancient and relatively minor philosophical method of eclecticism, which was established by Potamo in Alexandria at the end of the second century: Potamo broke with the conventions of discipleship imposed by the ancient schools of philosophy and encouraged his pupils to select instead what seems best from other philosophical doctrines and create a synthesis out of them. But in writing about an ancient philosophical method, Diderot actually writes about, and even defines, the modernity of eighteenth-century Enlightenment *philosophie*:

L'éclectique est un philosophe qui foulant aux pieds le préjugé, la tradition, l'ancienneté, le consentement universel, l'autorité, en un mot tout ce qui subjugue la foule des esprits, ose penser de lui-même, remonter aux principes généraux les plus clairs, les examiner, les discuter, n'admettre rien que sur le témoignage de son expérience et de sa raison ... Les sceptiques et les éclectiques auraient pu prendre pour devise commune, *nullius addictus iurare in verba magistri*.[21]

(The eclectic is a philosopher who, trampling underfoot prejudice, tradition, age-old ways, received wisdom, authority, in a word everything which subjugates the masses, dares to think for himself, to work back to the clearest general principles, examine them, discuss them, and accept things only on the basis of his experience and his reason ... The sceptics and the eclectics could have had as their motto *nullius addictus iurare in verba magistri*.)

Diderot offers here a clear definition of the modern freethinking *philosophes* at precisely the time when they were beginning to coalesce into a more readily identifiable group: individuals who, like their ancient forebears, refuse authority, question received wisdom and search for truth.[22] And more than that, Diderot also grounds this very contemporary vision of critical enquiry in a Latin tag which he does not identify but which is actually taken from Horace's *Epistles* I.I: 'nullius addictus iurare in verba magistri.'[23] ('I am not bound over to swear as any master dictates.') In this poem Horace explains that he wants to abandon poetry in favour of philosophical enquiry, and he indicates his intention not to follow any particular school, but to pursue instead the philosophical ideal of virtue. In Diderot's hands, though, the line is invested with new meaning: Horace is talking about virtue, but Diderot is defining the *philosophe*. Diderot lends to Horace's words a much broader, and much more subversive, meaning than they originally had. The Horatian context does not justify the distinctively freethinking philosophical interpretation which Diderot lends to the line: instead, displacement enacts a change in meaning, from the moral to the 'philosophical' in the open-ended eighteenth-century sense of the word.[24]

A similarly subversive, freethinking use of tags drawn from Horace is found in the *Promenade du sceptique*, which has four epigraphs – one at the beginning of the text as a whole and one at the beginning of each of the three *allées* (paths) which make up the text – from Horace's *Satires* II.3, a poem about the follies of humankind.[25] The epigraphs stress relativism, scepticism and anti-dogmatism. For example, the first *allée* along which the character Cléobule ventures is the 'Allée des épines' ('path of thorns'), an allegorical satire of a Roman Catholic nation; it begins with the epigraph: 'Quone malo mentem concussa? timore deorum.'[26] ('What is the illness that has stricken her mind? Fear of the gods.') Through both his allegory and his choice of ancient epigraph, Diderot exposes superstition as one of humankind's follies.

Diderot finds further support for his critique of religious superstition in Lucretius' Epicurean poem *De rerum natura* (*On The Nature of the Universe*), which tries to show humankind the way to happiness through freedom from fear of the gods and of death.[27] For example, in the *Salon de 1767*, he begins his account of Gabriel-François Doyen's painting *Le Miracle des ardents* (*The Miracle of the Fervent*), painted for the church of St Roch in Paris and commemorating the miraculous intervention in 1129 of the relics of St Genevieve, which were said to have saved Parisians from an epidemic of ergot poisoning, with an epigraph from Lucretius: 'multoque, in rebus acerbis / acrius advertunt animos ad religionem.'[28] ('In their bitter days they direct their minds far more eagerly to religion.') Calamities and self-interest, Diderot suggests, make people who fear death turn to their gods. Less explicitly, in the *Pensées philosophiques* Diderot echoes Lucretius when he condemns superstitious belief in a god who is made to appear fickle and vengeful and when he observes: 'L'on serait assez tranquille en ce monde, si l'on était bien assuré que l'on n'a rien à craindre dans l'autre: la pensée qu'il n'y a point de Dieu n'a jamais effrayé personne, mais bien celle qu'il y en a tel que celui qu'on me peint.'²⁹ ('People would be quite happy in this world if they were sure there was nothing to fear in the next: the thought that there is no God has never frightened anyone, but what has is the thought that there is one that is like the one that is painted to me.') Tellingly, Voltaire detected the echo and annotated his copy of Diderot's text accordingly: 'Et qu'on a toujours peint *eternas quoniam poenas in morte timendum*, Lucrèce.'³⁰ ('And which has always been painted *eternas quoniam poenas in morte timendum*, Lucretius.')

In Lucretius Diderot also finds a precursor of the founding metaphor of the Enlightenment. The epigraph to the *Pensées sur l'interprétation de la nature* (*Thoughts on the Interpretation of Nature*) is loosely based on *De rerum natura*: 'Quae sunt in luce tuemur e tenebris.'³¹ The quotation is from Lucretius' discussion of the Epicurean theory of vision, according to which we can see things in the light from the dark because, after the dark air has filled our eyes, bright air, which is quicker and more powerful, purges them and enables sight. Diderot uses an ancient author as a means of celebrating modernity; he also uses Lucretius to define the critical, dynamic, non-dogmatic character of experimental philosophy, proceeding from ignorance to discovery, from darkness to light.

However, Lucretius' influence on Diderot goes further still: there is more to it than a metaphor or a spirit of anti-superstition. In fact, there is a fundamental connection between Diderot and Lucretius in terms of their shared exploration of the natural universe. Lucretius' *De rerum natura* owes its inspiration to the teaching of Epicurus, who in turn revived, and partly modified, the ancient atomist theory developed by Leucippus and his pupil Democritus. Like Lucretius, Diderot conceives of a wholly material and unified universe with no divine agency responsible for its creation; he asserts the existence of matter as sole reality; and he argues that all matter is in an eternal flux and that no particle may exist apart from the whole. Lucretius' ancient atomist philosophy helped prepare the way for Diderot's atheist materialism.³²

Echoes of Lucretius' theory of the universe can be heard in Diderot's works from as early as the *Pensées philosophiques*, where he evokes the notion of the fortuitous concourse of atoms and the principle of the immortality of matter.³³ This same principle is evoked by the dying Saunderson in the *Lettre sur les aveugles* as he argues against Holmes's belief in the immortality of the soul. In response to the Protestant clergyman's harangue on the wonders of nature, the blind mathematician retorts with arguments about the origin of the world, matter in motion, evolution from chaos and the absence of any purposeful design, all of which are derived ultimately from Book 5 of *De rerum natura*.³⁴

But perhaps the text which resounds with the clearest echoes of Lucretius
is *Le Rêve de d'Alembert* (*D'Alembert's Dream*), which Diderot wrote the year
after working with La Grange on his translation of *De rerum natura* and
which he had originally considered presenting as a conversation between
Democritus, Hippocrates and Leucippus.[35] When the dreaming d'Alembert
declares that 'tous les êtres circulent les uns dans les autres, par conséquent
toutes les espèces . . . tout est en un flux perpétuel' ('all beings circulate within
each other, and thus all species . . . everything is in constant flux'),[36] he
echoes, like Saunderson before him, Book 5 of *De rerum natura*. Swept
along by his vision of the material universe as one of dynamic transformation,
he exclaims that 'tout change, tout passe, il n'y a que le tout qui reste'
('everything changes, everything passes, only the whole remains'),[37] thus
echoing Books 2 and 3 of *De rerum natura*. And as d'Alembert goes on,
Diderot quotes (inexactly) one of the most famous lines from Virgil as he
expresses in condensed form his dynamic materialist vision of the world:
'Dans cet immense océan de matière, pas une molécule qui ressemble à une
molécule, pas une molécule qui se ressemble à elle-même un instant: *Rerum
novus nascitur ordo*, voilà son inscription éternelle.'[38] ('In this immense ocean
of matter, not one molecule resembles another, not one molecule resembles
itself for a second: *Rerum novus nascitur ordo*, that is its eternal motto.')
Diderot presents the line from Virgil as the motto of nature, and inherent
in nature is change: change is constant; matter constantly changes its nature
and has no stable existence; matter provides substance, but only motion can
provide form. The quotation is based on a famous line from the fourth of
Virgil's *Eclogues*: 'Magnus ab integro saeclorum nascitur ordo.'[39] ('The great
line of the centuries begins anew.') Diderot, who was known to have been
alive to Lucretian echoes in Virgil's poetry, may well have detected here
echoes of Lucretius' account of the history of the world in Book 2 of *De rerum
natura*.[40] What is also striking about this line is that it is precisely the line in
which medieval readers of Virgil, including Dante, saw him predicting the
coming of Christ. In other words, the line had acquired a Christian interpretation which, in reappropriating it, Diderot effectively jettisons: for the
Lucretian Diderot, the only reality is not divine, but material.[41]

THE POLITICS OF THE *PHILOSOPHE*,
ANCIENT AND MODERN

If the ancients helped Diderot to think about philosophy, they also helped
him to think about himself and his place in the world as an intellectual.
Diderot habitually thinks through, and sees himself in, a series of

emblematic figures, notably Socrates, Diogenes, Aristippus and Seneca, in a process of self-definition that speaks loudly of his creative relationship to the past.

Diderot famously identified himself with Socrates.[42] He translated Plato's *Apology* while imprisoned at Vincennes for having published the *Lettre sur les aveugles* (*Letter on the Blind*).[43] Socrates now became a reality for him, even a mirror-image of himself: the man of self-sacrifice and irreproachable integrity, an enlightened champion against obscurantism, a martyr to truth. It is unsurprising that Socrates was an emblematic figure for the persecuted *philosophes* in eighteenth-century France, but it was Diderot more than any who sought to establish clear parallels between them. Writing in the *Correspondance littéraire* of 1 August 1762, Grimm attributes to Diderot precisely such a parallel: 'Socrate, au moment de sa mort, était regardé à Athènes comme on nous regarde à Paris ... Mes amis, puissions-nous en tout ressembler à Socrate, comme sa réputation ressemblerait à la nôtre au moment de son supplice!'[44] ('Socrates, at the time of his death, was regarded in Athens as we are in Paris ... My friends, may we be just like Socrates, just as his reputation might resemble ours at the time of his trial!') Diderot had by this stage already planned in his *De la poésie dramatique* a moving and instructive *drame philosophique* about Socrates,[45] which in the event he never wrote, but which appears to have inspired other dramatists, foremost amongst them Voltaire.[46]

Diderot saw in Socrates an embodiment of the still very contemporary struggle of free thought against superstition. In Book 19 of the *Histoire des deux Indes* (*History of the Two Indies*), for instance, he celebrates him for offering a moral code free from religion:

Il y a plus de deux mille ans que Socrate, étendant un voile au-dessus de nos têtes, avait prononcé que rien de ce qui se passait au-delà du voile ne nous importait, et que les actions des hommes n'étaient pas bonnes parce qu'elles plaisaient aux dieux, mais qu'elles plaisaient aux dieux parce qu'elles étaient bonnes: principe qui isolait la morale de la religion.[47]

(More than two thousand years ago, Socrates, stretching out a veil above our heads, declared that nothing that happened beyond the veil was of any importance to us and that man's actions were not good because they were pleasing to the gods, but that those actions were pleasing to the gods because they were good: this principle separated morality from religion.)

And in the *Réfutation d'Helvétius* (*Refutation of Helvétius*), he defends Socrates' bravery in dying for truth, asking: 'Oserez-vous blâmer l'homme courageux et sincère qui aime mieux périr que de se rétracter, que de flétrir par sa rétraction son propre caractère et celui de sa secte?'[48] ('Will you dare blame the brave and sincere man who prefers to die than to retract and thus blacken his own character and that of his sect?')

However, Diderot could not identify with Socrates completely, not least because Socrates believed in the immortality of the soul.[49] He therefore turned to Diogenes, the mad Socrates, as Plato famously described him, the strong-willed Cynic who lived a life of poverty and moral integrity and became known for the boldness of his words and actions and for his refusal to compromise. In part, Diogenes represented for Diderot a humorous or satirical possibility, a style of comically wilful, scornful philosophy; hence his presence in *Le Neveu de Rameau* (*Rameau's Nephew*), a work inspired by ancient Cynicism insofar as it is a work of contempt (directed at the enemies of the *philosophes*) and about contemptibility, namely that of the avowedly base nephew, who explicitly identifies himself with Diogenes.[50]

The Cynicism of Diogenes also represented a philosophical and moral ideal for Diderot: the ideal of autonomy, the free and self-sufficient life, and the exemplary quality of candid impudence. Diderot describes Diogenes as 'une âme indépendante et ferme' ('an independent and steadfast soul') in the *Essai sur les règnes de Claude et de Néron* (*Essay on the Reigns of Claudius and Nero*); he also observes: 'Dans Athènes ... j'aurais pris la robe d'Aristote, celle de Platon, ou endossé le froc de Diogène.'[51] ('In Athens ... I would have assumed the robe of Aristotle or Plato or donned the dress of Diogenes.') Diderot sees in Diogenes a provocative figure, one who is prepared to keep the powerful at arm's length rather than cosy up to them. In his *Encyclopédie* article 'Cynique' ('Cynic'), he describes him thus:

Il fut plaisant, vif, ingénieux, éloquent. Personne n'a dit autant de bons mots ... Personne n'eut plus de fierté dans l'âme, ni de courage dans l'esprit, que ce philosophe. Il s'éleva au-dessus de tout événement, mit sous ses pieds toutes les terreurs, et se joua indistinctement de toutes les folies ... Voilà ce que nous devons à la vérité, et à la mémoire de cet indécent, mais très vertueux philosophe.[52]

(He was amusing, lively, ingenious, eloquent. Nobody ever said as many witticisms as he did ... Nobody had a prouder soul nor a braver mind than this philosopher. He rose above every event, he trod underfoot all fears and he toyed indiscriminately with all follies ... This is what we owe to the truth and to the memory of this indecent but very virtuous philosopher.)

Elsewhere, however, Diderot distances himself from Socrates and Diogenes, both of whom prove too idealistic, and turns instead to the more compromised figure of Aristippus, a sometime pupil of Socrates and the founder of the Cyrenaic school of philosophy. The ambiguities in Diderot's position emerge in the *Salon de 1767*, in which he stages a debate between Socrates and Aristippus: subverting the historical record, Diderot implies that the stubbornly principled Socrates called for civil disobedience, and he has Aristippus define virtue in terms of obeying laws, be they good or bad, and argue that one can better influence the law-makers, not by rebelling against them in the name of truth, but by keeping on good terms with them: 'Je ferai ma cour aux maîtres du monde; et peut-être en obtiendrai-je ou l'abolition de la loi mauvaise, ou la grâce de l'homme de bien qui l'aura enfreinte.'[53] ('I shall court the masters of the world, and perhaps I shall obtain from them the abolition of a bad law or a pardon for the good man who had broken that law.') And, significantly, in his *Mélanges pour Catherine II* (*Miscellaneous Pieces for Catherine II*), the more 'politicised' Diderot makes a clear contrast between Socrates' unwavering position and the greater flexibility of Aristippus, who, like 'B' in the last part of the *Supplément au Voyage de Bougainville* (*Supplement to Bougainville's Voyage*),[54] favours obedience to the law, not least as it avoids the risk of social unrest.[55]

Similarly, Diderot shifts allegiance to Aristippus from Diogenes. In 1769, in his *Regrets sur ma vieille robe de chambre* (*Regrets for my Old Dressing Gown*), Diderot calls himself a disciple of Diogenes, while acknowledging that he is nevertheless irresistibly drawn to the more self-indulgent lifestyle of Aristippus, with the 'robe de chambre' representing precisely Diderot's position in the social and political order: 'O Diogène, si tu voyais ton disciple sous le fastueux manteau d'Aristippe, comme tu rirais! ... J'ai quitté le tonneau où tu régnais pour servir sous un tyran.'[56] ('O Diogenes, if only you could see your disciple wearing the fine coat of Aristippus, how you would laugh! ... I have left the barrel where you reigned in order to serve under a tyrant.') Aristippus becomes for Diderot an emblem of political flexibility; through him, Diderot thinks about his own role as a kind of courtier and the extent to which he too needs to bend to political expediency.

It is a small step for Diderot from the pleasure-loving Aristippus to the worldly Seneca, the Stoic philosopher through whom Diderot thinks further about his position in the world of politics. The choice might seem odd, since Diderot the materialist might not be expected to identify himself with a Stoic, given that Stoicism placed its faith in the resolute mind alone. But Diderot in fact has an ambivalent attitude towards Stoicism, as he suggests in his *Essai sur les règnes de Claude et de Néron*, a revised and expanded version of his *Essai sur la vie de Sénèque* (*Essay on the Life of Seneca*), which had first been published as the final volume of La Grange's translation of

Seneca's works: 'Plus j'y réfléchis, plus il me semble que nous aurions tous besoin d'une teinte légère de stoïcisme.'[57] ('The more I think about it, the more it seems to me that we all need a little touch of stoicism.') The key phrase is 'teinte légère', since Diderot is wary of 'l'âpreté de cette philoso- phie dans la spéculation, et ... son impossibilité dans la pratique' ('the severity of this philosophy in speculation and ... its impossibility in practice').[58] In Seneca, crucially, Diderot finds a 'stoïcien mitigé, et peut- être même éclectique, raisonnant avec Socrate, doutant avec Carnéade, luttant contre la nature avec Zénon, et cherchant à s'y conformer avec Épicure, ou à s'élever au-dessus d'elle avec Diogène' ('a Stoic only in part, and perhaps even an eclectic, reasoning with Socrates, doubting with Carneades, fighting against nature with Zeno, and trying to conform to it with Epicurus, or to rise above it with Diogenes').[59]

But more than that, in Seneca Diderot also finds a political counterpart. Written in the wake of his experiences in Russia at the court of Catherine the Great, the *Essai sur les règnes de Claude et de Néron* shows Diderot identifying with Seneca as a disillusioned freethinker, a wise counsellor who was unable to play out his political role to the full. If Socrates was the martyr for truth, Seneca was the martyr to power: 'O Sénèque! tu es et tu seras à jamais, avec Socrate, avec tous les illustres malheureux, avec tous les grands hommes de l'Antiquité, un des plus doux liens entre mes amis et moi, entre les hommes instruits, de tous les âges, et leurs amis.'[60] ('O Seneca! You are, and you always will be, together with Socrates, all the great victims and all the great men of Antiquity, one of the sweetest links between my friends and me, between learned men of all ages and their friends.') Once again, Diderot holds up the ancient world as a mirror of the present: for ancient Rome we are invited to read modern-day Paris.[61] Diderot's reflection on Seneca's relationship with Claudius and Nero is a pretext for exploring the present, and in particular his own relationship with the powerful, including Catherine. Tellingly, of the *Essai sur les règnes de Claude et de Néron* he observes: 'C'est autant mon âme que je peins que celle des différents personnages qui s'offrent à mon récit.'[62] ('It is as much my own soul that I am painting as that of the different characters who figure in my account.') He defends Seneca against his critics, presenting him, significantly, as the victim of a 'rage antiphilosophique' ('anti-philosophical rage').[63] To this deliberate anachronism he adds the observation that 'les ennemis de nos philosophes ressemblent quelquefois merveilleusement aux détracteurs de Sénèque'.[64] ('The enemies of our *philosophes* sometimes bear a striking resem- blance to Seneca's detractors.') And perhaps most strikingly of all, there is a powerful moment of critical introspection in which Diderot and Seneca effectively merge into one, and Catherine is implicitly compared to Nero:

Les Grands une fois corrompus ne doutent de rien … et lorsque nous ne nous avilissons pas à leur gré, ils osent nous accuser d'ingratitude. Celui qui, dans une cour dissolue, accepte ou sollicite des grâces, ignore le prix qu'on y mettra quelque jour. Ce jour-là, il se trouvera entre le sacrifice de son devoir, de son honneur, et l'oubli du bienfait; entre le mépris de lui-même et la haine de son protecteur.[65]

(The powerful, once they become corrupt, question nothing … and when we do not debase ourselves as much as they would like, they dare accuse us of ingratitude. The man who, in the midst of a corrupt court, accepts or solicits favours does not know the price he will have to pay one day. That day he will find himself caught between sacrificing his duty and his honour and neglecting the benefit; between contempt for himself and hatred of his protector.)

Reading the ancient past allows Diderot to engage politically with his own present.

CONCLUSION

Diderot turns to the past in search of lessons for the present and the future: for him, antiquity is both old and new, familiar and unknown. His approach might seem excessively magpie-like, reflecting the observation he makes in the *Mélanges pour Catherine II* on his working method: 'Si je trouve quelque chose dans les auteurs qui me convienne, je m'en sers.'[66] ('If I find something I like in an author, I use it.') But what is of interest is the way in which Diderot assimilates and reworks ancient writers for a whole range of polemical ends. He is no blind follower of the ancients,[67] nor, contrary to expectations, is he straightforwardly one of the 'moderns'.

Diderot's relationship to the past is more complex, as he himself suggests. In his letter to Falconet in February 1766, to which I referred at the beginning of this chapter, Diderot presents life in the present as a delicate balancing act, with humankind perched 'sur la pointe d'une aiguille' ('on a pinhead'), his nature being to 'osciller sans cesse sur ce *fulcrum* de son existence' ('oscillate constantly on this fulcrum of his existence'); but these oscillations are not limited in either time or space, as two telling examples illustrate: 'Épicure sur sa balançoire, porté jusque par-delà les barrières du monde, heurte du pied le trône de Jupiter; Horace dans la sienne fait un écart de deux mille ans et s'accélère vers nous, son ouvrage à la main, en nous disant: Tenez, lisez et admirez.'[68] ('Epicurus on his seesaw, carried over the barriers of the world, kicks Jupiter's throne; Horace on his lunges forward two thousand years and hurtles towards us, his works in his hand, saying: Take this, read it and admire it.') Diderot, too, participates in this boundless oscillation, this ongoing dialogue with the past and the future. He sees the ancients in the context of his own times, and he uses them as a basis for the development of new ideas: the legacy of the past plays a vital role in his understanding of the present. He is, put simply, the most 'ancient' of the 'modern' *philosophes*, the writer who, more than any of his contemporaries, sought, as he put it in the *Salon de 1767*, to 'parler des choses modernes à l'antique' ('speak about modern things in an ancient way').[69]

NOTES

1. DPV, vol. xv, p. 5.
2. Ibid., p. 47.
3. There is to date no overall treatment of this question. Useful starting points include Jean Seznec, *Essais sur Diderot et l'Antiquité* (Oxford: Clarendon Press, 1957), which focuses largely on Diderot and the visual arts; Raymond Trousson, 'Diderot et l'antiquité grecque', *Diderot Studies*, 6 (1964), 215–45; and France Marchal, *La Culture de Diderot* (Paris: Champion, 1999), pp. 119–84. For general background on interest in antiquity in eighteenth-century France, see Chantal Grell, *Le Dix-Huitième Siècle et l'antiquité en France, 1680–1789*, SVEC, 330–1 (Oxford: Voltaire Foundation, 1995).
4. See DPV, vol. I, p. 12.
5. Denis Diderot, *Œuvres*, ed. Laurent Versini, 5 vols. (Paris: Laffont, 1994–9), vol. III, p. 454. On Diderot's reading of Homer, see Raymond Trousson, 'Diderot et Homère', *Diderot Studies*, 8 (1966), 185–216.
6. DPV, vol. xIV, pp. 278–9.
7. See Raymond Trousson, 'Diderot et la leçon du théâtre antique', in Anne-Marie Chouillet (ed.), *Colloque international Diderot (1713–1784): Paris, Sèvres, Reims, Langres, 4–11 juillet 1984* (Paris: Aux Amateurs de livres, 1985), pp. 479–92.
8. DPV, vol. xx, p. 105.
9. On Diderot's reading of ancient Greek tragedy, particularly in Pierre Brumoy's translation, see Lucette Pérol, 'Diderot, les tragiques grecs et le père Brumoy', *SVEC*, 154 (1976), 1593–1616.
10. DPV, vol. x, pp. 119–20.
11. Ibid., p. 179; Horace, *Ars poetica*, 156–7. References to Horace are from *Satires, Epistles and Ars poetica*, ed. H. R. Fairclough (Cambridge, MA: Harvard University Press, 1929). For further discussion, see Russell Goulbourne, 'Diderot et Horace, ou le paradoxe du théâtre moderne', in N. Cronk (ed.), *Études sur 'Le Fils naturel' et les 'Entretiens sur le Fils naturel' de Diderot* (Oxford: Voltaire Foundation, 2000), pp. 112–22.
12. See DPV, vol. x, pp. 403–4. See also Dorval's discussion of Terence's *Hecyra* in the third of the *Entretiens* (ibid., p. 129).
13. See ibid., p. 397.
14. DPV, vol. xIII, p. 460. Diderot knew Terence's theatre well, having over a number of years read and revised in manuscript Guillaume-Antoine Le Monnier's translation, which was finally published in 1771: see Raymond

Trousson, 'Diderot et Térence', in *Mélanges à la mémoire de Franco Simone*, 4 vols. (Geneva: Slatkine, 1980–83), vol. IV, pp. 351–63.

15. DPV, vol. X, p. 101.
16. Ibid., pp. 116–17. See also Chapter 10 of *De la poésie dramatique*: 'La nature m'a donné le goût de la simplicité, et je tâche de le perfectionner par la lecture des Anciens' (ibid., p. 366). ('Nature has given me a taste for simplicity, and I try to perfect it by reading the ancients.')
17. Diderot, *Œuvres*, ed. Versini, vol. III, p. 420.
18. DPV, vol. II, p. 116. See also Diderot's *Encyclopédie* article 'Pyrrhonienne ou sceptique, philosophie' ('Pyrrhonian or Sceptical Philosophy'), in which he observes that, in response to any question put to him, the Pyrrhonian is equally ready to argue for or against, whereas the sceptic avoids expressions indicating formal denial or affirmation (DPV, vol. VIII, pp. 143–4).
19. DPV, vol. II, p. 35.
20. Ibid.
21. DPV, vol. VII, pp. 36–7.
22. See Paolo Casini, 'Diderot et le portrait du philosophe éclectique', *Revue internationale de philosophie*, 148–9 (1984), 35–45.
23. Horace, *Epistles*, I.1. 14.
24. For further discussion, see Russell Goulbourne, 'Appropriating Horace in Eighteenth-Century France', in L. B. T. Houghton and M. Wyke (eds.), *Perceptions of Horace: A Roman Poet and his Readers* (Cambridge: Cambridge University Press, 2009), pp. 256–70.
25. See DPV, vol. II, pp. 85, 114, 139.
26. Horace, *Satires*, II.3. 295.
27. For Diderot's knowledge of Lucretius, see Johan W. Schmidt, 'Diderot and Lucretius: The *De rerum natura* and Lucretius's Legacy in Diderot's Scientific, Aesthetic, and Ethical Thought', *SVEC*, 208 (1982), 183–294. See also Eric Baker, 'Lucretius in the European Enlightenment', in S. Gillespie and P. Hardie (eds.), *The Cambridge Companion to Lucretius* (Cambridge: Cambridge University Press, 2007), pp. 274–88, especially pp. 278–80.
28. DPV, vol. XVI, p. 256; Lucretius, *De rerum natura*, III.53–4. References to Lucretius are from *De rerum natura*, ed. W. H. D. Rouse and M. F. Smith (Cambridge, MA: Harvard University Press, 1982).
29. DPV, vol. II, p. 20. See also Diderot's allusion to Plutarch's essay on superstition to support his argument that superstition is more pernicious than atheism (ibid., p. 21).
30. Ibid., p. 20, n. 11. The quotation, meaning 'everlasting punishment is to be feared after death', is from *De rerum natura*, I.III.
31. DPV, vol. IX, p. 27; cf. Lucretius, *De rerum natura*, IV.337: 'E tenebris autem quae sunt in luce tuemur.' ('Again we see out of the dark what is in the light.')
32. See Paolo Quintili, 'Les matérialistes anciens chez Diderot', in M. Benítez *et al.* (eds.), *Materia actuosa: Antiquité, âge classique, lumières. Mélanges en l'honneur d'Olivier Bloch* (Paris: Champion, 2000), pp. 487–512.
33. See DPV, vol. II, pp. 28–30.

34. DPV, vol. IV, p. 50; cf. *De rerum natura*, v.828–31, 837–54. For further discussion, see Christine M. Singh, 'The *Lettre sur les aveugles*: Its Debt to Lucretius', in J. H. Fox *et al.* (eds.), *Studies in Eighteenth-Century French Literature Presented to Robert Niklaus* (Exeter: University of Exeter Press, 1975), pp. 233–42. Similarly, Lucretian physical notions abound in the *Pensées sur l'interprétation de la nature*, particularly in *pensées* 50, 51, 56 and 58 (DPV, vol. IX, pp. 77–85, 88–98). On the ancient principle of the immortality of matter, see also Diderot's *Encyclopédie* article 'Impérissable' ('Imperishable') (DPV, vol. VII, p. 507).

35. For a discussion of some of the echoes of Lucretius in *Le Rêve de d'Alembert*, see Ian H. Smith, '*Le Rêve de d'Alembert* and *De rerum natura*', *Journal of the Australasian Universities Language and Literature Association*, 10 (1959), 128–34, and Alain Gigandet, 'Lucrèce vu en songe: Diderot, *Le Rêve de d'Alembert* et le *De rerum natura*', *Revue de métaphysique et de morale*, 3 (2002), 427–39. On Diderot's plans for an 'ancient Greek' version of *Le Rêve*, see Jean Varloot, 'Le projet "antique" du *Rêve de d'Alembert*', *Beiträge zur romanischen Philologie*, 2 (1963), 49–61. On Democritus and Leucippus, see Diderot's *Encyclopédie* article 'Éléatique' ('Eleatic') (DPV, vol. VII, pp. 140–6).

36. DPV, vol. XVII, p. 138. Cf. Lucretius, *De rerum natura*, v.828–31. A similar echo of Lucretius is found in Diderot's *Encyclopédie* article 'Jordanus Brunus', where he discusses the idea of matter being in a state of constant flux (DPV, vol. VII, pp. 559, 561).

37. DPV, vol. XVII, p. 128. Cf. Lucretius, *De rerum natura*, II.999–1003, III.964–71.

38. DPV, vol. XVII, p. 128.

39. Virgil, *Eclogues*, v.4. References to Virgil are from *Eclogues, Georgics, Aeneid 1–6*, ed. H. R. Fairclough and G. P. Goold (Cambridge, MA: Harvard University Press, 1999).

40. See Lucretius, *De rerum natura*, II.1144–74. Cf. DPV, vol. XVIII, pp. 10–11.

41. For further echoes of Lucretius, see Diderot's *Encyclopédie* article 'Épicuréisme' ('Epicureanism') (DPV, vol. VII, pp. 270–9).

42. See Seznec, *Essais sur Diderot et l'Antiquité*, pp. 1–22, and Raymond Trousson, *Socrate devant Voltaire, Diderot et Rousseau: la conscience en face du mythe* (Paris: Minard, 1967), pp. 45–65.

43. See DPV, vol. IV, pp. 245–80; see also Raymond Trousson, 'Diderot helléniste', *Diderot Studies*, 12 (1969), 141–326. Significantly, after his imprisonment in Vincennes, Diderot decided to keep many of his most subversive works to himself, and in this respect he may have been influenced by Socrates' fate just as Plato was, according to Diderot's *Encyclopédie* article 'Platonisme' ('Platonism') (DPV, vol. VIII, p. 115).

44. Grimm, *Correspondance littéraire, philosophique et critique*, ed. M. Tourneux, 16 vols. (Paris: Garnier, 1877–82), vol. V, p. 134. See also Diderot's letter to Falconet in February 1766, in which he paraphrases a passage from Plato's *Apology* (38d–39c) before asking: 'Est-ce que nous ne sommes pas tous deux dans Athènes?' (DPV, vol. XV, p. 41). ('Are we not both of us in Athens?')

45. See DPV, vol. X, pp. 339–41, 412–16. See also his letter about his planned drama to Jacob Vernes of 9 January 1759 (*Corr.*, vol. II, p. 107).

46. See Russell Goulbourne, 'Voltaire's Socrates', in M. Trapp (ed.), *Images and Uses of Socrates from Antiquity to the Present* (Aldershot: Ashgate, 2007), pp. 229–47.

47. Diderot, *Œuvres*, ed. Versini, vol. III, p. 629.

48. DPV, vol. XXIV, p. 590. See also Diderot's letter to Jeanne-Christine de Maux in summer 1769 concerning his debate with d'Holbach and friends about the value of Socrates' self-sacrifice (*Corr.*, vol. IX, pp. 112–13).

49. Cf. Diderot's exclamation in his *Encyclopédie* article 'Socratique' ('Socratic'): 'Ah Socrate, je te ressemble peu; mais du moins tu me fais pleurer d'admiration et de joie!' (DPV, vol. VIII, p. 317). ('Oh Socrates, I am not really like you; but at least you make me shed tears of admiration and of joy!')

50. See DPV, vol. XII, pp. 192–3. See also Jean Starobinski, 'Diogène dans *Le Neveu de Rameau*', *Stanford French Review*, 8 (1984), 147–65; Heinrich Niehues-Pröbsting, 'The Modern Reception of Cynicism: Diogenes in the Enlightenment', in R. B. Branham and Marie-Odile Goulet-Cazé (eds.), *The Cynics: The Cynic Movement in Antiquity and its Legacy* (Berkeley: University of California Press, 1996), pp. 329–65, especially pp. 347–53; and Louise Shea, *The Cynic Enlightenment: Diogenes in the Salon* (Baltimore, MD: Johns Hopkins University Press, 2010), pp. 56–73.

51. DPV, vol. XXV, pp. 53, 102.

52. DPV, vol. VI, pp. 538–9. See also Diderot's response in the *Salon de 1767* to Jean-Bernard Restout's painting *Diogène demandant l'aumône aux statues* (*Diogenes Asking the Statues for Alms*): DPV, vol. XVI, pp. 427–8.

53. DPV, vol. XVI, p. 204.

54. See DPV, vol. XII, p. 643.

55. See Diderot, *Œuvres*, ed. Versini, vol. III, p. 349.

56. DPV, vol. XVIII, p. 52. See also Diderot's 1754 *Encyclopédie* article 'Cyrénaïque' ('Cyrenaic'): DPV, vol. VI, pp. 548–9.

57. DPV, vol. XXV, p. 372. There is a series of useful articles on this text by Laurence Mall: 'Une autobiolecture: l'*Essai sur les règnes de Claude et de Néron* de Diderot', *Diderot Studies*, 28 (2000), 111–22; 'Sénèque et Diderot, sujets à caution dans l'*Essai sur les règnes de Claude et de Néron*', *Recherches sur Diderot et sur l'Encyclopédie*, 36 (2004), 43–56; and 'Une œuvre critique: l'*Essai sur les règnes de Claude et de Néron* de Diderot', *Revue d'histoire littéraire de la France*, 106 (2006), 843–57.

58. DPV, vol. XXV, p. 374.

59. Ibid., p. 54. See also Diderot's *Encyclopédie* article 'Stoïcisme' ('Stoicism'), in which he argues that the Stoics were 'matérialistes, fatalistes et à proprement parler athées' ('materialists, fatalists and, frankly, atheists') (DPV, vol. VIII, p. 339).

60. DPV, vol. XXV, p. 39.

61. This was recognised by contemporary readers: see, for example, Grimm's account of the text in March 1782 (*Correspondance littéraire*, vol. XIII, p. 104).

62. DPV, vol. XXV, p. 36.

63. Ibid., p. 172.

64. Ibid., p. 210.

65. Ibid., p. 74.

66. Diderot, *Œuvres*, ed. Versini, vol. III, p. 355.

67. See, for instance, in the *Salon de 1763*, Diderot's attack on those who uniformly dismiss contemporary artists as inferior to their ancient forebears (DPV, vol. XIII, p. 531), and the letter, possibly written to Naigeon in 1774, in which he defends his literary taste, while admitting that no ancient writer is perfect (*Corr.*, vol. XIV, pp. 18–19).

68. DPV, vol. XV, p. 50.

69. DPV, vol. XVI, p. 352.

CHAPTER 2

Diderot's earlier philosophical writings

Marian Hobson

Diderot's standing as a philosopher is decidedly non-standard.[1] It is odd in a number of ways. First, he worked for much of his life as a part of various socio-professional groups[2] – different ones succeeding each other from the 1740s on: the *Encyclopédistes* during the later 1740s and the 1750s when he acted as the director of the great *Encyclopédie*; painters, architects and doctors in the 1760s, their information, and sometimes their personalities, brought into the trilogy *Le Rêve de d'Alembert* (*D'Alembert's Dream*) and into his art criticism, the great *Salons* of the 60s; the team round Raynal putting together the history of colonialism and European expansion, *Histoire des deux Indes* (*A History of the Two Indies*) during the 1760s and 1770s; the very wealthy Baron d'Holbach's coterie from about 1752 on, and the materialist–atheist volumes it produced. Most of Diderot's most important philosophical work is connected with these groups, written for them and their project, or sometimes inspired by them, in the sense of being commentary literally written in the margins of their works: Helvétius with the *Réfutation d'Helvétius* (*Refutation of Helvétius*), written in 1773; the Dutch philosopher Hemsterhuis (about the same date); or of works these were interested in – the Roman philosopher Seneca who committed suicide on Nero's orders (Diderot wrote twice: *Essai sur la vie de Sénèque le philosophe, sur ses écrits, et sur les règnes de Claude et de Néron* (*Essay on the Life and Works of the Philosopher Seneca, and on the Reigns of Claudius and Nero*), written between 1776 and 1778 at the instigation of d'Holbach, and then as if in the margins of Seneca's writings and his own work on Seneca, in the *Essai sur les règnes de Claude et de Néron* (*Essay on the Reigns of Claudius and Nero*), written between 1779 and 1781.) Although various members of the above-mentioned groups were treated by enemies and friends alike as a social set and labelled 'les philosophes', the singular version 'le philosophe' was attached to Diderot alone, as if it were a generic. No doubt this use refers to the very public role he played as leader of the battalion and chief executive officer of the work expressly entitled as that of a group:

Encyclopédie, ou Dictionnaire raisonné des sciences, des arts et des métiers, par une société de gens de lettres (*Encyclopedia, or an Analytical Dictionary of the Sciences, Arts and Trades, by a Society of Men of Letters*).

A second oddity: some of his most successful philosophical work – successful in the sense of having survived today in the reading of the general public – is written not in discursive form but as dialogues, or novels in dialogue. These include *Le Rêve de d'Alembert* and *Le Neveu de Rameau* (*Rameau's Nephew*). I shall leave these two aside, since they are covered in other sections of this volume.

A third oddity, possibly a result of the two preceding: he would probably not now be considered a philosopher at all, at any rate not by some cultural measures. Two instances of this side-lining: his work seems never to appear in the texts set for the *agrégation de philosophie* written exams, though it does occasionally in the orals, and his appearance in English histories of philosophy is usually fleeting.[3] In spite of his generic title, Diderot's present-day institutional standing as a philosopher is then altogether less secure than that of his friend and later enemy Jean-Jacques Rousseau, of Montesquieu, or even of Helvétius.

Why should this be? When one surveys the main writings that could be called philosophical, a main reason seems to emerge: they are not cast in the form of self-standing treatises of philosophy, but in much looser or shorter form, often of commentary, allowing an appearance, and sometimes the reality, of disconnectedness. This is not just the effect on his production of his having cast much of it in the form of the *Encyclopédie* articles on the history of philosophy. It is more than a result of that career necessity, or choice. It is as if he wrote best, or most easily, either in article form, or in an open way, as a kind of annotation; he seems to have been little concerned with using any formal or pre-existing shape to express his ideas.

In the case of what is conventionally proposed as Diderot's first philosophical work, *Principes de la philosophie morale ou Essai de M. S.*** sur le mérite et la vertu* (*Principles of Moral Philosophy, or Shaftesbury's Essay concerning Virtue and Merit*) of 1745,[4] it is difficult to decide even whether it is actually his, for it is close to being a paraphrase of a work by Shaftesbury. The footnotes are said to be entirely the translator's, whereas in fact, though they are sometimes original, more often they are derived from other works by Shaftesbury.[5] Conversely, in French the translation sometimes reads as rather far from Shaftesbury in its effect, and that slippage, if it can be so called, from the English works in the same direction as some of the notes which appear to be entirely his. Now, Diderot at this time was already scratching a living as a translator and a team manager. He had begun James's

Dictionary of Medicine as the head of a team and completed Temple Stanyan's three-volume *Grecian History* (1707, 1739) on his own, as far as we know; the *Encyclopédie* begins as a project for a translation of Chambers' *Cyclopaedia*, which Diderot takes over and vastly expands into a monumental team effort (seventeen double-columned folio volumes; eleven volumes of prints). So though the *Essai sur le mérite et la vertu* is treated as his first book, it has a somewhat ambiguous status. Derived but also deviating from Shaftesbury, the choice of text seems to have been Diderot's: out of a collection of essays round ethics and aesthetics, he picks an 'Inquiry' on the relation between ethics and happiness. Diderot much later appears to confirm the connection between his early choice of Shaftesbury and what he says is his own permanent worry about the motivation for ethical action: What is the good of being good? Will it increase our happiness? 'J'étais bien jeune lorsqu'il me vint en tête que la morale entière consistait à prouver aux hommes, qu'après tout, pour être heureux, on n'avait rien de mieux à faire que d'être vertueux; tout de suite je me mis à méditer cette question, et je la médite encore.'[6] ('I was pretty young when it entered my head that the whole of morality consisted in proving to mankind that after all, in order to be happy, the best thing to do was to be virtuous; I began to meditate this question immediately, and I am still meditating it.')

The preliminary discourse of the *Essai* sketches out the two main directions his future work will take: scientific and moral. It presents both as objects of empirical investigation. But we will see later that his concern with experience as action can encompass speculation – which is after all an *activity* of the mind, though designed as a kind of internal experiment restricted to thinking and writing, and thus, in another sense, highly unempirical. Diderot's view of man is anthropological. Man is a 'creature', a term which places him in a group with all other animals, and he is said to have, like them, a natural tendency towards his individual well-being (*bien-être*). Now it might seem that Diderot/Shaftesbury has merely developed a topos of eighteenth-century thought: man is naturally sociable, and his sociability and his egoism are not in conflict:

> ... God and Nature link'd the gen'ral frame,
> And bade self-love and social be the same.[7]

But in fact, even in this *Essai*, even this early in his intellectual cursus – though not his life; Diderot is a late starter – he moves beyond this eighteenth-century cliché. His view of man is generalising and broad; anthropological in tendency, it treats man as a group, a species. Yet Diderot also sees man as an individual, and this allows him to hint at a darker side. If, as an individual, man should also have tendencies which prevent his attaining that good, that well-being, then he is 'denatured' – so altered that he has lost his human nature. This word will come into important resonance some ten years later with Rousseau, for whom in his Second Discourse (1755) man is not 'denatured' but 'depraved' by his capacity to think, or rendered crooked, if the word is taken etymologically. In other words, he has taken a wrong path in his evolution (*dépravé* is a word associated with morals): 'Si elle nous a destinés à être sains, j'ose presque assurer, que l'état de réflexion est un état contre Nature, et que l'homme qui médite est un animal dépravé.'[8] ('If nature had destined us to be healthy, I dare nearly affirm that the state of reflection is a state against nature, and that who meditates is a depraved animal.') Whereas, for Diderot, if a man cannot attain happiness for himself by harmony with the world, he has not merely taken a wrong turning in his development. It is significant that Diderot should use *dénaturé*. Such a man is quite simply altogether outside nature, and his situation is not to be connected with any particular turning in human historical development.

That the ego and the more general social interests should not conflict is not surprising in the *Essai*. The world is just so ordered that this is so: being eaten by a spider is not agreeable for the fly, but is natural, a part of the web of things. Diderot uses the word 'sacrifice' where Shaftesbury does not, but the good of the spider is not the result of a willing sacrifice on the part of the fly. The fly's existence is necessary so that the spider thrives: 'L'existence de la mouche est nécessaire à la subsistance de l'araignée.'[9] ('The fly's existence is necessary to the sustenance of the spider.') This is a strange argument: a treatment of the food chain as the model for ethics. When developed, it will lead to the world of the marquis de Sade's imagination. In such a world, there is no justice, merely a relation of forces. It is a system which preserves itself, but not those within it. There is no absolute evil, only relative evil, for evil becomes a relative evil when placed within a more encompassing system. And these ordered systems have a kind of harmony, a kind of beauty; working with them is virtuous, so that beauty and goodness merge. Appreciation of them is an effect of reason – in fact, a relation to God. Hence Diderot can claim in his *avant-propos*: 'point de vertu, sans croire en Dieu; point de bonheur sans vertu' ('No virtue without belief in God; no happiness without virtue').[10] In this, however, there is a failure to make an important distinction, which for many years runs like a fault-line through Diderot's experience of his own thinking. He will not distinguish between the interests of the species, or society, and the interests of the individual. It is the main source of his intellectual and personal differences with Rousseau. The distinction will be confronted and questioned by two works, both of which bear traces of his reflection on Rousseau's thought: *Le Paradoxe sur le comédien* (*The Paradox on the Actor*), and *Le Neveu de Rameau*, both dating for their conjectural main redaction from around 1772.

In the *Essai*, then, virtue is not related to self-denial, but to a course of action according to the advantage or disadvantage of each man's own 'system', which in turn is set up in accordance with the encompassing system or systems; where this is not the case, the man is *dénaturé*. It is obvious here why Rousseau, when ten years later he puts together his politics and his ethics (fairly developed already in the *Encyclopédie* article 'Économie politique', 1755), will feel the need for a notion like *social contract*. Rousseau needs to be able to make clear that the system he envisages is not merely personal, nor is it anthropological but is on a different level; it is political, public, an object of choice.[11] Diderot will suggest (or develop in reaction to Rousseau, as we shall see) a very different position: to act in relation to one's own good is only evil when incompatible with a wider system's good, or with nature as a whole.

For Rousseau such an action must be free, and any sacrifice voluntary. Seemingly Diderot already in 1745 does not think man is free. Man cannot choose self-denial freely, but only when unnaturally constituted; his will, which is not free, can only be self-denying if his 'choice' is a kind of unavoidable perversion. Now, such a view relies on the notion of a structure of constraining causes acting as a unified system: in the long run, things will pan out. Like its distant descendants, the 'rational market theories' of the recent credit crunch, it is only plausible if our intellectual and ethical world were to be closed, sealed from the random and the mixed-up, were a self-sufficient system shut off from the random or the totally unexpected, from the 'black swan'.[12] We will see that a mere four years later, in his *Lettre sur les aveugles* (*Letter on the Blind*), Diderot will try thought experiments to see whether this unified causal field can be deemed to exist both for man's experience and for the whole universe. The unity necessary to the system in 1745 will in 1749 be put under severe strain.

Some arguments very largely latent in the *Essai* are expanded by Diderot in a kind of continuation, the *Pensées philosophiques* (1746), a set of 'philosophical thoughts'. The first *Pensées* clear mainstream Christianity out of the way by stressing that the passions which many Christians aim to repress are the source of energy and greatness in man. The text then becomes a discussion between a sceptic, a deist and an atheist about arguments for the existence of God. The discussion is developed in a wily fashion – the epigraph 'Quis leget haec?' ('Who will read this?') is taken from the Roman satirist Persius and we will see briefly later the importance of satire in

Diderot's thought, not as a theme, but as a mode, a way of writing, a development of his argument not so much explicitly as through manner of exposition.[13] Diderot's book seems to have been a great publishing success, judging by the number of bootleg copies and refutations it inspired. This may be because it is intellectually titillating. Much of the argument is conducted as if in order to disorientate the reader: it prods and puzzles him or her. In what could do duty as a summing up we are told: 'Le scepticisme est . . . le premier pas vers la vérité'.[14] ('Scepticism is the first step to truth.') But scepticism is not just the beginning: it seems the only conclusion possible from the last two *Pensées*, one of which (LXI) opts for Christianity, but only just, the other opting for that natural religion which is common to all the great religions, their common denominator.[15] We will see, however, that the scepticism in Diderot is less a set of positions (however odd such a description of doubt and scepticism is) than a mode of writing, a way of injecting hesitation and complication into what is being expressed.[16]

The *Pensées philosophiques* move further towards atheism than the *Essai sur le mérite et la vertu*. The discussion, although fragmentary, is put forward as a narrative in the first person. Scientific arguments are used by the narrating 'I', which in effect build up the argument from 'Intelligent Design' as it is now called. This was the then current justification for deism, where an architect-God creates the world but afterwards leaves it to develop on its own.[17] The argument 'I' advances is one of the wondrous functionality of the world, especially the miniature world, the eye of a mite or a fly for instance. 'I' is putting forward here the arguments of the biologists associated with the scientist Réaumur (1683–1757), using the microscope as a kind of counterpart to the earlier discoveries through the telescope.[18] It is at this point that the atheist produces his trump card, one that so impressed Diderot's then friend, Rousseau. From an explanation of causality through antecedence in time in *Pensée* XXI, the argument moves to treating causality as a question of mathematical probability. This causality is statistical: given enough time, the world could develop through the random combination of particles of matter. The argument is that of the monkey who, playing long enough on the computer keyboard, could produce the works of Shakespeare.[19] Not unlike the monkey, Diderot is said to have written this work in a fit of intellectual drunkenness, in 'intempérances d'esprit', to make money for his mistress. One can wonder about this – he nevertheless wrote an 'Addition' to the *Pensées* some fifteen years later, and this tradition about the piece's origin should warn us that we need to reflect on the concepts of 'purpose' and 'intention', and indeed on the nature of organisation in his writing. A work may seem composed of fragments but Diderot may take pains to shape them so that the work itself can be twinned with another earlier one, through which a kind of form emerges retrospectively. This will be discussed briefly later, in regard to the *Lettre sur les sourds et muets* (*Letter on the Deaf and Dumb*) and to the *Pensées sur l'interprétation de la nature* (*Thoughts on the Interpretation of Nature*).

The *Pensées* did not please the theological or the police authorities. Diderot was spied on, denounced by his local *curé*, but left at large, unlike other writers of irreverent or irreligious brochures. However, in 1749 he took one step too far. His *Lettre sur les aveugles* goes far beyond irreligion in its examination of man's experience and beliefs; it goes far beyond in its examination of order. Diderot was arrested and imprisoned for some three months in the castle of Vincennes, until released after a humiliating confession and retraction, and after powerful friends and his publishers had urged his release on the government. This 'letter', written partly in a jocular, bantering style, had developed Locke's thesis that all knowledge in the mind is derived from the input of the senses.[20] But its concluding part had taken to its limits a problem already put to Locke after his first edition by his Irish friend, William Molyneux, whose wife was blind: do all senses give the same information, or is there a qualitative difference between them? In particular, will a man blind from birth be able to put together, through touch and hearing alone, a knowledge of those visual elements of the world that his handicap makes him miss? Could he do it through sound and language and what people tell him? How would this world be different from that of a sighted man?

In other words, as suggested already, Diderot is examining whether one can claim that there is one unified field of experience, in which all the senses are coordinated one with another. His letter starts by investigating a particular blind man and the way he lives. The blind man conducts his life at least as well as most people: he can tidy his house, he teaches his son to read using raised print, but is puzzled by optical instruments such as mirrors and microscopes. At first, we have a set of remarks and anecdotes; but quite rapidly Diderot questions the blind man about values, about beauty and honesty. For the blind man, beauty is what sighted people say is beautiful, it is completely conventional, with no real basis in the outside world; he does not value bodily modesty, because he cannot understand why showing one part of the body is worse than showing another. And honesty does not much matter to him either, except in so far as he fears not just that the sighted will steal from him, but that they will see him if he tries to thieve himself. Up to here, the investigation of the blind man suggests how much 'la morale des

aveugles est différente de la nôtre'.[21] ('How different from ours is the
morality of the blind.') There is a general conclusion: the body influences
the mind and its ideas quite radically – 'nos idées les plus purement
intellectuelles ... tiennent de fort près à la conformation de notre
corps'.[22] ('Our most purely intellectual ideas are very closely linked with
the conformation of our bodies.') What goes on in the head of a blind man
has no analogy whatsoever with what goes on in ours,[23] because when we do
geometry, we combine what we see, but the blind man can only combine
the points he can touch. So far, then, the case of the blind man suggests that
our knowledge, and more worryingly our morals, are relative to our body.
But mathematical knowledge is supposed to be non-relative: a blind man's
geometry should be the same as that of the sighted.

Diderot turns at this point to a blind mathematician who had actually
existed, Nicholas Saunderson, the holder of the Lucasian chair of mathematics in Cambridge from 1711 to 1739 (a subsequent holder being Stephen
Hawking). He explores Saunderson's tactile world, and after discussing
(and illustrating) how Saunderson calculated, using a kind of abacus on
which he could feel different numerical values, Diderot discusses the idea of
the infinite, necessary in mathematical operations. But here he strikes out,
away from the idea of the infinite in mathematics to the idea of the infinite
in natural history, one that takes us away from the possibility of an actual
infinite, associated in some Western and Islamic philosophy with the idea of
God, with the actual presence of God in the wonders of the world. He turns
to the 'negative' infinite, which, like the natural numbers, continues to
infinity, but only by a series of finite steps, each separately attainable by
merely human man. He has thus created the context in which he can
imagine the dying Saunderson saying: 'Si vous voulez que je croie en
Dieu, il faut que vous me le fassiez toucher.'[24] ('If you wish me to believe
in God, you must make me touch him.') To a blind man, or a doubting
Thomas, touching is believing. But Diderot goes much beyond this tying of
our belief in God to the particular state of our senses. For the blind man is
by his very disability a sign of lack of order in the world, a monster. In a kind
of vision, Saunderson sees a primeval chaos existing before the present
world, where animal forms were not as they are now, but monstrous,
some without heads, some without stomachs, and where the non-viable
forms failed to persist, leaving what is present now. But such an order –
'quelque arrangement dans lequel ils puissent persévérer' ('some arrangement in which they could persevere')[25] – is only momentary. The world, he
says, is 'un composé sujet à des révolutions qui toutes indiquent une
tendance continuelle à la destruction; une succession rapide d'êtres qui

s'entre-suivent, se poussent et disparaissent; une symétrie passagère; un ordre momentané' ('a composite, subject to revolutions which all indicate a continual tendency to destruction; a rapid succession of beings which follow on after each other, push each other and disappear; a passing symmetry, a momentary order').[26] The atheism is not abstract here, but is turning into a materialism; matter has not just self-organising power, but a kind of energy both creative and destructive; what it does not seem to have is direction, for the stability is purely statistical, and unlike the idea of system in the *Essai sur le mérite et la vertu*, the panning out into stasis is only momentary.

Saunderson's very last words push to a relativity so extreme that the possibility of relation and thus order in the cosmos has disappeared: 'Le temps, la matière et l'espace ne sont peut-être qu'un point.'[27] ('Time, matter and space are perhaps only a point.') The third part of the *Lettre* repeats this in psychological terms, for at its very end it puts in doubt the existence of the most basic sort of order, the physiological. Diderot does this by means of the problem put to Locke by Molyneux: could a blind man whose sight was restored distinguish a sphere from a cube by sight alone? Or would he need to have recourse to his tactile memory, and touch it? Diderot goes even further, and asks what would happen if the subject of the experiment had all his senses misaligned and in contradiction? For Diderot, the result would be more disquieting than any mere relativity in the information supplied by the senses: the whole relation between passive and active would be disturbed: that is, the very basis of our subjectivity and our self.

Diderot in this *Lettre* has systematically questioned all ideas of natural order: social, cosmic, epistemological. The fact that our senses are finally not contradictory is not the result of cosmic arrangement, nor of divine intention; it is a socio-physiological fact, constructed out of the geometry of our world and the regularity in our sense perceptions; to which are added the normalising effects of language and of education: 'Il est évident que la géométrie, en cas qu'il en fût instruit, lui fournirait un moyen infaillible de s'assurer si les témoignages de deux sens sont contradictoire ou non.'[28] ('It is evident that geometry, if he had been instructed in it, would furnish him with an infallible means to be certain whether the two senses are contradictory or not.') The *Lettre* is thinking about the relation of mathematics to order, in the universe, in our perceptions: could mathematics be merely a matter of convention? Or does it represent a non-relative foundation to our thought? The question is continued in the *Lettre sur les sourds et muets* (1751), but this time posed in connection to language. Do the very different temporalities of sense experience and language mean that any order is imposed, half-hearted and arbitrary? Do the serious differences between natural languages mean that that there is no frame of comparison? Or can we rely on a kind of Chomskian deep order, a 'natural order' in language, as the eighteenth-century calls it, which ensures meaning? In both letters, a social practice, in the first case education, in the second language, allows order to arise out of potential disorder.

In 1782, two years before his death, Diderot writes *Additions à la Lettre sur les aveugles* (*Additions to the Letter on the Blind*), partly no doubt to emphasise its formal relation to the *Lettre sur les sourds et muets*, and to make them more of a structural pair in their treatment of the nature of knowledge. But one can wonder whether earlier, in his work on the *Encyclopédie*, there is not also the drive to create philosophical patterns in this way. Many articles are derived from or are developments of Brucker's *Historia critica philosophiae*.[29] But in at least one or two important cases, it is as if he constructs an opposing twin, this time not with himself but with Rousseau. Rousseau, for reasons that are even now ill understood, was given or accepted to write only one article on political thought for the *Encyclopédie*: 'Économie politique' ('Political Economy'), published in 1755 but in all likelihood requested earlier. Yet Diderot, who was close to him from the early 1740s till their final quarrel in 1757, must have known at least something of his friend's brilliant ideas. He certainly knew a great deal about the first two discourses, correcting the proofs for the first, and being considered by Rousseau as the inspirer of parts of the second. 'Économie politique' is even held to be in part a draft or variant of parts of *Du contrat social* (*The Social Contract*). How does it then fit in with other political articles in the *Encyclopédie*? In the first volume (1751), there is an article 'Arithmétique politique' written by Diderot, which takes an opposing position to that of Rousseau on 'political arithmetic'. Diderot recounts the development by William Petty (1623–87) of that science – in other words, of the use of demography and statistics in public administration – to conclude his first paragraph, but in effect the whole article, by the statement 'Le monde politique, aussi bien que le monde physique, peut se régler à beaucoup d'égards par poids, nombre et mesure.'[30] ('The political world, just like the physical world, can be regulated in many ways by weight, number and measure.') The driving idea of 'political arithmetic', that man's political life can be regulated not perhaps by political and moral choice but by statistics, is not Rousseau's, as he has made clear in the First Discourse and will do so again in 'Économie politique'.[31]

In fact it is as if Diderot and Rousseau at this point in their lives define and refine their ideas in relation to each other. Both endorse the initial statement of Diderot's article 'Autorité politique' ('Political Authority'), in the first volume of the *Encyclopédie*: 'Aucun homme n'a reçu de la nature le droit de commander aux autres.'[32] ('No man has received from nature the right to command others.') The article caused a political storm in France on its first publication, for its implicit attack on the doctrine of the Divine Right of Kings, the official political doctrine of the state: 'la couronne, le gouvernement, et l'autorité publique, sont des biens dont le corps de la nation est propriétaire', writes Diderot.[33] ('The crown, the government, and public authority are possessions belonging to the body of the nation.') Both Rousseau and Diderot proclaim the sovereignty of the people. But their discussion through the *Encyclopédie* and Rousseau's political manuscripts[34] takes an increasingly divided and divisive aspect. For in volume v, the very same volume as 'Économie politique', Diderot publishes his article on 'Droit naturel' ('Natural Law', or 'Natural Right'), in which the idea of the 'General Will' is launched, later to be altered and much developed by Rousseau. Diderot's General Will is that of the 'genre humain', the whole human species. It is the will of an agglomeration of beings, not a political entity, and the 'natural right' is anthropological not political. Man's conformity of physiology with others of his species regulates everything else. If he has no free will, then his goodness is animal, a factor of his physical make-up: like the abstract system of the *Essai sur le mérite et la vertu*, he is just good or bad as a function of his relation to a wider system – his existence is fundamentally social, which is something that Rousseau comes to realise he can never accept.

In the 'Droit naturel' Diderot turns to man's consciousness of this relation: either he can accept it, and pass judgement on himself as on others, which will produce a 'do as you would be done unto' morality; or he allows exactly the same freedom to others to hurt him as he wishes to take himself, in another anticipation of Sade. What, Diderot asks, can be the right reply to such an argument, to such a monster? That even this argument has at its basis a moral argument, one of equity or reciprocity. And this reply is not to be justified by individual proclivities, but by the will of the human species, 'le genre humain'. It is this he calls the 'General Will'. For Diderot, it can be found among particular societies, even amoral ones, among brigands hidden in their caves. At this point, most tellingly, Diderot lets slip that, for him, this is still an anthropological, and not an ethical or political notion: he evokes the chief problem in contemporary natural history: whether species are fixed or in 'perpetual flux'. If the latter, he says, his argument is still valid: the nature of natural rights would not change; it would always be related to the General Will. So his 'General Will' parts company with what will become Rousseau's: it belongs to a species, there is a physiological element in it, it is described as a 'désir commun', a desire held in common. It is accessible by human reason, without which man is 'dénaturé' and to be treated as such, placed outside the system of the world, as earlier in the *Essai*.

With the publication of Rousseau's manuscript material, the aim of Diderot's article has become quite clear.[35] When he writes 'l'homme n'est pas seulement un animal, mais un animal qui raisonne' ('man is not only an animal, but a reasoning animal'), and asserts that whoever refuses to use reason in all domains 'renonce à la qualité d'homme, et doit être traité par le reste de son espèce comme une bête farouche' ('renounces his humanity, and must be treated by the rest of his species as a wild beast'),[36] he is contradicting the famous statement in Rousseau's Second Discourse, to the effect that the man who meditates is a depraved animal. The natural law in this formulation by Diderot has disquieting implications. It is based on a sociability which is universally inherent in man, one that allows violent treatment of those who are deemed excluded, 'dénaturé' – outside nature. Even more seriously, in an imperious way that makes the article's jocular tone slightly menacing, it implies at the end that he who does not accept its conclusions is equally irrational, outside the pale of nature, and 'doit être traité comme un être dénaturé' ('must be treated as an unnatural being').[37]

At more or less the same moment, or only slightly earlier, Diderot was working on a complement and development to his *Pensées philosophiques*, the *Pensées sur l'interprétation de la nature* (*Thoughts on the interpretation of nature*) of 1753. It is the first piece where an original engagement with sciences other than mathematics is revealed (in the 1746 work, he was repeating scientific commonplaces). The Divinity has been left behind in all but the tone: the first oracular words, 'Jeune homme, prends et lis' ('Young man, take [this book] and read')[38] offended the 41-year-old Frederick the Great of Prussia. He didn't recognise the quotation from Plato, but thought he recognised a pretension to legislate. However, the text is difficult – difficult precisely because it speculates rather than legislates about science. It is an attempt to create a pattern in the development of the sciences in the past and for the future. Diderot recommends an attention to experiment in the natural sciences; he suggests that work in mathematics, 'une affaire de conventions' ('an affair of conventions'),[39] be dropped by scientists. Mathematics has developed as far as it can go. And it is of little use, whereas the natural sciences are opening out. Diderot proceeds to produce examples of problems which have not been settled, but which all suggest that Nature is a kind of experimental laboratory: it produces through variation. The first is in the physiology of quadrupeds: is what we now see the result of a set of versions of a basic form? He suggests that the species of quadrupeds are these variations, but that at their confines we have an indeterminate area populated by beings that one cannot assign with certainty to one species or the next. Clearly here there is much more knowledge of contemporary science than was present in the *Lettre sur les aveugles* – Diderot is in fact referring to the work of the naturalist Buffon on the definition of species, and to his disagreements with Maupertuis. There is also, as a kind of consequence of his editing of the *Encyclopédie*, with its many articles on trades, a much greater emphasis on experience, on technical experimentation, on its necessary slowness, on its openness to what turns up. But typically, knowing the history of science, Diderot, in developing his advocacy for experiment, also reminds us how many discoveries have resulted almost accidentally: spin-offs from work on abstract problems in mathematics which turn out to be impossible to solve. For he is defining experiment in a way that can be related to inspiration, or indeed the judgement of art 'comme les gens de goût jugent des ouvrages d'esprit, par sentiment' ('as people of taste judge works of the mind, through feeling').[40]

The work admires experiment with tools but it conducts very clearly its own active tests on ideas through speculation. Diderot, goes very far towards suggesting that there is no sharp line between the mental and the physical. By using indirect speech, by placing the responsibility for these suppositions with the scientist Maupertuis, by using the hypotheses like so much experimental material, he moves in a brilliant but allusive way to ideas clearly ancestors of those which a hundred years later will be expressed round *The Origin of Species*. The time that organisms can be allotted for development is nearly infinite, the whole world is interconnected, and Diderot makes of it an integrated whole, 'un système infini de perceptions' ('an infinite system of perceptions'), a kind of animal. It could be God. The figure of Spinoza and other late-seventeenth-century thinkers, the mathematician Raphson for instance, are in the shadowy background here. For matter, it is suggested at the end, is eternal: it is living or dead, but not in stable fashion – the quality of life or death can be exchanged between molecules. The last thought in a conditional tense suggests we turn to the useful sciences, to our 'bien-être', in a phrase already picked up as important in his earlier work. But this very way of putting this suggests the value of such speculation, and incorporates it in an almost dialectical way into the purpose he is giving to human activity, technological or scientific, which is to improve life on earth.

These ideas have extraordinary range: they bring together contemporary work in biology, chemistry and the theory of reproduction. But in a way typical of Diderot, they also contain a theory of what they are: the 1753

Pensées examine the nature of speculation at the same time as they put forward cutting-edge science. In this work of successive 'thoughts', he insists on the need to connect. Yet a connection with his reader is not made easy by his choice of material, nor by the lack of a construction in regularly rhythmed steps, nor by his use of satire, a literary mode whose boundaries are often difficult to determine. His philosophical writing, like his great literary works, retains something of the rococo mode, a flickering light, not a permanent steady spotlight on a problem. In a note to the Dutch philosopher who is the addressee of the *Réfutation d'Hemsterhuis* (*Refutation of Hemsterhuis*), he explains this in terms of censorship: 'Voltaire . . . a-t-il été inconséquent? ou a-t-il eu peur du docteur de Sorbonne? Moi, je me suis sauvé par le ton ironique le plus délié que j'aie pu trouver, les généralités, le laconisme, et l'obscurité.'[41] ('Voltaire . . . was he lacking in logic? Or was he frightened of the Sorbonne theologians? As for me, I have got out of this by the most agile tone that I could find, by generalities, laconism, and by obscurity.') With all the respect one owes him, one can still wonder whether there is not in his oblique exposition of his ideas more than self-protection. The already thought-out, the standard position, are not what interest him. His atheism, his materialism hardly waver; but both less and more than theses, they are complex, questioning tools for a thinking-over of science and morals. They guide him in what type of causality to admit; by keeping their status as hypotheses always in his mind, they force a recognition from his reader of all that is not known. They keep everything always open.

NOTES

1. For a thorough, trustworthy view, see Colas Duflo, *Diderot philosophe* (Paris: Champion, 2003).
2. The historian Margaret C. Jacob in an important book has called this kind of group a 'sodality': *The Radical Enlightenment: Pantheists, Freemasons and Republicans* (London: George Allen and Unwin, 1981).
3. See, for instance, Simon Critchley, *The Book of Dead Philosophers* (London: Granta, 2008), p. 180.
4. Shaftesbury's text *An Inquiry Concerning Virtue, or Merit* was originally published as one of a collection of treatises entitled *Characteristicks of Men, Manners, Opinions, Times*, 3 vols. ([London]: [printed by John Darby], 1711). The *Inquiry* is contained in vol. II (pp. 2–176).
5. See Franco Venturi, *Jeunesse de Diderot, 1713–1753* (Paris: Skira, 1939) – still the most learned and accurate account of Diderot's early years.
6. LEW, vol. VIII, p. 167. This remark is thought by some scholars to be part of a review of a work by Jean-François Dreux du Radier: *Le Temple du bonheur, ou Recueil des plus excellents traités sur le bonheur, extraits des meilleurs auteurs anciens*

et modernes (*The Temple of Happiness, a Collection of the Most Excellent Treatises on Happiness, Taken from the Best Authors Ancient and Modern*), 4 vols. (Bouillon: aux dépens de la Société typographique, 1770), which at least supplies an approximate date, if the supposition is accepted.

7. Alexander Pope, *An Essay on Man and Other Poems* (New York: Dover, 1994), ll. 317–18.

8. Jean-Jacques Rousseau, *Œuvres complètes*, ed. Bernard Gagnebin and Marcel Raymond, 5 vols. (Paris: Gallimard, 1959–95), vol. iii (1964), p. 23.

9. DPV, vol. i, p. 312.

10. Ibid., pp. 20–1.

11. Cf. Bronislaw Baczko, *Rousseau, solitude et communauté* (Paris: Mouton, 1974).

12. The 'black swan' is Nassim Nicholas Taieb's phrase for that which is very unlikely: cf. *The Black Swan: The Impact of the Highly Improbable* (New York: Random House, 2007). The book is dedicated to Benoît Mandelbrot, the great mathematician and explorer of fractals (i.e. broadly speaking, structures exploring the statistical distribution of irregularity).

13. To my mind, in this he resembles Michel de Montaigne and Jacques Derrida.

14. DPV, vol. ii, p. 35 (*Pensée* xxxi).

15. See DPV, vol. ii, pp. 51–2.

16. See the important article by Jean-Claude Bourdin, 'Matérialisme et scepticisme chez Diderot', *Recherches sur Diderot et sur l'Encyclopédie*, 26 (1999), pp. 85–97.

17. See DPV, vol. ii, pp. 26–8 (*Pensée* xx).

18. Cf. Jacques Roger, *Les Sciences de la vie au xviiie siècle* (Paris: Colin, 1959).

19. The argument is about throwing down printer's letters randomly to produce Homer's *Iliad* (DPV, vol. ii, pp. 28–9, *Pensée* xxi). Diderot was a gifted amateur mathematician; his first publication which is both authorised by the government censorship and entirely his own is *Mémoires de mathématiques* (*Mathematical Memoirs*) of 1748.

20. See John Locke, *An Essay Concerning Human Understanding*, ed. Roger Woolhouse (London: Penguin, 1997), p. 109 (Book ii, chap. i, §2).

21. Denis Diderot, *Lettre sur les aveugles, Lettre sur les sourds et muets*, ed. M. Hobson and S. Harvey (Paris: Flammarion, 2000), p. 38.

22. Ibid., p. 37.

23. Ibid., p. 40.

24. Ibid., p. 59, ll. 1006–7.

25. Ibid., p. 62.

26. Ibid., pp. 62–3.

27. Ibid., p. 63.

28. Ibid., p. 81.

29. Jacques Proust, *Diderot et l'Encyclopédie* (Paris: Colin, 1962).

30. DPV, vol. v, p. 475.

31. See the discussions of taxes and salaries in the 'Économie politique' article – and we should remind ourselves of the opposing arguments round the question of financiers' salaries and 'bonuses' in 2010.

32. DPV, vol. v, p. 537.

33. Ibid., p. 540.
34. After the Second Discourse and 'Économie politique', there is a gap for Rousseau, who published *Du contrat social* in 1762.
35. The man who argues that he will not reason is still using reason. The article 'Droit naturel' calls him 'notre raisonneur violent' ('our violent reasoner'); see DPV, vol. VII, p. 26. Rousseau answers this in a beautiful and famous passage discovered in his manuscripts, which clearly shows that they are replying textually one to the other: 'Que notre violent interlocuteur soit lui-même le juge de nos travaux, montrons lui dans l'art perfectionné la réparation des maux que l'art commencé fit à la nature' (Rousseau, *Œuvres complètes*, vol. III, p. 479). ('Let our violent interlocutor be himself the judge of our work. Let us show him in art perfected the reparation of all the ills that the arts once begun did to nature.') Cf. the important article by Jean-Claude Bourdin, 'L'Effacement de Diderot par Rousseau dans l'article *Économie politique* et le *Manuscrit de Genève*', in Franck Salaün (ed.), *Diderot–Rousseau: un entretien à distance* (Paris: Desjonquères, 2005), pp. 36–50.
36. DPV, vol. VII, pp. 26.
37. Ibid., p. 29.
38. DPV, vol. IX, p. 26.
39. Ibid, p. 29 (§ III).
40. Ibid, p. 48 (§ XXX).
41. DPV, vol. XXIV, p. 409. The DPV edition presents the *Réfutation* under the title: *Observations sur la Lettre sur l'homme et ses rapports de Hemsterhuis* (*Observations on Hemsterhuis's Letter on Man and his Relations*).

CHAPTER 3

The Encyclopédie: *innovation and legacy*

Daniel Brewer

Conceived by a Parisian printer as a modest business venture, a French translation of Ephraim Chambers' two-volume *Cyclopaedia* printed in London in 1728, the *Encyclopédie* far outstripped all initial plans. Entrusted to Jean le Rond d'Alembert and Denis Diderot, the project quickly took on vaster proportions, ultimately becoming one of the greatest commercial and intellectual enterprises of eighteenth-century France. The first volume of the work appeared in Paris in 1751. When the final volumes were completed two decades later in 1772, the *Encyclopédie* had grown to become the most massive single reference work in Europe. It comprised seventeen folio volumes containing 71,818 articles, eleven folio volumes of 2,885 plates, and five supplemental volumes. A group of more than 150 contributors supplied articles to the work, which was directed by Diderot alone after d'Alembert withdrew from the project in 1757. (Much of the work fell to Louis de Jaucourt, who some scholars have credited with more than 17,500 articles or 27 per cent of the total number.) The *Encyclopédie* was sold by subscription in France and throughout Europe to some 4,500 individuals. Prior to the French Revolution in 1789, five subsequent editions, either reprints or revisions, were produced in Italy and Switzerland, with roughly half of these 25,000 copies sold to readers in France.

But numbers alone only begin to tell the story of the *Encyclopédie* and its significance, both in the eighteenth-century socio-intellectual context and for us today. To assess that significance, we can start by taking the encyclopedists at their own word, by considering the descriptive title that frames the work: *Encyclopédie, ou Dictionnaire raisonné des sciences, des arts et des métiers, par une société de gens de lettres* (*Encyclopedia, or an Analytical Dictionary of the Sciences, Arts and Trades, by a Society of Men of Letters*). Behind this long title lies a particular relation to the question of knowledge, its value and usefulness, and the principles according to which it can be ordered. As an analytic or descriptive dictionary, the *Encyclopédie* provided definitions that stated the general principles and essential details pertaining to all branches of science and the liberal and mechanical arts of the eighteenth century. It was the arbitrary order of the alphabet that governed the arrangement and accessibility of such knowledge. There was little that was innovative in the idea of a dictionary, a genre in which the encyclopedists had many precedessors, including the dictionary of the Académie Française (begun in 1638), Louis Moréri's *Grand dictionnaire historique* (1674), and Pierre Bayle's *Dictionnaire historique et critique* (1697). The encyclopedists made free use of more technically oriented dictionaries as well, including Antoine Furetière's *Dictionnaire universel des arts et des sciences* (1690), Thomas Corneille's *Dictionnaire des termes d'arts et de sciences* (1723), and Jacques Savary-Desbrulon's *Dictionnaire universel de commerce* (1723).

At work in the encyclopedic project, however, was a second and more profound structuring and revaluing of knowledge. As encyclopedia, the work aimed to establish and display the fundamental interconnectedness of all forms of human knowledge. The encyclopedic *mappemonde* or knowledge network was designed to map and thus reflect the order that the encyclopedists believed that thought imprints upon the world, an order that is represented visually in the encyclopedic *tableau des connaissances humaines* or table of human knowledge. In addition, the editors argued that the *Encyclopédie* would generate new orders of knowledge, new linkages between articles, ideas and modes of knowing that would result from the inquisitive and critical use to which the work's readers would put it. A vast reference work stemming from a decades-long collective documentational enterprise, the *Encyclopédie* reflects the most powerful tenet of Enlightenment thought, namely, the belief in the individual's power to understand the world critically, the world as it comes to be grasped, ordered and mastered by the rational mind. Encyclopedia and dictionary – in the pages of the *Encyclopédie* two ways of structuring knowledge are at work, two modes of evaluating this knowledge and of putting it to use. Two protocols of reading are implied here as well, which involve ways of understanding the objectives set for the encyclopedic project and the challenges confronting it.

Besides describing their work as a knowledge map or epistemological net, the encyclopedists also viewed it as a storehouse, a capacious text that accumulated all that was useful and valuable to know in order to preserve it over time and transmit it to future generations. For the *Encyclopédie* to succeed in such a transmission, the encyclopedists were well aware that language had to be carefully attended to. In the article 'Encyclopédie', for instance, a kind of user's manual that represents the work's most self-reflexive entry, Diderot voices concern that the treatment of language (as opposed to grammar) might be the work's weakest part. One way to strengthen that potential weakness is to employ a language that is accurate. But according to whom? In all the articles involving the trades and mechanical arts, Diderot notes, it is the everyday, practical language of the worker and the workshop that must be used, not exclusively the language of the scholar, whose definitions risk remaining abstract, ideal and theoretical, cut off from language in its everyday and practical use. Illustrating this view of language, as editor Diderot left the writing desk while composing numerous technical articles involving the arts and trades, venturing to the workshop to consult with artisans themselves. In the 'Prospectus' to the *Encyclopédie*, Diderot writes: 'On a trop écrit sur les Sciences: on n'a pas assez bien écrit sur la plupart des Arts libéraux: on n'a presque rien écrit sur les arts méchaniques.'[1] ('Too much has been written on the sciences; not enough has been written well on most of the liberal arts; almost nothing has been written on the mechanical arts.') Elsewhere, in the article 'Art', Diderot notes that the time-honoured distinction between the liberal and the mechanical arts, based on the division between the work of the mind and that of the hands, has unfortunately resulted in 'avilissant des gens très estimables et très utiles' ('demeaning highly estimable and useful people').[2] A look at the plates shows the value the encyclopedists attached to the world of manufacturing, the trades and the mechanical arts. As Diderot notes, a mere glance at these images conveys far more knowledge than the lengthy descriptions that accompany them. It is as if the encyclopedic gaze these images imply cuts through their object, just as the surgeon's scalpel cuts through the body in the surgical plates or as sight penetrates machines in the cross-sectional engravings, in order to reassemble those objects in the form of a diagram, that is, a kind of representation that is less concerned with depicting the real than with conveying both know-how and knowledge.

For the *Encyclopédie* to achieve its goals, attention would have to be paid to language, as Diderot stresses in the article 'Dictionnaire' ('Dictionary'). Serving as a kind of in-house style sheet, the article describes in detail the practical issues pertaining to definition that the author of each entry had to resolve, such as distinguishing between literal and figurative definitions, the limits of the definable, the role of synonyms, the influence of pronunciation upon spelling, the importance of etymology, as well as the use that could be made of other works, such as rhyming, historical and scientific dictionaries. These are practical questions, but beneath them lie the more intractable problems of linguistic usage and historical change, issues that were repeatedly grappled with in the eighteenth century. According to the linguistic theory of the time, massively influenced by the seventeenth-century grammarians of Port-Royal, the word reflects the idea, with the workings of language mirroring the mind's analysis of sense perceptions and its generation of ideas. Gradually, however, language specialists, as well as *philosophes* who approached language in its relation to other ways of knowing (such as aesthetics, history or ethics), were drawn to questions involving the temporality of the usage of language and the latter's inherent historicity. Through these questions history encroached upon linguistics in the last half of the eighteenth century, revealing the theoretical shortcomings and blind spots of Port-Royal language theory. Thus, Diderot will argue that words reflect ideas, but also that they are vessels laden with the memory traces of past cultures. Consequently, language offers Diderot a yardstick for measuring the degree of progress, philosophical as well as technical, that past civilisations have attained. Looking forward, what this view of language means, and what the encyclopedists grapple with, is that temporal and historical change permeates language. New words will be coined to refer to new discoveries, techniques and ideas. Thus they fear that linguistic flux, the very historicity of language, might well render the *Encyclopédie* incomprehensible to future generations. Here, as in so many areas of eighteenth-century intellectual enquiry, time enters the equation, creating a situation the encyclopedists will seek to resolve and indeed to turn to their advantage.

The alphabetical ordering of definitions made the *Encyclopédie* usable, allowing the reader to access the knowledge that the work systematised according to the alphabetical code. But the encyclopedists aimed at a much more critical goal. They sought, as Diderot puts it, to 'changer la façon commune de penser' ('to change the general way of thinking').[3] This restructuring of thought aimed to remake and reform a culture's worldview, in part through the work of definition, a semantic struggle that had philosophical, institutional and political dimensions. In the area of religion, for instance, the encyclopedists' efforts to change opinions and received ideas is seen in the borrowings Diderot made from the Jesuits' own reference work, the *Dictionnaire de Trévoux*, published between 1704 and 1771. In some borrowings, Diderot contests the religious doctrine and metaphysics that infused articles in the Trévoux dictionary by offering a slight but telling recasting of the Jesuits' definitions.[4] In other borrowings, Diderot's definitions refute the grounding of judgement on the transcendental principles of religion or idealist metaphysics, suggesting instead that judgement should be based on the sensing, material body, understood through the philosophical lens of empiricism, sensationalism and materialism.[5]

Besides definitions, the cross-referencing system of the *Encyclopédie* also plays a critical role in the encyclopedists' programme. Scholars have repeatedly stressed the importance of the cross-references, not only for the way they highlight textual and epistemological order by creating connections between various branches of knowledge, but also for the ironic, subversive effects they produce. Numerous cross-references have as their primary function to produce other, less predictable linkages that serve to undercut unity, resist the imposition of closure and monological order, and open up counter-discursive subtexts and the possibility of dialogical critique, notably of received ideas and institutionalised truths. These cross-references represent a more generalised textual practice characterising an intellectual culture of resistance that directed strategies of irony and dissimulation against a social and political order that forcibly repressed those intellectual developments that were perceived as a threat. If the cross-references are subversive, it is not so much because they convey particular political and philosophical views, which of course they do, but more broadly because they point to and indeed perform a more generalised and productive relation to knowledge. These cross-references, in this sense an extended synecdoche of the entire text, create an irresolvable tension between order and disorder, structure, and process, knowledge and knowing. They stand for a general reading practice that spreads across the entire work, understood as a vast set of textual, epistemological connections, switch points and nodes designed to make possible a virtually, yet not absolutely, limitless series of readings.

Diderot's comments in the article 'Encyclopédie' are but another instance of his self-reflexive highlighting of this performative production of knowledge. Here as elsewhere, Diderot takes no pains to cover over the *Encyclopédie*'s mosaic-like assemblage, its textual heterogeneity, its network of intertexts. Instead he promotes and exploits the effect on the reader and upon reading that such a situation produces. In a strikingly self-reflexive article, 'Éclectisme', Diderot sometimes incorporates word-for-word borrowings from Johann Jacob Brucker's *Historia critica philosophiae*. Yet the article does not so much reflect poorly hidden plagiarism as it performs the critical act of eclectic philosophising, borrowing an argument from here or there, rejecting an argument from elsewhere, all the while displaying the critical activity of philosophical judgement, signalled in the article by first-person reference to the writing–judging 'I'. This eclectic borrowing, which is found in Diderot's articles and above all in those of Jaucourt, often dismissed as a simple 'compiler', can also be understood self-reflexively as signalling not simply the intertextual nature of dictionary and encyclopedic production, but the fundamentally interdiscursive nature of knowledge as presented in the *Encyclopédie*.

Diderot consistently advanced the sensationalist argument, taken from John Locke and developed in France by Étienne Bonnot de Condillac, according to which ideas derive not from innate ideas, infused in the mind by God, but rather from the senses. Rejecting all divine, transcendental causality, Diderot claims that it is the sensing body that, in its immediate and material contact with the world, offers the surest, most rational way of knowing that world. In Diderot's additions to articles on the soul, and in other articles he wrote himself, such as 'Nature', 'Périr' ('Perish'), 'Volonté' ('The Will'), 'Délicieux' ('Delicious'), and 'Locke', he mounts a virulent critique of religion, based on a sensationalist relativism that situates knowledge in relation to the body. Here Diderot participates in a more general eighteenth-century rehabilitation of the passions, whereby sentiments are divided into good and bad, the unruly passions and the civilising ones. In this view of the passions, the body is freed from a subordinate position in relation to reason and mind, coming to be viewed as capable of playing a determinate, even autocratic, role in shaping human conduct. It is but one step from embracing the civilising function of certain passions, notably sympathy, as it was valorised in the moral philosophy of the period (influenced profoundly by Adam Smith), to devising mechanisms to generate the experience of such passions, such as the sentimental novel.

Although there are several articles in the *Encyclopédie* that rehearse established points of religious doctrine, in general the encyclopedists were tireless in denouncing what they took to be the repressive passion of superstition and fanaticism. Instead, they promote critical enquiry and religious tolerance. They sap the foundations of Christian doctrine and the authority of the Catholic church, missing no opportunity to present other beliefs favourably. At times this attack is made obliquely, by means of an artful use of rhetoric. For example, a harmless article that presents an orthodox statement of Christian dogma might be followed by a cross-reference to another article that mounts a virulently atheistic denunciation of theology from the pen of Baron Henri Thiry d'Holbach, and to a deistic apology for religious tolerance. Or else the seemingly harmless article 'Capuchon' ('Hood') turns out to be a forceful critique of the monastic orders. With their duplicitousness and irony, these cross-references bring philosophical perspectives into conflict, forcing the reader to rethink accepted ideas. In this fashion they are emblematic of the critical dimension of the *Encyclopédie*, which incites its reader to engage in constant interpretation, understood as a conflictual process.

It is not surprising that the encyclopedists soon found themselves embroiled in conflicts with the faculty of theology at the University of

Paris and the Jesuit editors of the *Dictionnaire de Trévoux*. Following an attempt against the life of Louis XV, as well as the storm of opposition aroused by the publication of Claude-Adrien Helvétius's materialist *De l'esprit*, Pope Clement XIII condemned the *Encyclopédie*, which the church placed on its index of forbidden books; in 1759 the crown revoked the text's *privilège* or royal authorisation to publish. (The authorisation would soon be restored, in part because the authorities recognised the commercial impact of the enterprise.)

These political struggles concerning the relation between individual rights and sovereignty are played out in the pages of the *Encyclopédie* as well. In Diderot's major entries on political authority and natural law, 'Autorité politique' and 'Droit naturel', he argues that individuals assign authority not to an individual but to a sovereign body. In return, the function of the sovereign is to guarantee the free play of natural laws, based on the notion of private property, which it is the sovereign's principal duty to protect. The theory of contractual monarchism expressed in the *Encyclopédie* reflects the growing dissatisfaction with absolutism, in theory and in practice, a dissatisfaction played out in the political struggle of the *parlements* during the 1750s and 1760s to win greater autonomy and power from the crown. The brand of contractual monarchism expressed in the pages of the *Encyclopédie* is by no means insurrectionist or revolutionary, however. It can best be understood as the political corollary of the encyclopedists' economic liberalism. Thus Louis de Jaucourt will critique despotism in the name of natural political laws, a critique that meshes with Anne-Robert-Jacques Turgot's physiocratic defence of laissez-faire capitalism in the name of supposedly equally natural economic laws. Various articles on economics, in particular those by François Quesnay, promote reforms in accordance with such laws, including limitations on the power of guilds and monopolies, tax reforms, and increased recognition of the importance of agriculture, trade and the merchant class.

Once again, language provides a lens through which to view these philosophical and political struggles, as well as the encyclopedists' reforming impulse. For if the power of church and crown could effectively be contested in the pages of the *Encyclopédie*, it was because this work and its authors found themselves in a political and discursive situation in which the authorised meanings of words could no longer be maintained intact, protected from debate and critique. No authoritative instance, whether political or religious, could succeed in channelling dispute in the public sphere, let alone neutralise such dispute and put an end to it.[6] This situation was not a limitation upon the encyclopedic project, but rather its enabling condition. The encyclopedists sought not only to collect, communicate and expand knowledge but to revise and reshape it as well. To achieve that goal they had to design a text, and with it a way of knowing, that would reconfigure the relation between the subject of knowledge, its object and the language that linked subject and world. It was through its structure, which was supposed to reveal the order and linkage between all forms of human knowledge, that the encyclopedic text would redesign the relation between epistemological subject and his or her world.

In describing the order that structures their work, the encyclopedists reject any absolute or transcendent order that can be perceived only by divine vision. Such an ideal and impossibly godly view from nowhere is one that humans can never acquire. The encyclopedists argue instead that any ordering of the world, be it that of ancient philosophy, medieval scholasticism or contemporary encyclopedism, is ultimately arbitrary. In other words models for structuring knowledge do not belong instrinsically to the object of knowledge; instead they are fashioned by the practitioner of knowledge. Thus it falls to the knower to determine the criteria according to which he or she lays claim to know the world. It is for this reason that the *Encyclopédie* is both dictionary and encyclopedia, for the alphabetical order of the dictionary is supplemented by an encyclopedic order, an order based moreover on the human mind at work as it processes sense perceptions and produces knowledge of its world. The *arbre généalogique des connaissances* or genealogical tree of knowledge displays both this mental order and the textual order that is derived from it, figuring the dynamic interconnection between categories of knowledge and groups of encyclopedic articles. Diderot explains the dovetailing of epistemological and encyclopedic order thus: judgement acts upon perception in one of three ways – by enumeration, examination or imitation. This process of judgement results in ideas that are divided into three categories of thought – history, philosophy and poetry. By continuing this process of subdividing categories of thought and of knowledge, the encyclopedists derive a complex 'tree of knowledge', a kind of epistemological flow chart that reflects both a mental order and a textual one.

In affirming the arbitrariness of epistemological models, the encyclopedists lay the ground for their argument that any model, any way of organising and evaluating knowledge, must be judged in terms of its usefulness to the knowing subject. In this sense the encyclopedists were less interested in knowing things in and for themselves than in experimenting with how they may be known most effectively. Contesting the authority and legitimacy of idealist explanatory systems, seeking to eradicate residual idealism in philosophy, science and ethics, as in the article 'Âme' ('Soul'), the encyclopedists sought to demystify knowledge by presenting it as the result of a more empirical, materialist and utilitarian way of knowing. And yet, although the encyclopedists criticised Cartesian philosophy and science for being idealist and reductive, for valuing abstract systematicity over systematic and practical knowledge, they too wished in effect to realise Descartes's dream of putting knowledge to use to ensure a way of attaining mastery and possession of the world, or 'nous rendre comme maîtres et possesseurs de la nature' ('make ourselves, as it were, masters and possessors of nature').[7] As we see in the encyclopedic plates, the world of the *Encyclopédie* is one where objects are ordered by being placed in relation to a knowing subject. The objects that fill the world of the encyclopedists are known above all by their use value and their usefulness. Thus, if the encyclopedists lay no claim to knowledge in and of itself, leaving that understanding to God and its pursuit to theologians and metaphysicians, it is because that knowledge has little value for them. What they wish for instead is useful knowledge, produced and ordered in relation to the human subject. Usefulness is indeed the value that founds encyclopedic knowledge. For the encyclopedists it is useful knowledge that makes it possible to understand more fully the workings of the natural world, to create more efficient and productive machines that improve and enrich life, to establish social and political structures designed to better the lives of the greater number, and finally to dispel all forms of error and superstition that yoke individuals to inefficient ways of knowing at best, and harmful, exploitative and destructive forms of knowledge at worst.[8]

The new relation to knowledge can certainly be phrased in terms of an Enlightenment humanism, provided one thinks somewhat critically about the term. Diderot's comments on the ordering principle of the *Encyclopédie* provide one way to do so. Reflecting on the work's order, Diderot asks: 'Pourquoi n'introduirons-nous pas l'homme dans notre ouvrage comme il est placé dans l'univers? Pourquoi n'en ferons-nous pas un centre commun? . . . L'homme est le terme unique d'où il faut partir, et auquel il faut tout ramener.'[9] ('Why do we not place man in our work the way he is positioned in the universe? Why do we not make him the work's common centre? . . . Man is the single term from which all must be derived and to which all must be reduced.') Instituting the notion of 'man' as creator and user of knowledge, the *Encyclopédie* lays claim to providing an index to the world by relating everything to this ideal and imaginary centre. At times in the *Encyclopédie* 'man' refers to a seemingly non-gendered, undifferentiated and universal subject of knowledge; at others, the term implies the white

European male subject of privileges and the social order in which he has his place. Thus it would be incorrect and equally reductive to read the *Encyclopédie* either as simply a manifesto of proto-capitalist bourgeois ideology, on the one hand, or as the heroic expression of a timeless humanism, on the other. The *Encyclopédie* does not so much reflect an eighteenth-century sense of self (whether we call it the 'man' of European humanism or the 'bourgeois individual' of early modern capitalism) as it sets in place a narrative, figural, representational mechanism that rationalises and naturalises certain actions and institutions, certain beliefs and values. It does so, moreover, by employing the powerful figure of 'man' as a driving force in the production of knowledge. In a striking metaphor, Diderot calls the *Encyclopédie* a machine. This text is indeed a knowledge machine, designed to generate both a knowledge of things and a complex, multifaceted subject who uses the *Encyclopédie* and in the process comes to know both things and self through the pages of the work.

Diderot and d'Alembert insist that the encyclopedic text they envision cannot be the work of one person, for practical as well as theoretical reasons. No one individual could claim mastery over all the areas of knowledge and technical expertise the *Encyclopédie* sought to make accessible. Only what Diderot, expanding upon the work's title, calls 'une société de gens de lettres et d'artistes' could aspire to such coverage: a group of learned individuals and artists '[qui sont] occupés chacun de sa partie, & liés par l'intérêt général du genre humain, & par un sentiment de bienveillance réciproque' ('[who are] each involved with their own share and are joined by their general interest in humankind and by a feeling of mutual goodwill').[10] The article 'Philosophe', attributed to Du Marsais, privileges the *philosophe* as the figure who, anticipating the latter-day French intellectual, best represents this humanitarian disinterestedness. Whether this figure rises above particular interests, or whether it was in fact a role that many eighteenth-century writers fashioned for themselves precisely to serve such interests, the relation to the conception, production, dissemination and use of knowledge that the *Encyclopédie* inaugurates is not only critical and disciplinary; it is collective as well. Diderot and d'Alembert defend their work against critics representing crown and church by claiming that the encyclopedic team represents nothing so much as disinterested and well-intentioned experts labouring for the greater good of humankind.

In this way the *Encyclopédie* project dovetails with the larger critical and reformist project of the Enlightenment. The *Encyclopédie* has often been presented as a kind of multi-volume manifesto of Enlightenment, a major document in the centuries-long intellectual tradition of humanism, and one of the inaugural texts containing the origins of a modern way of knowing. Especially if one focuses selectively on d'Alembert's 'Discours préliminaire', with its intellectual history of the long march from shadows to light, or on the philosophical articles in which empiricism and sensationalism crowd out idealism, or on the cultural–historical articles designed to undermine religious doctrine, the *Encyclopédie* indeed appears to promote Enlightenment rationalism, freethinking and reform. But scholars have questioned whether the notion of a monolithic 'Enlightenment project' adequately accounts for the complexity of the intellectual, social and cultural field of the eighteenth century. Indeed, the view of a liberal, liberalising, even heroic Enlightenment, such as may be derived from Immanuel Kant's celebrated 1784 essay 'Beantwortung der Frage: Was ist Aufklärung?' ('Answering the Question: What is Enlightenment?'), has been subjected to increasing scrutiny and questioning, even if, paradoxically, the terms and method of such questioning are those of Enlightenment critique itself. Nonetheless, we have become highly sceptical of the ideal of a liberating, modernising project of Enlightenment. Consequently, attempts have been made to decouple Enlightenment and the *Encyclopédie*, making it possible to view the *Encyclopédie* from other vantage points so as to be at once faithfully historical and compellingly contemporary, in a way moreover that allows us to assess more critically our own present-day relation to the encyclopedic text and the origins we locate there.[11] In other words we have come to read the *Encyclopédie* with the critical awareness that origins come into sight retrospectively, taking shape with an inevitable delay and thus after the fact. This paradoxical logic suggests that origins are not autonomous, never radically distinct from all that follows and proceeds from them, and from all that in fact constitutes these origins as such.

What of the *Encyclopédie* today? Thanks to facsimile editions in both paper and electronic format, as well as to a collaborative on-line translation project, this vast text has become more accessible and more readable.[12] Digitised web-based versions in particular have enabled a hypertextual reading of a new, powerfully searchable object in which the essential interconnectedness of the *Encyclopédie*, its textual, epistemological self-reflexivity, becomes newly discoverable. For technical reasons, the Pergamon reprint, the Redon CDRom, and the ARTFL website cannot duplicate or replace the eighteenth-century original. Does this mean though that the *Encyclopédie* has become yet another autonomous, dehistoricised reference work, produced, marketed and consumed in a culture in which everything is information, or at least appears to be, in the absence of a criterion for judgement? Certainly we no longer consult the *Encyclopédie* to obtain information about the objects in our world, as Mme de Pompadour supposedly did in order to learn the chemical composition of face powder. But in many respects it still maintains its meta-critical function, offering us the opportunity, through reading, to come to grips with how we know those objects, as well as why we desire to know them in the first place.

NOTES

1. *Encyclopédie*, vol. i, p. 4.
2. Ibid., vol. i, p. 714.
3. Ibid., vol. v, p. 13.
4. See 'Damnation', 'Irréverence', 'Jehovah', 'Irréligieux' ('Irreligious'), 'Croire' ('Belief') and 'Imaginaire' ('Imaginary').
5. See 'Involontaire' ('Involuntary'), 'Volonté' ('The Will'), 'Inné' ('Innate'), 'Spinosiste' ('Spinozist'), 'Naturaliste' ('Naturalist'), 'Naître' ('To be born'), 'Néant' ('Nothingness'), 'Rien' ('Nothing'), 'Imperceptible' and 'Harmonie' ('Harmony').
6. This argument is made by Keith Michael Baker, 'Epistémologie et politique: pourquoi l'*Encyclopédie* est-elle un dictionnaire?', in Philippe Roger and Robert Morrissey (eds.), *L'Encyclopédie: du réseau au livre et du livre au réseau* (Paris: Champion, 2001), pp. 51–8.
7. René Descartes, *Discours de la méthode* ed. Geneviève Rodis-Lewis (Paris: Garnier Flammarion, 1966), p. 84; *'Discourse on Method' and 'The Meditations'*, ed. and trans. F. E. Sutcliffe (London: Penguin, 1968), p. 78. The quotation is taken from the 'Sixième Partie' (pp. 83–95).
8. The emergence of postcolonial studies has brought renewed attention to the treatment of the question of race in the *Encyclopédie*, as well as systems of exploitation that definitions of race were taken to legitimate. See, for example, the articles 'Hottentots', 'Nègre' ('Negro'), 'Esclave' ('Slave' – pertaining primarily to slaves in antiquity), and 'Sucrerie' ('Sugar Plantation').
9. *Encyclopédie*, vol. v, p. 614.
10. Ibid., p. 636.
11. For a collection of essays that explore this issue, see Roger and Morrissey, *L'Encyclopédie*. I propose a reassessment of our relation to the Enlightenment in *The Enlightenment Past: Reconstructing Eighteenth-Century French Thought* (Cambridge: Cambridge University Press, 2008).
12. See www.hti.umich.edu/d/did/intro.html.

CHAPTER 4

Diderot, Rousseau and the art of craft

Angelica Goodden

Diderot to Rousseau: as social to solitary, atheist to believer, urban to rustic, progressive to primitive, *bon viveur* to ascetic, mechanist to Luddite, matter to spirit? There is some truth in these antitheses, though none reflects a straightforward reality. An article written by Jean Fabre nearly half a century ago drew attention to the common principles that underlay an apparently oppositional relationship, focusing primarily on philosophical matters.[1] But there is another avenue worth exploring in connection with the rapport between these 'frères ennemis'. It generates a new set of contrasts – between dexterity and genius (or hand and mind), deed and thought, fact and fancy – that on further scrutiny resolve into a kind of likeness; but its origins lie far back in the lives of both men.

Diderot's daughter Mme de Vandeul relates how in his early youth the future *philosophe* declared that he wished to abandon his studies. His cutler father (Didier) put him to work making knives and other instruments. After four or five days during which Denis ruined many pieces, he decided to resume his education, declaring: 'J'aime mieux l'impatience que l'ennui.'[2] ('I prefer impatience to boredom.') He had clearly changed by the time he came to edit the *Encyclopédie*, for which he wrote a number of entries on the crafts, including 'Coutelier' ('Cutler'). This new Diderot was so determined to gain first-hand experience of different trades that he visited workshops, consulted artisans, operated their machines and used their tools, almost – as he notes in the Prospectus to the *Encyclopédie* – becoming an apprentice himself. Raising the status of craft, arguing the case for *métiers* ('trades' or 'crafts') along with science (in the then current sense of 'that which is rationally known') and art, had from the outset been a specific goal of the *Encyclopédie*, enshrined in its subtitle *Dictionnaire raisonné des sciences, des arts et des métiers* (*An Analytical Dictionary of the Sciences, Arts and Trades*).

Yet the entry 'Artisan' ('Artisan' or 'Craftsman'), which might have seemed made for this purpose, lightly but firmly denigrates its subject. Why? According to its anonymous author, the title was the 'nom par lequel on désigne les ouvriers qui professent ceux d'entre les arts mécaniques qui supposent le moins d'intelligence. On dit d'un bon cordonnier que c'est un bon artisan; et d'un habile horloger, que c'est un grand artiste.' ('name designating those workmen who practise the manual arts that require the least intelligence. It is said of a good cobbler that he is a good craftsman; and of a skilled watchmaker, that he is a great artist.') One reason for this disparagement may be that watchmaking required a range of precision skills outstripping those needed by cobblers, and took longer to master; another, that clocks and watches used more expensive materials and seemed to elevate the craftsman working them accordingly.[3] And although the entry 'Artisan' explicitly ranges both activities among the 'arts mécaniques' ('mechanical arts'), neither of them was extensively mechanised in the modern sense of the word in mid- to late eighteenth-century Europe (a fact that made their products comparatively dear). Is this, indeed, the principal reason why the author calls both of them arts rather than *métiers*? What, in that case, was meant by 'métier'? One of its senses conflates what in English is labelled *either* a trade *or* a craft; yet, as the *Encyclopédie* entry 'métier' reminds us, in French the word also designates a concrete object, the loom. And although the degree of automation varied from model to model and age to age, the loom was a machine that enabled its operative to do almost mechanically what previously could be done only by 'knowing' and independent hands. Were they, though, a *craftsman's* hands?

To answer this question we must return to the first, broader definition of 'métier'. In this sense the word designates 'toute profession qui exige l'emploi des bras, et qui se borne à un certain nombre d'opérations méca-niques qui ont pour but un même ouvrage, que l'ouvrier répète sans cesse' ('any profession that requires the use of labour, and which is limited to a certain number of mechanical operations that contribute to the same product, and which the worker repeats endlessly'). The word 'mécanique' itself conveys one of two things in this definition: either that a procedure required little conscious input or attention from the human worker, or that it was automated, automatic. Only in the first sense may the word imply a moral judgement, as it does when, in the eighth Promenade of the *Rêveries du promeneur solitaire* (*Reveries of the Lone Walker*), Rousseau polemically describes his enemies as 'des êtres méchaniques qui n'agissoient que par propulsion' ('mechanical beings who only acted when acted upon').[4] Cor-respondingly, the *Encyclopédie* entry makes clear that a high degree of mechanisation or, put differently, the absence of a need for much human skill may cause a 'métier' to be judged lowly, despite the *Encyclopédie*'s stated mission to correct the social bias against crafts and trades. It was, after all, clear enough that some practical occupations required more expertise than others. The *Encyclopédie's* revisionist enterprise is clarified further on in the entry, where it is said of artisans: 'Je laisse à ceux qui ont quelque principe d'équité, à juger si c'est raison ou préjugé qui nous a fait regarder d'un œil si dédaigneux des hommes si essentiels. Le poëte, le philosophe, l'orateur, le ministre, le guerrier, le héros seroient tout nuds et manqueroient de pain sans cet artisan objet de son [*sic*] mépris cruel.' ('I leave it to those who have some sense of fairness to judge whether it is reason or prejudice that makes us view such essential men with such disdain. The poet, the philosopher, the orator, the minister, the warrior, the hero would be quite naked and have nothing to eat without this artisan who is the object of their cruel contempt.')

The disparagement of artisans, similarly, was relative to the degree of reflective thought their activities demanded, and was, according to Diderot's article 'Art', often both snobbish and perverse: 'Quelle bisarrerie dans nos jugemens! nous exigeons qu'on s'occupe utilement, et nous méprisons les hommes utiles.' ('What bizarre judgements we make! We require that people are usefully occupied, and we despise useful men.') But this disparagement has had the predictable result that 'les artisans se sont crus méprisables, parce qu'on les a méprisés; apprenons-leur à mieux parler d'eux-mêmes' ('artisans have believed themselves to be despicable, because we have despised them; let us teach them to speak better of themselves'). This might, though Diderot does not say as much, be as useful an application of the encyclopedists' ambition to 'changer la manière commune de penser' ('change the general way of thinking') as any other.

The familiar qualitative distinction between liberal arts governed by the mind and manual crafts dependent (to an unspecified degree) on physical function continued to be made in Enlightenment culture, however artificial it had appeared to writers, thinkers and artists themselves over the ages. In a deliberate challenge to this orthodoxy, Colbert had charged the Académie des sciences in 1675 to begin a systematic description of the so-called mechanical arts, an enterprise which by the middle of the following century had yielded the twenty-seven-volume *Description des arts et métiers* (*Description of the Arts and Trades*) edited by Duhamel de Monceau.[5] (Its enormous selection of illustrative plates would be used by Diderot in the *Encyclopédie*, though not always updated to take account of technological developments over the intervening years.) Even Colbert's influence, however, proved insufficient to change the assumption – prevalent since classical antiquity, and in France perhaps reinforced by the philosophy of Descartes – that work of the mind was inherently superior to work of the body. The distinction drawn in Leroy's *Encyclopédie* entry 'Horloger' between different types of watchmaker suggests an opposition of craftsman and mere 'homme de métier' that is relevant to this discussion. A workaday journeyman horologist, Leroy claims, cannot stand comparison with an 'horloger mécaniste' ('watchmaker-mechanist'), an *artist* who must also be a mathematician, engineer, physicist and astronomer, as well, of course, as a competent 'main-d'œuvre' ('manual worker') capable of making the most delicate cogs, the finest springs and the most polished escapements. The contrast with the entry 'Artisan' is implicit. The preliminary discourse to the *Encyclopédie* had even observed that the inventors of the watch escapement were as worthy of fame as any great algebraist, which in turn raised the question whether horology was a science, an art, or the two together. If it was an art, it certainly seemed to count as 'liberal' (a qualitative distinction the encyclopedists in theory deprecated). Even within horology, however, negative comparisons might still be made, as the entry 'Horloger' makes clear: all the years of apprenticeship – normally eight – might still leave them mere makers.

For whatever reason, Rousseau did not, any more than Diderot, show any early desire to be a craftsman, nor any talent for his work. The *Confessions* describe the young Rousseau and his cousin massacring his horologist grandfather David's tools trying to make watches just as Diderot abused his father's implements during his brief rebellion against school.[6] And just as Diderot's schoolboy assault on cutlery had been both short-lived and abortive, Rousseau's taste of the craftsman's life endured less than three years of his projected five-year term apprenticed to the surly young master engraver Abel Ducommun. Curiously enough, the family profession of horology seems never to have been considered for him, though Ducommun was an 'horloger graveur' ('watchmaker-engraver'),[7] and he remained for much of his adolescence opposed to any idea of earning a 'respectable' living. All he retained from the time of his apprenticeship, in fact, was a taste for good engravings and the ability to write beautiful script – a considerable 'all', as it turned out, given that his elegant hand later made him a fine copyist of music, his own chosen *métier*.

All manual activities, for Rousseau, stood at a distance (often it seemed a blessed distance) from the perils of imagination, which he would blame for the 'disaster' of a literary career that earned him proscription and persecution.[8] Another opposition he articulated – that between craft activity and machine – reflected his antagonism towards the materialist world of the eighteenth century that Diderot and other encyclopedists more often celebrated. Diderot's apparent support for the incipient industrialism of eighteenth-century France partly reflects his citified nature: he was simply more comfortable than Rousseau in urbane (and urban) environments, and his *Encyclopédie* entries 'Bas' ('Stocking') and 'Métier à bas' ('Stocking Loom') accordingly offer an unequivocal welcome to the machine age anticipated by Colbert's seventeenth-century project and positively proclaimed by the *Encyclopédie* itself. But if this attitude possessed its own idealism, so too did Rousseau's ambivalent proto-Luddism. The ambivalence emerges in the seventh *Rêverie*, with the walker's description of his shocked discovery on a botanising ramble in the Swiss mountains of a 'manufacture de bas' ('stocking manufactory') – more probably a domestic loom than a factory, but even so distressing enough in what he has perceived to be the untamed natural world.[9] But at least cottage industries of this kind maintained the spirit of fraternity and freedom Rousseau so valued, corresponding as they did to the localised governments of the Swiss federation. The time would come when textile production that had previously been a small-scale enterprise – the Clarens estate in *La Nouvelle Héloïse* describes one such model[10] – maintaining a worker/entrepreneur structure unconstricted by the relations of urban master/merchant on the one hand and downtrodden artisan on the other,[11] proved powerless to resist the machine-based urbanisation of cotton textile spinning, leaving handloom weavers increasingly dissident. This trend would later be accelerated by the advent of conquering French revolutionary troops and their Swiss allies. The Revolution claimed Rousseau as a precursor: the irony of his having thus accelerated the decline of the Swiss rural economy would surely not have escaped him.[12]

The more gregarious Diderot, metropolitan man against countryman, unequivocally opposed the machine pessimism[13] that came so naturally to his former friend; and it is a further irony that a Rousseau of the late nineteenth, twentieth or twenty-first century would certainly have witnessed in the individualised fabrication and ecological integrity of the Arts and Crafts, 'Slow' and Green Movements a (usually expensive) resurrection of practices that in his own time were beginning to be displaced by uniform mass production. Diderot's attitude to all these matters has its complexities, however 'Fast', impenitently citified and machine-minded he often appears. A writer and thinker more than a practical doer (for all his work with craftsmen as *Encyclopédie* editor), he was never associated with the kind of industrialised production of consumer goods Voltaire would set up with his watchmaking colony at Ferney. Nor, of course, did he ever display quite the unabashed hedonism Voltaire celebrates in his poem *Le Mondain*: he included a satire on luxury in the *Salon* of 1767, and famously preferred his stained old dressing-gown to a new one he had been made to accept. Diderot and Rousseau were inherently moderate in ways that perhaps reflect their bourgeois upbringing. Diderot never earned enough money to live lavishly, and worried so much about providing his daughter's dowry that Catherine II of Russia bought his library for the Hermitage, while leaving him free possession of it during his lifetime; Rousseau, having discarded his own children, partly, he claimed, because he could not have afforded to raise them, turned down pensions offered by the kings of France and England, insisted that he enjoyed the music-copying that others thought an unworthy profession for an author who had once had literary Europe at his feet, but none the less refused to do more work than was strictly necessary to support his basic requirements and those of Thérèse Levasseur, his companion from 1745 to the end of his life. Proceeding otherwise, he thought, would both compromise his freedom and betoken base materialism, exemplifying the general rule of consumerism which holds that people will always acquire more than they truly need if they are able to do so, indulging in a spirit of conspicuous waste that quickly becomes the unashamed love of luxury. Diderot, whilst disapproving of Rousseau's hermit-like existence away from Paris, examines some of these issues without prejudice in *Le Neveu de Rameau* (*Rameau's Nephew*), anatomising the alienation that accompanies man's development as an urban animal, but declining to argue that it annihilates the folk spirit prevalent in less advanced economies. Even without its disappearance, according to the dialogue, civilisation brings a new taste for the adventitious rather than the habitual, as those whose palates are corrupted by lavishness or excess seek stimulus in eccentricity or the unexpected. Rousseau's nostalgia for the simple life was mocked by contemporaries unable or unwilling to see how the stability it promoted might be preferable to the febrile thrust of urban existence, while Diderot's quicksilver mind, the changeability he associated with natives of his own birthplace of Langres, made him at home in a city such as Paris, where his playful self-opposition (brilliantly expressed in *Le Neveu de Rameau* and other dialogues) and swift adaptation to new climates of thought could be given free rein. Yet he might still be worsted by those whose temperament was slower and patience greater than his own. It is unsurprising, for instance, that the 'Slow' Rousseau regularly beat him at chess when they started playing together late in 1742.

Despite his habitual liking for the natural, Rousseau was not inherently hostile to mechanical and other forms of advance where they served an evident purpose; what he disliked was the invention of needs associated with artificial environments. Certainly, he required small, carefully crafted implements as his passion for botanising developed in the early 1760s onwards. (Might a cutler Diderot – son Denis rather than father Didier – have found a way back to his former friend's heart by custom-making such implements?) Given the watchmaking and barometer-constructing reportedly done by villagers in Môtiers (Rousseau's refuge after the condemnation of *Émile* and *Du contrat social*) during the winter months, one might have expected precision instruments of the kind he needed also to be manufactured there, particularly as many of them resembled tools used in horology. As it was, however, they had to be ordered for him by various friends – Deluc the younger, Du Peyrou, d'Ivernois and Julie de Bondeli.[14] (The instruments included magnifying glasses, even though he had, according to Bernardin de Saint-Pierre, very good close vision.) The seventh Promenade of the *Rêveries* gives a celebrated account of the comparative pleasures of investigating, often by dissection, different members of the natural scene, contrasting the smiling world of flora with all that is repulsive in the animal and mineral realms (abhorrent when the investigator must slice up dead creatures, unhealthy when he has to extract minerals from a grudging earth), but excluding even the examination of flowers if the purpose is medicinal rather than what Rousseau calls 'purely' curious[15] – which seems to signify a combination of the disinterestedly scientific, in the spirit of Linnaeus, and the aesthetic. But was it not provocative to insist that using the tools of progress was acceptable provided they served non-utilitarian purposes? The encyclopedists – to whose number, as d'Alembert reminded him, Rousseau himself belonged as author of the entries on music, but from whose spirit he in many ways so radically dissented – would have disagreed. If man was unique in being a tool-making animal,[16] what was wrong with using tools for a variety of purposes that might help humans live, among them machine construction and other kinds of industrial development? D'Alembert was not the only *philosophe* to signal his broad agreement with much of Rousseau's argument in the *Discours sur les sciences et les arts* (*Discourse on the Arts and Sciences*),[17] but few saw his hostility towards culture as tenable in the long term.

An element in man's uniqueness as a tool-making entity is surely his possessing the faculty of imagination, that inventive power Rousseau would come to bemoan as a principal cause of his persecution, and the source of those writings for which he would be first arraigned and then exiled. (Rousseau's mistrust of the imagination was a deeply rooted Genevan trait, directly connected with the city's liking for whatever was utilitarian and practical.) His hostility towards the imagined would also become associated with a type of anti-rationalism that further marked his split with Diderot and the *Encyclopédie*. For Rousseau, more specifically, imagination spelt the danger of what had first been reflected on and then channelled into freely conceived compositions of the sort the guardians of convention deplored – precisely, in fact, what occurred when he withdrew from Paris to write in the late 1750s. As a mode of thought, then, it undeniably belonged in spirit to the *Encyclopédie*'s declared ambition to change the general way of thinking, itself to be punished by repeated censorship and prohibition. Only its focus was different.

If one claim for originality that Diderot makes in the Prospectus to the *Encyclopédie* is misleading – namely, that the emphasis laid on 'arts mécaniques' was new – his direct consultation with those who actually worked the machines partly justifies it. As he comments, his presence in *ateliers* was the more vital for the fact that most of the workers were unable to explain the mechanical operations performed there. It is all a far cry from the ideal of transparent language he formulates in the article 'Encyclopédie' in connection with the need to have entries written by experts, and further explains his own determination to gain the requisite knowledge by mastering the processes involved in different types of manufacture. Significantly, understanding modes of commercial production does not appear ever to have induced any of Rousseau's pessimism in him: the *Encyclopédie*'s radical determination to look forward precluded such a response. Diderot's workhorse de Jaucourt addresses some of these matters in his entry 'Industrie' ('Industry'), but denies that the proliferation of machines might ever work against man by creating unemployment, insisting, rather, that the development of industry necessarily conduces to social wellbeing. Rousseau's fear that multiplying instruments and devices intended to increase man's control of the external environment must simply result in severing him from his essential nature is not addressed.

Perhaps this situation is reflected in the absence of the human factor from a range of *Encyclopédie* entries, and particularly the plates accompanying them; the work in its entirety may have been meant to change the general way of thinking, but there were risks implicit in thought's disembodied nature. More specifically, the thought involved in creating machinery that dehumanised the manufacturing process might come perilously close to appearing its own justification, with the operatives simply its servants. How should we judge an abstraction that in the end controls the lives both of those who originate it and those who give it practical form? The plea for both theory and practice to be measured against the needs of humanity is not heard merely in Rousseau; to an extent it is also present in Diderot, who famously wrote: 'Je suis homme, et il me faut des causes propres à l'homme.'[18] ('I am human, and I must deal in human causes.') But Rousseau's sense of alienation was always more urgent and anguished, and Diderot's statement is not incompatible with the kind of thoroughgoing determinism Rousseau deplored. For the latter, estrangement could best be cured by returning man to intact nature, not nature bent to human will; yet as his two *Discours* both concede, regaining this state of wholeness is impossible. Human will and the power of rationality, on the other hand, enable man to defy nature, and their combined force is the object of the *Encyclopédie*'s exaltation: less man as machine (though Diderot's materialist thought, pushed to its limits, acknowledged this as a fact) than man as maker, then user, of machines.

In keeping with his convictions, Rousseau's *Projet de constitution pour la Corse* (*Proposed Constitution for Corsica*) of 1765 focuses on what mankind can do on the small scale and in practical terms to defend itself against forces that threaten its survival, a process detailed more extensively in *Du contrat social*. Salvation, predictably enough, is seen to rest in the motions of practical life, in doing rather than reflecting, and in *creatively* doing rather than passively operating (which might leave operatives dangerously free to think): what this small island needs are blacksmiths, carpenters and weavers, hands-on workers rather than the machine-using alienated souls of nascent industrialism – in fact the same sturdy craftsmen whom the *Projet de constitution* finds in the uncorrupted Swiss people of times past.[19] Some lines from the fourth *Rêverie*, referring back to Rousseau's boyhood, poignantly describe a skill since made redundant in the mechanised modern world, a hand movement familiar to weavers that would soon have been excluded altogether from the weaving process thanks to the ingenuity of Jacques de Vaucanson (1709–82), the famous maker of automata who also invented the first fully automated loom: a matter of sensuously feeling fabric as it is being woven to determine the tension of the threads and thus the closeness of the weave.[20] But the degree of automation was in another respect insufficient, as Vaucanson would show; for when Louis XV wanted the variable quality of silk weaving to be corrected by eliminating the human factor, Vaucanson applied to the loom's mechanism the knowledge of breathing he had gained in making his mechanical flautist 'play' (the precise finger movements originally engineered having been insufficient for the required 'performance'), with the result that threads were now mechanically maintained at the right tension, with a precision no human hand could achieve.[21] So weavers became dispensable – until, that is, a further revolution in taste would for the first time make the human element in craft production positively

desirable, and irregularity preferred to a machine-contrived smooth-
ness. Well before that time, however, Vaucanson had made the situation for human operatives even worse by designing machines capable
of creating complex patterns of flowers and birds and then having
donkeys power them. Late in his career, in the *Paradoxe sur le
comédien* (*Paradox on the Actor*), Diderot would describe the achieve-
ment of such 'repeatability' as a mark of genius when applied to
human dramatic performance rather than the working of machinery;
but it is an aesthetic preference which his readers – whether or not
supporters of craft individualism – may decline to share.

   If in the *Encyclopédie* article 'Bas' Diderot could refer without apparent
regret to the fact that mechanisation had left human labour little part to play
in the weaving process he described, at about the same time Rousseau's
feelings about this particular product of the loom took a decidedly negative
turn. What provoked the negativity, however, had nothing to do with
mechanisation in itself – the creeping (or, depending on point of view,
triumphant) industrialisation of society. The problem with the stockings he
discarded was their dainty whiteness, and to remedy it all he had to do was
replace them with rougher ones. His growing disenchantment with the
civilised world, proclaimed from the late 1740s onwards, makes him representative of what has been called the Counter-Enlightenment,[22] yet in other
respects he still subscribed to progressive trends in society, if selectively.
Consider, for example, his adoption of Linnaean principles, evidenced in
his personal writings, in his *Lettres sur la botanique* (*Letters on Botany*) and in
his *Dictionnaire botanique* (*Botanical Dictionary*) – a (rationalist) commitment
to taxonomy implicit in the *Encyclopédie* itself; or his admittedly abortive
attempt to develop what he called a 'pasigraphie' of botanical form, a total
ideogrammatic system for designating plant and floral types.[23] There was also
his abortive new scheme of musical notation based on numbers rather than
the existing symbols which he had brought with him to Paris in 1742, and
presented without success to the Académie des sciences.[24]

   Other proofs exist of Rousseau's attraction to enlightened modern views in
contemporary society. Ignore the first *Discours*'s anti-scientism (that is, hostility towards work that contributed to the advancement of human knowledge), a reworking of the story of Genesis to the effect that man had been
born for goodness and innocence but fatally tasted the fruit of the tree of
knowledge: d'Alembert's preliminary discourse to the *Encyclopédie* would
provide an answer to this attack. But set against it the rather telling fact of
Rousseau's attendance (like Diderot's) at the lectures on science given by
peripatetic popularisers such as Nollet and Rouelle in the early 1740s, when,

according to the *Confessions*, 'Je m'attachais à la Chymie' ('I was becoming keen on chemistry') while barely mastering its basic principles. There is the equally irrefutable truth of his close friendship with Diderot, the science-mad encyclopedist about whom, as late as 1757, Rousseau was being told by a mutual acquaintance, Deleyre, that 'il songe à vous et vous aime tendrement; mais je ne sais quoi se met entre vous deux ... cette maudite chimie le tient toujours à la chaîne' ('he thinks of you and loves you dearly; but something or other is getting between you ... he is still in thrall to that cursed chemistry').[25] Their enthusiasm for one another in the early days was patent and unembarrassed. Diderot eulogised his friend in the article 'Encyclopédie' in terms that would soon invite the ridicule of the anti-encyclopedists: 'Ô Rousseau, mon cher et digne ami, je n'ai jamais eu la force de me refuser à ta louange: j'en ai senti croître mon goût pour la vérité, et mon amour pour la vertu.'[26] ('O Rousseau, my dear and worthy friend, I have never been capable of refraining from praising you; and in doing so, I have felt my thirst for truth and my love of virtue grow.') And Rousseau responded in kind, for instance in the *Lettre sur la musique française* (*Letter on French Music*), which additionally ranges Rousseau himself among the *philosophes* in championing Italian music against French.[27] Even in 1765, when the long-absent hermit was passing through Paris on his way to England, holding court during his brief transit at the mansion of the prince de Conti, Diderot confided in Sophie Volland that he was tempted despite everything to see Jean-Jacques again, though in the end he decided not to;[28] as late as 1773, in the *Réfutation d'Helvétius* (*Refutation of Helvétius*), he called Rousseau's principles wrong but his conclusions right;[29] and he dissented from the extreme materialist view of some *philosophes* in the third dialogue of *Le Rêve de d'Alembert* (*D'Alembert's Dream*) in terms that might have drawn him closer to the tortured anti-*philosophe* Rousseau had become. Diderot rarely agreed with the view that science explains all of experience; nor did he deny the possibility that a transcendent realm of truth exists above the world of sensation, however single-mindedly the *Lettre sur les aveugles* (*Letter on the Blind*) of 1749 had allowed the blind mathematician Saunderson to call it into question, and notwithstanding Diderot's obvious attraction to the empirical claims of modern science.

The post-Rousseau reaction to the hard doctrines of materialism and rationality would be called Romanticism; but its anticipation is already present in the first *Discours* and, later, the *Lettre à d'Alembert* (*Letter to d'Alembert*) as it would be throughout the works in which Rousseau insists on the guiding light of inner conviction and spiritual life against the evidence of outward form and the mastery of nature. Yet the encyclopedic enterprise, opposed in so many ways to the 'natural' philosophy of Rousseau, may also demonstrate the fatal weakness of all totalising systems that, while claiming to offer empowerment, actually lead to disenchantment with the process of reasoning itself. As the modern world contemplates the ruined project of subjugating nature by mimicking or mastering its processes (the power of mechanical exploitation turned against itself, to devastating effect), so we may be assured that merely instrumental reason carries within itself the seeds of its destruction.[30] If sense be rooted in the earthly, lacking any transcendent dimension, it can no more fight than help the earthly when the material resources on which it relies have been exhausted. And since in rationalism all that matter are means and ends, it can offer no reference point for moral action – one of the dispiriting conclusions Diderot seemed to draw in *Le Neveu de Rameau*.

What should mankind then do? Rousseau thought that pity, in the constructive sense of care of and for the vulnerable, was the most humane response to this predicament, but the more *human* one may be to do nothing. Rather than Stoic endurance, what this signifies in both writers is spiritual self-suspension of the kind that Diderot celebrates in the *Encyclopédie* article 'Délicieux' ('Exquisite') and Rousseau in the experience of reverie,[31] for both men a condition quite other than the vacancy of machine operatives. But a call to action may also be heard in such circumstances, even in a world robbed of fixed moral purpose: Habermas located it in the public sphere[32] (the same body Rousseau evokes in *Du contrat social*), a community inevitably different from the brotherhood created amongst the *Encyclopédie*'s readers, but sharing some of its attributes. If Rousseau's political works were to find an audience ready to attempt the changes they proposed, then so might the great enterprise of Diderot and (originally) d'Alembert: not, ironically, by showing men how to master the world by technology, but by enlightening them sufficiently in the long term for the 'harder' doctrines of rationalism to be weakened.

On this interpretation, we may see the world that Rousseau thought disenchanted by pitiless reason[33] as manifesting a new enlightenment, one resembling the transfiguration he experienced on the road to Vincennes (where he visited the incarcerated Diderot) rather than the often explosive force of human hegemony envisaged in the *Encyclopédie*. To a post-Enlightenment world experiencing ecological and other kinds of humanly engineered catastrophe Rousseau's natural doctrine has obvious attractions, if not in the passive form his reveries suggest; the requisite harmony, it now appears, must be achieved by will and action rather than their antithesis. What is needed, in other words, is less Heidegger's 'Gelassenheit zu den

Dingen'[34] ('relaxedness about or releasement towards things') than a modest effort of nature retrieval. Such a goal, for many readers, holds the moral appeal of a Rousseauist counter-revolution, a move against the man- and brain-centred world inherited from the eighteenth century (or from whatever point man's tool-making propensities grew into a guiding philosophy), but fit for the world we have made and must live in.

Diderot, and Rousseau in his botanical works, write for those who wish to understand or must be made to understand – to be, in some sense, replenished by knowledge, 'added to' in something like the way Rousseau's being is 'supplemented' by the process of reverie, to the point where it 'doublera pour ainsi dire [son] existence' ('doubles, so to speak, [his] existence').[35] If we are so Romantically inclined that rational enlightenment seems an unacceptable substitute for the sensory 'dédoublement' ('splitting') of reverie, we may also remain stubbornly convinced, as Wordsworth was, that technology and industrialism simply impoverish the human spirit in their deployment of human reason. On such an interpretation, the 'outing' of mineral from rock, the process Rousseau deplores in the seventh *Rêverie*, is tantamount to rape, the seizing from nature of what it does not freely give. But most of the processes and techniques described in the *Encyclopédie* do the same, to the same end, making what is inert move before our eyes, separable from its related parts and in some sense active. For Heidegger this making of matter into a standing reserve ('Bestand') for our purposes would be a form of diminution, the lessening of wonder. To judge by the seventh *Rêverie*, Rousseau anticipated him in deploring the denaturing of nature by man and by nature itself. On the evidence of the *Encyclopédie*, however, Diderot saw the true wonder of turning nature into supernature, i.e. a product of matter, creative imagination and the work of human hands.

NOTES

1. Jean Fabre, 'Deux frères ennemis: Diderot et Jean-Jacques', *Diderot Studies*, 3 (1961), 155–213.
2. DPV, vol. 1, pp. 1–39 (p. 10).
3. For useful background, see Antoine Babel, *Les Métiers dans l'ancienne Genève: histoire corporative de l'horlogerie, de l'orfèvrerie et des industries anciennes* (Geneva: A. Jullien, Georg et Cie, 1916), pp. 171–2.
4. Jean-Jacques Rousseau, *Rêveries du promeneur solitaire*, in *Œuvres complètes*, ed. Bernard Gagnebin and Marcel Raymond, 5 vols. (Paris: Gallimard, 1959–95), vol. 1, p. 1078.
5. See Bertrand Gille, 'L'*Encyclopédie*, dictionnaire technique', in Suzanne Delorme and René Tatou (eds.), *L'*Encyclopédie* et le progrès des sciences et des techniques* (Paris: Presses Universitaires de France, 1952); also Arthur H. Cole

and George B. Watts, *The Handicrafts of France as Recorded in the 'Description des arts et métiers 1771–1788'* (Cambridge, MA: Harvard University Press, 1952) and Roger Hahn, *The Anatomy of a Scientific Institution: The Paris Academy of Science, 1666–1803* (Berkeley, CA: University of California Press, 1971).

6. Rousseau, *Œuvres complètes*, vol. I, p. 25.
7. Ibid., p. 31.
8. In a letter of 26 November 1758 to Dr Théodore Tronchin of Geneva, Rousseau wrote that he should have been a watchmaker. See Rousseau, *Correspondance complète*, ed. R. H. Leigh, 52 vols. (Oxford: Voltaire Foundation, 1965–98), vol. V, p. 242. A related point is made in the *Confessions*: see Rousseau, *Œuvres complètes*, vol. I, pp. 43–4.
9. See Rousseau, *Œuvres complètes*, vol. I, p. 1071. See also his letter of 20 January 1763 referring to the Val de Travers, where 'on trouve ... des manufactures dans des précipices, des ateliers sur des torrents' ('one finds ... manufactories perched in precipices, and workshops over torrents').
10. See Rousseau, *Œuvres complètes*, vol. II, p. 551.
11. See Charles Tilly, *Contention and Democracy in Europe, 1650–2000* (Cambridge: Cambridge University Press, 2004), p. 185.
12. See also the 'Dédicace à la République de Genève' ('Dedication to the Republic of Geneva') attached to the *Discours sur l'inégalité* (*Discourse on Inequality*) in Rousseau, *Œuvres complètes*, vol. III, pp. 111–21, especially p. 113.
13. See Paul Greenhalgh, 'The Progress of Captain Ludd', in Peter Dormer (ed.), *The Culture of Craft* (Manchester: Manchester University Press, 1997), pp. 104–15 (p. 105).
14. See, for instance, Rousseau, *Correspondance*, vol. XXII, pp. 240, 256.
15. On this general concept see Neil Kenny, *Curiosity in Early Modern Europe: Word Histories* (Wiesbaden: Harrassowitz, 1998).
16. Benjamin Franklin's phrase, endorsed by Karl Marx in *Das Kapital*. See Paul A. Rahe, 'The Political Needs of a Tool-Making Animal: Madison, Hamilton, Locke, and the Question of Property', *Social Philosophy and Policy*, 22.1 (January 2005), 1–26 (p. 8).
17. See, for instance, Jean le Rond d'Alembert, *Discours préliminaire de l'Encyclopédie* (*Preliminary Discourse of the Encyclopédie*), ed. Michel Malherbe (Paris: Vrin, 2000), p. 143.
18. DPV, vol. XXIV, p. 523.
19. See Rousseau, *Œuvres complètes*, vol. III, p. 914.
20. See ibid., vol. I, p. 1036.
21. See Richard Sennett, *The Craftsman* (London: Allen Lane, 2008), p. 87.
22. See Isaiah Berlin, 'The Counter-Enlightenment', in Henry Hardy and Roger Hausheer (eds.), *The Proper Study of Mankind* (New York: Farrar, Straus and Giroux, 2000), pp. 243–68; Graeme Garrard, *Rousseau's Counter-Enlightenment* (Albany: State University of New York Press, 2003); Darrin McMahon, *Enemies of Enlightenment* (Oxford: Oxford University Press, 2001).
23. See Jacques-Henri Bernardin de Saint-Pierre, *La Vie et les ouvrages de Jean-Jacques Rousseau*, ed. M. Souriau (Paris: Cornélie et Cie, 1907), pp. 162–3; also

A. Matthey-Jeantet, *L'Écriture de Jean-Jacques Rousseau (sa pasigraphie, ses abréviations)* (Le Locle: Courvoisier, 1912).

24. See Rousseau, *Œuvres complètes*, vol. I, pp. 272–3, 281, 284–7.
25. *Corr.*, vol. I, p. 244.
26. DPV, vol. VII, p. 244.
27. See Rousseau, *Œuvres complètes*, vol. V, p. 306.
28. See *Corr.*, vol. V, p. 226.
29. See DPV, vol. XXIV, p. 720.
30. See John Gray, *Enlightenment's Wake: Politics and Culture at the Close of the Modern Age* (London: Routledge, 1995), especially pp. 145–8.
31. See Roland Mortier, 'À propos du sentiment de l'existence chez Diderot et Rousseau', *Diderot Studies*, 6 (1964), 183–95.
32. See Jürgen Habermas, *The Structural Transformation of the Public Sphere*, trans. Thomas Bürger (Cambridge: Polity Press, 1989).
33. There is a considerable body of writing on Max Weber's notion of (modern) disenchantment by reason, but a useful summary is contained in Jeffrey E. Green, 'Two Meanings of Disenchantment', *Philosophy and Theology*, 17.1–2 (2006), 51–84.
34. See Martin Heidegger, *Discourse on Thinking*, trans. John W. Anderson and E. Hans Freund (London: Harper and Row, 1966), pp. 45–56.
35. Rousseau, *Rêveries*, p. 1001.

CHAPTER 5

Diderot's anti-colonialism: a problematic notion

Anthony Strugnell

Throughout the nineteenth century and well into the twentieth, Diderot's reputation as the most radical opponent of European colonialism among the *philosophes* rested almost exclusively upon the evidence of the *Supplément au Voyage de Bougainville* (*Supplement to Bougainville's Voyage*) which was not published in printed form until 1796. In the section of that work entitled 'Les Adieux du vieillard' ('The Old Man's Farewell') Diderot delivers a devastating critique of the arrogant European assumption that any territory not belonging to a recognised power was up for grabs without regard to its inhabitants. In a brief and brilliant inversion the old Tahitian destroys utterly the legitimacy of European colonisation of the lands of supposedly primitive peoples. In response to the literal way of staking a claim by thrusting a blade into the ground, inscribed with '*Ce pays est à nous*' ('This country is ours'), he retorts, '*Ce pays est à toi? et pourquoi? parce que tu y a mis le pied? Si un Tahitien débarquait un jour sur vos côtes, et qu'il gravât sur une de vos pierres ou sur l'écorce d'un de vos arbres: Ce pays est aux habitants de Tahiti, qu'en penserais-tu?*'[1] ('This country is yours? And why? Because you have entered it? If one day a Tahitian landed on your shores and carved onto one of your stones or the bark of one of your trees: *This country belongs to the inhabitants of Tahiti*, what would you think?') The question is unanswerable and it was to form the basis of anti-colonialist argument in France in the years leading up to the French Revolution. Foremost in the debate on the rights and wrongs of European colonisation in the Americas and the Orient was the abbé Raynal's monumental history of European trade and settlement across the globe, the *Histoire philosophique et politique des établissemens et du commerce des Européens dans les deux Indes* (*Philosophical and Political History of European Establishments and Trade in the Two Indies*) to give it its full title, or the *Histoire des deux Indes* in short. And since the arrival at the Bibliothèque Nationale in 1951 of the most important collection of Diderot's manuscripts, the Fonds Vandeul, we know that those sections of the *Histoire des deux Indes* that promote the most radical rejection of European colonial activity came from his pen, much of it written at the same time as the *Supplément.*

Recent work on the *Histoire des deux Indes* has demonstrated incontrovertibly the long-held view that was circulating in Raynal's lifetime that, far from being the sole author, he headed a team of writers who, through the three editions published in 1770, 1774 and 1780,[2] were responsible for researching and writing the vast compendium of historical and contemporary information of the trading and colonial enterprises of the European nations. In the words of Gianluigi Goggi, 'l'*Histoire des deux Indes* était le résultat d'un travail collectif coordonnée par l'abbé, qui doit donc être considéré comme le rédacteur en chef de son ouvrage' ('the *Histoire des deux Indes* was the result of a collective enterprise coordinated by the abbé, who must therefore be considered chief editor of his work').[3] Among his collaborators some are known. These include the naturalist Jussieu; the *philosophes* Saint-Lambert, Suard and Deleyre; probably Condorcet; and, most importantly, Diderot.[4] There were others, possibly twenty or more, but their participation is based more on surmise than evidence. What is significant is that there is not one voice, Raynal's, that speaks through the pages of the *Histoire des deux Indes*, but a number of voices. As the variants from one edition to the next demonstrate,[5] Raynal revised their contributions to create as far as possible a common style, yet the contents and the arguments remained those of their authors. As a consequence, while the *Histoire* promotes a generally progressive, secular view of the world, it does not attempt to offer a single, coordinated and coherent perspective (and in both respects it can be compared with its predecessor, the *Encyclopédie*). On any issue, the reader will find a number of approaches, which range from the moderately conservative through to the militantly radical, and are at times frankly contradictory.

Diderot's contributions to Raynal's history are situated at the radical end of the spectrum. On commerce, he rejects mercantilism and monopoly for the new mantra of free trade; in politics, he consistently espouses progressive Lockean principles of popular sovereignty; on religion, he argues for scepticism and tolerance; on education, he believes in a practical, formative pedagogy. By and large, it can be said that Diderot adopts a fairly consistent and unequivocal position in all of these major areas of contemporary debate. However, while it has been argued that his anti-colonialism is similarly unambiguous, the object of this study is to demonstrate that in that respect such an interpretation of Diderot's position is misconceived, and that, although he does indeed adopt a radical stance, it is that of a man of his time. It is a mistake to attribute to a representative of the Enlightenment the kind of unqualified hostility to any kind of European influence over the lives of non-European peoples that we associate with the anti-colonialism of the twentieth century.

The standard reading of an uncompromising hostility towards colonialism expressed in Diderot's contributions to the *Histoire des deux Indes* was most fully formulated by Yves Benot in a highly influential book, *Diderot, de l'athéisme à l'anticolonialisme*, and in two articles in which he advanced the same line.[6] His interpretation has exercised a preponderant influence on discussion of this aspect of Diderot's thought ever since. It must be left to the individual reader to explore Benot's extremely knowledgeable book-length analysis of Diderot's contributions to Raynal's history; but in many respects – at least as regards his anti-colonialism – it is an elaboration of his earlier, shorter, but equally influential article, 'Diderot, Pechmeja, Raynal et l'anticolonialisme' ('Diderot, Pechmeja, Raynal and Anti-colonialism'). In that more condensed study, Benot had already adopted an unequivocal stance summed up in his conclusion: 'Nous sommes en droit de juger que c'est bien à lui [= à Diderot] que l'on doit la transformation de l'œuvre "réformiste" de Raynal en un manifeste anticolonialiste.'[7] ('We are entitled to conclude that it is indeed to Diderot that we owe the transformation of Raynal's "reformist" work into an anti-colonial manifesto.') Quoting from a passage in Book VIII that Diderot contributed to the third edition, Benot is in no doubt that he categorically rejects the right to colonise:[8]

D'après ces principes, qui me paroissent d'éternelle vérité, que les nations Européennes se jugent & se donnent à elles-mêmes le nom qu'elles méritent. Leurs navigateurs arrivent-ils dans une région du Nouveau-Monde qui n'est occupée par aucun peuple de l'ancien, aussi-tôt ils enfouissent une petite lame de métal, sur laquelle ils ont gravé ces mots: *Cette contrée nous appartient.* Et pourquoi vous appartient-elle? N'êtes-vous pas aussi injustes, aussi insensés que des sauvages portés par hasard sur vos côtes, s'ils écrivoient sur le sable de votre rivage ou sur l'écorce de vos arbres: *Ce pays est à nous?*[9]

(According to these principles, which seem to me to be eternally true, let the European nations judge themselves and give themselves the name they deserve. If their navigators arrive in a region of the New World that is not occupied by any people from the Old, they immediately bury a small metal blade on which they have engraved these words: *This land belongs to us.* And why does it belong to you? Are you not as unjust, as insane as savages brought by chance to your shores would be if they wrote on the sand of your beaches or the bark of your trees: *This country is ours?*)

Reading these lines, one may be inclined to conclude with Benot that Diderot's opposition to colonialism is absolute, admitting of no qualification, unless one takes into account his remark made in the previous paragraph that 'Une contrée déserte & inhabitée, est la seule qu'on puisse s'approprier' ('A deserted, uninhabited land is the only kind that one can claim'). Diderot has not wavered in his conviction over the eight years that separate the *Supplément* from the third edition of the *Histoire*; the images and vocabulary are similar, and Benot's argument seems to be incontrovertible. However, if we examine the premises on which he bases his conclusions, we will find that they are less secure than they at first appear.

The principal weakness in Benot's interpretation of the uncompromising nature of Diderot's anti-colonialism lies in what he understands by colonialism. If we turn to Véron de Forbonnais's article 'Colonie' in the *Encyclopédie*, he identifies six types. The first four need not concern us as they refer to the colonies of the Ancient World, but the last two define contemporary forms of colonisation. The fifth kind of colony refers to the 'colonies d'entrepôts et comptoirs' ('colonies of warehouses and trading posts'), established for the purposes of trade, typified by the European possessions in Asia and Africa; the sixth is identified with the colonies of the Americas '[qui] ont eu le commerce & la culture tout-à-la-fois pour objet de leur établissement' ('which have had both trade and crop-growing as the purpose of their establishment'). Benot's conclusions regarding Diderot's anti-colonialism derive almost entirely from an extended examination of his writings on the latter, American type of colony. He does, it is true, draw attention to Diderot's impassioned defence of indigenous populations in the first five books of the *Histoire*. His 'Apostrophe aux Hottentots' ('Address to the Hottentots') in Book II, in which he calls on them to flee the Dutch who have occupied the Cape of Good Hope, and his call to the Indians to rise up against their British oppressors at the end of Book III, are singled out as clear examples of Diderot's hostility to European colonialism in Africa and Asia.[10] But, as we shall see, Diderot's contributions to these first five books where attention is focused on the Orient are less unequivocally opposed to colonialism in any guise than is the case with his much more substantial participation in the later books devoted to European activity in the New World. The prime reason for this lies in the difference in kind of colonial settlements in the Americas as opposed to those of Asia, the difference identified by Véron de Forbonnais in his *Encyclopédie* article.

For both Diderot and Benot, whose personal history as an anti-colonial activist in postcolonial West Africa attracted him to the radicalism of the *Histoire*, the history of the Spanish conquistadors in South America, of the plantation owners in the Caribbean, and of the settlers in North America are variations on a common theme. The aim of the Europeans was not principally trade, as in Asia, but territorial appropriation and settlement, with the concomitant servitude or removal of the indigenous peoples, or, worse, their annihilation. To compound matters, the large-scale cultivation of tropical crops, such as sugar, cotton and tobacco, for the home markets required a workforce capable of operating in the extreme climatic conditions of the plantations, a problem to which black African slaves provided the solution. European colonialism in the Americas was inseparable from territorial dispossession and, in much of the settled territory, from slavery. Diderot's indictment of slavery in Book XI of the *Histoire* (Chapters 10, 22 and 24) is perhaps the most heartfelt, impassioned and moving moment in the whole of Raynal's work. After refuting the theological, racial and economic arguments justifying slavery and the exploitation of men and women for material gain through the permanent deprivation of the freedom which is their birthright, he invokes the rise of a black Spartacus who will raise the standard of liberty and lead the oppressed in an armed struggle to regain their fundamental human rights. For Benot, in that heroic figure, a prophetic prefiguration of Toussaint-Louverture who led the slave revolt in Haiti in 1791, 'l'aspect encore humanitaire de la lutte contre l'esclavage, et l'aspect plus strictement politique de la lutte contre le principe de la colonisation se sont finalement confondus' ('the still-humanitarian aspect of the struggle against slavery, and the more strictly political aspect of the struggle against the principle of colonisation finally merged').[11] Diderot's anti-colonialism can admit of no compromise because the colonial projects of the Europeans are utterly dependent on the enslavement of thousands upon thousands of Africans, robbed of their humanity by a racist ideology generated by greed. Diderot finds such a situation utterly repellent both morally and philosophically. It is a situation that admits of only one response: revolt by the oppressed under their own leadership, with the unqualified support of all those in Europe who lay claim to enlightened values. There is a clear identification with the Enlightenment *philosophe* and his evocation of the emancipated slave, liberator of his people, on the part of the twentieth-century radical intellectual and scholar Benot, whose idealism led him to move to West Africa to lend his support first to the newly independent Guinea of Sekou Touré, and then the Ghana of Kwame Nkrumah.[12]

Unfortunately, noble as his idealism was, Benot's identification with Diderot's hostility to a New World colonialism, based on the deprivation of the liberty of black people and their cruel exploitation, led him to present Diderot's anti-colonialism in a twentieth-century garb. Lacking any real interest in European colonial activities in Asia, he fails to pay sufficient attention to what Diderot has to say on that front. In order to readjust the balance, it will not be enough simply to examine Diderot's response to those activities. We must also understand what he meant when he argued that commercial relationships between Europeans and indigenous peoples should be conducted according to enlightened principles. Also, in a broader context, it is important to explore his view of indigenous culture from his own self-proclaimed enlightened perspective. For the European presence in Asia is of a quite different, and in some ways a more complex, order than the European presence in the Americas. We have mentioned the difference in the type of settlement, the 'colonies d'entrepôts et comptoirs'; but, equally, the cultural profile of populations receiving the Europeans in their midst is profoundly different. In the place of 'savages', noble or otherwise, there are sophisticated, literate peoples with long histories, and their own social, moral, spiritual and intellectual systems are even more ancient than those of the European nations. If it is to be reliable, an assessment of Diderot's response to colonial activity in the Orient must adopt a holistic approach, and examine his wider response to Indian civilisation.

We will focus our attention on Diderot's contributions to the *Histoire*'s survey of the European powers' trading and colonising activities in the Indian subcontinent, since it is here that the rivalry between them was most intense and the interaction between the European and indigenous interests most complex. Briefly, let us recollect that by the time of the publication of the third edition of the *Histoire* the effective European presence in India had been reduced to Britain and France. Moreover, the influence of the latter had been severely curtailed by the 1765 Treaty of Paris, which had translated the defeat of the French by the British in the Seven Years War into the loss of all their territories with the exception of a number of trading counters. This humiliation was felt not only by the French government, which acquiesced to its losses and concentrated on supporting the rising insurgency in the British North American colonies, but also by French public opinion, largely driven by the *philosophes*. If their government had given up the fight over India, they most certainly had not; and the weapons they brought to bear in that struggle were twofold. On the one hand, they actively promoted the translation of the most significant English studies of both Indian society and British influence in India, primarily through the East India Company in Bengal. On the other, they conducted a sustained critique of that influence, primarily in the pages of the *Histoire*, the object being to understand both the culture of an indigenous population which had been so easily dominated, and the mechanics of that domination as operated by the British. This enquiry was conducted in the name of *les Lumières*, the specifically French version of enlightened thought with its ostensible commitment to universal human values, and a rather less overt belief that a French reading of those values should prevail. No one was more eloquent in this pursuit than Diderot.

Before turning to Diderot's discussion of colonialism in the Indian subcontinent, and what he conceived should be an enlightened form of European, and more particularly French, commercial and administrative engagement with native populations, we should take into account his broader assessment of Indian culture. This will provide us with the context necessary for an evaluation of his arguments. Without that contextual colouring, one is likely to miss the true steer of his more general statements. Of the translations of contemporary English publications on India, five stand out among a dozen or so as having been exploited for information by Raynal and his team, and consequently as having influenced the perception of European colonial activity in India, of Indian society itself, and of their interaction. They are, to give them their French titles, Bolts' *État civil, politique et commerçant du Bengale*, Dow's *Dissertation sur les Hindous*, Halhed's *Code des Loix des Gentoux ou Réglemens des Brames*, Holwell's *Événemens historiques intéressans, relatifs aux provinces de Bengale, & à l'empire de l'Indostan*, and Orme's *Histoire des guerres de l'Inde*.[13] Of these, Halhed's extensive description and analysis of Brahmanic jurisprudence in his *Code of Gentoo Laws* attracted Diderot's most detailed attention; and it is in his commentary on Halhed's work in Book 1 of the *Histoire* that his attitude towards Indian civilisation is revealed.

Chapter 8, in which Halhed's work features, is entitled 'Religion, gouvernement, jurisprudence, mœurs, usages de l'Indostan' ('Religion, Government, Jurisprudence, Mores and Customs of Indostan'). It is exceptionally long, extending to thirty-three pages in the 1780 quarto edition, and as its title suggests covers in some detail the salient aspects of Indian life. Apart from a few opening and concluding paragraphs, Diderot contributed the whole text, drawing from Halhed, but also from the French translations of Holwell and Dow. In his comments, Diderot demonstrates a deep interest in India and the Indians, but *à sa manière*, just as in the *Supplément au Voyage de Bougainville* he had shown himself to be deeply interested in Tahiti and the Tahitians. But whereas Bougainville's *Voyage autour du monde* (*Journey Around the World*) had inspired Diderot to exploit his account of Tahitian society to create a 'natural' benchmark by which to judge the shortcomings of civilised European, and particularly French, society, here he reverses the process. Halhed, Holwell and Dow are drawn upon to fashion a model of an aberrant society which has lost sight of its origins and historical dynamic to be caught up in an atemporal stasis in which the good, bad and the unaccountably bizarre are permanently set in an unchanging juxtaposition.

If one compares Diderot's selective summary of Halhed's translation of the Gentoo laws and his accompanying comments with Halhed's own commentary as it appears in his Translator's Preface, differences are immediately apparent. Where Diderot adopts the acerbic, not to say dogmatic, tone of the secular *philosophe*, Halhed's is that of a latitudinarian Anglican, widely tolerant of all forms of belief even if he does not find them credible. The consequences of these markedly different intellectual stances reflect the conceptual differences between modern French and English notions of tolerance and ultimately of freedom at their origins in the eighteenth century. Let us start with Diderot's comments on the Brahmanic doctrine of creation which he summarises in order subsequently to discredit the mythical foundation of a society based on the immutability of the caste system. He has no interest in attempting to understand the social and historical origins of the phenomenon, but sees it purely in terms of a device engineered by the Brahmans to ensure their enduring domination of Indian society: 'La distribution des Indiens en castes, qui s'élèvent les unes au-dessus des autres, caractérise la plus profonde corruption, & le plus ancien esclavage. Elle décèle une injuste & révoltante prééminence des prêtres sur les autres conditions de la société, & une stupide indifférence du premier législateur pour le bonheur général de la nation'.[14] ('The distribution of Indians among hierarchically disposed castes is characteristic of the deepest corruption and the most ancient slavery. It reveals an unjust and revolting pre-eminence of the priests with regard to the other social ranks, and a stupid indifference on the part of the original legislator towards the general happiness of the nation.') The distinctive character of Brahmanic founding mythology is a matter of indifference to Diderot, who sees in it only the manipulation of the past characteristic of all mythologies in which religion is exploited by an adroit group of individuals who seek to control the population for their own selfish ends. It is only through the progress of civilisation and enlightenment, argues Diderot, that one has become emboldened to examine these beliefs and one has begun to blush at one's credulity.[15] Halhed, by contrast, is much more prudent, displaying a relativism and a sense of historical evolution which is all but absent from Diderot's account. Arguing against a Christian rejection of Hindu doctrine, rather than the rationalist one adopted by Diderot, Halhed advances the following view: 'We are not justified in grounding the standard and criterion of our examination of the Hindoo religion upon the known and infallible truth of our own; because the opposite party would either deny the first principles of our argument, or insist upon an equal right on their side to suppose the veracity of their own scriptures uncontrovertible.'[16]

These different starting points, the one rationalist, the other latitudinarian, produce strikingly different responses: contemptuous dismissal on the part of Diderot and respectful agreement to differ from Halhed. It is the latter whose initial stance provides him with a basis for a fruitful enquiry into the obscurities and complexities of a different culture which the former, viewing them exclusively through the grid of his own culture, perceives as palpable absurdities. As if he were seeking to pre-empt the arguments based on the progress of the human mind advanced by Diderot, Halhed warns against the temptation to adopt an ahistorical approach to religious mythology which sees in it nothing other than the fruit of ignorance and superstition. On the contrary, it should be looked upon as 'the first step towards an emersion from savage barbarism, and the establishment of civil society'.[17] With reference to Hindu belief, it makes no sense to subject their doctrines to comment or reinterpretation from the intellectual vantage point of a more advanced culture, since that fails to recognise and consequently respect the genuine belief of the Hindus in what they hold to be 'simple and plain matter of fact'; 'nor can it be otherwise', concludes Halhed, 'unless the progress of science, instead of being slow and gradual, were quick and instantaneous; unless men could start up at once into divines and philosophers from the very cradle of civilisation, or could defer the profession of any religion at all, until progressive centuries had ripened them into a fitness for the most abstracted speculation'.[18]

In a modern perspective, Halhed's apparently tolerant orientalism might be seen as extending patronising approval to a culture whose conservative and multifaceted nature served the interests of a nascent British imperialism. Diderot's criticism implies a different but equally fundamental assumption about the superiority of enlightened European values. This is reinforced by his reference to 'la haute réputation de la sagesse des brames, dans les siècles les plus reculés' ('the lofty reputation of the wisdom of the brahmans, in the most distant times').[19] The parallel between an ancient priesthood who supposedly fulfilled the role of philosophers in ancient India and the modern French *philosophes* is inescapable. In mitigation of Halhed, it could be said that he lived in India, entered into dialogue with the Brahman community, spoke Hindi, was accomplished in Persian and had gained a grasp of Sanskrit. Diderot, in contrast, could lay claim to none of these achievements, and, indeed, was entirely dependent on Halhed and others with first-hand experience of India for his knowledge of that civilisation. His criticisms, therefore, if too intelligent to be dismissed as the manifestation of a crass Eurocentric arrogance, none the less denote an inability to escape the straitjacket of a European sense of superiority. From today's postcolonial perspective it can be construed as potentially an 'epistemic' aspect of colonial violence, that is 'an attack on the culture, ideas and value systems of the colonised peoples'.[20]

A comparable sense of superiority feeds the argument that Diderot puts forward in Book IV in support of an enlightened response to relationships with Indian communities which, if implemented, would promote French interests in the subcontinent once the inevitable indigenous reaction against British oppression and rapaciousness set in. In the final chapter of Book IV, entitled 'Principes que doivent suivre les François dans l'Inde, s'ils parviennent à y rétablir leur considération & leur puissance' ('Principles which the French must follow in India, if they succeed in re-establishing their good reputation and power there'), he offers a practical guide to what is in effect an enlightened form of colonialism. On the face of it, it sets out an entirely equitable and honourable model for relationships between European traders and the Indian communities with which they trade. The lesson is one of moderation:

Un peuple sage ne se permettra aucun attentat ni sur la propriété, ni sur la liberté. Il respectera le lien conjugal; il se conformera aux usages; il attendra du temps le changement dans les mœurs. Il ne fléchit pas le genou devant les dieux du pays, il se gardera d'en briser les autels. Il faut qu'ils tombent de vétusté. C'est ainsi qu'il se naturalisera.[21]

(A wise people will not allow itself any attacks on property or freedom. It will respect the bond of marriage; it will conform to local ways of doing things; it will rely on time itself to change customs. Whilst not bending its knee to the gods of the country, it will be careful not to destroy their altars. These must fall into disuse over time. In this way, the wise people will become assimilated.)

But that does not preclude a degree of social engineering of the native population to accelerate the natural process of change: 'En quelque endroit que vous vous fixiez si vous vous considérez, si vous agissez comme des fondateurs de cités, bientôt vous jouirez d'une puissance inébranlable. Multipliez-y donc les conditions de toutes les espèces; je n'en excepte que le sacerdoce. Point de religion dominante.'[22] ('Wherever you establish yourselves, if you consider yourselves, if you act like founders of cities, soon you will enjoy an absolute power. Therefore multiply all kinds of ranks and occupations; I only except the priesthood. Let there be no dominant religion.') Nor does it preclude the organised immigration of young Europeans who will presumably intermarry with locals to further advance that process: 'Le vaisseau qui transporteroit dans vos colonies de jeunes hommes sains & vigoureux, de jeunes filles laborieuses et sages, seroit de vos bâtimens le plus richement chargé. Ce seroit le germe d'une paiz éternelle entre vous & les indigenes'.[23] ('The vessel that transported into your colonies healthy, vigorous young men and hardworking, respectable young women, would be the one carrying the most precious cargo of all your ships. It would carry the seeds of an eternal peace between you and the indigenous people.') Diderot's idealism fails to disguise the disparity in the encounter between a technologically advanced civilisation and one that is conservative and traditional, and therefore, from a European standpoint, backward and needing encouragement to advance. It is a disparity which places all the initiative on the side of the coloniser and must consequently play to his advantage, however seemingly noble and humane his intentions.

   Despite Benot's best efforts, we must conclude that on the question of colonialism Diderot may have been a man ahead of his time, to use a convenient oxymoron, but in a truer sense he was a man of his time. His unfettered hostility to the form of European colonialism manifest in the Americas, which required the territorial expropriation of indigenous peoples, and in many cases the importation of slave labour, was radical, but it was the direct culmination of the body of belief in human rights and freedoms which had been growing at least since the Renaissance, and had taken on a renewed vigour with the advent of the Enlightenment. However, when Diderot turns his attention to the east, he does not escape the strictures which, since Said,[24] have been directed at all those European writers who have cast a critical gaze on the Orient. In this context, he cannot be cast as an anti-colonialist. On the contrary, there is no escaping the fact that his vision for the future of the Indian subcontinent is, beneath its conscientious philanthropy and enlightenment, inescapably imperialistic.

NOTES

1. DPV, vol. XII, p. 591.
2. A full descriptive bibliography can be consulted in Anatole Feugère, *Bibliographie critique de l'abbé Raynal*, new edn (Geneva: Slatkine Reprints, 1970). Unless otherwise stated, all further references to *Histoire des deux Indes* are to the third edition, published in four volumes (Geneva: J. L. Pellet, 1780).
3. See the recent edition: Guillaume Raynal, *Histoire philosophique et politique des établissements et du commerce des Européens dans les deux Indes*, ed. Anthony Strugnell *et al.*, 5 vols. (Ferney-Voltaire: Centre international d'étude du XVIIIe siècle, 2010–), vol. I, p. xxx.
4. For a tabulation of Diderot's contributions see Michèle Duchet, *Diderot et l'Histoire des deux Indes ou l'Écriture fragmentaire* (Paris: Nizet, 1978), pp. 64–105. A more detailed and accurate identification of the contributions has been undertaken by Gianluigi Goggi for the aforementioned critical edition.

5. The variants of Books I–V of the 1770 and 1774 editions are published in the recent critical edition.

6. Yves Benot, *Diderot, de l'athéisme à l'anticolonialisme* (Paris: Maspero, 1970); 'Diderot, Pechmeja, Raynal et l'anticolonialisme', *Europe*, January–February 1963, republished in Yves Benot, *Les Lumières, l'esclavage, la colonisation*, ed. Roland Desné and Marcel Dorigny (Paris: La Découverte, 2005), pp. 107–23 (my references are to this version); 'Diderot, Raynal et le mot "colonie"', in Peter France and Anthony Strugnell (eds.), *Diderot. Les dernières années, 1770–1784* (Edinburgh: Edinburgh University Press, 1985), pp. 140–52.

7. Benot, 'Diderot, Pechmeja, Raynal', p. 123.

8. The 1780 edition is divided into nineteen books: the first five cover the Orient, Books VI–XVIII the New World, and Book XIX provides a lengthy conclusion on all the major themes discussed in the body of the work.

9. Raynal, *Histoire*, vol. II, pp. 251–2.

10. Benot, *Diderot*, pp. 176–8 and 183–4.

11. Benot, 'Diderot, Pechmeja, Raynal', p. 117.

12. Roland Desné and Marcel Dorigny, 'Présentation. Un homme, une œuvre', in Benot, *Les Lumières*, pp. 9–10.

13. Their original titles are William Bolts, *Considerations on India Affairs; Particularly Respecting the Present State of Bengal*, 3 vols. (London: J. Dodsley, etc., 1772–5); Alexander Dow, *The History of Hindostan*, 3 vols. (London: T. Becket and P. A. De Hondt, 1770–2) (originally a translation from the Persian of M. Firishtah, this is a second edition revised, altered and greatly enlarged by Dow); Nathaniel Brassey Halhed, *A Code of Gentoo Laws, or, Ordinations of the Pundits* (London, 1776); John Zephaniah Holwell, *Interesting Historical Events Relative to the Provinces of Bengal and the Empire of Indostan* (London: T. Becket and P. A. De Hondt, 1765); Robert Orme, *A History of the Military Transactions of the British Nation in Indostan* (London: J. Nourse, 1763–78). For a discussion of these books and their French translations see Anthony Strugnell, 'Mixed Messages: Orientalism and Empire in the Early British Histories of India and their Reception in France', in Hans-Jürgen Lüsebrink (ed.), *Das Europa der Aufklärung, und die außereuropäische koloniale Welt* (Göttingen: Wallstein, 2006), pp. 287–301.

14. Raynal, *Histoire*, vol. I, p. 39.

15. Ibid.

16. Halhed, *A Code of Gentoo Laws*, p. xiii.

17. Ibid.

18. Ibid., p. xvi.

19. Raynal, *Histoire*, vol. I, p. 48.

20. Ana Loomis, *Colonialism/Postcolonialism* (London: Routledge, 1998), p. 54.

21. Raynal, *Histoire*, vol. I, p. 545.

22. Ibid., p. 546.

23. Ibid.

24. Edward W. Said, *Orientalism* (London: Routledge, 1978); *Culture and Imperialism* (London: Vintage, 1994), pp. 289–90.

CHAPTER 6

Diderot's letters to Sophie Volland

Pierre Saint-Amand

The *Letters to Sophie Volland* are a documentary record of Diderot's relationship with Louise-Henriette Volland (1716–84), whom the *philosophe* decides to call 'Sophie', a name evoking wisdom.[1] As Sophie's own letters have disappeared without trace, this correspondence can seem like a long monologue on Diderot's part, a drawn-out plaint from the man of letters who has fallen in love, an extended apostrophe. Jacques Chouillet uses the striking phrase 'un dialogue à une voix' ('a one-voice dialogue') to describe the collection.[2] To add to this effect, history records almost nothing about Louise-Henriette. Trousson is only able to furnish the sparsest of details. He notes: '[elle] était fille d'un avocat au Parlement de Paris, ensuite directeur des gabelles – l'impôt sur le sel' ('she was daughter of a lawyer at the Paris *parlement*, who went on to become director of *gabelles* – the salt tax'), adding that Diderot remembers her mother's maiden name (Carlière) when he writes one of his short stories.[3] So we have no choice but to follow the example of Odile Richard-Pauchet and reconstruct 'Sophie' from the image which Diderot has bequeathed in his correspondence. His object of love is also his ideal addressee: 'Épistolière esthète et philosophe à ses heures, lectrice enthousiaste d'une œuvre qui n'a pas donné toute sa mesure, sensible et indépendante, telle est Sophie.'[4] ('A letter-writer capable of being an aesthete and a philosopher; the enthusiastic reader of a work that has not yet fully blossomed; sensitive and independent: such is Sophie.') Part of this correspondence (the first five years) has disappeared; we do not have the first 134 letters written in the years following Diderot's earliest meeting with Sophie. So from the outset we must bear in mind that we only have fragments of an incomplete whole which bears the marks of material absence and dispersal.

TIME TO LOVE

The Diderot–Sophie letters allow access to the *philosophe*'s private life; many passages also provide a chronicle of his social life amongst friends.

Diderot deploys his skills as a humorist as he writes what he calls 'the Grandval gazette'.[5] Grandval was the country estate where the baron d'Holbach and his wife entertained a small and colourful group of guests. Regularly present were d'Holbach's mother-in-law Mme d'Aine, Père Hoop, and d'Alainville. Other, more peripheral figures occasionally had a walk-on part – these included Grimm and Mme d'Épinay. At Grandval, Diderot was able to spend long hours in meditation. The baron's hospitality extended to the provision of a personal study, which became a home from home: 'a small, separate apartment, perfectly quiet, jolly and warm'.[6] Diderot reveals in his letters that he loves his rue Taranne study in Paris 'more than ever',[7] but Grandval provides him with the perfect rural replacement. The *philosophe* sets out a detailed account of his activities at the estate: there is time to read, spent 'between Horace and Homer';[8] the guests relax around the dining table or play billiards or chess; there is conversation and there are philosophical walks.[9] The gentle activities of Grandval provide respite from the turmoil of Diderot's Parisian life. He finds this liberating, except for the ascetic separation from his mistress. So when he is at the baron's estate, his letters to Sophie constantly return to the bucolic romance of this 'little society'. Diderot misses only one person in this place so conducive to reverie. As indicated in the letter of 1 October 1759, he takes with him Sophie's portrait,[10] that obligatory memento, a talisman that is supposed to overcome physical distance; even so, the geography of Grandval intensifies his sense that his cherished object is elsewhere. The *philosophe* does little to hide his melancholy. On 25 September 1760 he writes: 'I have revisited those slopes where I have taken so many walks accompanied by your image and my reverie; I have revisited Chennevières atop the hill, and Champigny that spreads beautifully around it like an amphitheatre, and the River Marne that winds its way from Langres, which is also my first home – the river and I are sad compatriots.'[11] In the letter dated 28 October of the same year, Diderot returns to the theme of how he spends his time at Grandval. Having told Sophie how each free hour is spent, from getting up to going to bed, Diderot concludes: 'What can one possibly miss in the middle of such occupations? Nothing, except one's Sophie.'[12] From Grandval once again, on 1 October 1759, the *philosophe* writes as though time spent away from Sophie is cursed. The leisure offered by country life is not conducive to work, and the time that might be devoted to study is eroded by thoughts of love:

I work a great deal, but with difficulty. One idea keeps intruding and pushes away all others: I am not where I want to be. My friend, I can only be happy in your presence. I have told you a hundred times and it is the absolute truth. If I were condemned to living here for a long time without being able to see you, it is certain that I would not survive; one way or another I would die. The hours seem long; the days never end; the weeks are eternal.[13]

It is not only 'studious leisure' that threatens to disrupt the euphoric time devoted to love. Even more demanding are the activities necessitated by urbane social intercourse, the details of negotiations and interactions that draw the *philosophe* into the whirlwind (*le tourbillon*),[14] the social maelstrom. And in his letter of 20 May 1765 Diderot laments this situation as follows:

One of the great drawbacks of living in society is the sheer number of ways to spend one's time, and above all the way one enters lightly into commitments that sap one's chances of happiness. One marries, one takes up an occupation, one has a wife and children, all before the age of common sense. 'Ah! If only I could start over!' This is a constant lament and I have applied it to everything I have done, excepting, dear and loving friend, the sweet bond I contracted with you. If I regret something, it is every instant that is taken away from that.[15]

Diderot contrasts time crammed with business with utopian time, which is time shared by lovers. The *philosophe* imagines an alternative timetable of activities that would consist of euphoric repetition of the hours reserved for *amour*. In a letter of 21 July 1765, Diderot describes this Arcady, in which he would have a 'little refuge', the perfect place to indulge in *otium*:

Have a tiny place prepared for me, near you, where I can shelter far from all these worries that assail me ... Is that little refuge ready? Do you want to share it? We will meet each morning; on waking I will come to you to inquire how you slept; we will converse; we will part with a burning desire to see each other again. We will take our midday meal together. We will walk far, far away, until we have found a hidden spot beyond prying eyes. There we will tell each other of our love and we will indeed love each other ... We will do justice to our supper, for we will be hungry. We will lie on lovely soft bedding, our souls content, our minds free, our bodies healthy, looking forward to tomorrow, which promises to be as beautiful as today.[16]

The letters to Sophie constantly contrast time spent in business with time given to love. Diderot's negotiations represent a truly negative time, an obstacle to leisured love. On 25 November 1760, Diderot writes: 'Lovers need retreat, rest and silence. No one is more fatigued by the hurly-burly of cities than lovers. They yearn for nightfall. Only when sleep imprisons all those noisy beings who distract and importune them are lovers reunited with their sweethearts.'[17] These two types of time (time for love versus time for business) give rise to two distinct spaces. Diderot gives the following account of this phenomenon:

I tell you in no particular order, without thinking things through or making logical connections between them, everything that occurs in the space I occupy and beyond that space; in my own location and the place where others are moving; in the place where I feel every moment that I love you madly and the other place, where everyone else is worrying about a hundred thousand tiny things.[18]

The letter dated 1 December 1760 gives an idea of this terrible hurly-burly which can only be remedied by making time for letter-writing: 'I have a thousand things to do. I should be at the Hôtel des Fermes; I should be seeing Monsieur de Saint-Julien's cashier; I should be at Madame d'Épinay's; and I am with you, and I cannot bring myself to part from you.'[19]

'WHAT A CIRCUIT!'

The epistolary link with Sophie is subject to the post and its vagaries. The time it takes for letters to arrive increases Diderot's sense of the cherished one's absence. He ceaselessly makes arrangements for the sending and receipt of letters. As those written by Sophie cannot be sent to the rue Taranne, a series of intermediaries is brought in to ensure an efficient delivery system: Gaudet and Damilaville are called upon, especially the latter, through whose hands most of the missives pass.[20] The *philosophe* effectively portrays the complicity of his faithful go-between who thoughtfully adds to Diderot's own precautions. The longed-for letter from Sophie becomes part of a scene of secrecy, of the clandestine; in a perfect, painterly description Diderot creates a genre scene that reveals the forbidden object. Let us follow him as he surreptitiously enters Damilaville's study. The privacy provided by this room protects the secrecy of the extra-marital affair:

Today is Sunday. He has been obliged to leave his study. He had no doubt that I would come this evening; for I never fail to do so when I am hoping for a letter from you. He left his key and two lighted candles on a table, and between the two candles your little letter, and an extremely obliging note signed by him. I read and re-read your letter; I am alone and I will now reply to it.[21]

The quai des Miramionnes – Damilaville's address – appears in the *Letters to Sophie* to be a fateful address, in more than one sense: it is the unavoidable address, but it is also cursed, when the letter box (so to speak) is empty.[22]

The *philosophe*'s contacts help him by exploiting postal bureaucracy. This is especially true of Damilaville, who has the use of two counter-signatures: his own and that of Monsieur de Courteilles.[23] This ensures that the delivery of the letters, and arrangements for payment, are treated with all possible discretion. So it is to Damilaville's home that Diderot repairs to collect his longed-for mail. And he runs: 'It is late, I must be countersigned;

and if I do not make haste to the quai des Miramionnes, I will find everyone has left.'[24] When Diderot is at Grandval, the letters that he addresses to the rue des Vieux-Augustins (the Vollands' Parisian home) go via Charenton. Diderot explains the arrangement carefully to his mistress. The 'epistolary pact' – that neurotic contract (will the lovers write regularly? When will the replies arrive?) – depends above all, in this case, on technical and logistic considerations.[25] The letter from Grandval dated 1 October 1759 spells out the necessary details: 'A servant who receives my orders will carry my letters to Charenton. You will address yours to the Director of the post with instructions for them to be delivered to me by that same servant.'[26]

The *Letters to Sophie* offer an interesting insight into the state of postal services in Diderot's time.[27] One major factor that disrupts the post is obviously bad weather.[28] Diderot therefore complains when it is excessively wet or windy, which causes many interruptions to the lovers' dialogue: 'I am sorry that the irregularity caused by the postal services or by our contacts is from time to time so hard for you to bear.'[29] In the same letter the *philosophe* resorts to a system of affective compensation which he theorises as follows: 'To delay our enjoyment is often to serve us. To make one's friend wait for happiness is to afford him a pleasant prospect; it is to deal with him as the reliable bursar who invests the idle sum entrusted to him at a high rate of interest.'[30] But more often, waiting for Sophie's letters taxes her lover's patience. Worrying delays in receiving the promised post repeatedly give rise to panic. One letter in particular, probably written on 15 October 1759, shows the *philosophe* rushing to a chest of drawers which he was using as a letter box. This is the scene:

The servant left yesterday at half past two. I had instructed him to put my letters in the chest of drawers, explaining that I would leave the key in the drawer. At six in the evening, I thought he might have returned. Never have I passed a longer evening. I went up. I opened the drawer: there were no letters . . . In the middle of the game [of cards], I rose and left. I went to look, and I found nothing.[31]

Later, he rushes back to the chest of drawers, and worries again. The absence of letters leads to frenzied activity, an intense expenditure of energy.

The lovers' correspondence is organised around the theme of suffering. It bears the marks of absence and separation, exacerbated by geographical distance. In Paris especially, distance can become the pretext of all kinds of recriminations and the effect of every hitch in communications is magnified. On 8 October 1759, Diderot writes: 'I came to find my posy, a loving word, a kiss, a caress . . . And you knew that I would arrive, and that it was my Saint's day, and you are not there!'[32] The *philosophe* feverishly imagines that the postal system is capable of anything, however crazy: letters may have been diverted or intercepted. And on those occasions he writes letter upon letter, trying to compensate for Sophie's silence by the amount of correspondence he sends her: 'I have written to you twice at Monsieur La Touche's address; a third time at your address, by messenger, and a fourth today by special messenger. This is my fifth letter.'[33] Diderot's despair at not receiving a reply, or at the disruption of postal services, sometimes culminates in a threat to visit Sophie in person, to compensate for the unreliability of his chain of substitutes: 'Impatience will overcome me. One morning, I will get dressed and leave for Paris.'[34] The expression 'sur-le-champ' (straight away) emerges, in the letter of 8 October 1760, as the watchword of the letter-writer, an ideal contraction of time that eliminates all delay.[35] Elsewhere Diderot writes: 'I beg you, sweetheart, not to complain of my negligence. I will answer you straight away.'[36]

When the post works, joy replaces torment. The *philosophe* then experiences moments of true euphoria, in which the dreamt-of merging with the other that is Sophie becomes a reality: 'I would not be sufficiently loved if the days when post arrives were not for you as for me days of celebration, nor would I love sufficiently.'[37] But the *philosophe*'s trips, and the time Sophie spends at Isle-sur-Marne (an exile imposed by her mother), more often produce a confusion in the destination of the lovers' letters, a switching back and forth between addresses that renders communication still more difficult and brings a greater risk of misdirected mail: 'As soon as I arrived in Paris I ran to the quai des Miramionnes, for I had to have your letters, if any had arrived for me, and I had to stop those same letters from trying to reach me at Grandval, which I had left, and where I had assured Damilaville that I would remain until Tuesday.'[38] Diderot is constantly aware of this and always regards the carriage of letters with a degree of anxiety, as in the letter of 8 October 1760: 'I am leaving tomorrow to spend the rest of autumn at Grandval. I cannot tell you, my dear friend, how difficult it is for me to tear myself away from here ... How will your letters reach me? How will you receive mine? What a circuit!'[39] On 31 August 1760, Diderot, who has set out in hope of finding a letter from Sophie, is pacing the streets of Paris. He traces a hectic topography of expectation and pursues a breathless pilgrimage of love: 'As you have used Grimm's and Damilaville's addresses alternately, when I find nothing at the quai de Miramionnes I run quickly to the rue Neuve-Luxembourg ... With all that, I never regret the comings and goings, and if I sometimes feel tired, it is when I return empty-handed.'[40]

The correspondence is vulnerable to the many setbacks that disrupt the lovers' plans. They cannot escape the imperfections of postal technology: its hit-and-miss nature, its unpredictability, its separate stages, its changes of timetable. Diderot notes in his letter of 12 October 1761: 'These letters arrive whenever they can, and my replies do the same.'[41] Often delays are caused by the carelessness of one of Diderot's go-betweens. For instance, he blames Gaudet in his letter of 9 September 1762: 'There was a time that I received your replies the very same day I wrote to you, every Thursday and Sunday; now I scarcely hear from you except on Wednesday evenings. Sometimes it pleases the great Gaudet not to open his packages for three or four days at a stretch.'[42] In *La Carte postale* (*The Postcard*), the philosopher Jacques Derrida offers metaphysical considerations on communication by post (which, he maintains, acts as 'parasite structure' in relation to non-postal communication). Of relevance here is the pithy statement: 'poster, c'est envoyer en "comptant" avec une halte, un relais ou un délai suspensif' ('to post [a card or letter] is to send something whilst "counting" on an interruption, a relay or a delay').[43] It is impossible, then, to vanquish absence, or to overcome distance. The post is the proof of this catastrophe. Diderot complains on 2 September 1760:

This evening I was waiting for a word from you to reassure me concerning the fate of my last two letters. It is seven o'clock; the mail has been opened; and there is nothing at Grimm's. What am I to think? Curiosity, malice, faithlessness, unforeseen setbacks, and who knows what else. Does everything conspire against the sweetness of our intercourse, and take from us the only thing we still have, the one consolation we possess and which we so need?[44]

This recalls the passage in Voltaire which Derrida cites ironically, as if (but only as if) to contradict the idea of postal 'différance' ('difference/deferral'), which is to say the delay built into its very structure. The passage in question is the article of the *Dictionnaire philosophique* (*Philosophical Dictionary*) entitled 'Poste', in which we read the following optimistic declaration: 'la poste est le lien de toutes les affaires, de toutes les négociations; les absents deviennent par elle présents; elle est la consolation de la vie' ('the post is the link connecting all business, all negotiations; by means of the post the absent become present; it is life's consolation').[45] This 'consolation' of the post, 'the only consolation we still have',[46] is also mentioned in the letter of 31 August 1760, but it always ends, ineluctably, in disappointment.

A lost letter (and his fear of a series of such losses) causes Diderot to plunge into a technological reverie on possible modes of telecommunication. It is inspired by a certain Nicolas Ledru Comus who claimed to have invented a system that allows unmediated correspondence to take place between persons in separate rooms. In a fantastic prefiguration of the modern fax machine (and other technologies of communication), Diderot imagines the following development of Comus's 'secret':

If Comus were one day to extend correspondence from one town to another, from one place to another several hundred leagues away: what a fine thing! All that would be needed is for each correspondent to have a box. These boxes would be like two small printing works where everything printed in one would suddenly be printed in the other.[47]

ON THE INTERPRETATION OF LOVE

The correspondence with Sophie provides Diderot with an opportunity to pursue his philosophical reflections, for instance by working on a contri-bution to the *Encyclopédie* or a page of the *Salons*. However, at the end of such passages the love letter always resumes where it left off. Often, the lover's discourse assimilates that of the *philosophe*; the latter legitimates the former. The *Letters* thus contain a certain number of brief philosophical experiments, in the conjectural style favoured by Diderot. One of his reveries, possibly written on 15 October 1759, ponders the eternity of matter: 'What lives has always lived, and will live for ever.'[48] It includes the following statement of some of the great principles that will be developed in *Pensées sur l'interprétation de la nature* (*Thoughts on Interpreting Nature*) of 1754 and *Le Rêve de d'Alembert* (*D'Alembert's Dream*) of 1769: 'The only difference which I know between death and life is that for now you are living as a mass and that, once you have been dissolved into molecules, in twenty years' time you will live in small, separate pieces.'[49] Philosophical conjecture will be extended into a hypothesis on the survival of the love which he and Sophie share, its post-mortem duration, its material transformation:

O my Sophie, then perhaps I can still hope to touch you, to feel you, to love you, to seek you out, to unite and be one with you, when we no longer exist. If we were ruled by a law of affinity; if we were in the future to form a single being between us; if as the centuries passed I were to form a whole with you once again; if the scattered molecules of your lover were to oscillate, to move and to seek out your own, wherever they were to be found in the whole of nature![50]

We notice that Diderot's love for Sophie contradicts the idea that time is irreversible; it pushes the *philosophe*'s materialist theses onto new ground. It is the opposite of the arrow of time; it transcends the ephemerality of individual lives. In a letter of 28 July 1765, Diderot asserts: 'Time dissipates all illusions, and all passions end. The more I have seen you, the more I have loved you. Time only increases my tenderness for you; this is because it was based on qualities whose reality and value I have felt more keenly with every day that passes.'[51] The *philosophe*'s faithfulness, indeed, defies the instability of material objects and the change which time brings. The following thought is dated 2 September 1760: 'Everything that is around you can change, except for my feelings. They are immune to time and to events ... If I had to speak about my Sophie, I would say this: the more time I spend with her, the more virtues I find in her, the more beautiful she becomes, the more I love her, the more I am bound to her.'[52] This reasoning finds a parallel in Diderot's response to the vagaries of the post – to clamour for reliability in spite of its bureaucratic contingency and the unpredictable flux of letters. Love stands firm against the chaotic meandering of the mail, its capricious wanderings, its always improbable circulation, its material disorder: 'I am punctual and the postal system functions; but my letters languish for three or four days at a time on the desk of the Deputy Superintendent of Post and meanwhile you complain and I despair.'[53] To take another example: 'I have received your letters. They arrive later, because of the vicissitudes of their journey.'[54] The philosopher of flux and contingency who was to write: 'tout est en flux général'[55] ('everything is in general flux') paradoxically practises, in matters of the heart, a precise arithmetic: Sophie's letters and his own are counted, a schedule is imposed (Thursday and Sunday for Diderot's letters), and the letters are obsessively numbered. To take an example at random, the communication dated 14 July 1762 demonstrates the *philosophe*'s watchfulness: 'How is it that I have just received your seventh letter, and that you have only received the first four of the nine which I have written to you, counting this one? But let the deliveries run as they will; they could never run as fast our love would wish them to.'[56] In the same spirit of accountancy, Diderot emphatically warns his correspondent in November 1760: 'I do not like it when you upset my calculations.'[57]

GOODNIGHT, SOPHIE

We have seen that the correspondence between Diderot and Sophie is an ongoing attempt to overcome absence. But it reminds the *philosophe* of their being in different places, of their failure to coincide. The letter of 2 September 1760 speaks of this catastrophe: 'You complain of the place where you are living, of the claims on your time ... but do you think that things are better here? No, dear friend, everything here is as bad as it is there, because you are not here, because I am not there.'[58] The letter literally transmits the tragedy of desire, its impossibility. Diderot expresses it perfectly by playing on the ideas of absence and presence: 'Nothing would be missing where you are; I would have nothing to desire where I am, if I were there, if you were here.'[59]

But above all the love letter as penned by Diderot reveals something unsurprising about itself. The letter speaks only of itself; it is the pure repetition of its own speech. The signifiers contained in these letters are empty of all other content. So what does the letter say, in the sheer volume of its writing? 'Nothings. But these nothings, placed end-to-end, form the most important of all histories: that of our heart's love.'[60] One famous letter, a gift to anthologists, provides a perfect dramatisation of this self-referential aspect of the love letter. It says both everything and nothing. It expresses a dual impossibility: the letter-writer cannot overcome the emptiness of absence, and (worse still) he cannot conjure up the absent subject. Indeed, the letter mimes or *copies* this absence. In the passage in question, Diderot composes an erotic interior scene. The room where letters are written is transformed into a virtual, spectral space. The letter-writer's scribbling produces ghostly signs, hieroglyphs of his passion. The resulting letter, written on 10 or 12 July 1759, is worth citing in full:

I write without seeing. I came here. I wanted to kiss your hand and return. I will return, but without this reward. But will I not have reward enough, if I have shown you how much I love you? It is nine o'clock. I am writing to you that I love you, at least I want to write that to you, but I do not know if my quill obeys my desire. Will you not come here so that I can tell you [that I love you] and fly from here? Adieu, Sophie, good night. Does not your heart tell you that I am here? This is the first time I have written anything in the dark. This situation should inspire very tender thoughts in me. Only one occurs to me: I cannot leave this place. The hope of seeing you here for a moment keeps me here, and I continue to speak to you, not knowing whether my hand is forming characters. Everywhere you find a gap, read that I love you.[61]

Whatever Diderot says, the day will come when this love fades. The return of the routine negotiations, the many details of daily life, will henceforth provide the substance of the letters to Sophie. Diderot relates his trips to Grandval, to La Chevrette,[62] but also, towards the end of the correspondence, those longer journeys to the Hague and to Saint Petersburg (in the letters of 1773–4). The lovers' space shrinks as more and more people crowd in. And even as Diderot continues to complain about the gap between sending and receiving letters, he writes less frequently. Finally, the letters cease to resemble the long happy ones of former times. Diderot no longer writes to his mistress alone; he also includes Sophie's two sisters, Mme Legendre and Mme de Blacy. They are the 'good friends' to whom he addresses himself from now on. This is highlighted when Diderot indicates on or around 7 March 1766 that he wishes to be read by his mistress alone: 'This letter is for you and you alone. Do you understand?'[63] Of course, even in his 'open' letters the *philosophe* may still direct some protestations of love towards Sophie alone: 'Tell me only that you are well and that you love me; let me see a sample of your hand once again.'[64] But the drama of love and the affects of earlier times are now examined nostalgically, as though consigned to a distant past. Thus, in the letter of 22 November 1768, Diderot asks:

What happened to the time when my impatience, my chagrin, my rage, would have pleased you greatly? When you would have been delighted if I had anticipated the too-slow arrival of my letters to you and your replies? When you would have reproached me for not writing to you for two days as if I had been silent for two whole weeks? Today you would find such reproaches unjust.[65]

The chronicle of that exclusive 'sweet bond' has become part of Diderot's account of his social relationships in general.

NOTES

1. A useful summary of Diderot's relationship with Sophie Volland can be found in a recent biography: Raymond Trousson, *Diderot* (Paris: Gallimard, 2007), pp. 115–22.
2. Jacques Chouillet, *Denis Diderot – Sophie Volland. Un dialogue à une voix* (Paris: Champion, 1986).
3. Trousson, *Diderot*, p. 118. The story in question is usually known by the title *Mme de La Carlière*; see DPV, vol. XII, pp. 549–75.
4. Odile Richard-Pauchet, 'Sophie Volland et Denis Diderot dans les *Lettres à Sophie Volland* (1759–1774): une amitié particulière', *Recherches sur Diderot et sur l'Encyclopédie*, 39 (2005), 20–1. See also, by the same author, the cultural and poetic study *Diderot dans les 'Lettres à Sophie Volland'. Une esthétique épistolaire* (Paris: Champion, 2007).
5. *Corr.*, vol. III, p. 222. All translations of Diderot's letters are the editor's and are based on the Roth–Varloot edition of the *Correspondance* used throughout this volume. For easy reference to other editions of the *Correspondance*, the date of each letter cited is given either in the main text or in the notes.
6. *Corr.*, vol. II, p. 264 (1 October 1759).
7. Ibid., vol. V, p. 236 (30 December 1765).
8. Ibid., vol. II, p. 264 (1 October 1759).
9. Ibid., vol. III, p. 206 (28 October 1760).
10. Ibid., vol. II, p. 264 (1 October 1759).
11. Ibid., vol. III, p. 86.
12. Ibid., p. 206.
13. Ibid., vol. II, p. 266.

14. Ibid., vol. v, p. 169 (12 November 1765).
15. Ibid., p. 37.
16. Ibid., pp. 59–60.
17. Ibid., vol. III, p. 264.
18. Ibid., vol. IV, p. 43 (14 July 1762).
19. Ibid., vol. III, p. 282.
20. In his edition of a selection of the *Lettres*, Jean Varloot notes that Étienne-Noël Damilaville (1723–68) was 'premier commis au bureau du vingtième' ('chief assistant at the office of the *vingtième*' (a 5 per cent tax on income)), and that in this capacity he allowed his friends to benefit from the postal arrangements available to the Ministry of Finance. See *Lettres à Sophie Volland*, ed. Jean Varloot (Paris: Gallimard, 1984), p. 381 (n. 73).
21. *Corr.*, vol. III, 245 (9–10 November 1760). For an assessment of the role and importance of such private places, see Orest Ranum, 'Les Refuges de l'intimité', in Philippe Ariès and Georges Duby (eds.), 5 vols. *Histoire de la vie privée* (Paris: Seuil, 1999), vol. III, pp. 225–8.
22. The French word 'fatal', translated here by 'fateful', can mean 'fatal' or 'inevitable'.
23. On the use of 'contreseings' (countersignatures), see E. Vaillé, *Histoire générale des postes francaises*, 7 vols. (Paris: Presses Universitaires de France, 1953), vol. VI, part I, pp. 138–49.
24. *Corr.*, vol. IV, p. 78 (28 July 1762).
25. I borrow the notion of the epistolary pact from Benoît Melançon, *Diderot épistolier. Contribution à une poétique de la lettre familière au XVIIIe siècle* (Quebec: Fidès, 1996). See also Anne-Marie Boilleau's exhaustive study, *Liaison et liaisons dans les lettres de Diderot à Sophie Volland* (Paris: Champion, 1999).
26. *Corr.*, vol. II, p. 265.
27. On this point see Richard-Pauchet, *Diderot*, pp. 55–74.
28. *Corr.*, vol. III, p. 135 (14–15 October 1760).
29. Ibid., p. 155.
30. Ibid., p. 154.
31. Ibid., vol. II, pp. 279–80.
32. Ibid., p. 267. As Georges Roth indicates on the same page (n. 3), the feast of Saint Denis falls on 9 October.
33. Ibid., p. 287 (18 October 1759).
34. Ibid., p. 288 (18 October 1759).
35. Ibid., vol. III, p. 122.
36. Ibid., vol. VIII, p. 221 (15 November 1768).
37. Ibid., vol. III, p. 44 (31 August 1760).
38. Ibid., p. 218 (3 November 1760).
39. Ibid., p. 122.
40. Ibid., p. 44.
41. Ibid., p. 336.
42. Ibid., vol. IV, p. 145.

43. Jacques Derrida, *La Carte postale* (Paris: Flammarion, 1980), p. 73.
44. *Corr.*, vol. III, p. 49.
45. Cited in Derrida, *La Carte postale*, p. 77.
46. *Corr.*, vol. III, p. 44 (31 August 1760).
47. Ibid., vol. IV, p. 74 (28 July 1762). On these 'ghostly' arrangements, see Gilles Deleuze, *Kafka. Pour une littérature mineure* (Paris: Minuit, 1975), p. 55.
48. *Corr.*, vol. II, p. 283.
49. Ibid., p. 283.
50. Ibid., p. 284.
51. Ibid., vol. V, pp. 71–2.
52. Ibid., vol. III, p. 52.
53. Ibid., p. 61 (10 September 1760).
54. Ibid., p. 201 (28 October 1760).
55. DPV, vol. XVII, p. 136.
56. *Corr.*, vol. IV, pp. 38–9.
57. Ibid., vol. III, p. 238.
58. Ibid., p. 51.
59. Ibid. On Diderot's treatment of this commonplace of love letters, see Melançon, *Diderot épistolier*, pp. 59–76.
60. *Corr.*, vol. III, p. 188 (26 October 1760).
61. Ibid., vol. II, pp. 168–9.
62. Ibid., vol. III, p. 340 (19 October 1761).
63. Ibid., vol. VI, p. 156.
64. Ibid., vol. XIII, p. 41 (13 August 1773).
65. Ibid., vol. VIII, p. 228.

PART II

Novels

CHAPTER 7

Les Bijoux indiscrets: *transition or translation?*

Anne Deneys-Tunney

For some considerable time, Diderot's novel *Les Bijoux indiscrets* (*The Indiscreet Jewels*) was relegated to a place amongst the minor and even obscene works, in the *Enfer* of the Bibliotheque Nationale, Paris.[1] Now, however, it is considered to be one of Diderot's major works, and its philosophical importance is widely recognised. The *philosophe* wrote this, his first novel, in 1747. More than twenty years later, between 1770 and 1775, he added three chapters that enhance the philosophical significance of the work: 'Le Rêve de Mangogul' ('Mangogul's Dream'), 'Des Voyageurs' ('The Explorers') and 'De la figure des insulaires et de la toilette des femmes' ('On the Islanders' Appearance and their Women's Style of Dress').[2] In writing *Les Bijoux*, Diderot made use for the first time of the form known as the 'philosophical novel', a hybrid genre with which he will come to be closely associated.

As Diderot combines philosophy and the (libertine) novel for the first time in his writing career, he produces a formally complex work that deserves to be called seminal. On one level, the *bijoux* ('jewels', or women's genitals) of the title permit a symbolic or allegorical representation of the new (or newly perceived) world which the Enlightenment *philosophes* will not cease to try to interpret – or rather, in this case, to hear. Taken together, the thirty-one trials of the magic ring given to the sultan Mangogul by the good genie Cucufa constitute a truly encyclopedic world tour, or at least a tour of the 'feminine' world of sex and pleasure, a journey subject to various twists and turns, vicissitudes, surprises and discoveries. (Let us not forget that Diderot was writing *Les Bijoux* at roughly the same time as he and d'Alembert were entering into a contract to become joint editors of the *Encyclopédie*.[3]) The female sex is thus explored, listened to and represented in this novel as a series of 'jewels' that are alternately talkative, muffled, boastful, musical, mute, etc.[4] The *bijou* becomes the emblem of a new reality, repressed until now: and philosophy sets itself the task, henceforth, of representing it as a new origin of truth – a scandalous, scabrous origin, but in spite of this (or precisely because of this) all the more essential, necessary and desirable.[5]

But this is not the only way in which philosophy and the novel intersect in this work. While Diderot's libertine tale suggests that the *bijoux* give voice to what classical, metaphysical philosophy has repressed – the body and sex – certain chapters (which Diderot himself explicitly designates as philosophical) tackle the mainstream metaphysical questions of his day. These include the nature of the soul and its location in the body; Cartesian dualism; whether animals use language; the development of the human body in terms of practical aims, needs, sensation and pleasure; and the possibility of a political system in which sexual characteristics would determine the arranging of 'good' marriages based on physiology and therefore, perhaps, conducive to happiness.[6] So even if the novel is often obscene, it is punctuated by moments of high philosophy, explicitly presented as such. And at such moments, all the key terms of metaphysics appear: 'truth', 'pineal gland', 'soul', etc. The reader is supposed already to possess a firm grounding in the key concepts.[7]

By its constant use of such terms, which evoke the great metaphysical debates of the day, the novel repeatedly engages with an external philosophical discourse which is parodied, displaced and integrated into an unfamiliar discursive context (an obscene oriental tale) that serves to debase it. Diderot thus deconstructs metaphysical language from within, taking its key terms and causing them to 'drift', as the novel veers from the literal to the metaphorical or vice versa, creating series of increasingly surreal images that may leave us reeling. One example of many is afforded by the chapter mentioned above ('Métaphysique de Mirzoza'), in which we are offered a vision of an alternative world where each person would be reduced to the body part (or parts) which is the most important to him/her, and in which Mirzoza argues that the soul must therefore reside (the feet and legs of dancers, the throats of singers, the *bijoux* of 'most women', etc.).[8]

In what follows, I will focus on a very short chapter of the novel: 'La Petite Jument' ('The Little Mare').[9] The chapter in question is at once comical, obscene and philosophical. It is so short that it may easily be overlooked on first reading, but it is situated in a position that seems to signal its importance. For Diderot placed it between two of his overtly philosophical chapters: Chapter XXVII of Volume I, 'Suite de la conversation précédente' ('Continuation of the Preceding Conversation'), which is itself preceded by 'Métaphysique de Mirzoza. Les âmes',[10] and Chapter XXIX of the same volume, entitled: 'Le meilleur peut-être et le moins lu de cette histoire. Rêve de Mangogul, ou voyage dans la région des hypothèses'

('Perhaps the Best and the Least Read [Part] of this Story. Mangogul's Dream, or a Journey into the Region of Hypotheses').[11] We will see that the chapter in question, which is structured as a simple anecdote, in fact inflects the meaning of the novel as a whole, pulling it towards a kind of enquiry – at once central to the novel and latent within it – into the question of language and its relationship (or non-relationship) to meaning.

What is the theme of the chapter in question? Mangogul has already used his magic ring twelve times. These trials have all 'worked', in the sense that they have revealed the universal passion for pleasure shared by the women whose *bijoux* have spoken. At this point, the sultan suddenly decides to interrogate the *bijou*, not of one of the court favourites, but of his mare: a new 'altar of truth'.[12] The chapter relates how the mare at first produces sounds which no one in Mangogul's entourage can understand or interpret. (The chapter becomes increasingly bizarre until its conclusion, in which the discourse of the mare's *bijou* is finally deciphered.) So the sultan decides to call on a series of scholars and specialists of foreign languages to translate the 'jewel''s discourse into a comprehensible form. Every effort meets with failure. All the translators produce different versions, equally wrong, of the sounds produced by the mare. They fail to identify its meaning and even its language:

Le prince en fit distribuer sur-le-champ des copies à tous ses interprètes et professeurs en langues étrangères, tant anciennes que modernes. L'un dit que c'était une scène de quelques vieilles tragédies grecques qui lui paraissait fort touchante; un autre parvint, à force de tête, à découvrir que c'était un fragment important de la théologie des Égyptiens: celui-ci prétendait que c'était l'exorde de l'oraison funèbre d'Annibal en carthaginois. Celui-là assura que la pièce était écrite en chinois, et que c'était une prière fort dévote à Confucius.[13]

(The prince immediately had copies distributed to all his interpreters and teachers of foreign languages, both ancient and modern. One said that it was a scene from some ancient Greek tragedy, which he found highly moving; another managed, after much deliberation, to discover that it was an important fragment of Egyptian theology; yet another claimed that it was the exordium of Hannibal's funeral oration, in Carthaginian. Someone else asserted that the extract was written in Chinese, and that it was a deeply devout prayer addressed to Confucius.)

The chapter is only two pages long, and yet for the first illustrated edition of the novel (brought out in two volumes in 1748), it was decided that the episode deserved an engraving, suggesting that it was extremely popular – or that the engraver considered it highly significant or particularly striking. The illustration in question is reproduced in the Pléiade edition of the novel.[14] It depicts a magnificent horse looking at its reflection in a large mirror, while a scholar sits at a nearby desk, trying to catch the mare's words. The detail and exquisite luxury of the background, with its windows, rich draperies and neo-Renaissance sculptures, match the narrative style adopted by Diderot. The chapter opens with a comical list (comical, that is, because it is a horse and not a woman that is being described) of the mare's various claims to beauty:

Je ne suis pas grand faiseur de portraits. J'ai épargné au lecteur celui de la sultane favorite; mais je ne me résoudrai jamais à lui faire grâce de celui de la jument du sultan. Sa taille était médiocre: elle se tenait assez bien; on lui reprochait seulement de laisser un peu tomber sa tête en devant. Elle avait le poil blond, l'œil bleu, le pied petit.[15]

(I am no great describer of characters. I have spared the reader a description of the sultan's favorite wife; but I will never be able to withhold that of the sultan's mare. She was of medium height, and had good posture; the only fault that some found in her was that she held her head too low. Her coat was blonde, her eyes were blue, her hooves were small.)

The engraver of the 1748 edition manages to convey this joke in visual/ spatial terms.

At the end of the chapter, once all the translators' and scholars' efforts have ended in a fiasco, Mangogul has recourse to a character from another novel: the eponymous hero of Jonathan Swift's *Gulliver's Travels:*[16]

Tandis que les érudits impatientaient le sultan avec leurs savantes conjectures, il se rappela les voyages de Gulliver, et ne douta point qu'un homme qui avait séjourné aussi longtemps que cet Anglais, dans une île où les chevaux ont un gouvernement, des lois, des rois, des dieux, des prêtres, une religion, des temples et des autels, et qui paraissait si parfaitement instruit de leurs mœurs et de leurs coutumes, n'eût une intelligence parfaite de leur langue. En effet, Gulliver lut et interpréta tout courant le discours de la jument, malgré les fautes d'écriture dont il fourmillait. C'est même la seule bonne traduction qu'on ait dans tout le Congo.[17]

(While the scholars were testing the sultan's patience with their erudite conjectures he remembered *Gulliver's Travels,* and felt sure that anyone who had lived as long as this Englishman on an island where the horses have a government, their own laws, kings, gods, priests, a religion, temples and altars, and who therefore seemed so perfectly knowledgeable concerning those horses' customs and traditions, would have a complete grasp of their language. Indeed, Gulliver read and interpreted the mare's speech without a hitch, in spite of the spelling mistakes in every line. It is the only good translation in all of the Congo.)

Beyond implying a homage to Swift, the arrival of Gulliver in Diderot's novel has a symbolic significance. Fiction, here, comes to the aid of the failed or impossible interpretation of the discourse of the mare's *bijou.* It seems that only a fiction-within-a-fiction has the power to understand the discourse in question and translate it into human language; this suggests such a possibility is (so to speak) especially fictional.

We must remember that when Diderot wrote *Les Bijoux indiscrets* the question of whether animals use language had been a major philosophical question since the previous century. Had Descartes been right or wrong to assert that animals only create an illusion of possessing language, that the 'language' of animals was in fact a mechanical imitation of meaning without soul (or without thought and intelligence, and therefore without creativity of any kind)? To assert that animals possess language, for Descartes, is equivalent to saying that they have a soul, a possibility which he firmly refutes. In the *Discours de la Méthode* (*Discourse on Method*), he raises the question of the soul and the language of animals, given that he sees a connection between the soul and the ability to use (true) language. Descartes proceeds to argue that animals have a mere semblance of language (consisting in the imitation of sounds), and that they do not possess thought (or the soul), without which meaning, and so (true) language, cannot be produced. Thus, in Part v of the *Discours*, after discussing other matters (e.g. the planets and the circulation of blood within the body), Descartes declares that he will broach 'la différence qui est entre notre âme et celle des bêtes' ('the difference between our soul and that of animals'). Descartes's argument can be summarised as follows: if we were capable of creating extremely sophisticated machines resembling humans, then:

Nous aurions toujours deux moyens très certains pour reconnaître qu'elles ne seraient point pour cela de vrais hommes. Dont le premier est que jamais [les machines corporelles] ne pourraient user de paroles ni d'autres signes en les composant, comme nous faisons pour déclarer aux autres nos pensées ... Et le second est que, bien qu'elles fissent plusieurs choses aussi bien, ou peut-être mieux, qu'aucun de nous, elles manqueraient infailliblement en quelques autres, par lesquelles on découvrirait qu'elles n'agiraient pas par connaissance, mais seulement par la disposition de leurs organes.[18]

(We would still have two very certain means of recognising that they were not, for all that, real men. Of these the first is, that they could never use words or other signs, composing them as we do to declare our thoughts to others ... And the second is that, although they might do many things as well as, or perhaps better than, any of us, they would fail, no doubt, in others, whereby one would discover that they did not act through knowledge, but simply through the disposition of their organs.)[19]

For Descartes, the use of language and signs does not belong to the realm of the *cogito*. Linguistic expression, a concept Descartes extends to the use of signs, does not contain thought as such. This is in contrast to the sceptics' view that there is no firm distinction to be made between the souls of animals and those of humans. If in the seventeenth century La Fontaine portrays speaking animals in his Fables, it is because he is not a Cartesian but a Gassendist, and therefore a sceptic.[20]

These comments suffice to show that, in the chapter we are examining, Diderot revisits this major philosophical question, and does so in a farcical and parodic fashion.[21] At the end of the chapter, we have seen, Gulliver is able to interpret the mare's discourse, and so 'solves' the riddle of whether animals use language.[22] (In the following chapter, Mangogul has a dream in which it is revealed that metaphysics is a temple that rests on a void.[23]) But, in fact, the episode goes beyond discussion of this particular question. The anecdote of the little mare dramatises the struggle to interpret and translate one language (that of the sex and the body, which happens to be the body of a mare and therefore a female body, the male body and sex being left out of account) into another language (the human language of thought): in philosophical terms, this is the question of phenomenological sensation and its relation to intellection. At the end of Chapter 28 of Volume I, we have seen, only a character from fiction (Gulliver) can interpret and translate the language of sex (which is, moreover, an equine version of that language) into human terms: this suggests that the interpretation or translation of that language into ours can only ever occur in fiction: that it is, in fact, a purely fictional possibility. So the chapter implies an enquiry into the very possibility of translation – of one language being substituted for another, the verbal language of intellection for the language of sex and the body. Diderot implies that to 'express' the language of the body in human language always requires an act of translation, but that such an act is never unproblematic and might even be impossible. The intervention of the 'doubly fictional' Gulliver, being parodic, offers no definitive answer to the question of how to achieve the transition/translation from the language of an animal (the mare) into a human language (in this case French, the language spoken by most of the human *bijoux* in the novel).

Elsewhere in the novel, the question of the language spoken by the human *bijoux*, and the possibility of hearing and understanding it, are repeatedly problematised. There is the case of the polyglot *bijou*; and also all those gaps and crossings-out in the manuscript of the novel which prevent the reader from completely making out what the *bijoux* 'originally' said. There are also the suffocated *bijoux*, which are inaudible because of the muzzles which their owners have attached to them.[24] Such comical episodes (like that of the mare) problematise the idea of speaking *bijoux*: how they might achieve expression, language and meaning. In each of these cases, it is as though full, comprehensible meaning were always absent. It is significant that at the end of the novel Mangogul dares to do what he had promised not to: turn the gem set in his magic ring in the direction of Mirzoza, who has fallen into a deep swoon. But Mirzoza wakes as her *bijou* is still speaking, so that its confession remains partial and unfinished:

Il tourne sa bague sur elle; mais le bijou de Mirzoza, qui s'était ennuyé au sermon ... et qui se sentait apparemment de la léthargie, ne murmura d'abord que quelques mots confus et mal articulés ... Mangogul transporté de joie, ne s'aperçut pas que la favorite sortait insensiblement de sa léthargie, et que s'il tardait à retourner sa bague, elle entendrait les dernières paroles de son bijou. Ce qui arriva.[25]

(He pointed his ring in her direction and turned it; but Mirzoza's jewel, which had been bored during the sermon ... and which apparently felt lethargic, brought forth, at first, nothing more than a few indistinct and poorly articulated words ... Mangogul, transported with joy, did not notice that his favourite was gradually coming to, nor that if he did not hurry to turn his ring in the reverse direction, she would hear the last words uttered by her jewel – which is what happened.)

In the episode of the mare, as in the others just mentioned, something in the discourse of the *bijoux* ineluctably escapes the ear of the listener – which is to say Mangogul's and the reader's ear. Some 'thing' is trying to find expression and be understood, but that thing cannot be distinctly heard or reliably interpreted. Thus the obscene oriental tale that is *Les Bijoux indiscrets* raises the whole question of Diderot's reflection on hermeneutics. Can the real world ever be saturated with meaning? Is it possible that we can attain a complete knowledge, at least, of (the) sex? Or will we only find gaps, missing elements, muffled and ultimately untranslatable noises that suggest a realm beyond the reach of knowledge and meaning? Given the failures of communication and meaning portrayed in *Les Bijoux indiscrets*, the reader may well ask: is reality itself full of holes? Or are the missing parts merely gaps in our knowledge of reality, which fails to achieve total comprehension of phenomena in their wholeness and diversity? Will Enlightenment progressively fill the most important gaps, given time? Or will reality stubbornly resist 'translation' and prevent us from approaching a perfect match between words and things, between the 'raw material' of reality and our understanding of it? The discourse of the *bijoux* poses this question in a particular form: how to translate what belongs in the realm of sex, the body, desire, the animal, into human language? Can these two 'worlds', which co-exist in reality, be made to correspond to each other? Are the language of sex and the body and that of the novel and philosophy compatible, or are they fundamentally heterogeneous and mutually exclusive? How can human ears be brought to hear the unfamiliar discourse of sex and animality?[26]

In an article on 'le pyrrhonisme du matérialisme' ('materialist pyrrhonism') in the eighteenth century, Francine Markovits argues that rationalist discourse always evades the question of language.[27] In such discourse, statements are supposed to possess, as it were, an intrinsic truth and clarity. The relationship between such truths and the speaking subject, or such truths and the language in which they are expressed, indeed the relation between *énoncé* ('utterance') and *énonciateur* ('producer of the utterance'), is neither indicated nor treated as problematic in rationalist authors: it is skirted around. It is striking that, by contrast, Diderot's fable of supposedly 'indiscreet' *bijoux* portrays the expression of a new reality, i.e. of the repressed content of metaphysical discourse (sex and the body), as the appearance of a new language.[28] This new language is explicit in certain episodes of *Les Bijoux*; at other times, it is indecipherable, untranslatable, ambiguous or incomplete. Diderot, we have seen, uses a wide range of novelistic procedures to question the phenomenon of language and the relationship between *le sujet de l' énonciation* ('the subject of the enunciation') and *le sujet de l'énoncé* ('the subject of the utterance'). He offers many examples foregrounding utterances that are true only from the point of view of the speaker (in this case, the *bijoux*, be they human or equine). This technique in fact revives a nominalist critique that has its roots in scepticism. It does so by revealing the opacity of language, the difference between languages (that of philosophy versus that of the *bijoux*), the dependence of meaning on the perceptions of the subject, and a certain autonomy and arbitrariness belonging to language-as-mechanism. If Diderot is moving towards materialism in 1748, it is to be found in the aporetic, dialogic, alogical, critical and self-critical form of his novel. Markovits asserts that 'le discours sceptique apparaît comme celui qui implique l'énonciateur dans la structure de l'énoncé' ('sceptical discourse implicates the speaker in the structure of the utterance').[29] Diderot's recourse to the *bijoux* early in his writing career suggests that he is already aware of the necessity to invent a new language to express the ideas of a new philosophy.

Let us sum up. The oriental tale allows Diderot to construct the fiction of another language, a new language, and, at the same time, point to its aporia.[30] The magic ring provided by Cucufa does allow female genitals to be heard, but often, we have seen, something limits the listener's understanding of their 'confessions'. The episode of the little mare, then, becomes symbolic of the novel as a whole: something tries to find expression and make itself heard – or is given voice, but cannot be understood or translated, except by the novel itself, with its characters and its fictions. In other words, meaning always depends on a construction; meaning is a form which the novelist confers, or in which he 'clothes' phenomena that are fundamentally irreducible, in their strangeness and difference.

If Diderot dramatises in *Les Bijoux* the entry into discourse of sex and the 'feminine', and if he does indeed inaugurate, as Michel Foucault eloquently argues, 'the age of sexuality',[31] the discourse in question remains in so many ways inaudible or untranslatable. Diderot's first novel suggests that sex and pleasure push towards expression in language, and yet it also emphasises the limits of such expression, suggesting that these may always leave a vital 'remainder' unsaid. The episode of the little mare is exemplary in this respect: it tells us that between real phenomena and our knowledge of them there is always an operation of the human mind. Meaning is not automatic; it cannot be directly accessed, it does not offer easy 'readability'; there must always be an act of translation – human and linguistic – with all its detours, follies, mistakes and, finally, its felicities. The dramatisation of the unavoidability of such translation, with all the problems it brings, reveals that language is far more than a simple conduit or transition from real phenomena to knowledge expressed in words. The insistent return to this problem in *Les Bijoux indiscrets* places it beyond any straightforward rationalism or mechanistic materialism. The episode of the mare in particular, with its emphasis on the precariousness of translation and meaning, impels the novel towards an infinitely open space of meaning, sense and nonsense. Thus it constitutes one of the great philosophical moments of the novel, and one that can be linked with Derrida's notion of the 'supplement' in *De la grammatologie*:

Mais le supplémént supplée. Il ne s'ajoute que pour remplacer. Il intervient ou s'insinue *à-la-place-de*; s'il comble, c'est comme on comble un vide. S'il représente et fait image, c'est par le défaut antérieur d'une présence. Suppléant et vicaire, le suppléant est un adjoint, une instance subalterne qui *tient-lieu*. En tant que substitut, il ne s'ajoute pas simplement à la possibilité d'une présence, il ne produit aucun relief, sa place est assignée dans la structure par la marque d'un vide. Quelque part, quelque chose ne peut se remplir *de soi-même*, ne peut s'accomplir qu'en se laissant combler par signe et procuration. Le signe est toujours le supplément de la chose même.[32]

(But the supplement supplements. It adds only to replace. It intervenes or insinuates itself *in-the-place-of*; if it fills, it is as if one fills a void. If it represents and makes an image, it is by the anterior default of a presence. Compensatory and vicarious, the supplement is an adjunct, a subaltern instance which *takes-(the)-place*. As substitute, it is not simply added to the positivity of a presence, it produces no relief, its place is assigned in the structure by the mark of an emptiness. Somewhere, something can be filled up *of itself*, can accomplish itself, only by allowing itself to be filled through sign and proxy. The sign is always the supplement of the thing itself.)[33]

Les Bijoux indiscrets can be read in the light of this perception. Whether the *bijoux* speak, shout, or sing at the top of their voices (when they are not reduced to silence), the noises they produce are to a significant degree stifled, ambiguous and inaudible, and must always be translated from one language to another. Their discourse thus introduces a destabilising supplement into the philosophical novel that contains (or fails to contain) it; the problems attached to hearing, understanding and translating what the *bijoux* have to say suggest the impossibility of any true match between word and thing, between existence and language. In this respect, Diderot's first novel inaugurates and symbolises, prophetically enough, the modern era's struggle with the problem of language and signifying systems.

NOTES

1. In 1830, the Bibliothèque Nationale's closely guarded collection of obscene, blasphemous or otherwise 'dangerous' works was named the *Enfer* ('Hell'). See Philippe Sollers, *Le Cœur absolu* (Paris: Gallimard, 1987), p. 312, where the author quotes Casanova writing in 1781 on the dangerous effects of certain 'récits voluptueux et lubriques' ('lewd, voluptuous tales'), including *Les Bijoux indiscrets*.
2. See DPV, vol. III, pp. 259–81.
3. Diderot and d'Alembert were approached after Gua de Malves had withdrawn from the enterprise, and their contract was agreed on 16 October 1747. See Raymond Trousson, *Diderot* (Paris: Gallimard, 2007), p. 46.
4. See DPV, vol. III, pp. 134–8.
5. Throughout the novel the *bijoux* are humorously referred to as 'autels de vérité' ('altars of truth'), for instance in the subtitle to vol. I, chapter VII: 'Second essai de l'anneau. Les autels' ('Second Trial of the Ring. Altars') (DPV, vol. III, p. 51). The irony of this designation emerges in the course of the chapter, where we read: 'Et chaque bijou répondant à son tour, on entendit sur différents tons: "je suis fréquenté, délabré, délaissé, parfumé, fatigué, mal servi, ennuyé, etc." Tous dirent leur mot, mais si brusquement, qu'on n'en put faire au juste l'application. Leur jargon, tantôt sourd et tantôt glapissant, accompagné des éclats de rire de Mangogul et de ses courtisans, fit un bruit d'une espèce nouvelle' (p. 53). ('And every jewel replied in turn. Those present heard the following words, pronounced in various tones: "I am much visited, I am in a sorry state, I am abandoned, perfumed, neglected, bored, etc." All the jewels had something to

say, but they spoke so rapidly that it was impossible to catch all the interesting details. The jewels' unfamiliar speech, which was by turns muffled and shrill, and to which was added the noisy laughter of Mangogul and his courtiers, made a sound such as had never been heard before.')

6. See especially DPV, vol. III, pp. 118–28, 130–4, 267–74.
7. See my article 'La Critique de la métaphysique dans *les Bijoux indiscrets* et *Jacques le fataliste* de Diderot', *Recherches sur Diderot et sur l'Encyclopédie*, 26 (April 1999), pp. 141–51.
8. See DPV, vol. III, pp. 118–25.
9. See ibid., pp. 128–30.
10. Ibid., pp. 118–28.
11. Ibid., pp. 130–4.
12. See n. 5 above.
13. DPV, vol. III, p. 129.
14. See Denis Diderot, *Contes et romans*, ed. Michel Delon *et al.* (Paris: Gallimard 2004), p. 233.
15. DPV, vol. III, p. 128.
16. *Gulliver's Travels* was translated into French by Desfontaines in 1727, a year after it first appeared in English. Diderot alludes to the episode in Part IV of the novel, in which Gulliver travels to the land of the Houyhnhnms.
17. DPV, vol. III, p. 130.
18. René Descartes, *Discours de la méthode*, ed. Geneviève Rodis-Lewis (Paris: Garnier Flammarion, 1966), pp. 78–9.
19. René Descartes, *'Discourse on Method' and 'The Meditations'*, ed. and trans. F. E. Sutcliffe (London: Penguin, 1968), p. 74.
20. For an interesting account of Descartes's views on 'ce qui est de l'entendement ou de la pensée que Montagne et quelques autres attribuent aux bêtes' ('the question of the understanding or thought which Montaigne and several others attribute to animals'), see René Descartes, *Œuvres*, ed. Charles Adam and Paul Tannery, 12 vols. (Paris: Vrin, 1964–74), vol. IV, pp. 573–5 (Letter to the marquess of Newcastle, 23 November 1646).
21. On the eighteenth-century revival of the debate over whether animals have souls, see Diderot, *Les Bijoux indiscrets*, in *Contes et romans*, p. 959 (n. 2).
22. I am not suggesting that this solution indicates Diderot's own position, given the parodic nature of the 'solution' in question.
23. DPV, vol. III, pp. 130–4; as noted above, the chapter is subtitled: 'Le meilleur peut-être et le moins lu de cette histoire. Rêve de Mangogul, ou voyage dans la région des hypothèses' ('Perhaps the Best and the Least Read [Part] of this Story. Mangogul's Dream, or a Journey into the Region of Hypotheses').
24. See ibid., pp. 79–81.
25. Ibid., p. 258.
26. At roughly the same time as he is writing *Les Bijoux*, Diderot raises related questions in *La Promenade du Sceptique* (*The Sceptic's Walk*); but in that text, despite its humour, Diderot employs more strictly philosophical (and sceptical) terms. See DPV, vol. II, pp. 63–155.

27. Francine Markovits, 'L'Antimachiavel-médecin', *Corpus, revue de philosophie*, 31 (1997), 207–36.

28. See my study *Écritures du corps, de Descartes à Laclos* (Paris: Presses Universitaires de France, 1992), especially chap. 1 ('Le corps et les signes ou les fantômes de la philosophie').

29. See Markovtis, 'L'Antimachiavel-médecin', p. 234.

30. This aporia is indicated by the gaps in the manuscript throughout the novel: 'La république des lettres aurait certainement obligation à celui qui nous restituerait le discours du bijou de Callipiga, dont il ne nous reste que les deux dernières lignes. Nous invitons les savants à les méditer, et à voir si cette lacune ne serait point une omission volontaire de l'auteur, mécontent de ce qu'il avait dit, et qui ne trouvait rien de mieux à dire' (DPV, vol. III, p. 180). ('The Republic of Letters would certainly be obliged to the person who might restore for us the words of Callipiga's jewel, of which we only have the last two lines. We invite scholars to meditate on them, and to see if this lacuna might not be a voluntary omission on the part of the author who was dissatisfied with what he had said, but who could not think of anything better.')

31. See Michel Foucault, *Histoire de la sexualité*, vol. I: *La Volonté de savoir* (Paris: Gallimard, 1976), pp. 101–5.

32. Jacques Derrida, *De la grammatologie* (Paris: Minuit, 1967), p. 208. It should be noted that in French, 'suppléer' can mean 'make up' or 'stand in for', and that Derrida plays on the double meaning of 'supplément' (completion/substitution).

33. Jacques Derrida, *Of Grammatology*, trans. Gayatri Chakravorty Spivak (Baltimore, MD: Johns Hopkins University Press, 1976), p. 145.

CHAPTER 8

Jacques le fataliste et son maître: *finding myself in the work of another*

Joseph Breines

Jacques le fataliste et son maître (*Jacques the Fatalist and his Master*) is one of Diderot's works known in his lifetime to a few select readers, including those with access to the *Correspondance littéraire* (*Literary Correspondence*). On one level, it tells the story of Jacques and his master travelling through France towards an unstated destination, an eight-day journey enlivened by the servant's on–off account of his *amours*, culminating in his wooing of his true love. But the stories told by Jacques to his master are repeatedly interrupted by the events of the journey; this gives rise to intercalated narratives, as the travellers meet people with a story to tell; and the master–servant dialogue is itself contained in an exchange between reader and author (which introduces yet more stories). Diderot's novel is striking on many counts, but perhaps especially for what might be termed its two spheres of reference. On the one hand it is a novel about life that insistently returns to the question of whether Jacques's 'fatalism' (a word that covers both fatalism and determinism in the eighteenth century) adequately accounts for his/our experience of the world. On the other hand it is also a novel about the novel, indeed about story-telling in all its forms: about readers and writers, tellers and listeners. And it is about all these things above all by virtue of its 'self-referential' passages – those in which the text calls attention to itself as text, as artefact, as literature. On account of this, it has sometimes been referred to as an 'anti-novel'.

In *Jacques le fataliste*, the author-figure quotes the hero as saying: 'Quelle que soit la somme des éléments dont je suis composé, je suis un, or une cause n'a qu'un effet; j'ai toujours été une cause une, je n'ai donc jamais eu qu'un effet à produire, ma durée n'est donc qu'une suite d'effets nécessaires.'[1] ('Whatever the sum total of the elements I am composed of I am still one entity. Now one cause only has one effect. I have always been one single cause and I have therefore only ever had one effect to produce. My existence in time is therefore nothing more than a series of necessary effects.'[2]) But does the author-figure recommend Jacques's philosophy to the reader without reservation? Does either he or Diderot implicitly share the belief that one cannot be other than oneself? I will offer answers to such questions below; and in the process, I will suggest a new perspective on the relationship between *Tristram Shandy* and *Jacques le fataliste*, Sterne and Diderot.

Various texts by Diderot put forward a persuasive case for a determinism based in monist materialism. *Le Rêve de d'Alembert* (*D'Alembert's Dream*), written in 1769, shortly before *Jacques le fataliste* is undertaken, is what Otis Fellows calls 'an altarpiece to Diderot's deterministic materialism'.[3] Indeed, in *Le Rêve*, Diderot affirms a determinist position with the classic determinist notion of the impossibility of doing 'otherwise'.[4] What I find unusual, in Diderot's case, is that he adds on an identity element – the idea that in doing otherwise, one would be other than oneself: 'Puisque j'agis ainsi, celui qui peut agir autrement n'est plus moi; et assurer qu'au moment où je fais ou dis une chose j'en puis dire ou faire une autre, c'est assurer que je suis moi et que je suis un autre.'[5] ('Since I act in this way, he who can act otherwise is no longer me; and to affirm that at the moment at which I do or say one thing, I can say or do another, is to affirm that I am myself and that I am another.') In *Jacques le fataliste* we find the eponymous hero, in the philosophical debate with the master, articulating the same view as if he were quoting (in this case, in a series of rhetorical questions) from *Le Rêve*: 'Puis-je n'être pas moi? et étant moi puis-je faire autrement que moi? Puis-je être moi et un autre?'[6] ('Can I be anything other than myself, and being me, can I act otherwise than I do? Can I be myself and somebody else?'[7]) In both instances, the classic determinist affirmation ('I cannot do otherwise') is followed by the implied impossibility of being other than myself, of being myself and another: 'que je suis moi et que je suis un autre' in *Le Rêve*, and 'Puis-je être moi et un autre?' in *Jacques*.[8]

It seems rather strange, for a number of reasons, that Diderot, as a particular writer and personality, would be insisting on fixed identity. In the same year that he writes *Le Rêve*, he begins his essay on acting, the *Paradoxe sur le comédien* (*Paradox on the Actor*), the thrust of which is precisely the necessity of being other than oneself. For a successful actor must cease to be himself: 's'il est lui quand il joue, comment cessera-t-il d'être lui?'[9] ('If he is himself when he is acting, how will he cease to be himself?') The actor is characterised not by the unity of self, but by a duality, a being oneself and another, as is clear in the following lines on the actress, La Clairon: 'Dans ce moment elle est double: la petite Clairon et la grande Agrippine.'[10] ('In this moment, she is double: the little Clairon and the great Agrippina.')

In this regard, one can also look at various critics' characterisations of Diderot. Herbert Dieckmann, for instance, intentionally uses Diderot's own terms from the *Paradoxe* as he notes a characteristic duality in Diderot. Dieckmann sees Diderot as at once the 'spectateur froid' ('cold spectator') – what, according to Diderot, the actor must be – and the 'homme sensible' ('sensitive man') – what the ideal spectator, but not the actor, must be – terms which Diderot opposes to each other. Dieckmann's lines appear in his groundbreaking article on the 'Préface-Annexe' ('Postscript-Preface') to *La Religieuse*. This article, the result of research on a manuscript in the Fonds Vandeul, seeks to show that the 'Préface-Annexe', explicitly attributed to Grimm, was to a large extent Diderot's work. The immediate context of Dieckmann's remark is his discussion of the anecdote of d'Alainville's visit to Diderot. Here is how Dieckmann introduces the anecdote:

Of particular interest are the insertions which Diderot wrote on the little piece of paper. The first is the famous anecdote of d'Alainville's visit to Diderot. He finds the philosopher all in tears; on asking him the cause of his grief, he receives the surprising answer: 'Je me désole d'un conte que je me fais' ['I'm upset by a story I'm telling myself']. The 'conte' is *La Religieuse* ... But nobody suspected or could suspect that Diderot and not, as it seems, Grimm was the 'author' of the anecdote and that it was Diderot who inserted it into the original text.[11]

It is in this context that Dieckmann remarks on Diderot's duality: 'But we must now add that Diderot was not only the "homme sensible", but also the "cold spectator" whom he so often opposed to the first, and that Diderot, the cold spectator, the man of judgement, could tell a good story about Diderot "homme sensible".'[12] There would thus seem to be a dissonant relationship between the identity element of the philosophical argument ('I cannot be myself and another') and the particular writer who, through his characters (Mademoiselle de Lespinasse in the *Rêve*, and Jacques in his last novel), appears to have affirmed it.

In an earlier essay, I suggested that the identity element in Diderot's determinist argument comes from Leibniz's doctrine of 'possible worlds', and more particularly, from the idea in Leibniz that there can be no identity across worlds.[13] Leibniz's correspondence with the French Jansenist Antoine Arnauld between 1686 and 1690 gives us numerous examples very much like the following: 'si dans la vie de quelque personne ... quelque chose allait *autrement* qu'elle ne va, rien ne nous empêcherait de dire que ce serait *une autre personne*'.[14] ('If in the life of any person, something were to happen otherwise than it actually does, nothing would prevent us from saying that this would be another person.') In tracing this theme back to Leibniz, my intent was not only to speculate on a possible source for what is found in

Diderot's texts, but also to suggest that *Jacques* represents both a playful breakdown of the Leibnizian separation of actual and possible (*Jacques* is a world in which things *can* happen otherwise) and an ironic calling into question of the impossibility of being other than oneself. The notion of 'possible worlds' is displaced, in Diderot's novel, to the level of what is generally called 'narrative possibilities': the alternatives for the fictional content, and the various possible relations of a narrator to the telling (what Genette, in his discussion of narrative metalepsis, refers to as 'a shifting but sacred frontier between two worlds, the world in which one tells, the world of which one tells').[15] At the same time, the identity element is called into question in relation to various stories. In one such story, the character named Gousse insists that he has only one body at a time, 'je n'ai qu'un corps à la fois', and claims that he is himself and no other, 'je ne suis pas un autre',[16] only to reveal, when the story is resumed twenty pages later, that in putting himself in prison, he has dealt with himself as if he were indeed another:

– Et comment vous y êtes-vous pris?
– *Comme je m'y serais pris avec un autre. Je me suis fait un procès à moi-même, je l'ai gagné*, et en conséquence de la sentence que j'ai obtenue contre moi et du décret qui s'en est suivi, j'ai été appréhendé et conduit ici.[17]

('And how did you go about that?'
'The same way I would have gone about having anyone else put in here. I sued myself. I won, and as a result of the sentence I obtained against myself and the warrant which followed I was apprehended and taken here.'[18])

I read the Gousse story as a version, *en abyme*, of Diderot's larger enterprise, that the novel is also a 'procès à moi-même', a trial against myself, an ironic and ludic calling to account in a fiction of the philosophical idea that I cannot be other than myself.

It is useful to connect this question with Diderot's openly stated 'plagiarism' of Sterne. There are a number of reasons for doing so. Plagiarism, by definition, involves a certain relation of self to other (passing off the work of another as one's own). In some of the examples cited above, Diderot seems to be playing with variations on this self–other relationship. Jacques, in the novel, is spouting lines ('Puis-je être moi et un autre?') that originally came from Mlle de Lespinasse in the *Rêve* ('que je suis moi et que je suis un autre'). There is also the case of the *Préface-Annexe*, which involves what might be considered a reversal of the plagiarism dynamic. The work was explicitly attributed to Grimm, who in the context of the d'Alainville anecdote refers to Diderot in the third person. What Dieckmann discovered, however, was that Diderot, and not Grimm, was the author; that is, Diderot had passed off his own work as the work of another. But Diderot's copying of Sterne's text is something else, or perhaps, more precisely, both the same and other. It too touches on the issues of identity and self and other, but in a more particular way, and in a very different way. That is what I would like to explore here.

On the last pages of *Jacques le fataliste* we are offered three possible endings to Jacques's love story. We are then informed, in a most playful manner, that the second of these endings has been plagiarised from Laurence Sterne's novel *Tristram Shandy*:

> Voici le second paragraphe copié de la vie de *Tristram Shandy*, à moins que l'entretien de Jacques le fataliste et de son maître ne soit antérieur à cet ouvrage et que le ministre Stern ne soit le plagiaire, ce que je ne crois pas, mais par une estime toute particulière de M. Stern que je distingue de la plupart des littérateurs de sa nation dont l'usage assez fréquent est de nous voler et de nous dire des injures.[19]

> (Here is the second paragraph, which has been copied from *The Life and Times of Tristram Shandy*, unless the conversation of Jacques the Fatalist and his master predates this work and the good minister Sterne himself is the plagiarist, which is something I do not believe, because of the particular esteem in which I hold Mr Sterne, whom I distinguish from the majority of men of letters of his nation whose quite frequent custom is to steal from us and then insult us.[20])

After we read this second ending, the references to plagiarism continue: 'Mais ce qui ne laisse aucun doute sur le plagiat, c'est ce qui suit. Le plagiaire ajoute: "Si vous n'êtes pas satisfait de ce que je vous révèle des amours de Jacques, Lecteur, faites mieux j'y consens".'[21] ('But what leaves no doubt at all as to the fact that this is a plagiarism is what follows. The plagiarist adds the following exhortation: "If you are not satisfied with what I have revealed to you of Jacques' loves, Reader, you may go away and do better – I consent to it".'[22]) Over time, it was discovered that this 'paragraph' was not the only bit that Diderot had lifted from Sterne. J. Robert Loy gives the most complete account of all such passages, showing that Diderot simply took the few pages that constitute Corporal Trim's love story in *Tristram Shandy* (Volume 8), broke it up into pieces through constant interruption, and with some very clever variations of his own, made it into Jacques's love story, which both begins and ends his own novel.[23] Loy notes that 'the actual copied passages are rather unimportant when brought to light',[24] and this is no doubt true. After all, the plagiarism involves nothing more than the character's account of how a bullet wound to the knee led to his falling in love with the young woman who was attending to him and giving him a massage above and below the knee. Since Loy's book, critics who have done comparative studies of Diderot and Sterne have, of course, referred to the lifted passages, but tend to leave them behind as they explore affinities elsewhere in the works of these two like-minded writers who were also good friends. Alice Green Fredman, for instance, in her book *Diderot and Sterne* (1955), sees fit not to include these passages, preferring instead to refer the reader to the relevant section in Loy's book.[25] And when critics have seized on something related to the lifted passages, they tend to be looking at Diderot's own variations and additions. One instance of this would be Georges May's famous article, 'Le maître, la chaîne et le chien dans *Jacques le fataliste*'.[26] Here May writes on the implications of a phrase at the very beginning of the novel, 'les chaînons d'une gourmette' ('the links of a horse's bit'),[27] that does not appear in Sterne.

I would like to adopt a different perspective on this question. While the passages Diderot lifted from Sterne (the several pages that constitute Corporal Trim's love story) may not, as Loy suggests, be important in relation to what was to become *Jacques le fataliste*, and that the obvious copying does not, as he goes on to say, 'deserve the accusation of plagiary',[28] the passages must have been very important to Diderot at the time he read them. So, I would like to put the focus back on Sterne's text in an attempt to answer the following two related questions. Why, of all the passages in Sterne's very long novel, did Diderot seize on these particular pages, and what did Diderot see in them that might have inspired him to include an explicit admission of plagiarism in his own novel? After all, what is remarkable about the plagiarism is not that Diderot plagiarised. As Fredman makes clear in her book, this sort of borrowing was not uncommon at the time: 'Actually, neither plagiarism nor its related practice, ghostwriting, was wholeheartedly decried in the eighteenth century . . . Neither Diderot nor Sterne regarded it a crime to use the work of others . . . Both men were adept at taking the writings of someone else as a point of departure and creating from these something entirely their own.'[29] What is remarkable about the plagiarism is that Diderot admits to it so explicitly, insistently and playfully. So, again, why would he do so, and why this particular bit?

To be sure, others have asked these questions before. So perhaps the difference is not in the asking, but rather in what is being looked at in order to answer them. I will not be looking at what have now become, thanks to the scholarship of others, the more obvious ideas. It is well known, for instance, that the first passage Diderot used included the ideas of predestination and inevitability, as well as the relationship of servant to master, both essential to a novel entitled *Jacques le fataliste et son maître*. And in a novel that famously thematises the notion of the second-hand, and the re-telling of stories, an explicit plagiarism would be one more instance of *redite* (a repetition, a retelling). What caught my eye and ear, however, and what I feel must have caught Diderot's, is something of a very different nature. Here is the first passage from *Tristram Shandy*:

King William was of the opinion, an' please your honour, quoth Trim, that every thing was predestined for us in this world; insomuch, that he would often say to his soldiers, that 'every ball had its billet.' – He was a great man, said my uncle Toby. – And I believe, continued Trim, to this day, that the shot which disabled me at the battle of Landen, was pointed at my knee, for no other purpose, but to take me out of his service, and place me in your honour's . . . Besides, said the corporal . . . if it had not been for that single shot, I had never, an' please your honour, been in love.[30]

In the next passage in Sterne, something begins to emerge in relation to this one: the conspicuous repetition of 'the knee':

There is no part of the body, an' please your honor, where a wound occasions more intolerable anguish than upon *the knee* –Except the groin, said my uncle Toby. An' please your honour, replied the corporal, *the knee*, in my opinion, must certainly be the most acute, there being so many tendons and what-d'ye-call-'ems all about it . . . The dispute was maintained . . . So that whether the pain of a wound in the groin . . . is greater than the pain of a wound in *the knee*, or whether the pain of a wound in *the knee* is not greater than a pain of a wound in the groin, are points which to this day remain unsettled.[31]

It is important to bear in mind that while Trim's love story, with its references to the knee, is told in the space of a few pages in Volume 8, Jacques's love story is constantly interrupted and thus spread out over the entire novel. References to the knee pervade the text from beginning to end. Some, of course, involve Jacques's knee, such as his bullet wound, 'un coup de feu au genou' ('a shot in the knee'),[32] or his idea that a wound to the knee is the most painful of wounds: 'je ne crois pas qu'il y ait de blessures plus cruelles que celle du genou'.[33] ('I do not believe there is any wound more painful than a wound in the knee.'[34]) Then there is the explicitly plagiarised passage at the end of the novel in which Jacques is getting a massage from his true love to sooth an itch in his knee wound: 'Mais ce n'était pas assez d'avoir éteint la démangeaison au-dessous du genou, sur le genou, il fallait encore l'éteindre au-dessus . . . Denise posa sa flanelle au-dessus du genou.'[35] ('But it wasn't enough to have cured the itching under the knee and on the knee. It still needed to be cured above the knee . . . Denise put her flannel above his knee.'[36]) Whereas in *Tristram Shandy* references to the knee are limited to the hero's anatomy, in Diderot's novel there are many knees other than Jacques's involved. There is the master's knee when he falls from his horse: 'son genou va s'appuyer rudement sur un caillou pointu' ('his knee came into violent contact with a pointed stone'), 'j'ai le genou cassée' ('my knee is shattered'), 'une blessure au genou' ('an injury to the knee'), 'ailleurs qu'au genou' ('any place other than the knee'), 'la blessure au genou' ('an injury to the knee'), 'à tous les genoux du monde' ('to all the knees in the world'), 'l'histoire de mon genou, qui est devenu le vôtre par votre chute' ('the story of my knee which has now become yours as well because of your fall').[37] The knee crops up in the sexual encounters with Justine and Suzanne: 'elle se jette à mes pieds, elle serre mes genoux'; 'Justine s'évanouit; ses genoux se dérobent sous elle'; 'ses genoux élevés rendaient ses jupons fort courts'.[38] ('She . . . threw herself at my feet and threw her arms around my knees'; 'Justine fainted. Her knees gave way under her'; 'since her knees were in the air her skirts didn't come down very far'.[39])

At other times, the knee becomes part of the master/servant theme. The master remarks that Jacques belongs to that race of men who 'ne fléchissent pas le genou' ('refuse to bend the knee').[40] Then, in the master's own love story, Saint-Ouin warns him that he must not show weakness towards Agathe's family or else 'il faudra fléchir le genou' ('you would have to bend the knee').[41] In the story of the landlady Madame de La Pommeraye we find: 'elle se jeta à genoux' ('she threw herself to her knees'); 'elle s'avança vers lui sur les genoux' ('she went forward to him on her knees'); 'la tête appuyée sur les genoux du marquis' ('her head pressed between the knees of the marquis').[42] There is also Jacques's true love's knee: 'elle avait un genou en terre, ma jambe était posée sur sa cuisse' ('she would have one knee on the floor; my leg would rest on her thigh').[43]

And it is not simply a question of the sheer number of references to the knee. In Diderot, there is a play of language in relation to the knee that is not found in Sterne. The fatalistic military aphorism from Sterne, 'Every ball has its billet', is translated as 'chaque balle qui part d'un fusil a son billet'.[44] This relatively cumbersome rendering of the English is immediately given a certain lightness as it is turned into a play on words in which 'son billet' is replaced by 'ton adresse', that is, at once the *billet de logement* (your billet, the military quarters where you lodge) and the 'genou' in which the bullet was destined 'to lodge': 'Le maître – Et tu reçois la balle à ton adresse. / Jacques – Vous l'avez deviné, un coup de feu au genou.'[45] Translated literally, this becomes: 'MASTER: And you receive the bullet at your address. / JACQUES: You've guessed it; shot in the knee.' There is also, after the master falls from his horse, the play on the idea that Jacques's love story is also a knee story: '[Jacques –] Mais pour en revenir à une peine que nous connaissons tous deux, l'histoire de mon genou qui est devenu le vôtre par votre chute . . . Le maître – Non, Jacques; l'histoire de tes amours qui

sont devenues miennes par mes chagrins passés.'[46] ('[JACQUES:] But to come
back to a pain with which we are both more familiar. The story of my knee
which has now become yours as well because of your fall. MASTER: No,
Jacques, the story of your loves which have become mine as well through my
own past sorrows.'[47]) And there is the playful interchange between the
master and Jacques at the end of the novel, as Jacques is describing how he
attached a garter to his true love's knee: 'Son maître lui dit: . . . selon toute
apparence tu touches à la conclusion de tes amours – Pas tout à fait. –
Quand on est arrivé au genou, il y a peu de chemin à faire. – Mon maître,
Denise avait la cuisse plus longue qu'une autre.'[48] ('MASTER: By all appear-
ances, you are nearing the end of the story of your loves. JACQUES: Not
quite. MASTER: When you get as far as the knee, there's not much farther to
go. JACQUES: Master, Denise's thigh was longer than many another girl's.'[49])
The play here, of course, is on the figurative sense of an itinerary (in a story
one tells, and in a sexual encounter), and it appears that in either case what
would be appropriately called the 'last leg' of the voyage will be problem-
atically long.

What I am suggesting, then, is that Diderot's attention must have been
drawn to the references to the knee in the passages in Sterne's novel that
were cited above ('upon the knee', 'the knee, in my opinion', 'a wound in
the knee . . . a wound in the knee'). In his own novel, he has clearly taken
the knee and 'run with it' in translation. As if he were doing what Saint-
Ouin warns the master he is at risk of doing ('il faudra fléchir le genou'), he
has bent the knee, inflected it, turning it towards some purpose of his own.
Given the constant circulation of the knee in the text, he has also inflated it,
like the various *billets d'échange* that circulate in the many stories told. Why
did he like it so much that he explicitly plagiarised the passages, essentially
framing his text with the knee (the fatalistic 'coup de feu au genou' ('shot in
the knee') at the beginning, and the massage of the 'démangeaison au-
dessous/dessus du genou' ('itch below and above the knee') at the end), and
then allowing 'le genou' to proliferate in between? And why, if in Sterne's
text, the 'knee versus groin' debate remains 'to this day unsettled', is the
corresponding debate settled, in Diderot's, so clearly in favour of the knee?
The answer seems so obvious, and at the same time entirely preposterous
(yet no more preposterous than the explicit plagiarism itself).

As all teachers of second languages know, there are certain cross-language
(and consequently imperfect) homonyms, and orthographic coincidences,
that cannot fail to produce a response in those learning a foreign language.[50]
In this regard, we must bear in mind that Diderot was not only plagiarising,
but he was also translating. Diderot wrote 'le genou' in his text, but what he

saw in Sterne's was 'the knee'. Does it really take much to imagine that Diderot, as reader of Sterne, and in anticipation of his own novel, must have been delightedly struck by the sound of this word, for as a Frenchman whose English pronunciation was not native, it would be so very close to the sound of his own name: *De-nis*? Diderot's response would have involved an imperfect cross-language homonym based on an English noun (the knee) and a French proper name (Denis). And given that Diderot had grown up with a favourite younger sibling named Denise, which would have already sensitised him to a playful coupling of sounds in relation to his own name, it is not hard to imagine that he was primed for this sort of thing when he encountered 'the knee' in Sterne's text (Denise, of course, sounding like a French pronunciation of 'the knees').

So how would all this serve to explain why Diderot made the plagiarism so obvious? Diderot could explicitly announce the plagiarism, and would indeed want to, because he had recognised it as more of an appropriation of a text in which his proper name was already sufficiently inscribed. In this sense, he owned Sterne's text more than his own. Like the *éponge* in the prose poems of Francis Ponge, *De-nis* is the author's signature.[51] Unlike the *sponge*, however, it is more thoroughly disguised in its translation, which would explain why readers have not noticed it. Moreover, it happens that *genou* (like 'the knee') is subject to homonym play, and quite famously so, though in this case it is not across languages, but rather a *calembour*. French speakers think of it grammatically, as first person singular–first person plural (*je–nous*), and more suggestively, as self (*je*), and self and other (*nous*). In the spirit of this word play, 'the knee' (singular) would become 'the knees' (plural), that is, the knee and its other. And it is certainly quite possible that the Diderot siblings, Denis and Denise, were familiar with this little joke.

So what Diderot will do after finding himself ('the knee') in the text of another, and disguising himself in translation (*le genou*), is to re-inscribe himself in his own text, not as himself, but rather as himself and another. In the love story in Sterne's text, Trim receives a knee massage from a young Beguine nun, referred to only as 'the Beguine'. Diderot could have given any name to the woman who performs a similar function in *Jacques*, and could conceivably have refrained from naming her at all. After all, in the case of his two eponymous characters, we are given only a generic name, and no name. But in the case of his masseuse, Diderot chooses not to go that way, and it is my sense that the choice of the proper name Denise is highly motivated (and not simply to give his younger sister's name some press). In fact, we have already seen this name in two passages cited above: in the massage, 'Denise posa sa flanelle au-dessus du genou', and earlier in the story, when Jacques is attaching a garter, 'Quand on est arrivé au genou, il y a peu de chemin à faire. – Mon maître, Denise avait la cuisse plus longue qu'une autre.'[52]

In these two principal scenes of Jacques's love story (the massage scene and the garter scene) there is, then, a simultaneous focus on the knee and Denise. This play is underscored not only by the fact that the French word for garter, *jarretière*, is already linked etymologically to the knee (being derived from 'jarret', or 'hollow of the knee'), but also by the fact that garters usually come in pairs, like the knees they are worn on. These two love scenes are also important in relation to each other because the element of chiastic reciprocation (Jacques attaches a garter to Denise's knee; Denise applies a piece of flannel to Jacques's) suggestively approximates a similar dynamic in Diderot's playful announcement, quoted above, of the plagiarism that frames the massage scene: 'Voici le second paragraphe copié de la vie de *Tristram Shandy*, à moins que l'entretien de Jacques le fataliste et de son maître ne soit antérieur à cet ouvrage et que le ministre Stern ne soit le plagiaire.'[53] ('Here is the second paragraph, which has been copied from *The Life and Times of Tristram Shandy*, unless the conversation of Jacques the Fatalist and his master predates this work and the good minister Sterne himself is the plagiarist.'[54]) Diderot seems to be saying: 'I copied from Sterne, unless my work came first, in which case Sterne copied from me.' This reciprocal dynamic of back and forth, of give and take, seems to characterise the relationship between these two writers. As Fredman notes, 'And if the *philosophe* was pleased that Sterne was able to discuss French authors with him, one can imagine Sterne's reactions to the keen interest and appreciation Diderot had with English writers.'[55] In fact, Diderot read Sterne's fiction and sermons, and shortly after they met Sterne was reading, at Diderot's request, Diderot's rough English trans-lation of *Le Fils naturel*, because Diderot wanted Sterne's opinion.[56]

Certainly, a principal consequence of Diderot's plagiarism of Sterne has been to link the two names for posterity. Again, to quote Fredman: 'starting with Diderot's own admission of copying a paragraph from *Tristram Shandy* for *Jacques le fataliste*, Diderot's and Sterne's names have been coupled by critics from the eighteenth to the twentieth century'.[57] How coincidental that Fredman's comment on 'the coupling of the names Diderot and Sterne' should find its counterpart in Jacques's words to his master which, with only a change of names, would seem to have proved curiously prophetic: 'après avoir si bien accolé votre nom au mien que l'un ne va jamais sans l'autre, et que tout le monde dit Jacques et son maître' ('after your name and mine have become so well linked that one never goes without the other and

everyone says: "Jacques and his Master""").[58] Above I quoted Jacques's line:
'Mon capitaine ajoutait que chaque balle qui partait d'un fusil avait son
billet', which is Diderot's rendering of Sterne's 'every ball has its billet'.
Michael Henry translates this as follows: 'My captain added that every shot
fired from a gun had someone's name on it.'[59] If 'a bullet with his name on
it' was destined to lodge in the knee and lead Jacques to his love story with
Denise, a short passage 'with my name in it', and the subsequent announcement of the plagiarism, was destined to lead critics to the story of friendship
between these two like-minded writers. And as chance would have it,
Jacques's line, 'l'un ne va jamais sans l'autre', which could apply so appropriately to the names Diderot and Sterne, brings us back to the knee, and more
particularly to that scene in which Jacques has just attached *une jarretière*
to Denise's knee. Here is Denise's mother as she walks in on the lovers:

Voilà une jolie jarretière, dit-elle, mais où est *l'autre?* – À ma jambe, lui répondit
Denise. Il m'a dit qu'il les avait achetées pour son amoureuse et j'ai jugé que c'était
pour moi. N'est-il pas vrai, Maman, que puisque j'en ai mis *une*, il faut que je garde
l'autre? – Ah! Monsieur Jacques, Denise a raison, *une jarretière ne va pas sans l'autre.*[60]

('That's a pretty garter,' she said, 'but where's the other one?'

'On my leg. He told me that he'd bought them for his lover and I imagined that they
were for me. Now that I've put one on I have to keep the other one, isn't that right,
Mother?'

'Ah! Monsieur Jacques, Denise is right. One garter doesn't go without the other.'[61])

Jacques never goes without the other, nor does the *jarretière*, nor does Denis.
It is precisely because Denis is 'the knee' that he can be himself and another.

NOTES

1. DPV, vol. XXIII, p. 190.
2. Diderot, *Jacques the Fatalist*, ed. Martin Hall, trans. Michael Henry (London:
   Penguin, 1986), p. 165.
3. Otis Fellows, *Diderot*, 2nd edn (Boston: G. K. Hall, 1989), p. 89.
4. I should note that the idea of 'the impossibility of doing otherwise' is as central to
   contemporary definitions of determinism as it was in Diderot's time. Here, for
   instance, is a passage in a book written in 1965 by Albury Castell. He is not a
   determinist, but he is presenting the argument from a determinist's point of view:
   'It is true . . . one feels as though one could do, or could have done, otherwise. But
   don't trust that feeling. It is the illusion of alternativity, of voluntariness. He being
   what he was, the circumstances being what they were, he never could have done
   other than he did do. The experience of voluntariness, could-have-done-
   otherwise, while no doubt an experience, is always and everywhere illusory . . .

The traditional ism-label for this claim is determinism, sometimes "hard determinism".' See Albury Castell, *The Self in Philosophy* (New York: Macmillan, 1965), p. 64. I should also note that while Castell uses the past conditional ('could have done') and gives the conditional as an alternative ('could do'), Diderot, in both *Le Rêve de d'Alembert* and *Jacques*, uses the present tense. If one were to read the present tense literally in Diderot's lines, the resulting meaning (because of the simultaneity) would be so silly, so goes-without-saying, that it is hard to imagine that Diderot would write such a thing (for example, 'Since I'm using a hammer, he who is using a screwdriver is not me'). My sense is that his statements imply what the conditionals express explicitly.

5. DPV, vol. XVII, p. 186. A variant of this quotation begins: 'Puisque c'est moi qui agis ainsi' ('Since it is I who act in this way'); see ibid., p. 186.

6. DPV, vol. XXIII, p. 28.

7. Diderot, *Jacques the Fatalist*, p. 25.

8. Sartre provides, though only indirectly, an interesting commentary on the question of 'being another in doing otherwise'. Sartre mentions Diderot (whose activities as a committed writer he admired) several times, but not in relation to determinism. Nevertheless, at the beginning of *L'Être et le néant* (*Being and Nothingness*), there is a critique of determinist thinking that could serve as an *explication de texte* and critique of the passages I have been considering. See Jean-Paul Sartre, *Being and Nothingness*, trans. Hazel E. Barnes (New York: Philosophical Library, 1970), p. 41.

9. DPV, vol. XX, p. 49.

10. Ibid., p. 51.

11. Herbert Dieckmann, 'The *Préface-Annexe* of *La Religieuse*', *Diderot Studies*, 2 (1952), 21–40 (p. 28).

12. Ibid., p. 28.

13. Joseph Breines, '"A Trial Against Myself": Identity and Determinism in Diderot's *Jacques le fataliste*', *The Romanic Review*, 90 (1999), 235–62.

14. Gottfried Wilhelm Leibniz, *Die Philosophischen Schriften*, ed. C. I. Gerhardt, 7 vols. (Berlin 1857–90; reprinted Hildesheim, 1960), vol. II, p. 53 (my italics and modernised spelling).

15. Gérard Genette, *Narrative Discourse*, trans. Jane E. Lewin (Ithaca, NY: Cornell University Press, 1980), p. 236.

16. DPV, vol. XXIII, p. 82.

17. Ibid., pp. 102–3.

18. Diderot, *Jacques the Fatalist*, pp. 89–90.

19. DPV, vol. XXIII, p. 289.

20. Diderot, *Jacques the Fatalist*, p. 252.

21. DPV, vol. XXIII, p. 290.

22. Diderot, *Jacques the Fatalist*, p. 253.

23. Robert J. Loy, *Diderot's Determined Fatalist* (New York: King's Crown Press, 1950), pp. 32–9, where Loy does a back-to-back comparison of all the relevant passages in the two novels.

24. Ibid., p. 32.

25. Alice Green Fredman, *Diderot and Sterne* (New York: Columbia University Press, 1955).

26. *Cahiers de l'association internationale des études françaises*, 13 (June 1961), 269–82.

27. DPV, vol. XXIII, p. 24.

28. Loy, *Diderot's Determined Fatalist*, p. 39.

29. Fredman, *Diderot and Sterne*, pp. 4–5.

30. Laurence Sterne, *Tristram Shandy* (New York: W. W. Norton, 1980), p. 401.

31. Ibid., p. 402 (my italics).

32. DPV, vol. XXIII, p. 24; Diderot, *Jacques the Fatalist*, p. 21.

33. DPV, vol. XXIII, p. 25.

34. *Jacques the Fatalist*, p. 23.

35. DPV, vol. XXIII, p. 289.

36. Diderot, *Jacques the Fatalist*, p. 253.

37. DPV, vol. XXIII, pp. 38–9; Diderot, *Jacques the Fatalist*, pp. 33–4.

38. DPV, vol. XXIII, pp. 213, 221.

39. Diderot, *Jacques the Fatalist*, pp. 185, 186, 192.

40. DPV, vol. XXIII, p. 91; Diderot, *Jacques the Fatalist*, p. 80.

41. DPV, vol. XXIII, p. 249; Diderot, *Jacques the Fatalist*, p. 217.

42. DPV, vol. XXIII, pp. 167–8; Diderot, *Jacques the Fatalist*, pp. 147–8.

43. DPV, vol. XXIII, p. 282; Diderot, *Jacques the Fatalist*, p. 246.

44. DPV, vol. XXIII, p. 23.

45. Ibid., p. 24.

46. Ibid., p. 39.

47. Diderot, *Jacques the Fatalist*, p. 34.

48. DPV, vol. XXIII, p. 285.

49. Diderot, *Jacques the Fatalist*, pp. 248–9.

50. To use two modern examples: for German speakers, the German noun 'Fahrt' is not funny, but for English speakers, when they first hear it, it is. For French speakers, the French word 'péter' is usually funny, and for English speakers, when they first encounter it in written form, it would be funny for two reasons, and might even be embarrassing if one's own name happens to be Peter. The hypothesis I am about to suggest combines aspects of these two examples.

51. For more on the signature in the prose poems of Francis Ponge, see Jacques Derrida, *Signéponge/Signsponge*, trans. Richard Rand (New York: Columbia University Press, 1984).

52. DPV, vol. XXIII, pp. 285, 289.

53. See ibid., p. 289.

54. See Diderot, *Jacques the Fatalist*, p. 252.

55. Fredman, *Diderot and Sterne*, p. 13.

56. Ibid., p. 6.

57. Ibid., pp. 3–4.

58. DPV, vol. XXIII, p. 181; Diderot, *Jacques the Fatalist*, p. 158.

59. Diderot, *Jacques the Fatalist*, p. 21.

60. DPV, vol. XXIII, pp. 283–4.

61. Diderot, *Jacques the Fatalist*, p. 248.

CHAPTER 9

La Religieuse: *Diderot's 'Richardsonian' novel*

James Fowler

The pioneering critic Georges May characterises *La Religieuse* as Diderot's novel 'à la manière de Richardson' ('in the manner of Richardson');[1] and in many respects it would be perverse to argue with this assessment. Richardson's *Clarissa* in particular became a source of plot elements, characters and themes without which *La Religieuse* would surely have been a very different work. In some ways, Diderot was bound to love the English author because he confirmed several of his own tendencies. The *philosophe's* writing before 1760 shows that he was drawn to the expressive possibilities of dialogue and gesture; and his theory and practice of the *drame*, developed in the 1750s, offer points of comparison with the middle-class, didactic aspects of Richardson. At the same time, mixed success had met his plays *Le Fils naturel* (*The Natural Son*) and *Le Père de famille* (*The Father*), in which base motives are banished by an all-conquering virtue. For Diderot, *Clarissa* proved that novels (if not plays) might morally improve their readers without showing virtue triumphant. Or as the *philosophe* puts it in the *Éloge de Richardson*: 'Qui est-ce qui voudrait être Lovelace avec tous ses avantages? Qui est-ce qui ne voudrait pas être Clarisse, malgré toutes ses infortunes?'[2] ('Who would want to be Lovelace, for all his advantages? Who would not want to be Clarissa, in spite of all her misfortunes?') Finally, it has often been remarked that, though *La Religieuse* is technically a memoir-novel, its narrator often forgets or defies the convention that the memoirist always knows the outcome of past events. For May, this means that Diderot embraced the aesthetic of 'writing to the moment', Richardson's term for using the epistolary form to create immediacy and suspense.[3]

But in spite of all such affinities, the author of *La Religieuse* adapted certain aspects of Richardson's most famous novel to the most 'un-Richardsonian' ends. For when it came to treating the theme of religion, the (by now) monist-materialist *philosophe* of the 1760s was unwilling to make concessions to his Puritan-leaning predecessor. This needs stating in opposition to May's eloquently expressed argument that, given Suzanne's unwavering piety, Diderot's novel attacks convents without undermining Christianity.[4] Below I will make the case that *La Religieuse* offers a subtle but sustained critique of religious belief as such, and so marks a limit to Richardson's influence even on the author of the *Éloge*.

La Religieuse is especially indebted to the opening instalments of *Clarissa*. Richardson's Harlowes are motivated by a combination of greed and ambition. The will left by Clarissa's recently deceased grandfather provides her with an estate and so the possibility of independence; her relations, especially her envious siblings, aim to keep this wealth in the family by having her marry the rich but odious Solmes, who though a miser agrees to generous marriage settlements. The heroine's father is even ready to challenge her grandfather's will in court.[5] In the *Éloge* Diderot writes that whilst reading *Clarissa*, he had seen 'les ressorts de l'intérêt et de l'amour-propre jouer en cent façons diverses' ('the impulses of self-interest and vanity working in a hundred different ways').[6] And when he creates the Simonin family, he endows them with similar motives. They wish to prevent Suzanne from inheriting a third of the family estate, and take all possible legal measures to do so.[7] When Suzanne asks why her sisters would allow this to happen, Père Séraphin exclaims: 'Ah! Mademoiselle, l'intérêt! l'intérêt!'[8] ('Ah! Mademoiselle, it's for their own good! Their own good!'[9]) And such selfish motives lead each fictional family, the Harlowes and the Simonins, to choose a sacrificial victim: Clarissa in one case and Suzanne in the other.

In Letter 13 of *Clarissa*, the heroine puts forward a hypothesis: 'were ours a Roman Catholic family, how much happier for me, that they thought a nunnery would answer all their views!'[10] We can imagine the *philosophe* reading this line and experiencing a 'eureka' moment. After all, having followed Richardson in imagining a family on the point of sacrificing its youngest child, he seems to build the rest of his novel around that fleeting thought of Clarissa's: what if she *had* been sent to a nunnery? It is also an intriguing fact of history that, in memory of Saint Clare, the nuns at Longchamp, Suzanne's first convent, were called 'les Clarisses' (the Gallicised version of 'Clarissa' which French readers, including Diderot, generally used to refer to Richardson's heroine).[11] And even if Suzanne enters the nunnery that is not available to Clarissa, Diderot continues to borrow elements from Richardson. The persecution which Clarissa undergoes at the hands of Lovelace and his harlot helpers finds a parallel in Suzanne's treatment by Sœur Sainte-Christine and her cronies. Moreover, though Suzanne escapes the rape inflicted on Richardson's heroine, the monk who helps her to escape from Sainte-Eutrope subjects her to some kind of sexual assault; and the threat of seduction is represented in Diderot's novel by the lesbian mother superior.[12]

But let us see how far Diderot diverges from Richardson, especially where religion is concerned. In Clarissa's Protestant world, the issue that initially divides her from her parents is that of 'relative duties' as expressed in Puritan conduct books. According to this system, children owe obedience to their parents while parents owe it to their children not to use their power unjustly. But what happens when parents wish to impose an arranged marriage on an unwilling child? One answer is that, barring defiance of God's law, obedience is owed even when parental authority is tyrannical. In *A Collection of Moral and Instructive Sentiments* (1755), Richardson writes: 'In reciprocal Duties, the failure on one side justifies not the failure on the other.'[13] Yet Clarissa adds nuance to this precept, and in the process she proves an impressive casuist – casuistry being on the decline but far from dead in mid-eighteenth-century England.[14] She argues that it is a sin to promise before God that she will honour a husband whom she cannot help despising: 'Let me not thus cruelly be given up to a man my very soul is averse to ... Had I a slighter notion of the matrimonial duty than I have, perhaps I might [be his]. But when I am to bear all the misery, and that for *life*; when my heart is less concerned in this matter than my *soul*; my *temporal* perhaps than my *future* good; why should I be denied the liberty of *refusing*?'[15] Her theology also helps her when she is drugged, raped and reduced to a mental state bordering on insanity. For then religious belief, and in particular meditation on the Book of Job, allows her to rediscover her own will in all its admirable force. Against all kinds of social pressure, she refuses to marry her abductor and rapist, arguing that 'it would be *criminal* in me to wish to bind my soul in covenant to a man so nearly allied to perdition'.[16] She also writes in capitals that all her trials have brought her to see that 'GOD ALMIGHTY WOULD NOT LET ME DEPEND FOR COMFORT ON ANY BUT HIMSELF'.[17] In brief, in Richardson's novel the lip service paid to religion by Clarissa's relatives (who are portrayed as 'whited sepulchres', so to speak) is opposed to her own glorious faith.

We have seen that Diderot's Simonins recall the greed, tyranny and self-ishness of Richardson's Harlowes. But where Lady Harlowe was a paragon of conjugal obedience, Suzanne's mother confesses to having had an extramarital affair of which Suzanne is the fruit. The mother's response to this is to try to obtain expiation for her adultery by persuading her daughter to become a nun. Now this plan clearly reflects Roman Catholic notions of expiation and intercession, for in Catholic tradition, the monastic religious are supposed to be able to help others towards certain spiritual benefits, such as a remission of time spent in purgatory. Barbara H. Rosenwein and Lester K. Little locate the beginnings of intercession through devotion in the Cluniac monasteries of the tenth and eleventh centuries. They note: 'The unique character of Cluniac prayer consisted not only in its length but also in the new use to which the additional liturgy ... was put, namely intercession.'[18] They also point out that, during the same period, and according to a similar logic, mendicant orders of Franciscan friars offered 'vicarious expiation', at least to those wealthy enough to afford it: a case of 'material support of these confident poor by the troubled rich'.[19]

A similar logic persuades Suzanne to enter the convent system some thirty pages into the novel. This fact is thrown into relief by her initial resistance to other kinds of logic. When Père Séraphin first urges her to take vows, the justification offered is not religious but materialistic, for apparently the marriage of Suzanne's sisters has deprived her of her own dowry: 'vos parents se sont dépouillés pour vos sœurs, et je ne vois plus ce qu'ils pourraient pour vous dans la situation étroite ou ils sont réduits'.[20] ('Your parents have spent all their money on your sisters, and I cannot see what else they could possibly do for you in their current straits.'[21]) But this argument carries no weight with Suzanne. (She subsequently agrees to become a novice only to gain time.) This Clarissean determination not to sacrifice her happiness for the sake of other people's worldly interests is dramatically illustrated when she publicly says 'no' at the profession ceremony where 'yes' is conventional.[22] Yet after she has returned to her parents' home, where she is imprisoned and largely ignored (like Clarissa), she changes her mind (unlike Clarissa, who continues to 'assert her negative'). The turning point comes when her adulterine origin is revealed to her. And this makes all the difference because she accepts to view this secret in a religious framework, as a sin whose atonement is to be achieved by an act of sacrifice. This is how her mother puts it shortly after Suzanne has been let into the secret: 'Dieu nous a conservées l'une et l'autre pour que la mère expiât sa faute par l'enfant.'[23] ('But God saved us both so that the mother might atone for her sin through her child.'[24]) And the mother reiterates her position in a deathbed letter: 'Votre naissance est la seule faute importante que j'aie commise; aidez-moi à l'expier, et que Dieu me pardonne de vous avoir mise au monde, en considération des bonnes œuvres que vous ferez.'[25] ('Giving birth to you is the only serious sin I have ever committed. Help me to atone for it, and pray that God, taking into account all the good works you will do, will forgive me for having brought you into the world.'[26]) By extension, Mme Simonin suggests that if Suzanne accepts the role of scapegoat for her mother's guilt, she dutifully imitates Christ. After all, it is perfectly orthodox (in both Catholic and Protestant traditions) to suggest that the Lamb of God is prefigured by the scapegoat of Leviticus, driven into the desert laden with the sins of the Israelites.[27] So Diderot represents Suzanne's own piety as the strongest weapon her mother and Père Séraphin are able to use against her; it succeeds where cajolery, threats and imprisonment have failed. Of course, if convents did not exist the Simonins would have been deprived of their cruellest option in dealing with 'their' daughter; but equally, if Suzanne were not pious, all the pressure exerted on her would not have succeeded in forcing her into the convent system.[28]

The purely spiritual level of Suzanne's motivation is confirmed in the following passage:

Je me renfermai dans ma petite prison. Je rêvai à ce que ma mère m'avait dit. Je me jetai à genoux, je priai Dieu qu'il m'inspirât; je priai longtemps, je demeurai le visage collé contre terre. On n'invoque presque jamais la voix du Ciel que quand on ne sait à quoi se résoudre, et il est rare qu'alors elle ne nous conseille pas d'obéir. Ce fut le parti que je pris. On veut que je sois religieuse, peut-être est-ce aussi la volonté de Dieu, eh bien, je le serai.[29]

(I locked myself away in my little prison. I reflected on what my mother had said to me. I knelt and prayed for God to inspire me. I prayed for a long time, my face pressed against the ground. The voice of God is usually only ever invoked when one does not know oneself what to do, and in those instances the voice almost always advises obedience. That was my decision. 'They want me to be a nun; perhaps that's what God wants too. Very well, I shall be a nun.'[30])

In the first three sentences of this extract, Diderot stresses Suzanne's solitude: at this critical moment no person, nor any institution, mediates between her and the God to whom she prays. And so it is not the intrusive influence of this or that mother superior but Suzanne's private interpretation of God's will that finally breaks down her resistance. The final sentence of the passage confirms this. 'On veut que je sois religieuse' functions as a summary of the collective will of parents and siblings, which Suzanne has so far resisted. What changes her mind is the additional thought: 'peut-être est-ce aussi la volonté de Dieu'. Even if she only believes that God wants her to enter the Convent 'peut-être', that 'perhaps' has a decisive effect on her actions.

So in *La Religieuse* piety itself provides the mechanism by which a young woman is brought to sacrifice all prospect of earthly happiness (which is of course the only kind we can obtain in a monist-materialist perspective).[31] In fairness to May, it must be conceded that *La Religieuse* portrays the convent as a fearsome trap, easy to enter and almost impossible to leave. Suzanne's *avocat* (lawyer) M. Manouri states emphatically: 'Il me semble pourtant que dans un État bien gouverné ce devrait être le contraire, entrer difficilement en religion et en sortir facilement.'[32] ('Yet it seems to me that in a well-governed state, the opposite should be the case: it should be difficult to enter the religious life and easy to leave it.'[33]) This type of statement clearly feeds the argument that *La Religieuse* makes a case for the dismantling of this social trap: convents might be abolished, or laws passed to facilitate the rescinding of vows. But in fact Suzanne's case shows that the evils of the convent can be fought on two levels. On the one hand, society might indeed create new laws; but, on the other, individuals might move beyond the beliefs that led to the founding of convents in the first place. Religious scepticism (or, of course, outright disbelief) could empty the monasteries as effectively as any legislation.

This point, incidentally, allows us to connect *La Religieuse* with other narratives by Diderot. For instance, in *Supplément au Voyage de Bougainville* (*Supplement to the Voyage of Bougainville*) civilisation's discontents are analysed by B. in the following terms: 'Voulez-vous savoir l'histoire abrégée de presque toute notre misère? La voici. Il existait un homme naturel; on a introduit au-dedans de cet homme un homme artificiel, et il s'est élevé dans la caverne une guerre continuelle qui dure toute la vie.'[34] ('Would you like to know the potted history of almost all human misery? Here it is: first there was natural man; then an artificial man was placed inside him, and within his body there arose a continual, life-long war.') According to B., religion (together with the law) produced this 'artificial man'. Therefore scepticism could sap the excessive power of this inner homunculus, preventing individuals such as Suzanne from becoming, as B. also puts it, 'des infortunés à propos de rien' ('people who are unhappy for no reason').[35]

The novel's attack on Catholic theology is continued by Diderot's characterisation of the well-intentioned Mme de Moni, Suzanne's first mother superior at Longchamp. Initially adopting a logic similar to Mme Simonin's, the superior asserts: 'Sœur Suzanne, la bonne religieuse est celle qui apporte dans le cloître quelque grande faute à expier.'[36] ('Sister Suzanne, the good nun is the one who brings with her into the cloister some great sin to expiate.'[37]) Thus she reassuringly suggests that the greater the sin, the greater the merit (and so the reward) of whoever expiates it. But Diderot shows Mme de Moni put under extreme stress by the approach of Suzanne's profession, and she subsequently dies as though fatally weakened by the challenge which her favourite's case represents for her own beliefs.[38] This crisis suggests that metaphysical systems on which we might call to square human suffering with divine justice are in critical cases unable to do what we ask of them – and so Diderot's text chimes in its way with Voltaire as well as, or rather than,

Richardson.[39] And the anti-theological thrust of *La Religieuse* surfaces yet again when Suzanne writes: 'Combien de mères comme la mienne expient un crime secret par un autre.'[40] ('How many mothers like mine atone for a secret crime by committing another!'[41]) This sentence shows how her beliefs have changed since she consented to atone for her mother's sin. For now Suzanne asserts that monastic expiation simply does not work: it serves only to compound a spiritual crime with one against individual freedom. In this passage, then, Diderot's heroine decides to disagree theologically with her mother after all; and Diderot presumably hoped that even pious readers, or at least the doubting pious, might follow suit.

Of course, Richardson too explores the theme of expiation, but it seems that his characters can only (at best) atone for their *own* sins, with the grace of God. Lovelace's dying words are, famously: 'LET THIS EXPIATE!'[42] Pointing us towards an intentionalist reading of this passage, the author wrote, using the breathless style he sometimes used in his letters: 'And at last with his wonted haughtiness of Spirit – LET THIS EXPIATE all his apparent Invocation and address to the SUPREME. Have I not then given rather a dreadful than a hopeful Exit, with regard to Futurity, to the unhappy Lovelace!'[43] (For the pious reader who enters into the fictional illusion, Richardson implies, Lovelace is as likely to end in Hell as Clarissa in Heaven.) At the same time, the novel reflects a specifically Protestant view of expiation, which reserves the role of vicarious victim for Christ alone. Clarissa subscribes to this theology when she says to Lovelace's friend Belford: 'Tell the poor man that I not only forgive him, but have such earnest wishes for the good of his soul, and that from considerations of its immortality, that could my penitence avail for more sins than my own, my last tear should fall for him by whom I die.'[44] It is only hypothetically that Clarissa's penitence could atone for Lovelace's sins.

Now the fact that expiation is treated differently in *Clarissa* and *La Religieuse* is a consequence in part of the simple fact that Richardson portrays a Protestant milieu and Diderot a Catholic one. But we should not let this superficial contrast, born of realism, distract us from a more fundamental, ideological one: the notion of expiation (together with its theological ramifications) helps Clarissa but harms Suzanne. Richardson insistently foregrounds the possibility that Clarissa atones for her initial, unreflecting pride through Job-like submission to God's will. In his Postscript, indeed, the author underlines the Christian interpretation according to which Clarissa will be rewarded for this in Heaven – or, as he puts it, almost as if he were shouting, 'HEAVEN'.[45] And even if we resist Richardson's direction on this point, it would be perverse to deny that after the rape Clarissa is comforted and strengthened by her faith. By contrast, we have seen that in *La Religieuse* the logic of (vicarious) expiation brings no benefit but only suffering to Suzanne (the innocent scapegoat). Diderot's heroine discovers no enduring comfort in her religion to counterbalance the trials it imposes on her.[46]

It remains to comment on the passage in which Suzanne consoles herself by identifying with Christ, which is so often taken as evidence that Diderot's strategy is to attack convents but not Christianity. Believing she is about to be killed by her fellow nuns for her defiance of Sœur Sainte-Christine, Diderot's heroine contemplates 'un grand Christ de fer sur mes genoux' ('a big iron crucifix on my lap'). This sight gives her strength: 'Voilà mon Dieu, et j'ose me plaindre! ... Je m'attachai à cette idée et je sentis la consolation renaître dans mon cœur. Je connus la vanité de la vie, et je me trouvai trop heureuse de la perdre avant que d'avoir eu le temps de multiplier mes fautes.'[47] ('"This is my God, and yet I dare to feel sorry for myself! ..." I clung to this idea and felt a renewed sense of consolation in my heart. I knew the vanity of life and found myself only too happy to lose it rather than have the time to commit yet more sins.'[48]) Here Suzanne echoes Clarissa, who had written to Lovelace: 'And I am indebted to you, *secondarily*, as I humbly presume to hope, for so many years of glory as might have proved years of danger, temptation, and anguish, had they been added to my mortal life.'[49] Each heroine, on the edge of death, piously welcomes the idea that God takes her to himself when she is in a spiritual state that promises well for the afterlife. May concludes: 'Ces quelques lignes de la méditation de sœur Suzanne, à elles seules, permettent d'affirmer que, quelquefois tout au moins, la *Religieuse* est un roman chrétien.'[50] ('These few lines of Sister Suzanne's meditation alone allow us to assert that, sometimes at least, *La Religieuse* is a Christian novel.') But this is to overlook the fact that Suzanne's surge of Clarissean hope is immediately followed by a fit of discouragement: 'Cependant je comptais mes années, je trouvais que j'avais à peine vingt ans, et je soupirais; j'étais trop affaiblie, trop abattue pour que mon esprit pût s'élever au-dessus des terreurs de la mort; en pleine santé, je crois que j'aurais pu me résoudre avec plus de courage.'[51] ('But I counted up my years and, realizing that I was barely twenty years old, I sighed. I was too weak and exhausted for my mind to rise above the horror of death. I think that had I been in full health, I would have been able to be bolder in my resolve.'[52]) Suzanne's identification with Christ passes before it can bring her any lasting benefit, that is according to her own beliefs. For had she died as she feared at the hands of the other nuns, it would have been in a state of terror which, to a believer, symptomises religious despair.

By way of conclusion we can usefully return to the *Éloge de Richardson*, written in 1762, which is to say after Diderot had started work on *La Religieuse*.[53] The *philosophe* defines Richardson's impact in various ways, but the most important is the following, in which he claims that the English author's most important legacy is a call to virtue for virtue's sake: 'S'il importe aux hommes d'être persuadés qu'indépendamment de toute considération ultérieure à cette vie, nous n'avons rien de mieux à faire pour être heureux que d'être vertueux, quel service Richardson n'a-t-il pas rendu à l'espèce humaine?'[54] ('If it is important for people to be persuaded that, independently of any consideration related to a future life, our best way to obtain happiness is through virtue, how can we overstate the service that Richardson has rendered to humanity?') Richardson, who opposed 'scoffers' and 'infidels' (deists and atheists), would have vehemently disagreed with the sentiments that Diderot here expresses in his name: that virtue can satisfactorily be defined outside a Christian context; that such virtue is our safest route to happiness; and that it should be pursued without a thought for the life everlasting. But Diderot also hints that he understands the message of *Clarissa* better than Richardson himself. For the passage continues: 'Il n'a point démontré cette vérité, mais il l'a fait sentir.'[55] ('He did not demonstrate this truth, but he made us feel it.') The truth that Diderot 'feels' on reading Richardson is somehow different from the truth that the English author explicitly demonstrates. Elsewhere in the *Éloge*, Diderot laments: 'Richardson n'est plus. Quelle perte pour les lettres et pour l'humanité! Cette perte m'a touché comme s'il eût été mon frère.'[56] ('Richardson no longer lives. What a loss for literature and for humanity! I felt this loss no less keenly than that of a brother.') But would he have wanted to publish the 'truth' of Richardson's novels while the author lived to contradict him? Two centuries before Roland Barthes announced the 'death of the author', Diderot offered his reading of *Clarissa* over Richardson's dead body. This justifies the paradoxical statement that *La Religieuse* is at once Diderot's most and least Richardsonian novel.

NOTES

1. Georges May, *Quatre visages de Denis Diderot* (Paris: Boivin, 1951), p. 160.
2. DPV, vol. XIII, p. 195.
3. See Georges May, *Diderot et 'La Religieuse': étude historique et littéraire* (Paris: Presses Universitaires de France, 1954), p. 215.
4. See ibid., pp. 161–96. This point continues to be made in readings of Diderot's novel; see, for instance, Raymond Trousson, *Diderot* (Paris: Gallimard, 2007), pp. 161–2.

5. Samuel Richardson, *Clarissa, or, The History of a Young Lady*, ed. Angus Ross, 2nd edn (London: Penguin, 2004), p. 80.

6. DPV, vol. XIII, p. 193.

7. DPV, vol. XI, p. 30.

8. Ibid., p. 106.

9. Denis Diderot, *The Nun*, ed. and trans. Russell Goulbourne (Oxford: Oxford University Press, 2005), p. 17. All further translations of passages from *La Religieuse* will be taken from this source, which also contains an extremely useful introduction by Goulbourne.

10. Richardson, *Clarissa*, p. 83.

11. See DPV, vol. XI, p. 114 (n. 33), where it is also stated that Longchamp was the convent in which Marguerite Delamarre, the real-life nun who tried unsuccessfully to have her vows rescinded in the 1750s, and whom Diderot's friend the marquis de Croismare had attempted to help, took her vows.

12. Rita Goldberg has examined various points of comparison and contrast between the two authors discussed here. See *Sex and Enlightenment: Women in Richardson and Diderot* (Cambridge: Cambridge University Press, 1984), especially pp. 169–208.

13. Cited in Thomas Keymer, *Richardson's 'Clarissa' and the Eighteenth-Century Reader* (Cambridge: Cambridge University Press, 2004), p. 95 (n. 35). This excellent study contains a chapter on 'Casuistry in Clarissa', with a section on the ethics of relative duty (pp. 85–141). Keymer usefully reminds us here that 'for Richardson's first [English] readers the case at Harlowe Place could not have been more finely balanced or more highly charged' (p. 97) – though to judge by his comments in the *Éloge*, Diderot was manifestly not one of the readers who thought the situation finely balanced.

14. See Keymer, *Richardson's 'Clarissa'*, p. 137.

15. Richardson, *Clarissa*, p. 221.

16. Ibid., p. 902.

17. Ibid., p. 1356.

18. Barbara H. Rosenwein and Lester K. Little, 'Social Meaning in the Monastic and Mendicant Spiritualities', *Past and Present*, 63 (1974), 4–32 (p. 7).

19. Ibid., p. 29. Later, of course, opposition to such developments was at the heart of the Reformation: 'The Protestant Reformers intended to correct a cluster of observances [including] prayers for souls in purgatory.' See *The Blackwell Encyclopedia of Modern Christian Thought*, ed. Alister E. McGrath, 6th edn (Oxford: Blackwell, 2000), p. 340.

20. DPV, vol. XI, p. 86.

21. Diderot, *The Nun*, p. 5.

22. DPV, vol. XI, pp. 100–1; Diderot, *The Nun*, pp. 13–14.

23. DPV, vol. XI, p. 109.

24. Diderot, *The Nun*, p. 20.

25. DPV, vol. XI, p. 126.

26. Diderot, *The Nun*, p. 31.

27. This remains the case even though some have argued that we owe the term 'scapegoat' to a mistranslation by William Tyndale of a Hebrew phrase which

may actually mean 'a goat for Azazel', the latter being perhaps a demon; and something similar happened in French translations of the Bible which use *bouc émissaire* as a translation of the Vulgate's *caper emissarius*. See Aron Pinker, 'A Goat to Go to Azazel', *Journal of Hebrew Scriptures*, 7.8 (2007), 1–25.

28. This argument stands even if Suzanne is 'physiquement aliénée' ('physically alienated') when she takes her vows, or is told she takes them (see DPV, vol. XI, p. 124; Diderot, *The Nun*, p. 30). For the key point here is that it is her religious convictions that lead her to re-enter the 'trap' that is the convent, whatever her subsequent thoughts on her own situation.

29. DPV, vol. XI, pp. 111–12.

30. Diderot, *The Nun*, pp. 21–2.

31. It is worth recalling that according to Suzanne's legal representative Manouri, the vow of celibacy renders all but 'quelques créatures mal organisées' ('a few abnormal creatures') unhappy. This quotation is taken from the following passage that summarises the case made by Suzanne's lawyer, M. Manouri: 'Ces vœux qui heurtent la pente générale de la nature, peuvent-ils jamais être bien observés que par quelques créatures mal organisées en qui les germes des passions sont flétris, et qu'on rangerait à bon droit parmi les monstres, si nos lumières nous permettaient de connaître aussi facilement et aussi bien la structure intérieure de l'homme que sa forme extérieure?' (DPV, vol. XI, p. 183). 'Can these vows, which fly in the face of our natural inclinations, ever be properly observed by anyone other than a few abnormal creatures in whom the seeds of passion have withered and whom we should rightly consider as monsters, if the current state of our knowledge allowed us to understand the internal structure of man as easily and as well as we understand his external form?' (Diderot, *The Nun*, p. 74).

32. DPV, vol. XI, p. 182.

33. Diderot, *The Nun*, p. 73.

34. DPV, vol. XII, p. 637.

35. Ibid., p. 643. B.'s phrase refers to various individuals made unhappy through Christian marriage customs. He thus suggests that not only the religious celibate, represented in the *Supplément* by the *aumônier* (chaplain), but Christians in general would benefit from abandoning religion.

36. DPV, vol. XI, p. 160.

37. Diderot, *The Nun*, p. 56.

38. See DPV, vol. XI, pp. 125–6; Diderot, *The Nun*, pp. 30–1.

39. In Voltairean vein, Diderot had written to Sophie Volland in October 1760 that he and the others at Grandval had discussed 'l'incompatibilité du mal physique et moral avec la nature de l'être éternel' ('the incompatibility of evil and suffering with the nature of the Eternal Being'). See *Corr.*, vol. III, p. 171. But elsewhere Diderot expressed a positive interest in Leibniz, whose philosophy had certain affinities with his own deterministic thinking. See Arthur M. Wilson, *Diderot* (New York: Oxford University Press, 1972), p. 380, and Joseph Breines' and Kate E. Tunstall's chapters in the present volume. In another context, it would be possible to explore the different responses to Optimism of Voltaire the deist and Diderot the atheist.

40. DPV, vol. XI, p. 186.

41. Diderot, *The Nun*, p. 76.

42. Richardson, *Clarissa*, p. 1488.

43. Cited in T. C. Duncan Eaves and Ben D. Kimpel, *Samuel Richardson: A Biography* (Oxford: Clarendon Press, 1971), p. 255.

44. Richardson, *Clarissa*, p. 1342.

45. Ibid., p. 1498.

46. I have argued elsewhere that Suzanne's religion also hampers her ability to analyse her own motives, for Diderot portrays her as though fear of damnation causes her to 'repress' her knowledge of sexuality, to damaging effect. This allows us to see connections with Diderot's other novels, especially *Les Bijoux indiscrets* (*The Indiscreet Jewels*). See James Fowler, *Voicing Desire: Family and Sexuality in Diderot's Narrative* (Oxford: Voltaire Foundation, 2000).

47. DPV, vol. XI, pp. 171–2.

48. Diderot, *The Nun*, p. 65.

49. Richardson, *Clarissa*, p. 1426.

50. May, *Diderot et 'La Religieuse'*, p. 168.

51. DPV, vol. XI, p. 172.

52. Diderot, *The Nun*, p. 65.

53. We know that Diderot had embraced the project of writing a novel entitled *La Religieuse* by August 1760, for in a letter written on the first of that month – the date is inferred by Roth with virtual certainty – Diderot writes to Damilaville: 'Je suis après ma *Religieuse*. Mais cela s'étend sous la plume, et je ne sais plus quand je toucherai la rive' (*Corr.*, vol. III, p. 40). ('I am busy with my novel *The Nun*. But it is becoming longer as I write, and I do not know when I will touch shore.')

54. DPV, vol. XIII, p. 195.

55. Ibid.

56. Ibid., p. 203.

PART III
Dialogues

CHAPTER 10

Eyes wide shut: Le Rêve de d'Alembert

Kate E. Tunstall

Le Rêve de d'Alembert (*D'Alembert's Dream*) is an exhilarating read.[1] It offers us a triptych of lively conversations, involving characters, three male and one female, one asleep and three awake, and topics that range from dualism, materialism and scepticism, to sensibility, selfhood and memory, to the origins of the universe and the workings of nature, from Siamese twins to a priest who underwent a gall bladder operation without feeling any pain, from masturbation to sex with goats. There is something for everyone here. The language and the form of the text are no less wide-ranging, combining philosophical and scientific language in a comic and theatrical dialogue, complete with stage directions. The first part, entitled 'La Suite d'un entretien entre M. d'Alembert et M. Diderot' ('Continuation of the Conversation between Diderot and D'Alembert'),[2] is a fairly typical philosophical dialogue involving a *philosophe* by the name of *Diderot*[3] and his friend, the mathematician, *d'Alembert*. The second, 'Le Rêve de d'Alembert' ('D'Alembert's Dream'),[4] set in *d'Alembert*'s bedroom, is, by contrast, formally much more complex and involves *Mlle de Lespinasse* reading out to the doctor, *Bordeu*, her transcription of what the geometer had been saying in his sleep, and the doctor interpreting and amplifying *d'Alembert*'s sleep-talk in conversation with *Mlle de Lespinasse* and, eventually, with *d'Alembert* once he has woken up. In the final part, called 'Suite de l'entretien précédent' ('Continuation of the Preceding Conversation'),[5] *d'Alembert* has gone out, and *Mlle de Lespinasse* and *Bordeu* have lunch and enjoy further conversation over a glass of Malaga and a cup of coffee.[6]

Despite the diversity of topics, situations and characters, readers have tended to reduce the text to a single message: there is no God, no soul, matter is all there is, and it has the ability to move, feel and think. In short, the text is materialist, though the nature of its materialism has received numerous qualifications, including 'biological',[7] 'chemico-vitalist',[8] 'enchanted',[9] and 'methodological'.[10] In this short essay, I want to suspend any advance knowledge of the text's materialist message and approach *Le Rêve* by way of a different philosophical tradition, namely scepticism, and I want to do so because, in staging a dream, Diderot is making use of a sceptical commonplace.[11] I want to show that he uses it in a highly original way with respect to the sceptical tradition, and with the aim of engaging with a particularly radical form of scepticism, one which goes as far as to doubt the very existence of matter and of a material world, external to the perceiving subject.

Such radical scepticism was identified with Berkeley, and this despite his overtly anti-sceptical position.[12] Exploiting Locke's acknowledgement in the *Essay Concerning Human Understanding* (1690; 2nd edition 1694) that the existence of material substance is a mere 'supposition' on the part of the perceiving subject, for s/he perceives only qualities or ideas,[13] Berkeley argued that ideas are, in fact, the only things that exist, together with God. Diderot and others took this view to be the ultimate in sceptical paradoxes, according to which sensory perception of the external, material world provides no sure grounds for believing that there is an external, material world to be perceived. Moreover, they understood it to have strongly solipsistic implications: not only might there be no material world, but the only ideas that exist might be my own. As Diderot put it in the *Essai sur les règnes de Claude et de Néron* of 1782: 'L'évêque de Cloyne a dit: soit que je monte au haut des montagnes, soit que je descende dans les vallées, ce n'est jamais que moi que j'aperçois; donc il est possible qu'il n'existe que moi.'[14] ('The bishop of Cloyne said: Whether I scale the mountaintops or plunge into the valleys, it is only ever myself that I perceive; therefore it is possible that I alone exist.')

There are in fact numerous references to Berkeley in Diderot's writing,[15] and this constant presence has caught the attention of a number of philosophers. While Jean Deprun argued that Diderot considered Berkeley to be 'le type même de l'adversaire prestigieux et dérisoire, insaisissable, invincible, et futile' ('the perfect example of an adversary, who is at once glorious and beneath consideration, elusive, invincible and pointless'),[16] Jean-Claude Bourdin and Colas Duflo have more recently argued that Diderot successfully refuted Berkeley's challenge to the existence of an external, material world.[17] Here I wish to engage with the latter claim in relation to *Le Rêve* and show that the text does not so much refute Berkeley's solipsistic idealism as offer a textual universe to rival, short-circuit and mirror it. I begin by exploring the link between scepticism, idealism, sleeping and dreaming to show that *Le Rêve* might fruitfully be approached in this way.

In Diderot's *Encyclopédie* article, 'Pyrrhonienne ou sceptique philosophie' ('Pyrrhonian or Sceptical Philosophy'), published in 1765,[18] he imagines a conversation with someone holding radically sceptical views:

Que dirai-je à celui qui prétendant que, quoi qu'il voie, quoi qu'il touche, qu'il entende, qu'il aperçoive, ce n'est pourtant jamais que sa sensation qu'il aperçoit; qu'il pourroit avoir été organisé de manière que tout se passât en lui, comme il s'y passe, sans qu'il y ait rien au dehors, et que peut-être il est le seul être qui soit? Je sentirai tout à coup l'absurdité et la profondeur de ce paradoxe; et je me garderai bien de perdre mon temps à détruire dans un homme une opinion qu'il n'a pas, et à qui je n'ai rien à opposer de plus clair que ce qu'il nie. Il faudrait pour le confondre que je pusse sortir de la nature, l'en tirer, et raisonner de quelque point hors de lui et de moi, ce qui est impossible. Ce sophiste manque du moins à la bienséance de la conversation qui consiste à n'objecter que des choses auxquelles on ajoute soi-même quelque solidité. Pourquoi m'époumonerai-je à dissiper un doute que vous n'avez pas? Mon temps est-il de si peu de valeur à vos yeux? En mettez-vous si peu au vôtre? N'y a-t-il plus de vérités à chercher ou à éclaircir? Occupons-nous de quelque chose de plus important; ou si nous n'avons que de ces frivolités présentes, dormons et digérons.[19]

(What shall I say to someone who claims that, whatever he sees, whatever he touches, whatever he hears, whatever he perceives, it is only ever his sensation that he perceives and that he may have been organised in such a way that everything happens inside him, without there being any outside, and that perhaps he is the only being there is? I shall immediately sense the absurdity and the profundity of this paradox, and I shall avoid wasting my time in ridding this man of an opinion that he does not really have and offering him nothing better by way of an objection than the very same things he denies. To convince him, one would have to be able to take him outside nature, and argue with him from some point outside him and me, which is impossible. This sophist offends the polite rules of conversation, which consist in not offering as objections the very things to which I myself give weight. Why shall I waste my breath in ridding you of a doubt which you do not have? Is my time of so little value in your eyes? Do you value your own so little? Are there no other truths left to seek or elucidate? Let us occupy ourselves with something more important, or if such frivolous things are all we can think of, let us sleep and digest.)

The sceptical paradox is, Diderot acknowledges, impossible to counter by philosophical demonstration, and so he asks his own set of questions that appeal instead to the rules of polite conversation and mutual respect, and finally he proposes an alternative to such 'frivolities',[20] namely that we go to sleep and digest. It is these two final imperatives that interest me here.

Bourdin has discussed them briefly in his *Diderot: le matérialisme*, arguing that for Diderot, sleeping and digesting overpower the sceptical position by virtue of their status as brute facts of existence: 'le lien entre l'envie de dormir et le scepticisme n'est pas fortuit', he says, 'il y a . . . quelque chose de plus fort que . . . l'absurde irréfutable de Berkeley, c'est la vie dans sa brutalité'.[21] ('The link between wanting to sleep and scepticism is significant; there is something stronger than Berkeley's irrefutable absurdity, namely life in its brutality.') On his reading, 'dormons et digérons' seems to be the Diderotian equivalent of Samuel Johnson's famous, 'I refute it *thus*', uttered as he kicked a stone.[22] It seems to me, however, that Diderot's concluding imperatives might also be taken to suggest exactly the opposite, for sleep is itself rich in sceptical connotations,[23] particularly when combined with a reference to eating.

In Pascal's *Entretien avec Sacy sur la philosophie* (1695–1700), Sacy describes readers of Montaigne as, 'des gens qui dorment, et qui croient manger en dormant' ('people who are asleep and who think they are eating as they sleep').[24] For Sacy (and eventually for Pascal once he has escaped the force of Montaigne's imagination),[25] it is the sceptics who sleep and eat, not their opponents. Diderot knew Pascal's text well, as Robert Niklaus has shown,[26] and if we read the final imperatives of the *Encyclopédie* article in the light of it, 'dormons et digérons' reads less like opposition to the sceptical position than like a (reluctant) acceptance of it. The shift from the third person 'ils' to the first person plural 'nous' strengthens this sense of acceptance, and the shift from 'manger' to 'digérer' even suggests that we might have polished off the sleep-food a while back.

The sceptic's activity par excellence is dreaming, perhaps most famously captured in Montaigne's chiasmus, 'nous veillons dormants, et veillants dormons' ('Sleeping we are awake, and waking asleep'),[27] the epistemological implications of which Descartes attempted to refute in the *Méditations* (1641). The sceptical challenge of dreaming occupies Diderot and the encyclopedists also, and in its most radical form. In the article 'Rêve', Diderot observes: 'L'histoire des *rêves* est encore assez peu connue; elle est cependant importante, non seulement en médecine, mais en métaphysique, à cause des objections des idéalistes.'[28] ('The history of dreams is still not very well known, but it is important not only in medicine, but also in metaphysics, owing to the idealists' objections.') Dreams support the 'idealists' in their claim that the only things that exist are our ideas because, he continues: 'nous avons en rêvant un sentiment interne de nous-mêmes, et en même temps un assez grand délire pour voir plusieurs choses hors de nous' ('when we dream, we have an inner sense of ourselves and, at the same time, we succumb to the madness of seeing various things outside ourselves').[29] Dream experience, so the 'idealist' or radical sceptic would claim, reveals what is at stake in waking experience: in neither case do we have any decent grounds for belief in the existence of anything other than our own ideas. The dream points, precisely, to the possibility that 'il n'existe que moi' ('I alone exist').[30]

There are then powerful sceptical connotations to sleeping and dreaming which, when combined with *Diderot*'s reference to Berkeley in the first

'Suite', lay the ground for a reading of *Le Rêve* as an engagement with radical scepticism and idealism. I begin by exploring that reference to Berkeley.

Having refuted dualism, dispensed with the soul and made the case that matter has the capacity for movement, feeling and thought, *Diderot* declares somewhat triumphantly to a rather sleepy *d'Alembert*:

Et pour donner à mon système toute sa force, remarquez encore qu'il est sujet à la même difficulté insurmontable que Berkeley a proposée contre l'existence des corps. Il y a un moment de délire où le clavecin sensible [*Diderot*'s metaphor for the material being[31]] a pensé qu'il était le seul clavecin qu'il y eût au monde, et que toute l'harmonie de l'univers se passait en lui.[32]

(And to give my system its full weight, notice also that it is open to the same insurmountable objection that Berkeley raised against the real existence of material bodies. There can come a moment of madness when a sensitive harpsichord imagines that it is the only one that has ever existed in the world, and that all the harmony of the universe is being produced by it alone.[33])

This presentation of Berkeley seems to me to be quite remarkable and different to the others in Diderot's writing.[34] It is clear in the first of the two sentences quoted that, far from seeking to refute Berkeley's challenge to the existence of material bodies or present it as futile, as Bourdin and Deprun have respectively claimed, *Diderot* appeals to its irrefutability as a standard by which to measure the success of his own system. His materialist system is, he declares, as impossible to refute as Berkeley's immaterialist one, and therein lies, precisely, 'toute sa force'. Perhaps it is its powerful irrefutability – its 'frivolité'? – that makes *d'Alembert* want to go home to bed: 'Dépêchez-vous', he tells *Diderot*, 'car je suis pressé de dormir.'[35] ('Well, don't be long, for I am anxious to get to sleep.'[36])

The second sentence might be taken, however, to contradict the first by presenting Berkeleyan solipsistic idealism as merely some kind of unavoidable mental blip on the part of the physical being, a kind of design fault causing temporary madness, 'un moment de délire'. We should be careful not to conclude as such too soon, however, for madness, along with its numerous cognates, such as 'galimatias' ('gibberish'),[37] 'folie' ('nonsense'),[38] 'des folies qui ne s'entendent qu'aux Petites Maisons' ('the sort of nonsense you only hear in the madhouse'),[39] are subsequently consistently used to describe not Berkeleyan idealism, but materialism itself. *Diderot* and Berkeley seem to be opposites and equals, and their systems as irrefutable and as mad as each other.

I turn now to 'Le Rêve' to explore the way in which it both undermines and amplifies the 'moment de délire', referred to in the 'Suite'. If 'Le Rêve'

stages a dreamer, the solipsistic figure par excellence, offering the sceptic and
the idealist grounds for thinking that there might be no external, material
world to cause his ideas, it also undermines any grounds for such a view by
means of its highly original *mise en scène*.

Most philosophical texts of the period, such as Descartes's *Méditations*,
Condillac's *Essai sur les connaissances humaines* (1746) and his *Traité des
sensations* (1754), place the perceiving subject centre-stage, a subject for
whom questions as to whether or not he is dreaming and whether there is
a world beyond his ideas are of great importance. *Le Rêve*, by contrast,
radically reconfigures this terrain. Adapting a term from Andrew Curran,
who has observed that *Le Rêve* proposes a 'de-formed' conception of selfhood, that is to say, a purely physical and physiological conception,[40] I wish
to argue here that *Le Rêve* also proposes a 'de-centred' conception of
philosophical enquiry.

What we learn about the dreamer and his dream comes through observations made by third parties. *D'Alembert* is referred to in the third person
by *Bordeu* and *Mlle de Lespinasse*: 'BORDEU: Est-ce qu'il est malade? MADE-
MOISELLE DE L'ESPINASSE: Je le crains; il a eu la nuit la plus agitéee'.[41]
('BORDEU: Is he ill? MADEMOISELLE DE LESPINASSE: I'm afraid so; he has
had a most disturbed night.'[42]) His mental state is accessed by others
through external signs and symptoms: *Bordeu* takes his pulse and temper-
ature,[43] and *Mlle de Lespinasse* reports on his earlier behaviour in the
following terms: 'Quand il a été couché, au lieu de reposer comme à son
ordinaire, car il dort comme un enfant, il s'est mis à se tourner, à se
retourner, à tirer ses bras, à écarter ses couvertures, et à parler haut.'[44]
('When he had been got to bed he didn't settle down in his usual way, for
he normally sleeps like a child, but began tossing and turning, throwing his
arms about, pushing back the bedclothes and talking out loud.'[45])
Moreover, we do not hear *D'Alembert* sleep-talk directly; rather his sleep-
talking is reported by *Mlle de Lespinasse*, who has noted down what he said
before the doctor arrived. In this way, *d'Alembert* appears as not so much a
perceiving subject as the perceived object of other people's observations, and
thus the conditions in which the sceptical challenge can arise are removed,
since the dreamer is not a subject wondering if there is anyone or anything
'out there' beyond his ideas, but rather is himself a physical object in an
external, physical world, whose existence is simply part of the *mise en scène*.

It is not only the grounds of epistemological enquiry that are thus
reconfigured. *D'Alembert's* sleep-talking also reorients the standard sceptical
questions related to language. The radical sceptic might object that just as
dreams reveal that normal experience offers no secure grounds for belief in

the existence of an external world, so sleep-talk reveals the absence of secure foundations for any linguistic communication. Locke had observed that, in a manner not dissimilar to that in which the perceiving subject merely 'supposes' the existence of material substance underlying his perceptions, the speaker merely 'supposes' that his words, by which he refers to the ideas 'within his own breast, invisible and hidden from others',[46] are 'the Marks of the Ideas in the Minds also of other Men, with whom they communicate'.[47] In fact, speaker and listener might attach radically different ideas to the same linguistic sign, though they would never know this was the case. In *Tristram Shandy* (1759), Sterne proposes a comic solution to such linguistic scepticism:

> If the fixture of *Momus*'s glass, in the human breast . . . had taken place . . . nothing more would have been wanting, in order to have taken a man's character, but to have taken a chair and gone softly, as you would to a dioptrical bee-hive, and look'd in, – view'd the soul stark naked; – observ'd all her motions, – her machinations; – traced all her maggots from their first engendering to their crawling forth; – watched her loose in her frisks, her gambols, her capricios; and after some notice of her more solemn deportment, consequent upon such frisks, *&c.* ---- then taken your pen and ink and set down nothing but what you had seen, and could have sworn to[.][48]

In the absence of such a window onto the soul, however, men must simply suppose that their words refer to the same ideas in someone else's soul. In *Le Rêve*, the sceptical view of language is voiced by *Bordeu*, but it receives comic treatment:

> D'ALEMBERT: Docteur, est-ce qu'on s'entend? est-ce qu'on est entendu?
> BORDEU: Presque toutes les conversations sont des comptes faits . . . Je ne sais plus où est ma canne . . . on n'y a aucune idée présente à l'esprit . . . et mon chapeau . . . et par la raison seule qu'aucun homme ne ressemble parfaitement à un autre, nous n'entendons jamais précisément, nous ne sommes jamais précisément entendus; il y a du plus ou du moins en tout: notre discours est toujours en deçà ou au-delà de la sensation.[49]
> (D'ALEMBERT: Doctor, do we understand what we are saying ourselves? Are we understood? BORDEU: Almost all conversations are like accounts (where on earth is my stick?) – I mean you have no clear idea in your mind (oh, and my hat?). And for the obvious reason that no two of us are exactly alike, we never understand exactly and are never exactly understood. There is always an element of more or less, our speech falls short of the real sensation or overshoots it.[50])

Here *Bordeu*'s linguistic theory is confirmed and undercut by his more mundane concerns: as he claims that words cannot be trusted because speakers often say one thing while thinking about something else, it is clear that he is himself thinking about something else as he interrupts himself with questions as to the whereabouts of his walking stick and hat. Comically then, his words translate his idea that words do not translate ideas. If we turn now to d'Alembert's sleep-talking, we see that it too may be read as engaging with the sceptical challenge, linguistic and epistemological.

Mlle de Lespinasse recounts to Bordeu what she heard d'Alembert say in his sleep in a passage that can be fruitfully compared with that from Tristram Shandy:

MADEMOISELLE DE L'ESPINASSE: Ensuite il s'est mis à marmotter je ne sais quoi de graines, de lambeaux de chair mis en macération dans de l'eau, de différentes races d'animaux successifs qu'il voyait naître et passer. Il avait imité avec sa main droite le tube d'un microscope et avec sa gauche, je crois, l'orifice d'un vase; il regardait dans le vase par ce tube et il disait: 'Voltaire en plaisantera tant qu'il voudra, mais l'Anguillard [Needham[51]] a raison; j'en crois mes yeux; je les vois, combien il y en a! comme ils vont! comme ils viennent! comme ils frétillent!' Le vase où il apercevait tant de générations momentanées, il le comparait à l'univers; il voyait dans une goutte d'eau l'histoire du monde.[52]

(Then he began mumbling something or other about seeds, bits of flesh pounded up in water, different races of animals he saw coming into being and perishing one after the other. He was holding his right hand to make it look like the tube of a microscope, and his left, I think, represented the mouth of some receptacle. He looked down the tube into the receptacle and said: 'That Voltaire can joke as much as he likes, but the Eelmonger is right; I believe my own eyes, and I can see them, and what a lot of them there are darting to and fro and wriggling about!' He compared the receptacle in which he could see so many instantaneous births, to the universe, and in a drop of water he could see the history of the world.[53])

Sterne's terms are both echoed and reversed here. There is some strikingly similar imagery in the two passages – 'frisky maggots' and 'wiggly eels', Momus's Glass and Needham's microscope[54] – but more striking are the differences, for where Sterne's Lockeanism has recourse to a conception of the mind that is located inside the body, access to which requires language and body to be stripped away, Diderot not only multiplies the layers of linguistic mediation, as Mlle de Lespinasse reads out what she transcribed of d'Alembert's earlier sleep-talk, and I shall return to this in a moment, but he also refuses any sense of interiority by having d'Alembert's body also express his ideas.[55] Indeed d'Alembert's gestures not only accompany his verbal references to microscopes and glass jars, they also reveal the erotic ideas that he attaches to those words, as his mime of a tube and an orifice culminates in orgasm, a comic version of 'spontaneous generation':

Il disait: Mademoiselle de l'Espinasse, où êtes-vous? – Me voilà. – Alors son visage s'est coloré. J'ai voulu lui tâter le pouls, mais je ne sais où il avait caché sa main. Il paraissait éprouver une convulsion; sa bouche s'était entr'ouverte, son haleine était pressée; il a poussé un profond soupir, et puis un soupir plus faible et plus profond encore; il a retourné sa tête sur son oreiller et s'est endormi. Je le regardais avec attention et j'étais toute émue sans savoir pourquoi, le cœur me battait, et ce n'était pas de peur.[56]

(Mademoiselle de Lespinasse, where are you? Here. Then his face became flushed. I wanted to feel his pulse, but he had hidden his hand somewhere. He seemed to be going through some kind of convulsion. His mouth was gaping, his breath gasping, he fetched a deep sigh, then a gentler one and still gentler, turned his head over on the pillow and fell asleep. I watched him very attentively, and felt deeply moved without knowing why; my heart was beating fast, but not with fear.[57])

Here the dreamer's body guarantees that ideas are accurately conveyed to the external world, just as the de-centred *mise en scène* confirms the existence of the dreamer's body in an external, material world. Solipsism and doubt, epistemological or linguistic, are formally and comically overcome here by positioning the dream *outside* the dreamer.

Yet other aspects of *Le Rêve* seem deliberately designed to suggest that there is no outside to the dream. In 'Le Rêve', the voices of the different characters merge, and it is not always clear who said what. Listening to *Mlle de Lespinasse*, *Bordeu* asks: 'Est-ce vous qui parlez?' and she clarifies: 'Non, c'est le rêveur.'[58] ('BORDEU: 'Is this you speaking? MADEMOISELLE DE LESPINASSE: No, it's the dreamer.'[59]) Moreover, *d'Alembert*'s sleep-talk is itself a kind of composite, as he was speaking in both his own voice and *Diderot*'s; *Mlle de Lespinasse* says: 'Il a ajouté en s'apostrophant lui-même: Mon ami d'Alembert, prenez-y garde, vous ne supposez que de la contiguïté où il y a continuité ... Oui, il est assez malin pour me dire cela.'[60] ('Well, he went on, addressing himself: "Friend d'Alembert, mind how you go, you are assuming that there is only contiguity, whereas there is continuity." Yes, he is artful enough to say that.'[61]) Perhaps most extraordinarily, *Bordeu* is able to predict what *Mlle de Lespinasse*, repeating *d'Alembert*, was going to say next:

MADEMOISELLE DE L'ESPINASSE: Rêvez-vous aussi?
BORDEU: Si peu, que je m'engagerais presque à vous dire la suite.
MADEMOISELLE DE L'ESPINASSE: Je vous en défie.
BORDEU: Vous m'en défiez?
MADEMOISELLE DE L'ESPINASSE: Oui.
BORDEU: Et si je rencontre?
MADEMOISELLE DE L'ESPINASSE: Si vous rencontrez, je vous promets ... je vous promets de vous tenir pour le plus grand fou qu'il y ait au monde.

BORDEU: Regardez sur votre papier et écoutez-moi.
MADEMOISELLE DE L'ESPINASSE: J'en suis confondue; c'est cela, et presque
   mot pour mot. Je puis donc assurer à présent à toute la terre qu'il n'y
   a aucune différence entre un médecin qui veille et un philosophe qui
   rêve.[62]

(MADEMOISELLE DE LESPINASSE: Are you dreaming, too? BORDEU: Far from dreaming, I would almost undertake to tell you what comes next. MADEMOISELLE DE
LESPINASSE: I bet you can't. BORDEU: You bet me? MADEMOISELLE DE LESPINASSE:
Yes. BORDEU: And if I hit on the right answer? MADEMOISELLE DE LESPINASSE: If
you hit on the right answer, I promise . . . I promise to consider you the biggest
madman in the world. BORDEU: Look at your notes and listen. MADEMOISELLE DE
LESPINASSE: I really am amazed; that's what he said, almost word for word. I can
now proclaim to all the world that there is no difference between a doctor awake
and a philosopher dreaming.[63])

We might be tempted to conclude that *Bordeu*'s strange powers of prediction
reveal that what *d'Alembert* said has the status of fact, and certainly that is what
Bordeu himself thinks.[64] However, there are many reasons why we should
resist an identification of *Bordeu* with Diderot,[65] and so, rather than arguing
that *Bordeu*'s continuation of *d'Alembert*'s sleep-talk grounds *Diderot*'s theory
in scientific reality or supplies it with medical proof, I wish to argue that the
peculiar discursive set-up of *Le Rêve*, in which characters repeat each other's
words or finish other character's sentences, both performs the materialist thesis
and suggests a kind of shared delirium, even a communal dream.

   In his sleep, *d'Alembert* explained how the material body has a sense of
self, how individual molecules that are physically contiguous to each other
can provide the feeling of a continuous self, and this is the explanation that
Mlle de Lespinasse repeats:

Non, c'est le rêveur . . . Je continue . . . Il a ajouté en s'apostrophant lui-même:
Mon ami d'Alembert, prenez-y garde, vous ne supposez que de la contiguïté où il y
a continuité . . . Oui, il est assez malin pour me dire cela . . . Et la formation de cette
continuité? Elle ne l'embarrassera guère . . . Comme une goutte de mercure se fond
dans une autre goutte de mercure, une molécule sensible et vivante se fond dans
une molécule sensible et vivante . . . D'abord il y avait deux gouttes, après le contact
il n'y en a plus qu'une . . . Avant l'assimilation il y avait deux molécules, après
l'assimilation il n'y en a plus qu'une. . . La sensibilité devient commune à la masse
commune.[66]

(No, it's the dreamer. I'm going on . . . Well, he went on, addressing himself.
Friend D'Alembert, mind how you go, you are assuming that there is only
contiguity, whereas there is continuity. And how is this continuity formed?
He'll find no trouble about that . . . Just as a globule of mercury joins up
with another globule of mercury, so a sensitive, living molecule joins up with

another sensitive and living molecule. First there were two globules, but after contact there is only one. The same sensitivity is common to the whole mass.[67])

The way in which the voices merge together may be said to perform an equivalent of the molecules merging together to form a continuity. *Mlle de Lespinasse's* 'je continue' is thus comic, as indeed is the fact that the first part of the text is entitled 'Suite': it was not simply a standard comic opening *in medias res*, but, we realise in retrospect, a suggestion of a continuous chain extending backwards in time, as well as forwards.[68]

This peculiar discursive set-up, in which characters repeat and continue each other's sentences, has also been explored by Wilda Anderson in *Diderot's Dream* (1990). She describes it in terms of 'one single supermind that can think thoughts that each alone perhaps would not have been able to produce'.[69] I want to adapt this image and refer instead to 'one single super-discourse' – perhaps even to a 'hyper-text'? – and to observe that it bears a strange resemblance to the one single mind of Berkeleyan idealism of the 'Suite' that contains within it all the sounds of the universe. *Le Rêve's* super-discourse, encompassing all the characters, is a material equivalent to the Berkeleyan universe, in which the subject 'lives, thinks and has his being', that is, God.[70]

Briefly to conclude: I do not wish to claim that *Le Rêve* offers a sceptical or an idealist message, but I do wish to suggest that it does not so much refute either of those philosophies as offer a *mise en scène* to short-circuit them, and a textual materialism, which is itself as irrefutable – and perhaps as much of a 'frivolité' – as they are. As a result, reading *Le Rêve* places us in the same position with respect to materialism as that in which Jacques and his master find themselves in relation to the château that bears the inscription: Vous y étiez avant que d'y entrer, et vous y serez encore quand vous en sortirez.'[71] ('You were here before you entered and you will still be here after you have left.'[72])

NOTES

1. All references to *Le Rêve* are to DPV, vol. XVII, pp. 25–209. This edition should be complemented by that of Colas Duflo (Paris: Garnier Flammarion, 2002), in which the punctuation is significantly different. The history of this 1769 text is complex; see Jean Varloot's introduction in DPV, vol. XVII, pp. 25–66 (pp. 25–7). All translations are taken from Denis Diderot, *'Rameau's Nephew' and 'D'Alembert's Dream'*, trans. Leonard Tancock (London: Penguin, 1966). I have modified Tancock's 'L'Espinasse' throughout to 'Lespinassse'; any other local modifications are signalled. Unless otherwise stated, all other translations from French are my own.

2. DPV, vol. XVII, pp. 89–113; *D'Alembert's Dream*, pp. 149–57.

3. I shall italicise the names of the characters in the dialogue to distinguish them from their real-life homologues. For a study of the real Bordeu, Lespinasse and d'Alembert, see Yvon Belaval, 'Les Protagonistes du *Rêve de D'Alembert*', *Diderot Studies*, 3 (1961), 15–32. Further information on the real Bordeu can be found in Dominique Boury, 'Théophile de Bordeu: source et personnage du *Rêve de D'Alembert*', *Recherches sur Diderot et sur l'Encyclopédie*, 34 (2003), 11–34, and in Sophie Audidière, Jean-Claude Bourdin and Colas Duflo (eds.), *Encyclopédie du 'Rêve de D'Alembert' de Diderot* (Paris: CNRS, 2006), pp. 70–2.

4. DPV, XVII, pp. 115–94; *D'Alembert's Dream*, pp. 165–224.

5. DPV, XVII, pp. 195–207; *D'Alembert's Dream*, pp. 225–33.

6. For an analysis of the *mise en scène* see Herbert Dieckmann, 'Die Künstlerische Form des *Rêve de d'Alembert*', *Arbeitsgemeinschaft für Forschung des Landes Nordrhein-Westfalen*, 127 (1966). For an emphasis on the theatrical dimension of *Le Rêve*, see Béatrice Didier, *Diderot, dramaturge du vivant* (Paris: Presses Universitaires de France, 2001). For an analysis of the text's hybrid genre, see Jean Starobinski, 'Le Philosophe, le géomètre, l'hybride', *Poétique*, 21 (1975), 8–23, and Stephen Werner, 'Comédie et philosophie: le style du *Rêve de d'Alembert*', *Recherches sur Diderot et sur l'Encyclopédie*, 22 (April 1997), 7–23.

7. Laurent Versini in Denis Diderot, *Œuvres*, 5 vols. (Paris: Laffont, 1994–7), vol. I, p. 7.

8. Yvon Belaval, 'Sur le matérialisme de Diderot', in *Europäische Aufklärung: Festschrift für Herbert Dieckmann* (Munich: Fink, 1967), pp. 9–21.

9. Élisabeth de Fontenay, *Diderot ou le matérialisme enchanté* (Paris: Grasset, 1981).

10. Colas Duflo, *Diderot philosophe* (Paris: Champion, 2003), p. 187.

11. I therefore disagree with Jean-Claude Bourdin, who has claimed: 'Diderot ne fut sans doute jamais sceptique et on chercherait en vain dans son œuvre l'utilisation des "lieux communs" sceptiques' ('Diderot was probably never a sceptic and one would seek in vain for the use of sceptical commonplaces in his writing'). See Jean-Claude Bourdin, 'Matérialisme et scepticisme chez Diderot', *Recherches sur Diderot et sur l'Encyclopédie*, 26 (1999), 85–97 (p. 85). Another example of Diderot's use of sceptical commonplaces is the blind man; see my 'Pré-histoire d'un emblème des Lumières: l'aveugle-né de Montaigne à Diderot', in Isabelle Moreau (ed.), *Les Lumières en mouvement: la circulation des idées au XVIIIe siècle* (Lyon: École Normale Supérieure, 2009), pp. 173–97.

12. See H. M. Bracken, *The Early Reception of Berkeley's Immaterialism, 1710–1733* (The Hague: Nijhoff, 1959); Sébastien Charles, *Berkeley au siècle des Lumières: immatérialisme et scepticisme au XVIIIe siècle*, preface by Geneviève Brykman (Paris: Vrin, 2003).

13. Locke writes: 'Not imagining how these simple ideas can subsist by themselves, we accustom our selves, to suppose some Substratum, wherein they do subsist, and from which they do result, which therefore we call Substance. So that if any one will examine himself concerning his Notion of pure Substance in general, he will find he has no other Idea of it at all, but only a Supposition of he knows not what support of such Qualities, which are capable of producing simple

Ideas in us.' John Locke, *An Essay Concerning Human Understanding*, ed. Peter Nidditch (Oxford: Clarendon Press, 1975), p. 295.

14. DPV, vol. xxv, p. 291. This phrase is very close to the opening of Condillac's 1746 *Essai sur les connaissances humaines* (*Essay on the Origin of Human Knowledge*), which Diderot explicitly compares to Berkeley in the *Lettre sur les aveugles* (*Letter on the Blind*); see DPV, vol. iv, p. 44.

15. See Jean Deprun, 'Diderot devant l'idéalisme', *Revue internationale de philosophie*, 38 (1984), 67–78. We should add to Deprun's inventory of references the following, from the entry 'Chardin' in the *Salon de 1765*: 'S'il est vrai, comme le disent les philosophes, qu'il n'y a de réel que nos sensations, que ni le vide de l'espace, ni la solidité même des corps n'ait peut-être rien en elle-même de ce que nous éprouvons, qu'ils m'apprennent ces philosophes quelle différence il y a pour eux, à quatre pieds de tes tableaux, entre le Créateur et toi' (DPV, vol. xiv, p. 117). ('If it is true, as the philosophers say, that there is nothing real except our sensations, that perhaps neither empty space nor even solid bodies possess those qualities we perceive in them, then let those philosophers explain to me what difference they see, when they stand at four feet from your pictures, between you and the Creator.') For an analysis, see René Démoris, 'Condillac et la peinture' in Jean Sgard (ed.), *Condillac et les problèmes du langage* (Geneva: Slatkine, 1982), pp. 379–93.

16. Deprun, 'Diderot devant l'idéalisme', p. 67.

17. See Jean-Claude Bourdin, *Diderot. Le matérialisme* (Paris: Presses Universitaires de France, 1998), p. 94, and Duflo, *Diderot philosophe*, pp. 180–1.

18. DPV, vol. viii, pp. 138–60.

19. Ibid., p. 160. The shift in pronoun from 'he' to 'you' here is characteristic of Diderot's writing; see Marian Hobson, 'Déictique, dialectique dans *le Neveu de Rameau*', in Georges Benrekassa, Marc Buffat and Pierre Chartier (eds.), *Études sur le Neveu de Rameau et le Paradoxe sur le comédien de Denis Diderot. Actes du Colloque organisé à l'Université Paris VII les 15 et 16 novembre 1991, Cahiers Textuel*, 11 (1992), 11–19.

20. It is unclear whether the term 'frivolité' is ironic: on the one hand, the question as to the existence of the material world might be said to be far from frivolous, while on the other, its unanswerability makes it frivolous. There is a similar uncertainty in *Le Rêve* as to whether the subjects under discussion are serious or not. See DPV, vol. xvii, p. 133; *D'Alembert's Dream*, p. 177.

21. Bourdin, *Diderot*, p. 94.

22. For recent discussions, see Douglas Lane Patey, 'Johnson's Refutation of Berkeley: Kicking the Stone Again', *Journal of the History of Ideas*, 47.1 (1986), 139–45; Bruce Silver, 'Boswell on Johnson's Refutation of Berkeley: Revisiting the Stone', *Journal of the History of Ideas*, 54.3 (1993), 437–48.

23. Bourdin does acknowledge this: 'opposer ... le sommeil à la longue justification matérialiste revient à fragiliser, à son tour, la supposition fondamentale' ('to oppose ... sleep to the long materialist justification amounts to undermining, in its turn, the fundamental supposition'); see Bourdin, *Diderot*, p. 92. He does not, however, develop this remark any further.

24. Blaise Pascal, *Entretien avec Sacy sur la philosophie*, ed. Richard Scholar (Arles: Actes Sud, 2003), p. 42.
25. For an interesting discussion, see Richard Scholar, 'La Force de l'imagination de Montaigne: Camus, Malebranche, Pascal', *Littératures classiques*, 45 (2002), 127–38.
26. Robert Niklaus, 'Les *Pensées philosophiques* de Diderot et les *Pensées* de Pascal', *Diderot Studies*, 20 (1981), 201–17 (pp. 214–17). Diderot also knew St Augustine's *Confessions* well, and Pascal's use of food metaphors is Augustinian. See Pascal, *Entretien*, p. 42, n. 3.
27. Michel de Montaigne, *Essais*, ed. Albert Thibaudet (Paris: Gallimard, 1950), p. 673; *The Complete Works*, trans. Donald Frame, intro. Stuart Hampshire (London: Everyman, 2003), p. 548.
28. DPV, vol. VIII, p. 218.
29. Ibid., p. 218. The problem is referred to once again in the article 'Somnambule', written by the doctor Ménuret de Chambaud: 'Les plus grandes preuves que le philosophe donne de l'existence des corps sont fondées sur les impressions qu'ils font sur nous; ces preuves perdent nécessairement beaucoup de leur force, si nous ressentons les mêmes effets sans que ces corps agissent réellement; c'est précisément le cas du *somnambule*' (*Encyclopédie*, vol. XV, p. 342). ('The greatest proofs which philosophy gives that material bodies exist are founded on the impressions which they make on us; but these proofs necessarily lose a great deal of their force if we feel the same effects without these bodies actually acting upon us; this is precisely the case of the sleepwalker.') For Diderot's knowledge of Ménuret de Chambaud, see Colas Duflo, 'Diderot et Ménuret de Chambaud', *Recherches sur Diderot et sur l'Encyclopédie*, 34 (2003), 25–44.
30. In fact, Berkeley's attitude to dreams is rather uninteresting; see George Berkeley, *Three Dialogues between Hylas and Philonous* in *The Works of George Berkeley*, ed. A. A. Luce and T. E. Jessop, 9 vols. (London: Nelson, 1964), vol. II, pp. 163–263 (p. 201).
31. For a discussion of this particular metaphor, see Delon, 'Le *Rêve de D'Alembert*', pp. 173–4.
32. DPV, vol. XVII, 108–9.
33. *D'Alembert's Dream*, p. 161.
34. See above, n. 15.
35. DPV, vol. XVII, p. 111.
36. *D'Alembert's Dream*, p. 163.
37. DPV, vol. XVII, p. 116; *D'Alembert's Dream*, p. 166.
38. DPV, vol. XVII, p. 137; *D'Alembert's Dream*, p. 177.
39. DPV, vol. XVII, p. 125; *D'Alembert's Dream*, p. 172.
40. Andrew Curran, 'Monsters and the Self in the *Rêve de D'Alembert*', *Eighteenth-Century Life*, 21.2 (1997), 48–69, and *Sublime Disorder: Physical Monstrosity in Diderot's Universe*, SVEC 2001:01 (Oxford: Voltaire Foundation, 2001).
41. DPV, vol. XVII, p. 115.
42. *D'Alembert's Dream*, p. 165.

43. DPV, vol. xvii, p. 115.
44. DPV, vol. xvii, pp. 116.
45. *D'Alembert's Dream*, p. 166.
46. Locke, *Essay*, p. 405.
47. Ibid., p. 406.
48. Laurence Sterne, *The Life and Opinions of Tristram Shandy, Gentleman*, ed. Melvyn New and Joan New, introductory essay Christopher Ricks (London: Penguin, 2003), p. 65.
49. DPV, vol. xvii, pp. 192–3.
50. *D'Alembert's Dream*, p. 222.
51. For an explanation of Needham's experiment, the ensuing dispute with Voltaire and the place of Needham in materialist thought, see Jacques Roger, *Les Sciences de la vie dans la pensée française au xviiie siècle* (Paris: Vrin, 1963); Shirley Roe, 'Metaphysics and Materialism: Needham's Response to d'Holbach', *SVEC*, 284 (1991), 309–42; José-Michel Moureaux, 'Un épisode inconnu de la querelle Voltaire-Needham', *SVEC*, 5 (2000), 29–45.
52. DPV, vol. xvii, pp. 127–8.
53. *D'Alembert's Dream*, pp. 173–4.
54. We might also note the shared use of the bee metaphor. For its use in *Le Rêve* and in philosophical and medical literature of the period, see 'Grappe d'abeilles' in Audidière *et al.*, *Encyclopédie du 'Rêve'*, pp. 201–4, and Annie Ibrahim, 'Maupertuis dans *Le Rêve de D'Alembert*: l'essaim d'abeilles et le polype', *Recherches sur Diderot et sur l'Encyclopédie*, 34 (2003), 72–83.
55. For another approach to the question of interiority in Diderot, see Olivier Tonneau, '"Ah! Si vous pouviez lire au fond de mon coeur. . .": Diderot et le mythe de l'intériorité', *SVEC*, 12 (2006), 291–8. For a study of exteriorisation in another text by Diderot, see Jean Starobinski, 'L'Incipit du *Neveu de Rameau*', *Nouvelle Revue Française*, 347 (1981), 42–64. For the notion of privacy in Diderot, see Caroline Warman, 'Intimate, Deprived, Uncivilized: Diderot and the Publication of the Private Moment', in Andrew Kahn (ed.), *Representing Private Lives of the Enlightenment, SVEC* (forthcoming). I am grateful to Caroline Warman and Andrew Kahn for their helpful discussion of a much earlier version of this essay. See also Jack Undank, *Diderot: Inside, Outside and In-Between* (Madison, WI: Coda, 1979).
56. DPV, vol. xvii, p. 129.
57. *D'Alembert's Dream*, pp. 174–5.
58. DPV, vol. xvii, p. 117. It is noteworthy that Ménuret de Chambaud also did the article on ventriloquism; see 'Ventriloque', in the *Encyclopédie*, vol. xvii, p. 33.
59. *D'Alembert's Dream*, p. 167.
60. DPV, vol. xvii, pp. 117–18. This is all the more interesting since *Mlle de Lespinasse* and *Bordeu* later observe that the only dream that it is impossible to have is one in which one dreams one is someone else.
61. *D'Alembert's Dream*, p. 167.
62. DPV, vol. xvii, pp. 121–2.

63. *D'Alembert's Dream*, pp. 169–70.
64. He provides medical evidence for *Diderot's* claims, as dreamt by *d'Alembert*: 'MADEMOISELLE DE L'ESPINASSE: Il a continué: "Eh bien! Philosophe, vous concevez donc des polypes de toute espèce, même des polypes humains? . . . Mais la nature ne nous en offre point." BORDEU: Il n'avait pas connaissance de ces deux filles qui se tenaient par la tête, les épaules, le dos, les fesses et les cuisses, qui ont vécu ainsi accolées jusqu'à l'âge de vingt-deux ans, et qui sont mortes à quelques minutes l'une de l'autre' (DPV, vol. XVII, pp. 124–5). 'MADEMOISELLE DE LESPINASSE: He went on: "Well, Mr Philosopher, so you think there are polyps of all kinds, even human ones? But we don't find any in nature." BORDEU: He obviously hadn't heard of the two girls who were connected by the head, shoulders, back, buttocks and thighs, and lived in that condition, stuck together, up to the age of twenty-two, and then died within a few minutes of each other' (*D'Alembert's Dream*, p. 172).
65. We have already seen how Diderot treats his views on the relations between words and ideas in comic fashion, and we should also observe that his medical competence is questionable: 'BORDEU: Mais il est dix heures et demie, et j'entends du faubourg jusqu'ici un malade qui m'appelle. MADEMOISELLE DE L'ESPINASSE: Y aurait-il bien du danger pour lui à ce que vous ne le vissiez pas? BORDEU: Moins peut-être qu'à le voir' (DPV, vol. XVII, p. 163). 'BORDEU: But it is ten-thirty, and I can hear a patient calling for me right across the town! MADEMOISELLE DE LESPINASSE: Would he be in any danger if you didn't go and see him? BORDEU: Probably less than if I saw him' (*D'Alembert's Dream*, p. 201). Moreover, he admits to making things up: 'MADEMOISELLE DE L'ESPINASSE: Vous mentez. BORDEU: C'est vrai' (DPV, vol. XVII, p. 137). 'MADEMOISELLE DE LESPINASSE: That is not true. BORDEU: I know it isn't' (*D'Alembert's Dream*, p. 180). Indeed, as Alexandre Wenger has recently suggested, *Bordeu* might be compared to the confidence trickster, Desbrosses, in Diderot's *Mystification*, written the year before *Le Rêve*; see 'C'est Horace, qui est un de nos grands médecins, qui l'a dit', paper read at 'Celebrating Diderot Studies', Oxford, 29–31 October, 2009; forthcoming in *Diderot Studies*, 33.
66. DPV, vol. XVII, p. 117.
67. *D'Alembert's Dream*, p. 167 (translation slightly modified).
68. The chain of repetition might make us think of *Jacques le fataliste*, in which the narrator tells us in the opening pages that: 'Jacques disait que son capitaine disait que tout ce qui nous arrive de bien et de mal ici-bas était écrit là-haut' (DPV, vol. XXIII, p. 23); see Denis Diderot, *Jacques the Fatalist*, trans. Michael Henry, ed. Martin Hall (London: Penguin, 1986), p. 21.
69. Wilda Anderson, *Diderot's Dream* (Baltimore, MD: Johns Hopkins University Press, 1990), p. 66.
70. See Stuart Brown, 'Platonic Idealism in Modern Philosophy from Malebranche to Berkeley', in G. A. Rogers, J. M. Vienne and Y. C. Zarka (eds.), *The Cambridge Platonists in Philosophical Context* (Boston: Kluwer, 1997), pp. 197–214; Stephen H. Daniel, 'Berkeley's Pantheistic Discourse', *International Journal for Philosophy of Religion*, 49.3 (2001), 179–94. Diderot's

relationship to Leibniz is beyond the scope of this article. For existing studies, see Jean-François Marquet, 'La Monadologie de Diderot', *Revue philosophique de la France et de l'étranger*, 3 (1984), 353–70; Max W. Wartofsky, 'Diderot and the Development of Materialist Monism', *Diderot Studies*, 2 (1952), 279–329; Yvon Belaval, 'Diderot, lecteur de Leibniz?' in *Études leibniziennes: de Leibniz à Hegel* (Paris: Aubier, 1976), pp. 244–63; Claire Fauvergue, *Diderot, lecteur et interprète de Leibniz* (Paris: Champion, 2006). It is also beyond the scope of this essay to consider *Mlle de Lespinasse* and *Bordeu*'s discussion of a material God (DPV, vol. XVII, p. 143), but it merits attention for the way it relates to the article 'Spinosa' in the *Encyclopédie* and beyond that to the image of the spider. See Isabelle Moreau, 'L'Araignée dans sa toile. Mise en images de l'âme du monde de François Bernier et Pierre Bayle à l'*Encyclopédie*', in Moreau, *Les Lumières en mouvement*, pp. 199–228.

71. DPV, vol. XXIII, p. 43.
72. Diderot, *Jacques the Fatalist*, p. 38.

CHAPTER 11

Logics of the human in the Supplément au Voyage de Bougainville*

Andrew Curran

Diderot's 1772 text *Supplément au Voyage de Bougainville* (*Supplement to Bougainville's 'Voyage around the World'*) is a 'riff', as Lynn Festa puts it, on the explorer Louis Antoine de Bougainville's memorable account of his land-fall on Tahiti.[1] The final text within a trilogy of moralising tales that includes *Ceci n'est pas un conte* (*This is Not a Story*) and *Mme de La Carlière*, Diderot's Tahitian fable targets his era's constricting jealousies, petty passions and denatured conventions by juxtaposing Tahiti's 'natural society' with a series of European notions and customs.[2] The overall structure of this clash of cultures is worth recalling. In the opening pages of the *Supplément*, Diderot stages a discussion between the witty and inquisitive interlocutors A and B, both of whom are enlightened relativists. In this initial part of the text, the two friends jump quickly from topic to topic, speculating on continental drift, the mores of ancient peoples on isolated lands and the seemingly contradictory psychology of Bougainville himself. In the ensuing section, A and B 'read' together the hidden manuscript ostensibly found within Bougainville's orig-inal text. This first Tahitian section begins, as it were, with a forceful, regressive view of history delivered by an old Tahitian man who enumerates the inevitable consequences of colonisation: contamination, enslavement and perhaps the eventual extermination of the Tahitians. The subsequent portion of the text shifts to a different era, where we witness more fruitful contacts between Tahitians and Europeans. In particular, we meet the very philosoph-ically minded patriarch and chief, Orou, who begins a discussion with an *aumônier* (chaplain) regarding the backward and unnatural sexual restrictions imposed on the Catholic clergy. (This is also the section where B recounts the story of Polly Baker's incarceration for having had five children out of wed-lock.) The *suite* (continuation) to this section relates Orou's later interactions with the *aumônier* after the clergyman has succumbed to the charms of Orou's daughter, Thia. At this point, the two men discuss the logic of the Tahitian

---

* I would like to thank Emma Drew for her attentive advice on this article.

sexual economy (where children have a greater value than any other 'commodity') at the same time as they deconstruct supposedly sinful notions such as adultery and fornication. The final section of the text brings back A and B, who speak about the 'denaturing' of humankind as well as the feasibility or non-feasibility of creating nature-based institutions in Europe, such as a more natural version of marriage. The final assessment of the text as supplied by A and B – that one should 'prendre le froc du pays où l'on va, et garder celui du pays où l'on est' ('wear the dress of the country to which one goes, but keep that of the country where one is')[3] – seems to be a synthesis of cultural relativism and, on a certain level, pragmatic conservatism.

Long considered something of an outlier among Diderot's major contributions to eighteenth-century thought, this short text is now among the *philosophe's* most taught and perhaps even most studied texts. While this phenomenon might be attributed to the *Supplément's* relative accessibility and readability – as compared to *Jacques le fataliste* (*Jacques the Fatalist*), *Le Neveu de Rameau* (*Rameau's Nephew*) or *Le Rêve de d'Alembert* (*D'Alembert's Dream*) – the appeal of this series of framed dialogues can also be ascribed to the fact that the preoccupations of the *Supplément* overlap prominently with those of many eighteenth-century scholars today. Not only does this simultaneously dystopian and utopian assessment of Tahiti provide a foil for a series of Enlightenment-era social codes and assumptions (e.g. *pudeur* (modesty), chastity, abstinence, coquetry, marriage, legal systems and religion); Diderot puts the most pointed analysis of European mores in the mouths of his 'tropicopolitan' characters.[4] It is this 'savage criticism', to adapt Anthony Pagden's phrase, that separates Diderot's Tahiti from Bougainville's.[5] While the *philosophe's* portrait of Tahitian culture certainly draws important elements from Bougainville's account of a geographical space where, as the explorer put it, 'la seule passion [était] l'amour' ('the only passion was love'),[6] Diderot's Tahiti is less a paradise than a massive thought experiment where puppet-like Europeans and articulate indigenous islanders generate both a Montesquieu-type clash of worldviews, and a wider realisation regarding the potential horrors of the ongoing colonial project.

Given its richness, critics have come to look at the *Supplément* from a variety of perspectives. A number of scholars have examined the text in terms of Diderot's larger, late-career meditation on morality, a concern not only in the trilogy of which the *Supplément* is the third part, but also in contemporary texts such as the *Entretien avec la maréchale de **** (*Conversation with the Wife of the Maréchal de ****).[7] Other Diderot specialists have focused on this text as a springboard for an exploration of the *philosophe's* political views or his understanding of human sexuality.[8]

Almost all of the scholarship focusing on the *Supplément*, however, brings this text into dialogue with other Enlightenment-era conjectural histories and visions of the state of nature, particularly the fall of natural man found in Rousseau's so-called Second Discourse of 1755.[9] While most scholars now tend to emphasise the divergences rather than the obvious points of overlap between Diderot's state of nature and Rousseau's, they have also neglected a key difference: the *Supplément* does not present the Tahitian as the archetypal primitive man, but as one possible incarnation of *homme naturel* (natural man). In point of fact, Diderot's Tahitian is not at all like the 'ur-savage' of the Second Discourse. Whereas Rousseau's *homme naturel* moves progressively from the state of nature to the state of civilisation within a sweeping human chronicle, the Tahitian is a specific type of savage, the product of a series of particular geographical and demographic (Pacific Island) variables. Although A and B (and Orou and the Old Man for that matter) do indeed maintain that the Tahitians embody natural values in contrast to European artifice, within the overall structure of this text these islanders represent but one logic of the human. In the present discussion, I seek to explore the wider set of logics or natural histories of humankind that Diderot develops in the *Supplément*, a series of narratives that not only explains the very existence and comportment of the Tahitians, but where they stand vis-à-vis the inevitability of the colonial project.

POLYNESIAN PALINGENESIS

One of the core tenets of Diderot's worldview was that the ambitions of natural history should be kept in check by the parameters of the physical realm. And yet, more often than not, the *philosophe*'s use of natural history begins with naturalist 'facts' and finishes with capacious speculation on a variety of subjects that transcends the purely physical. In *Le Rêve de d'Alembert*, for example, Diderot draws on developments in the life sciences (e.g. theories on human monstrosities and the discovery of the hydra) in order to refute constructive metaphysics. In *Le Neveu de Rameau*, the *philosophe* looks to speculative microphysiology (moral fibres, hereditary 'molecules') as a means of explaining natural morality or a lack thereof. Natural history also serves as a springboard of sorts in the *Supplément*. This begins as early as the first question-and-answer session between A and B. Following a meteorological assessment of the fog which descends (significantly) when the two friends begin speaking about Bougainville's *Supplément*, A wonders aloud how wolves, foxes, dogs, deer and snakes ended up on the remote islands of the South Pacific. In a line reminiscent of d'Alembert's Lucretian musings on the origin of life in *Le Rêve*, B responds that animal life was separated during what we would now call continental drift: 'B. Qui sait l'histoire primitive de notre globe? combien d'espaces de terre maintenant isolés, étaient autrefois continus? Le seul phénomène sur lequel on pourrait former quelque conjecture, c'est la direction de la masse des eaux qui les a séparés. A. Comment cela? B. Par la forme générale des arrachements.'[10] ('B. Who knows the primitive history of our globe? How many tracts of land, now isolated, were once conjoined as one? The only phenomenon upon which we can base some kind of hypothesis is the orientation of those bodies of water that separated them. A. How so? B. By the general shape of their displacement.') Not surprisingly, this theory is quickly used to explain not only the existence of remote human populations, but the effect that this geological diaspora had on the genealogy of human morality as well.

In particular, A and B take up the case of the island of Akiaki (which Bougainville named L'île des lanciers (the island of lancers) in 1768, in light of the inhabitants' long pikes). Having already resolved the riddle of how such islands came into existence, B wonders aloud what would become of humans on such small islands once they began multiplying 'sur un espace qui n'a pas plus d'une lieue de diamètre' ('in an area no more than one league in diameter').[11] The answer is a far cry from what we find in Rousseau's peaceful state of nature: in this particular *état* (state), demographics and the quest for survival produce violent population control measures. According to the two interlocutors, the islanders must behave in one of the following ways: 'A. Ils s'exterminent et se mangent. B. Ou la multiplication y est limitée par quelque loi superstitieuse: l'enfant y est écrasé dans le sein de sa mère foulée sous les pieds d'une prêtresse. A. Ou l'homme égorgé expire sous le couteau d'un prêtre. Ou l'on a recours à la castration des mâles. B. A l'infibulation des femelles.'[12] ('A. They kill and eat one another. B. Or reproduction is limited by some superstitious law; a child is crushed in his mother's womb, trampled under the feet of a priestess. A. Or a man is sacrificed under the knife of a priest, his throat slit; or they resort to the castration of their males. B. Or to the infibulation of their females.')

In the examples above, the reaction to the variable of overpopulation is mechanical and logical. What is more, according to Diderot's interlocutors, these dire physical catalysts also engender a series of superstitious justifications and, ultimately, sanctify civil laws that often last well after the physical problems have disappeared: 'Les institutions surnaturelles et divines se fortifient et s'éternisent en se transformant à la longue en lois civiles et nationales, et ... les institutions civiles et nationales se consacrent et dégénèrent en préceptes surnaturels et divins."[13] ('The supernatural and divine institutions are strengthened and preserved by being transformed, over time, into civil and national laws; and the civil and national institutions become consecrated, degenerating into supernatural and divine commandments.')

At the end of this sweeping anthropological assessment of the genesis of human customs, A muses that this entire process can be seen as a deleterious 'palingenesis' (rebirth): 'C'est une des palingénésies les plus funestes.'[14] ('It is one of the most ill-starred of rebirths.') This analogy is telling. Two years after Charles Bonnet asserted in his 1769 text *Palingénésie philosophique* (*Philosophical Palingenesis*) that catastrophic events may have culled certain animal populations, and thereby produced an amelioration within the remaining group via natural triage, Diderot maintains that such physical hardships, on the contrary, may have actually given rise to the deleterious genealogy of metaphysics among humans. The birth of superstition and (religious) morality from the constraints of the physical world is, as he sees it, a degenerative or regressive story, an unfortunate and unintended development.

Diderot refines this broad-brush understanding of the birth of 'civilised' human society in subsequent portions of the text. Much of this examination implicitly has to do with the impending changes that the Tahitians may undergo as a people over time. Two basic tenets of Enlightenment-era epistemology are in play in this discussion: the first is the basic notion that cognition depends on the complexity of one's ideas, which in turn can be explained by the type of stimuli received through the senses since birth. More pertinent, perhaps, is the widely accepted corollary that different stimuli produced not only different types of minds, but different types of *ethnic* minds.[15] This latter belief in the environmental production of specific types of ethnic beings overlaps not only with Buffon's climate theory – which explains morphology, pigmentation, behaviour and occasionally intelligence as functions of the environment – but also with the era's conjectural histories of the human species itself. The pithiest example of how this stage theory functions is found in Locke's *Two Treatises on Government* (1690), in which the philosopher declares that 'in the beginning, *all the world was America'*.[16] Echoes of this idea can be found in the *Supplément* where B puts forward a similar vision of the indigenous, claiming that the Tahitian 'touche à l'origine du monde et l'Européen touche à sa vieillesse' ('[the Tahitian] is close to the origin of the world, and the European to its old age').[17]

One of the big differences between standard conjectural histories (one thinks of Locke, Hobbes, Rousseau, etc.) and the narrative that plays out on Diderot's Tahiti, however, is that the two actors traditionally involved in the transition from nature to civilisation (*l'homme naturel* and *l'homme civilisé*) occupy the same temporal space. This seeming collapse of time and space allows Diderot to demonstrate how Europeans are likely to pollute savage life with many of the same spurious abstractions that are at the root of European civilisation. To a certain extent, these are the most Rousseauistic (and readily accessible) moments of the text. As the Old Man states unequivocally during his *adieux* (farewell speech), the introduction of unprocreative sexual desire, property and religion on the island will inexorably pull the Tahitians from their so-called childhood – their infancy – into a nasty adolescence where competition and the desire of the individual will win out over the logic of the collective; in this future, Tahitians are likely to have all the disadvantages of civilisation without any of its advantages. While such moments certainly recall the pessimism of the Second Discourse, what the Tahitian loses in this exchange differs markedly from what Rousseau's *sauvages* give up. Whereas the inhabitants of Rousseau's state of nature leave behind a virtually sexless innocence stemming (initially) from the savage's isolation, the Tahitian forfeits a seemingly perfect equilibrium between natural processes (sex), natural morality and natural civil codes. In short, the Tahitian, unlike the European, and unlike other more warlike *sauvages* evoked in the *Supplément*, was unique in that he had achieved a form of unaffected wisdom based on natural values, desires and collective needs – needs that, on this island paradise, did not involve the cannibalism or infanticide practised in other states of nature.

One of the clear epistemological assumptions in Diderot's overall understanding of the genealogy of culture is that physical variables determine both natural human behaviour and subsequent moral and civil codes. In the *Supplément*, the most obvious variables involved in this process are climate, geography, food supply and demographics. Hovering above these determinants is also the emerging logic of race. Before getting into this subject, I should emphasise that the notion of race, in 1772, is anything but a clearly defined concept for Diderot or his era; to the extent that we can define it at this time, 'race' is a syncretic set of often contradictory beliefs, a curious admixture of ideas that far from expresses the irresistible biological destiny of a particular group. Indeed, in works including the *Supplément* and the *Histoire des deux Indes*, Diderot uses the term 'race' as a vague, albeit deterministic, marker that is attached, above all, to a monogenetic worldview according to which all of humankind's *variétés* or races sprang from a single prototype (white) race and morphed over deep time into the world's different groups. In sum, 'race' does not denote an immutable category in Diderot's thought but functions as a fundamentally dynamic concept according to which white could shift to black, and black to white, in specific climates. And yet, like many of the other dynamic notions evoked in the *Supplément*, race is not only part of human history; it has an explanatory and diagnostic role within the text.

As is usually the case in Buffon's and Diderot's thought, race functions first and foremost as a degenerative concept. From the Tahitian's perspective, for example, the civilised men of Bougainville's crew are often portrayed as having lost their strength and vitality; like domesticated animals, they have degenerated from their earlier and more potent selves. This is put in the starkest of terms by the Old Man, who mocks Bougainville's crew as the physical inferiors of the Tahitians:

Regarde ces hommes [the Tahitians], vois comme ils sont droits, sains et robustes; regarde ces femmes, vois comme elles sont droites, saines, fraîches et belles. Prends cet arc, c'est le mien, appelle à ton aide un, deux, trois, quatre de tes camarades, et tâchez de le tendre. Je le tends moi seul.[18]

(Look at these men, see how upright, healthy and strong they are; look at these women, see how upright, lively, healthy and beautiful they are. Take up this bow of mine, call one, two, three, four of your countrymen for help and try to bend it. I can bend it myself, alone.)

Much like the domesticated pig, for example, humankind has lost much of its power and life force in its civilised state.[19]

This regressive history of the white man's physicality is but the first treatment of race in the *Supplément*. Later in the text, Diderot's characters also suggest that much of the Tahitian experience can be interpreted in light of lineage and bloodlines. Curiously enough, it is Orou (the very articulate Tahitian) who introduces the particular logic of race into the overall conception of humankind. This happens when Orou deconstructs the so-called 'Tahitian courtesy', the seemingly disinterested offering of fertile Tahitian women to European men. In explaining this supposedly generous act, Orou makes clear that the decision was, in reality, far from entirely charitable or hospitable: in fact, without knowing it, the Europeans were offering a 'tribute' of genetic material to the child economy of Tahiti:

Nous ne t'avons point demandé d'argent, nous ne nous sommes point jetés sur tes marchandises, nous avons méprisé tes denrées; mais nos femmes et nos filles sont venues exprimer le sang de tes veines. Quand tu t'éloigneras, tu nous auras laissé des enfants; ce tribut levé sur ta personne, sur ta propre substance, à ton avis n'en vaut-il pas bien un autre?[20]

(We have not asked any money of you, nor have we thrown ourselves on your wares, we, in fact, look down upon your goods; instead, our wives and daughters have come and taken the blood from your veins. When you go on your way, you will have left us with your children. In your opinion, is not this tribute, which is paid of your very person, of your very essence, as worthy as anything else?)

On its most basic level, this contribution to Tahitian society is simply quantitative. On an island where, as Orou reveals, the Tahitians do not have enough fertile men to engender sufficient numbers of farm hands and soldiers (or to replace Tahitians killed by epidemics), harvesting European sperm is simply a means of increasing the population.

Orou's sanguine understanding of *métissage* (the mixing of races) contrasts markedly with the Old Man's point of view. Whereas Orou sees a practical advantage in race mixing, the ancient patriarch sees the introduction of European blood as a syphilitic death knell. And yet, if the Old Man and Orou diverge regarding the merits and the dangers of engaging in cross-racial sex, they also agree that there are significant physical differences between the pureblood Tahitian and his or her European counterpart: as we have seen, both Orou and the Old Man envision the European as the Tahitian's physical inferior. This fundamental difference between Europeans and Tahitians is the point of departure for what we might call Orou's biopolitics. According to the Tahitian patriarch, the fact that mixed-race children will clearly be weaker than the Tahitians means that they may not be worth as much as regular pureblood Tahitians. As a consequence, these same children (conceived first as a European 'tribute') may ultimately be passed on to a 'voisin oppresseur' ('oppressive neighbouring state') to live out their lives as slaves. And yet this is not the only reason that Orou has sanctioned and encouraged *métissage*. By sending some of their women to sleep with what he deems to be the more intelligent Europeans – Orou describes them in the same breath as 'une race meilleure' ('a better race')[21] – the Tahitian patriarch also hopes to profit from a cognitive *métissage*. This tropical eugenics is one of the key elements in this text.

In many ways, this final explanation of the Tahitian courtesy recalls other passages in Diderot's works where the *philosophe* dreams of harnessing nature's power through the sex act: in particular, Orou's hybridisation project calls to mind the final discussion in *Le Rêve de d'Alembert* where Bordeu and Mlle de Lespinasse fantasise about the creation of a race of *chèvre-pieds* (goat-men) whose destiny would be to replace the African slaves toiling in European colonies.[22] And yet, there are significant differences between *Le Rêve*'s hybrids and the view of *métissage* that we find in the *Supplément*. After all, the racial mixing in the *Supplément* is not fantasy: it is, rather, a more realistic thought experiment based on the era's clearly articulated assumptions regarding comparative racial (or varietal) capabilities, namely:

(1) the white race (or variety) is more intelligent than the Tahitian race;
(2) this intelligence can be transferred through *métissage*;
(3) therefore, intelligence is a transferable trait that is passed down from generation to generation within a given group;[23]
(4) intelligence is therefore not simply the product of environment alone.

Although placed in the mouth of a Tahitian, the implications of this view of humankind's taxonomy are quite revealing. While Diderot actually refutes the basis for such beliefs elsewhere, in this part of the *Supplément* the *philosophe* hints at a heredity-based view of intelligence that stands in stark contrast to either environmentalist explanations of human varieties (Buffon) or a Lockean view of the mind at birth, as 'white paper'.[24] This, in and of itself, is significant. In this syncretic text, where genealogies and epistemologies overlap and seemingly contradict each other, the logic of race remains an unquestioned presence. In fact, it is perhaps the 'superior' and racialised European mind – a mind that produces both pernicious abstractions and superior technology – that is destined to bring about the destruction of the Tahitians' harmonious lifestyle.

MISCEGENATION AND THE COLONIES

Reading the *Supplément* through the prism of racial categories is, of course, both revealing and misleading. On the one hand, the very fact that Diderot brings up the question of (biological) human races within the Tahitian context – as does Bougainville himself – reflects the critical place that the question of human categories was beginning to occupy in the era's thought during the 1770s; this was, after all, a decade when Buffon's anti-classificatory understanding of humankind's varieties was losing ground to the increasingly trenchant views of race put forward by a wide range of thinkers including Le Cat, de Pauw, Valmont de Bomare and Raynal, not to mention Blumenbach.[25] It would be misleading, however, to assert unequivocally that Diderot was reducing the relationship between Tahitians and Europeans (or between the 'indigenous' and the 'European') to an implacable racial logic. This is amply demonstrated if one looks beyond the *Supplément* to Diderot's later musings on race and miscegenation in the third, 1780 edition of Raynal's *Histoire des deux Indes*.[26]

Diderot examines the 'natural history' of the human and the problem of cultural contact in Book IX of the *Histoire*. His continued interest in this matter comes to light while he answers a more general question, namely: 'les Européens ont-ils bien connu l'art de fonder des colonies?' ('did Europeans truly understand the art of founding colonies?'). To respond to this rhetorical query, Diderot does not look to history or economics, as both he and Raynal do elsewhere in the *Histoire*. Instead, he undertakes a discussion of the role of national character in the colonial context. Describing national dispositions as both fascinating and readily understood, Diderot maintains that the respective physiognomy of any culture is the product of both 'constant' causes (e.g. climate and geography) and 'variable' causes (presumably religion and culture). Echoing key ideas from the *Supplément*, Diderot argues that the goal of any society – true happiness – can only be realised if the 'principes spéculatifs [d'une nation] conspirent avec sa position physique' ('a nation's speculative principles work in harmony with its physical position').[27] When these physical and moral constants exist in perfect harmony, he adds, a given society 's'avance à grands pas vers la splendeur, l'opulence et le bonheur' ('advances rapidly towards splendour, opulence and happiness'); if these causes do not obtain, the nation will be 'insensée' ('insane' or 'irrational').[28]

Up to this point, Diderot's stance regarding a given population's national character corresponds to the foundational ideas contained in the *Supplément;* in short, these essential traits can be explained by both environment and the moral and/or religious tenets that arose out of those same physical constraints. In the subsequent portion of the *Histoire*, however, Diderot puts forward a new variable in this understanding of national types: the *durability* of these heretofore immutable characteristics in relation to an individual's distance from his home country. This new element, which seemingly overrides all other forces, leads Diderot to advance a curious hypothesis regarding the Europeans who now travel the globe. If, as he asserts, 'les métropoles des empires sont les foyers de l'esprit national' ('the large cities of the imperial powers are the home of their national spirit'),[29] then the farther that Europeans wander from these same home capitals, the more they must lose their national character and, on a certain level, their humanity:

Passé l'équator, l'homme n'est ni Anglais, ni Hollandais, ni Français, ni Portuguais. Il ne conserve de sa patrie que les principes et les préjugés qui autorisent ou excusent sa conduite. Rampant quand il est faible; violent quand il est fort; pressé d'acquérir, pressé de jouir, et capable de tous les forfaits qui le conduiront le plus rapidement à ses fins. C'est un tigre domestique qui rentre dans la forêt. La soif du sang le reprend. Tels se sont montrés tous les Européens, tous indistinctement, dans les contrées du Nouveau Monde, où ils ont porté une fureur commune, la soif de l'or.[30]

(Once past the equator, man is neither English, French nor Portuguese. From his home country he only retains the principles and the prejudices that authorise or excuse his conduct. He crawls when he is weak; he is violent when he is strong. Eager to acquire, eager to achieve pleasure, he is capable of anything that will lead him quickly to his objectives. He is a domestic tiger who enters the forest. The thirst for blood overtakes him. Such has been the case for all Europeans in the New World, a land to which they all took a common madness: the thirst for gold.)

Diderot's solution to the widespread moral degeneration of the European colonist is quite revealing. Reminiscent of Orou's miscegenation scheme, the *philosophe*'s suggestion is that Europe should practise a 'softer' colonisation by sending young men and women who would share their 'blood' with indigenous populations: 'N'aurait-il pas été plus humain, plus utile et moins dispendieux, de faire passer dans chacune de ces régions lointaines quelques centaines de jeunes hommes, quelques centaines de jeunes femmes ... Les hommes auraient épousé des femmes, les femmes auraient épousé les hommes de la contrée.'[31] ('Would it not have been more human, more useful and less costly to send a few hundred young men and a few hundred young women to these far-off regions? The men would have married the [indigenous] women, the women would have married the men of the country.')

While the exact goal of this human hybridisation is not clear – is it colonial profit, human happiness, or both? – what Diderot suggests here is that miscegenation could offer a new symbiosis that, unlike most situations in the colonial world, would ultimately be in the interest of the indigenous as well as the European. According to this schema, the payoff for the European would be a new generation of mixed-race children who are morally superior to the 'brutes' who generally pollute the world's colonies; the advantage for the indigenous, however, comes in the form of technology and knowledge: 'Dans cette liaison intime, l'habitant sauvage n'aurait pas tardé à comprendre que les arts et les connaissances qu'on lui portait étaient très favorables à l'amélioration de son sort.'[32] ('In this intimate liaison, the savage inhabitant [forest dweller] would quickly understand that the arts and knowledge that he was receiving were beneficial to his fortune.') As is the case in the *Supplément*, European stock, despite its degenerative potential, has a superior value that ultimately reshapes the sexual mores, bloodlines, and *arts et métiers* (arts and crafts) of the community, all for the common good.

Coming into relief against his more properly anti-colonial tirades elsewhere, the fantasy that the 'European tiger' could be happily tamed through miscegenation reflects Diderot's ability to envision the colonial riddle (and the human riddle) from a variety of perspectives. In many ways, the *philosophe*'s speculation on the different variables that determine the relationship between Europeans and the indigenous might be fruitfully linked to his dynamic understanding of the physical world in his more properly materialist texts. While Diderot's overall discussion of colonisation may not give rise to the playful folly of a work such as *Le Rêve de d'Alembert*, his ethnological thought experiments certainly reflect a desire to engage (as in *Le Rêve*) with the multiple and competing logics of a given question, in this case the clash between the natural and the supposedly civilised.

NOTES

1. Lynn Festa, 'Life, Liberty, and the Pursuit of Tahitian *Jouissance*', *Romance Quarterly*, 54.4 (2007), 303–25 (p. 303). Although the best-known portion of his book, Bougainville's account of Tahiti occupied only two chapters in his *Voyage autour du monde par la frégate du roi La Boudeuse et la flûte l'Étoile en 1766, 1767, 1768, et 1769* (Paris: chez Saillant et Nyon, 1771).
2. All three *contes* were written in 1772.
3. DPV, vol. XII, p. 643. All translations of passages from this text are my own.
4. I borrow the term 'tropicopolitan' from Srinivas Aravamudan, who has proposed a theory of the colonial subject who was at once 'fictive construct' and 'actual resident' and who was potentially an 'agent of resistance'. See Srinivas Aravamudan, *Tropicopolitans: Colonialism and Agency, 1688–1804* (Durham, NC and London: Duke University Press, 1999), p. 4. Along the same lines see Doris L. Garraway's subchapter 'Parodic Mimicry and Utopia in Diderot's *Supplément au Voyage de Bougainville*' in Lynn Festa and Daniel Carey (eds.), *The Postcolonial Enlightenment* (Oxford and New York: Oxford University Press, 2009).
5. See Anthony Padgen, 'The Savage Critic: Some European Images of the Primitive', *Yearbook of English Studies*, 13 (1983), 32–45.
6. Bougainville, *Voyage*, p. 219.
7. See Diane Fourny, 'Ethics and Otherness: An Exploration of Diderot's *Conte moral*', *Studies in Eighteenth-Century Culture*, 27 (1998), 283–306; see also Christine Fremont, 'Les Contes de la culpabilité', *Stanford French Review*, 12.2–3 (Fall 1998), 245–64.
8. See: Festa, 'Life, Liberty'; Andrzej Dziedzic, 'Liberté, propriété et sexualité dans le *Supplément au Voyage de Bougainville*', *Chimères: A Journal of French Literature*, 25.2 (Spring 2001), 45–53; Georges Van den Abbeele, 'Utopian Sexuality and its Discontents: Exoticism and Colonialism in the *Supplément au Voyage de Bougainville*', *L'Esprit créateur*, 24.1 (1984), 43–52.
9. The true title of Rousseau's Second Discourse or *Second Discours* is: *Discours sur l'origine et les fondements de l'inégalité parmi les hommes* (*Discourse on the Origin and Foundations of Inequality Among Men*). Both Discourses can be consulted in the following single-volume edition: Jean-Jacques Rousseau, *Discours sur*

l'origine et les fondements de l'inégalité parmi les hommes; Discours sur les Sciences et les arts, ed. Jacques Roger (Paris: Garnier Flammarion, 1971).

10. DPV, vol. XII, p. 582. Aspects of this idea are borrowed from Buffon's 1749 'Théorie de la terre', which was published in the *Histoire naturelle, générale et particulière avec la description du cabinet du roy,* 36 vols. (Paris: Imprimerie royale, 1749–88), vol. I, pp. 3–64.

11. DPV, vol. XII, p. 583.

12. Ibid., p. 583.

13. DPV, vol. XII, p. 583.

14. Ibid., p. 584. The word is derived from the Greek *palin* (again) + *genesis* (birth).

15. Locke, like his contemporaries, advances an ethnocentric view of how this intellectual potential might best come to fruition, proposing the English as an archetype of using Earth's gifts to the full, and the American Indian as an archetype of the failure to make use of the freedom, reason and resources bestowed upon man from birth. See John Locke, *Two Treatises of Government,* 2 vols. (Cambridge: Cambridge University Press, 1967), vol. II, pp. 40–1, 314–15.

16. Ibid., pp. 49, 319.

17. DPV, vol. XII, p. 587. One significant difference here, however, is the implicit decadence of the Europeans in Diderot's text.

18. Ibid., p. 592.

19. See Buffon's chapter on the degeneration of animals: *Histoire naturelle,* vol. IV, pp. 311–74.

20. DPV, vol. XII, p. 623.

21. Ibid., p. 624.

22. DPV, XVII, pp. 205–7.

23. This was the definition of race offered by Buffon. To be a member of a real race, he argued, a given human had to be able not only to procreate with another member of this same group, but to produce offspring whose traits would, generation after generation, mirror those of the genitor in question. See Buffon, *Histoire naturelle,* vol. IV, p. 565.

24. John Locke, *An Essay Concerning Human Understanding* (Oxford: Clarendon Press, 1975), p. 104. See also Diderot's writings on the African, slavery and race in the 1780 edition of Raynal's *Histoire philosophique et politique des établissemens et du commerce des Européens dans les deux Indes,* 8 vols. (Geneva: Jean-Leonard Pellet, 1781), vol. VI, pp. 1–178. A new edition of the *Histoire,* edited by Anthony Strugnell et al., is forthcoming (Ferney-Voltaire: Centre international d'étude du XVIIIe siècle). To understand Diderot's refutation of nascent race theory, see Ann Thomson's important work on the evolution of the 1770 to 1780 editions of the *Histoire* in her article 'Diderot, Roubaud, l'esclavage', *Recherches sur Diderot et sur l'Encyclopédie,* 35 (2003), 69–93.

25. This is an indicative, not an exhaustive, list. In the 1760s, Claude Nicolas Le Cat and Cornelius de Pauw were interested in racial anatomy; Jacques-Christophe Valmont de Bomare was a Buffonian naturalist who was,

nonetheless, heavily influenced by anatomical views of the human, particularly after 1770. Raynal put forward a polygenist view of race in the 1770 edition of the *Histoire*. And in the same decade (1775) Blumenbach became one of the first thinkers to put forward a conceptual taxonomy for the human races based, in large part, on the new racialised anatomy available after the 1750s.

26. These musings are contained in a preface to a section dedicated to the Portuguese in Brazil.
27. Raynal, *Histoire*, vol. v, p. 2.
28. Ibid. But Diderot qualifies this notion. In the first place he maintains that this national *esprit*, 'qui doit présider au conseil des peuples, et qui n'y préside pas toujours, ne règle presque jamais les actions des particuliers. Ils ont des intérêts qui les dominent, des passions qui les tourmentent ou les aveuglent' ('which should (but does not always) preside over councils that govern peoples, almost never controls the actions of individuals. The latter are governed by their own selfish interests; they are tormented or blinded by their passions') (*Histoire*, vol. v, p. 2).
29. Ibid.
30. Ibid.
31. Ibid., p. 3.
32. Ibid., pp. 3–4.

PART IV

Plays and dramatic theory

CHAPTER 12

Diderot and Olympe de Gouges convert the tyrant and transform the family

Carol L. Sherman

One of the changes wrought by the bourgeois drama made its denouement emanate from a shift in the powerful character's mind rather than from reducing his authority through humiliation or legal manoeuvres. (Molière's *Tartuffe*, for example, is confounded both by members of his household, who set a trap to reveal his lascivious intentions, and by the King, who orders him imprisoned for financial misdeeds.) In *Le Fils naturel* (*The Illegitimate Son*), Diderot's five-act *drame* of 1757, Dorval, on the other hand, comes to virtue by observing it in others and through his own sense of right action, and thus he gives up Rosalie, his friend's betrothed.[1] In *Le Père de famille* (*The Father/The Family Man*), another five-act *drame* (composed in 1758), the father moves toward clemency both under the influence of his children's wishes and against his brother-in-law's brutality, and so he permits his son's marriage to Sophie, who is thought to be socially inferior.[2] Thirty years after these plays and ten years after *Est-il bon? Est-il méchant?* (*Is He Good? Is He Bad?*), a four-act *drame* of circa 1781,[3] Olympe de Gouges wrote in the same genre and dramatised conversions to a kind of virtue that is even more broadly conceived. She often portrays tyrants caught in a family crisis the stakes of which are more complex than the traditional *mariage à faire* (marriage to be arranged). Although thwarted young lovers are present in each play, the couples at the centre of her plots are usually married, and their dilemmas concern the stability of a family that already exists. The despotism of her 'family men' expresses itself through adultery and through other threats to their wives and children. For these reasons, her remedies focus less on purely individual autonomy – the right to choose one's life-partner, for example – than on the integrity of the family and on protection of its weaker members. She manages some of her conversions by depicting women who help each other in bringing the powerful male to value the family as the centre of affectionate relationships rather than seeing it only as a legal structure that protects the master's wealth and his genes. In this she repeats and expands the experiments Diderot performed when he replaced raw authority with forms of affective collaboration among members of the families and friends he imagined.[4]

One interest of such observations arises from the structural parallels between family and state under the *ancien régime* and from the fact that theatre, the most social of literary genres, endlessly represents families. Changes in dramatic presentation reflect ways in which societal identities and subjective identities are entering into conflict before the French Revolution and, with de Gouges, during it. The gradual increase in the value attributed to the individual accompanied the period's invention of natural right, and these shifts gradually affected patriarchal and absolutist views of both the family and the state.

De Gouges's three-act play *La Nécessité du divorce* (*The Necessity of Divorce*), written before 1790, explores the paradox of legalising divorce in order to stabilise marriage.[5] If this freedom were granted, she suggests, it would increase the couple's dedication to each other since their attachment would be constantly chosen rather than imposed. Echoing Hardouin's enterprising spirit in *Est-il bon? Est-il méchant?*, the bachelor Rosambert tricks the husband in her play by helping to arrange scenes through which he is converted to admiration for the wife he has been deceiving. He falsely announces in the last scene that divorce has just been approved by the National Assembly. This brings consternation and then reconciliation as the husband, believing himself free, reasserts his devotion to his wife and declares his intention to remain faithfully hers. Both authors have created a trickster who decentralises power and manipulates events in favour of the meritorious people around him. Among the latter are the weak – women, children and thwarted young lovers.

Two of de Gouges's characters in *La Nécessité* have the names of two of Diderot's: Constance in *Le Fils naturel* and Germeuil in *Le Père de famille*. In her play, these two are the young lovers. Knowing of the master's adultery and suffering themselves from Rosambert's refusal to let them marry, they discuss the conditions under which love does or does not endure. Constance – well named by both playwrights – sees the adulterer as bringing disturbance to families (1.3), and she speaks of what she takes to be desirable: that women be true partners in the family, and that they also play a role in the polis, in part by educating the couple's children, the state's new citizens. Her viewpoint replicates the parallel between familial and societal structures that is found among the *philosophes* as well as in antiquity. The difference for de Gouges lies in seeing the woman as different but equal partner both in the couple and in the state, which equality depends on the fidelity of both husband and wife.[6]

The demand for parity makes her theses about power concern areas of experience different from those taken up in Diderot's earliest plays: the drama for the couple Dorval and Rosalie takes place largely within themselves as they condemn their own impulses (1.2; v.2). A further difference in the shape each playwright gives to the family is that mothers are absent from both *Le Fils* and *Le Père*. In the latter, however, the father's conversion to sentiment and to empathy might be thought to be coded as womanly, perhaps in response to the maternal absence and in reaction to the other powerful figure, the commander.[7] De Gouges later offers a contrast to the relative isolation of hero and heroine: in most of her plays, many women – mothers and other mature females – protect the deserving young and work at balancing power in the home.

Diderot's lengthy debates between characters – those between Dorval and Rosalie and between Dorval and Constance, for example – lay down the views that are in conflict and make clear the pedagogy of the play itself. De Gouges too stages discussions that emphasise contrasting opinions and the possibility of their changing, a basis for the conversions to right attitudes that she and the bourgeois drama in general cause to be performed. Among such characters one finds traces of Molière as well as of Diderot. The lascivious abbé Basilic is a Tartuffe-like character who preys upon the wife of his host and so displays the hypocrisy often described in the period's anticlerical thread. He shows how for de Gouges the church's rules are far from supporting companionate marriage. Rosambert, who long appears to be an Arnolphe-like bachelor, argues with the cleric Basilic by stating both the society-wide importance of successful marriage and his belief that forbidding divorce weakens the probability of stable marriages (1.6). Another debate occurs between the master of the house of Azinval and Rosambert; they contrast bachelorhood with the married state, and the bachelor paints a regretful picture of what he misses by being single (1.10). This further paradox – praise of good marriage by a bachelor who refuses to engage in it – is part of de Gouges's moving to accumulate a picture of its desirable conditions, if and when it is chosen rather than imposed.

Another piece in the mosaic of debates is provided by a scene between Madame d'Azinval and the bachelor friend: they speak for and against divorce, the wronged wife fears it, and Rosambert fears to marry as long as both church and state forbid it (11.2). In those debates, de Gouges builds the thesis that will make the central dramatic conversion possible – that of the husband to marital fidelity.

Two other elements that resemble Diderot's practice are the early presentation of familial disorder – including the keeping of secrets – and the

staging of the conversion itself with the use of *tableaux* inviting contemplation of the new familial harmony. The first scene of de Gouges's *Nécessité* is
comparable in function to the first scene of *Le Père*. In both, a character has
disturbed the family's tranquillity by staying out all night. In *Le Père* Saint-
Albin's absence has kept everyone up. He has violated family rules by
visiting a young woman he loves but who is unacceptable to his father.
Consistent with de Gouges's focus on the parental generation, in *La
Nécessité*, it is the husband, d'Azinval, who is missing; and it is the young
lovers Germeuil and Constance who express their worry and report on his
wife's sleepless night.

   In both plays the powerful character's conversion depends in part on the
revelation of secrets that have been kept by the weaker members of the
household. The common theatrical contrivances that hide people from each
other and that have some overhear others' conversations play their part in
changing him. Family secrets are then exposed, and redemption takes place.
In *Le Père* the children have hidden Sophie in their rooms. She is the woman
whom the son loves and who is forbidden the household. They have sent
the daughter's maid to listen in on the father's and commander's conversation, the one in which the father begins to value his relationship with his
children more highly than the rules of inheritance (v.9). At stake are two
possible marriages, the son's, Saint-Albin's, with Sophie, and the adopted
son's, Germeuil's, with the daughter of the house, Cécile. Both marriages
are opposed by the commander and by the father, who is, *le drame bourgeois
oblige*, about to give up his resistance and to prefer his children's happiness
and a friendly relationship with them.

   The secrets – hiding and eavesdropping – take a more complex form in de
Gouges's *Nécessité*. Mme d'Azinval's response to learning of her husband's
adultery is to write a note, signed with her maiden name, asking his young
target to pay her a visit. Rosambert arranges for the husband to overhear the
conversation between the two. In this way, he witnesses his wife's courage in
facing the woman she might have believed her enemy. His conversion is
not, however, immediate; his first fear is that his mistress will abandon him
since his wife has told her he is married. He gets a second shock in the next
scene: hoping to seduce her himself, the abbé tells her more about her
husband's duplicity. Now d'Azinval knows that three people are working
against his selfish behaviour. The two women have displayed mutual
courtesy and understanding. The abbé wants to undermine the master's
power by stealing his property – his wife.

   After exchanging reproaches with Mme d'Azinval, whose given name
Eugénie he will pronounce only in the last, tender scene, and after saying he

hopes soon to be free of her, he undergoes conversion to fidelity when, in the final gathering, Rosambert falsely announces that divorce is legal and that Madame d'Azinval asks nothing better than to be rid of him. The tyrant then throws himself at her feet, swearing to base their mutual future on love, esteem, repentance and virtue. This change casts a positive spell on the whole company: Rosambert, who fears marriage, allows Mme d'Azinval to persuade him to permit his nephew Germeuil to wed Constance. De Gouges's central interest is protecting the union that already exists, and when it is secured its magic spreads happiness to other characters, especially the young couple. By another conversion, that of Rosambert who has feared to take such a step himself and who also forbade his nephew to marry, they are to be united in marriage.

While both Diderot and de Gouges stage transformations that take place within the assembled group, as just described, both sometimes imagine such changes as occurring in the offender while he engages in solitary contemplation of his own destructive urges, which he finally suppresses. In *Le Fils*, Dorval's change of mind takes place in II.5 and II.7. In the second of these scenes, he is not entirely alone, for he is accompanied by a letter in which Rosalie condemns herself and renounces him. He reads parts of it aloud and dialogues with its assertions, blaming himself and exonerating the young woman. In her five-act play *Le Philosophe corrigé* (*The Philosopher Put Right*), written in 1787 and published in 1788, de Gouges stages her marquis–*philosophe*'s transformation by placing him on stage in the company of a baby in a cradle, a female child that legally belongs to him but whom he takes to be the fruit of his wife's liaison with another man.[8]

This expansion of the soliloquy to include a speechless infant augments the drama of tyranny: the autocrat, this family man, expresses the torture and hatred he feels before this sign of his wife's betrayal (v.3). The play's audience already knows that the child is in fact his own. In events that preceded the action represented, because she felt abandoned and wished to interest the marquis and renew their love, she sought and accepted the help of a female friend, disguised herself and allowed him to seduce her. In that moment, the so-called *philosophe* cuckolded himself while thinking he was involved in the most banal of seductions to which he attached neither importance nor guilt. Now, on stage, he draws his sword, tempted to kill the child who is in fact the product of an insignificant commerce with his own wife. Weapon in hand, he thinks aloud, as did Dorval, about the right course of action. His higher nature finally tames his violent wishes. Reason and virtue return to dominance.[9]

The unusual confrontation between jealous absolutism and helpless infant magnifies the disparity between power and weakness. Dorval's advantage over Rosalie and the temptation to keep her as his own pale when de Gouges reflects the violence of ambient political events and her own indignation by multiplying the instances of physical threat to weaker characters. Another comes at the hands of one she names the commander, perhaps echoing the similarly tyrannical character in Diderot's *Le Père*: the marquis's uncle encourages him to punish his wife and to rid his house of the child (II.4). He expresses unmitigated (and legal) tyranny over both. He persuades his nephew to imprison his wife, reminding him of his rights over her and of the danger to his reputation if he shows clemency (IV.I). In both Diderot and de Gouges, the commander exhibits extreme forms of patriarchal tyranny against which both playwrights invent the more compassionate character who is their hero, the person converted to virtue and whose newly found moderation they wish the spectators to admire.

In Diderot's *Est-il bon?* (as noted above, c. 1781) and in de Gouges's five-act play *Le Siècle des grands hommes ou Molière chez Ninon* (*The Century of Great Men or Molière at Ninon's House*), written at the end of 1787 and the beginning of 1788, the writers abandon some of the traits of bourgeois drama.[10] The liberties already taken by the genre with regard to classical norms appear to loosen their hold on form and focus even further. Unity of action is abandoned in both, and plots multiply. De Gouges employs two places; Diderot, one. Both retain the unity of time, but the single day is a very busy one. Writers replace fathers, and their despotism is benevolent. Both playwrights make of an author their central and powerful character; in each case, the character in question does much good throughout the play. The multiplication of actions performed occurs in worlds represented as inhabited mostly by people who often act as equals rather than by observing hierarchies of power. A further kind of re-shaping is noticeable in the fact that many characters are close to the same age. They are also remarkably dynamic, moving on and off stage many times. Diderot's cast forms a populous and wide-ranging final gathering. De Gouges arranges several such assemblies; they punctuate the unfolding of her various plots. In both plays, general assemblies take place perpetually instead of occurring only at the end, and the participants compose a large and varied family of friends. The more classical in-dwelling family is replaced by many visitors and guests. Its tight structure is exploded, and the very idea of family undergoes expansion. The bonds of friendship take a central place, and its loyalties motivate the players' actions.

It is as if the freedoms they exercised in writing their dramas finally led both authors to imagine worlds containing new kinds of people facing dilemmas other and more numerous than a marriage and parental opposition to it. Diderot gives the resistance to a mother this time, to Mme de Vertillac, and has his writer conspire to undermine her authority: Hardouin is a trickster who rights wrongs. The tyranny he combats arises from unjust laws and prejudices that do further harm to the weak. In de Gouges's play, a father is the despotic parent who forbids his daughter to marry a young man whose origins are unknown, and the playwright overturns his refusal by having the unmarried parents of this natural son named and found acceptable.

As many have observed about *Est-il bon?*, several meta-theatrical moments result from making an author into a powerful figure. Both playwrights require their onstage writers to invent entertainments in the course of the action, and these are performed as part of each play. Hardouin solves all the problems brought to him, including his own, which is being summoned to design an impromptu comedy for a birthday celebration. He solves his own dilemma – too many demands – by meta-composition: he simply hires another writer whom he puts to work on the project. Creative density increases when he expresses the wish that Molière would come back to life and help him (II.I and III.12) – Molière is the writer that de Gouges will shortly place at the centre of her play – and Diderot makes reference to his own *Père de famille* (IV.12) by having the substitute poet, M. de Surmont, reprimand the young lover, saying he is more violent than Diderot's Saint-Albin. The meta-theatrical extends to making artistic creation part of the plays' plots and to integrating reference, explicit and implied, to theatre's history.[11]

Another kind of confrontation with tyrannical forms of authority emanates from the presence and multiplicity of new kinds of characters, among whom are the authorial ones just described, and from the activity of creative ingenuity, both moral and artistic, that creates dynamism. Almost every character is an artist of some kind. Both playwrights say and show that the houses they represent are filled with writers: Diderot's Mme de Chepy, who is planning the celebration, has the choice of authors on whom she might call: 'elle en a cinq ou six autour d'elle' (I.5). ('She has five or six of them around.') Besides putting on stage Molière, Scarron, Desyveteaux, poets, and the painter Mignard, de Gouges too extends the possibility of artistic production to all the characters. Ninon asks Molière to invent 'un agréable impromptu' ('a pleasant impromptu') (III.12), and she orders verses from other friends as well (III.14). All are urged to prepare something in honour of

Queen Christina of Sweden (III.12). Both playwrights make artistic creation
an important source of each play's action; in each case it is a question of
creating a celebration for the woman to be honoured (Mme de Malves in
the case of Diderot; Christina for de Gouges). A lesson is implied in both:
less rigid social structures favour artistic creativity, joyful spectacles and
hence national pride. Scarron takes poetic inspiration from helping to
resolve a disagreement between two powerful men and says, 'Cette dispute
est favorable à mes vers; je vais à son arrivée [Ninon's] lui en faire l'hom-
mage' (III.4). ('This dispute is favourable to my poetry; as soon as she comes
back, I shall pay tribute to her with some.') De Gouges shows even the artist
Mignard as inventing a new painting when he hears a story that has just
been told to him about another character (IV.6). De Gouges has Molière
design and execute various projects in Ninon's house. They include ballets,
choruses and verses in honour of the queen who has asked to visit. She is the
centre of attention, and the author takes the opportunity to make of her a
lesson for absolute rulers: the conversation she conducts with her hostess
reveals that she has given up even the possibility of tyranny. A good
autocrat, she resigned her office.[12]

Besides giving efficacy to the character of the writer, these plays either
represent or talk much about very young children, who were rarely present
in classical comedy.[13] Familial imaginings are expanding. De Gouges's
putting an infant on stage in *Le Philosophe corrigé* was surprising; having it
threatened with death by its father was dramatic. In *Molière chez Ninon*, the
latter speaks in the plural of the children to whom she has given birth and
whom she has subsequently lost, either to death or by having them taken
from her, unwed as she was (V.4). In this way the playwright prepares for her
recognising a lost son when he appears. He comes seeking to marry a young
woman whom Ninon has been protecting from the harm she has risked by
leaving her tyrannical father's house. The rehabilitation of this *fils naturel*, a
term pronounced twice in the scene (V.22), can take place in part because of
his mother's high standing among her friends and her obvious devotion to
her new-found child.

It is one of de Gouges's purposes to preserve and strengthen the core
family where it exists and to remove the stigma from unacknowledged
children by not allowing them to be thrown away. She wants to require
each father to be responsible for his offspring, most especially those born of
adultery, and she would have the system of justice believe the mother when
she names the father of her child.[14] She composes a scene (III.4) in which
two men argue over the paternity of an unnamed child, not in order to avoid
it, but because each wants to claim him. One of their reasons is their esteem

for Ninon, whom they know to be the mother. De Gouges offers this example that goes counter to the usual repudiation of illegitimate offspring. The law forbids a child to seek its father, and the playwright makes mention of this by stating its opposite: nothing stops fathers from looking for their children. She has one of them say so: 'Il n'y a point de rang ni d'état qui empêche un père de réclamer son enfant, et c'est en quoi je loue M. le président [his competitor in the dispute over paternity]' (III.4).[15] ('There is no rank or profession that stops a father from laying claim to his child, and it is for that reason that I praise the president.') Much earlier Diderot had imagined such a reversal: neither Dorval nor Rosalie has the right to search for their father, but throughout the first acts, he is coming toward them.

Real and imagined families populate the stage and the characters' references – another difference with the classical and one that shows a change in values. The exercise of the tyrant's will alone no longer occupies minds or hearts on the stage. Both *Est-il bon?* and *Molière chez Ninon* pay attention to offspring. In comic mode, Diderot's representation of very young children consists of Binbin, whose widowed mother seeks Hardouin's help, and of a crowd of young participants in the spectacle prepared for Mme de Malves. In a more sombre mode, de Gouges has Ninon evoke in the plural her own lost children before she finds one of them, learns his name and helps him obtain the wife he desires. One of Hardouin's tricks is to pretend to be the father of a child in need. The presence of small humans gives weight to the observation that the represented population has changed. In these plays, written in the last quarter of the century, the rigid and nuclear family, ruled by an autocratic father, seems to dissolve in favour of community and friendship. The little worlds implied in both plays include children, both present on stage and mentioned in their absence, to whom attention is paid and who are welcomed into the company of adults.

They and friendship in general create a changed emphasis and so a shift in worldview: Diderot's cast of twelve named characters calls four of them friend (*ami(e)*) of someone else and designates five others according to their profession or civil status: *veuve d'un capitaine*; *avocat*; *premier commis*; *poète*; *femme de chambre* ('captain's widow'; 'barrister'; 'first assistant'; 'poet'; 'maid'). Only the very youngest, Binbin, is named according to his biological relation to another character ('enfant de Mme Bertrand'). Mlle de Vertillac, the second-youngest person, who also has a mother in the cast, receives no label whatsoever in the list. Similarly, de Gouges's twenty-four characters include six designated as friend (*ami(e)*) of another, three as suitor (*amant*), past, present and/or future, of Ninon. Only the young lovers are identified as belonging to parents, and all the others are named according to their civil status or their position in Ninon's house.

Diderot begins and ends his play by making references to copulation and reproduction. In the very first scene, for fear that he might father a new child with his wife, Mme de Chepy forbids one of her servants to go home during the coming week. In the antepenultimate scene, when the children are ready to come on stage carrying their bouquets, the poet whom Hardouin has hired to do his job of writing an entertainment teases Mlle Beaulieu, who is herding the children, by suggesting that all of them are hers, each from a different father (IV.16). Whether one finds this amusing or not, the tone is that of an ancient comic thread. Like de Gouges's having two men vie for the paternity of an unnamed child, Diderot too declares that each of these children has a father and that he is known. In other words, the 'petit troupeau d'enfants' ('little flock of children') is made up of individuals recognised by their community (IV.16).

Friendship, not tyranny, motivates the action of both these later plays. It is named, described and praised by the characters; they count on it. Hardouin plays tricks on the stubborn and unjust in order to give advantage to his friends; he enjoys manipulating them all, and nothing is tragic. Ninon too is shown as a devoted friend who pays very close attention to her acquaintances' dilemmas. Her house is described as open, welcoming and the site of brilliant goings-on (I.17), which forms another contrast with the classical hierarchical household in which entrances and exits are strictly controlled. Le Grand Condé says, 'Ce n'est que dans cette maison que je vois régner la pure et simple amitié' (III.6). ('It is in this house alone that I see pure and simple friendship reign.') During the *grand spectacle* Mme Scarron sits beside Queen Christina's throne, and she is dressed as the goddess of Friendship. Music comes from a *chœur de l'amitié* ('friendship choir') (IV.17). Furthermore, many times the actors explicitly contrast passion and friendship in favour of the latter, which is seen as life-sustaining and is declared to be longer lasting than amorous attachment (I.17 and II.8). Cooperation, understanding and loyalty among equals here replace both naked authority and passion's tyranny. The equality presented is of an affective kind – emotion that joins people to each other and to beneficial outcomes. Its absolute link to social class appears to be weakened.

Schemes for empowering the disadvantaged come and go on stage and in discourse. For some, a society's ability to protect its weakest members is the measure of its worth. Diderot and de Gouges invent and expand a genre that portrays change in private habits of absolutism. They depict conversion of the powerful to understanding of others and to giving up tyrannical impulses. Fixed societal and familial identities conflict with new ideas of individual agency. The serious genre reflects the potential for social change. It is true that loosened political structures ended in the Terror and that Napoleon's civil code restored hierarchy and privilege. The previous years' theatre nonetheless portrayed friendship and cooperation as being of higher value than titles alone. For the good of all their members, those qualities united the little imagined communities.

Between 1751 and 1791 the new genre became a place in which de Gouges and Diderot appear to conduct private experiments for public edification. In the plays they wrote in the 80s – *Est-il bon?* and *Molière chez Ninon* – tyranny has almost disappeared. The misuse of absolute power is no longer the central conflict, and both households succeed in rectifying injustices by using friendships and sibling-like solidarities, even recuperating previously discounted children. If the nation's house too had evolved, constitutional monarchy, for instance, might have shared power and might have similarly distributed justice and benevolence; but as everyone knows, the revolutionary spectacle did not long remain a bourgeois drama.

NOTES

1. DPV, vol. x, pp. 1–162. All further references will be to this edition. In what follows, I will not be considering this play's relation to the *Entretiens sur Le Fils naturel*. I am reading *Le Fils naturel* (the play labelled *comédie* in 1757) as belonging to the *genre sérieux*. Several relevant discussions appear in Nicholas Cronk (ed.), *Études sur 'Le Fils naturel' et les 'Entretiens sur Le Fils naturel'* (Oxford: Voltaire Foundation, 2000). Particularly useful is the contribution by Marian Hobson, who identifies private performances as well as recalling what is accepted as the first public representation in 1771 at the Comédie Française (pp. 138–49).
2. Denis Diderot, *Le Père de famille*, ed. Jacques Chouillet and Anne-Marie Chouillet, DPV, vol. x, pp. 163–322. All further references will be to this edition. As editor, Anne-Marie Chouillet notes that during the play's iterations in 1770, 1771 and 1772, the label *comédie* was changed to *drame* (p. 176).
3. Denis Diderot, *Est-il bon? Est-il méchant?*, ed. Jack Undank, DPV, vol. xxiii, pp. 381–479. All further references will be to this edition.
4. De Gouges was born in Montauban in 1748 and moved to Paris in 1767 or 1768. She had ample opportunity to read *Le Fils naturel* or to see it in Paris or in the provinces (for instance in Vienne, during 1771), and to read or see *Le Père de famille* performed in private theatres enumerated by Anne-Marie Chouillet; see DPV, vol. x, p. 165. For her life, work and a much-needed revision of the ways in which she has been discounted, see Olivier Blanc, *Marie-Olympe de Gouges, une humaniste à la fin du xviiie siècle* (Cahors: René Viénet, 2003).

5. References to *La Nécessité du divorce* are based on Olympe de Gouges, *Œuvres complètes*, ed. Félix Castan (Montauban: Cocagne, 1993–), vol. 1, pp. 225–43.

6. Her demand is for equal rights and agency, but ignoring difference is never its condition. Claudia Moscovici efficiently treats the seeming paradox in *From Sex Objects to Sexual Subjects* (New York and London: Routledge, 1996), p. 80.

7. For reading the father as adopting maternal attributes and as using friendship for his model, see Carol L. Sherman, *The Family Crucible in Eighteenth-Century Literature* (Aldershot: Ashgate, 2005), pp. 27–32.

8. References to *Le Philosophe corrigé* are based on de Gouges, *Œuvres complètes*, vol. 1, pp. 105–42.

9. De Gouges reverses the gender roles of two myths, each of which gave its name to a work by Molière. In hers, the wife recalls Jupiter's deception by visiting her husband while she is disguised. Besides being the victim of that role, he resembles Psyche by receiving a lover he cannot see; he has no lamp. Another sign of Molière's presence emerges if one observes that de Gouges's plot is an *école des maris* ('school for husbands').

10. References to *Le Siècle des grands hommes ou Molière chez Ninon* are based on de Gouges, *Œuvres complètes*, vol. 1, pp. 143–91.

11. For a profound and ingenious reading of fatherhood in Diderot's three main plays and of them as intertexts of each other, see Lars O. Erickson, 'Reflection and Projection: Diderot's Theatrical Father' (unpublished master's thesis, University of North Carolina, Chapel Hill, 1997).

12. Like other *philosophes* before her, instead of attacking rulers' errors directly, de Gouges depicts them undergoing conversion from absolutism to wisdom and tolerance. She composed this play in 1787–8, when Louis XVI might still have modified his governance. She never wished the monarchy to be abolished, only that it be constitutional. This moderate view, which she fervently promulgated, led to her death under the Terror in September 1793.

13. A rare earlier example is the child Molière put on stage in 1673, in *Le Malade imaginaire* (*The Imaginary Invalid*). Louison is Argan's little daughter, sister of Angélique. She appears in one long scene (II.II); her father threatens her with violence in order to learn from her what has taken place between Angélique and her suitor. I am grateful to Professor F. W. Vogler for remembering this.

14. She says so clearly in the widely anthologised *Déclaration des droits de la femme et de la citoyenne* (*Declaration of the Rights of Woman and of the Female Citizen*) of September 1791. See de Gouges, *Écrits politiques 1788–1791* (Paris: Côté-femmes, 1993), pp. 204–15.

15. Président is the title of a member of the *parlement*, a court of law.

CHAPTER 13

Diderot and Destouches: Le Philosophe marié in Est-il bon? Est-il méchant?

Derek Connon

To say that Diderot's most famous contribution to the theatre is his invention of the *drame*, which combines sentimentalism and didacticism, is simply to repeat a commonplace. Yet one can argue that the sentimental strain was already well established in French theatre when he began his dramatic experiments in the 1750s, and that the recognition of the didactic possibilities of theatre went back much further. Nevertheless, it remains Diderot who gets the credit or, perhaps more often in the eyes of posterity, the blame for the combination of the two which would be such a dominant force in French theatre for the rest of the century. There was bound to be a reaction, and it came from within as well as from without: that staunch disciple of Diderot's dramatic theory Beaumarchais sought to reintroduce 'l'ancienne et franche gaîté' ('the uninhibited gaiety of the old days') into comedy in *Le Barbier de Séville* (*The Barber of Seville*) in 1773,[1] even if he did revert to his earlier ways in *La Mère coupable* (*The Guilty Mother*); and Sedaine followed his creation of one of the finest of the *drames*, *Le Philosophe sans le savoir* (*The Philosopher Who Doesn't Know It*) (1765), with the much more conventional comedy *La Gageure imprévue* (*The Unexpected Wager*) (1768).

A striking aspect of the burst of activity in which Diderot inaugurated the *drame* is its brevity: *Le Fils naturel* (*The Natural Son*), including the satellite texts that give it its fictional context and set out the dramatic theory behind it, dates from 1757, and *Le Père de famille* (*The Father*), together with *De la poésie dramatique* (*On Dramatic Poetry*), from 1758. Nothing that followed would be either as significant or as famous, although the impetus did continue for at least a couple of years: 1760 saw the translation of Edward Moore's domestic tragedy *The Gamester*, and in 1759, as Diderot tells Grimm,[2] he completed four dramatic plans. If the most important of these, the historical domestic tragedy *Le Shérif* (*The Sheriff*), and two others, *Madame de Linan* and *L'Infortunée* (*The Unfortunate Woman*), very obviously chime in with Diderot's current theatrical preoccupations,

Le Train du monde (*The Way of the World*) is a slightly risqué, but otherwise quite conventional, mix of *comédie de mœurs* (comedy of manners) and *comédie d'intrigue* (comedy of plot) so complex that it is no surprise it never made it past the planning stage.[3]

Diderot would, of course, go on to complete two more plays, neither as famous as their predecessors, but which mark a much more obvious bifurcation of activity between the *drame* and the more conventional comedy that marked a reaction against it. The first, the disastrously sentimental 'petite tragédie' ('little tragedy'), *Les Pères malheureux* (*The Unhappy Fathers*), in reality a *drame* with a happy ending,[4] apparently belongs to the early 1770s: an adaptation of Salomon Gessner's *Erast*, it represents to a certain extent a response to Marmontel's adaptation of the same work, *Sylvain* (1770). Diderot's interest in the German author would result in the publication of his own *Les Deux Amis de Bourbonne* (*The Two Friends from Bourbonne*) and *Entretien d'un père avec ses enfants* (*Conversation of a Father with his Children*) alongside works by Gessner in German in 1772, and in French in 1773. Nevertheless, at about the same time, he was also preoccupied by the pure comedy of the *Plan d'un divertissement domestique* (*Plan for a Domestic Entertainment*). It is impossible to date this text precisely, but its composition can be situated between January 1766, when Diderot wrote the last of three letters which recount to Sophie Volland the ongoing real-life incident which provides the main focus of the plot of the plan,[5] and November 1775, when Grimm included it in the *Correspondance littéraire* (*Literary Correspondence*).[6]

Whilst Diderot's interest in the *drame* diverted him from comedy in the late 1750s, this time the opposite is the case; for even if the *drame* is a completed play while the comedy is a mere plan, it is in the comedy that Diderot showed the greater confidence and invested further work. The brief preface to *Les Pères malheureux* already shows limited confidence, suggesting that it is unsuited to the public stage: 'Si l'on jouait ce drame en famille, je ne doute point que l'intérêt des auditeurs pour les personnages qui seraient en scène ne fût très vif. Peut-être n'en serait-il pas de même sur un théâtre public?'[7] ('If this *drame* were to be performed at home, I don't doubt that the audience would be keenly interested by the characters on stage. Perhaps it wouldn't be the same in the public theatre?') In the event, we have no indication that even a private performance ever took place.

Grimm's introduction to the plan in the *Correspondance littéraire* tells us, on the other hand, that, even in its fragmentary state, it was actually performed: 'Ce canevas a été rempli avec beaucoup de succès dans une troupe de société' ('This plan was fleshed out with great success by an amateur troupe'),[8] and

Diderot would go on to rework it into complete plays not once, but twice. The first version, *La Pièce et le prologue* (*The Play and the Prologue*), retains from the plan only the central autobiographical incident, weaving into it two other plots also with an autobiographical basis to form a complex one-act structure. The second, *Est-il bon? Est-il méchant?* (*Is He Good, or Is He Wicked?*), retains the material of *La Pièce et le prologue* with only very minor revisions, but adds two more plots, this time apparently fictional, to create an even more complex four-act structure.[9] We know that *La Pièce et le prologue*, designed for the name day of Diderot's friend Mme de Maux, received a performance *en société* (i.e. a private performance) with Diderot in the central role of Hardouin,[10] and that work on *Est-il bon?* continued until the year of his death – an allusion to Beaunoir's *Jérôme Pointu* must post-date the first performance of that play in June 1781, and Diderot corrected a transcription by his favourite copyist Girbal in February 1784.[11] Whilst in the case of *Les Pères malheureux* the retreat from the public theatre to domestic performance (which apparently never occurred) seems to represent a lack of confidence in the play, similar reservations expressed in the dedications to *La Pièce et le prologue* and *Est-il bon?*[12] perhaps have different implications. For it seems unlikely that Diderot would have devoted so much time to the elaboration and revision of works in which he had little confidence, and there are other reasons for not offering these plays to the public theatre. First, the domestic nature of the project is obvious both from the subject-matter in general and the incorporation into the denouement of elements of the name-day celebration. Second, the autobiographical nature of so much of the material and the clear references to other real individuals might not have been deemed suitable for public consumption, and not only might the multiple plot lines have seemed outlandish to audiences used to plays observing the unity of action, but the closing sequence plays fast and loose with both the unity of time and chronology generally in a way that risks being incomprehensible in the public theatre.[13]

However, perhaps Diderot also wished to avoid a public avowal of his disillusion with the very genre that he created, for the significant energy he devoted to the elaboration of the three versions of this work seems not only to show him yielding to the lure of the comic, but actually rejecting the *drame*: near the beginning of both complete versions, Hardouin, identified by the numerous autobiographical links as Diderot's alter ego, refers to 'un drame détestable, comme ils sont tous' ('a dreadful *drame*, just like they all are').[14] No other remark is quite as explicitly damning as this, but *Est-il bon?* adds two more which also apparently question the value of the genre. Coaching de Crancy in his role in the play he has written, the author de Surmont says: 'Souvenez-vous M[r] que vous êtes d'une violence dont le

St Albin du Père de famille n'approche pas' ('Remember, Monsieur, that you are passionate in a way that Saint-Albin from *The Father* doesn't come close to'), to which he receives the reply: 'Cela ne me coûtera rien' ('That's easy').[15] And when Hardouin, discussing his artistic reputation, complains of the lack of taste that has the public flocking to *Jérôme Pointu*, it is not on his own or anyone else's contributions to the *genre sérieux* (serious genre) that he feels their time would be better spent, but on *Le Tartuffe* and *Le Misanthrope* (*The Misanthrope*).[16]

There is a similar neglect of the *drame* in favour of the purely comic in the passage on which the rest of this essay will focus. In an exchange common to both plays, Mme de Chepy, seeking to cast the entertainment she is preparing for Mme de Malves, asks her *femme de chambre* (maid) Mlle Beaulieu which plays she has acted in, and then instructs her to recite a speech from one of them, namely Destouches's comedy *Le Philosophe marié* (*The Married Philosopher*):

MADE DE CHEPY: Et vous, dans quelle pièce avez-vous joué?

MADLLE BEAULIEU: Dans *Le Bourgeois Gentilhomme, La Pupille, Le Philosophe sans le savoir, Cénie, Le Philosophe marié.*

MADE DE CHEPY: Et dans celle-ci, que faisiez-vous?

MADLLE BEAULIEU: Finette.

MADE DE CHEPY: Vous rappelleriez-vous un endroit . . . un certain endroit où Finette fait l'apologie des femmes.

MADLLE BEAULIEU: Je le crois.

MADE DE CHEPY: Récitez-le.

MADLLE BEAULIEU:

Soit, mais telles que nous sommes,
Avec tous nos défauts, nous gouvernons les hommes,
Même les plus huppés; et nous sommes l'écueil
Où viennent échouer la sagesse et l'orgueil.
Vous ne nous opposez que d'impuissantes armes.
Vous avez la raison, et nous avons les charmes.
Le brusque philosophe, en ses sombres humeurs,
Vainement contre nous élève ses clameurs;
Ni son air renfrogné, ni ses cris, ni ses rides,
Ne peuvent le sauver de nos yeux homicides.
Comptant sur sa science et ses réflexions
Il se croit à l'abri de nos séductions;
Une belle paraît, lui sourit et l'agace?
Crac. Au premier assaut, elle emporte la place.

MADE DE CHEPY: Mais pas mal. Point du tout mal.[17]

(MME DE CHEPY: What play have you acted in?
MLLE BEAULIEU: In *The Bourgeois Gentleman, The Ward, The Philosopher Who Doesn't Know It, Cénie, The Married Philosopher.*
MME DE CHEPY: What part did you play in that one?
MLLE BEAULIEU: Finette.
MME DE CHEPY: Do you perhaps remember a part ... a certain part where Finette speaks out on behalf of women?
MLLE BEAULIEU: I think so.
MME DE CHEPY: Recite it.
MLLE BEAULIEU:

Be that as it may, just as we are, With all our faults, we rule over men,
Even the proudest; and we are the rock
On which their wisdom and pride are broken.
The arms you wield against us are powerless.
You have reason, we have charm.
The brusque philosopher, with his sombre disposition,
Protests against us in vain;
Neither his sullen appearance, his cries, nor his wrinkles,
Can save him from our man-killing eyes.
Counting on his knowledge and his thoughts
He believes himself immune to our seductive powers;
A beautiful woman appears, smiles at him and teases him?
Bang. At the first attack, she is victorious.

MME DE CHEPY: Not bad. Not at all bad.)

No further comment is made on the extract, yet it seems odd for one author to quote another at length in this way for no reason; after all, the dramatic point could have been made simply by asking Mlle Beaulieu if she has ever acted, without the need for either the list of her repertoire or the recital of an audition piece.

Let us begin with the list of plays in which Mlle Beaulieu has acted. Diderot's admiration for Molière as the greatest French comic dramatist is clear – we have already seen evidence in his horror at the lack of taste of audiences who go to *Jérôme Pointu* rather than *Le Tartuffe* or *Le Misanthrope*. Consequently, it is surprising that he should choose to mention here not one of those masterpieces, but another play by Molière, and one that he specifically criticises in the *Entretiens* (*Conversations on 'The Natural Son'*): 'Pour un homme de goût, il y a la même absurdité dans Castor élevé au rang des dieux, et dans le Bourgeois gentilhomme fait Mamamouchi. Le genre comique et le genre tragique sont les bornes réelles de la composition dramatique ... Il est impossible au genre comique d'appeler à son aide le burlesque, sans se dégrader.'[18] ('For a man of taste, it is just as absurd to see Castor made into a god, as it is to see the Bourgeois Gentleman made Mamamouchi. Comedy and tragedy are the true limits of dramatic composition . . . It is impossible for comedy to call on the burlesque to help it along without degrading itself.')

He even suggests that *Le Bourgeois* is successful simply because of who it is by.[19] So, whilst Diderot admires Molière in general, he certainly does not admire *Le Bourgeois Gentilhomme*, a fact that may be significant in our interpretation of the function of this list.

La Pupille (*The Ward*) (1734), Fagan's best-known play, is an early example of the strain of sentimentality in comedy that would lead to the *drame*. It owes a clear debt to Molière, in that Fagan has the ward of his title reject a younger suitor to marry her older guardian. The resemblance to the subsidiary plot of Molière's comedy *L'École des maris* (*The School for Husbands*) is underlined by the fact that Fagan's guardian and the older, more sympathetic brother of Molière's play (who, unlike the central character Sganarelle, is also successful in marrying his ward) both have the conventional name Ariste. Ariste is also the name of the central character of Destouches's comedy, and a link with that play is found in the assumption that a *philosophe* is immune to feminine charms, something that is disproved in *La Pupille* and *Le Philosophe marié* equally.

Le Philosophe sans le savoir, the one play in this list to figure only in *Est-il bon? Est-il méchant?*, is the *drame* that Diderot, and with him posterity, came to regard as the masterpiece of the genre – although for posterity certainly there is an element of damning with faint praise in that judgement. First performed in 1765 and published the following year, it certainly could have been mentioned by Mlle Beaulieu in *La Pièce et le prologue*. So why was it not? After all, as a famous passage of the *Paradoxe sur le comédien* (*Paradox on the Actor*) shows, Diderot was enthusiastic about it from the outset, apparently seeing it as the work that vindicated his creation of the *drame*.[20] Perhaps he felt that at that stage it had not been in the repertoire for long enough to be popular with amateurs. Perhaps he did not want to associate it with Hardouin's generalisation that all *drames* are 'détestables'. So, in adding it later, was his intention to give the credit due to the honourable exception to that generalisation, or are the implications more negative?

Could there also be some sense of giving credit where it is due in the next reference, which is to Françoise de Graffigny's *Cénie*? This comedy of 1750 had a huge success, making it one of the most important works in the sentimental vein that was so influential in the creation of the *drame*. Indeed, although it perhaps lacks the didacticism that would be part of Diderot's new genre, it is in many respects a *drame avant la lettre* (*drame* before its time) – and its success was a relatively recent phenomenon at the time of the composition of *Le Fils naturel*. It is, therefore, surprising that neither it nor its author receives the scantest mention in the dramatic theory of the 1750s – or perhaps not: as I have suggested elsewhere, for Diderot to acknowledge a debt to Mme de Graffigny or other similar precursors of his work like Nivelle de La Chaussée would have served to reduce the impact of his own innovation.[21] Does this mention here mark a late decision to redress the balance? Either way, Mme de Chepy dismisses all four of these works in favour of the last on Mlle Beaulieu's list, Destouches's *Le Philosophe marié* of 1727, a clear rejection of both the burlesque and the sentimental in favour of the conventionally comic. For Destouches's work predates the fashion for sentimentality; and although his addition of a clear moral to his comedies resulted in their designation as *comédies morales* (moral comedies), the potential link with the didactic aims of the *drame* is not something that is strongly felt in this particular work.

Like so many playwrights of the eighteenth century, Destouches goes unmentioned in Diderot's dramatic theory, although the fact that the *drame* owes him no obvious debt makes him a less striking omission than Mme de Graffigny or Nivelle de La Chaussée. Neither is his only mention in the surviving correspondence at all flattering: 'Qu'ils supportent après cela, s'ils le peuvent, Destouches et Lachaussée' ('Let them put up with Destouches and La Chaussée after that, if they can'),[22] although admittedly this was written in the full flush of the success of the revival of *Le Père de famille* in 1769 (which caused Diderot in the same letter to declare his superiority even to his admired Sedaine). And yet, unless they are all coincidences – the names of classical comedy are after all highly conventional and, for the most part, often repeated – certain echoes in his own works suggest that *Le Philosophe marié* was a text for which Diderot had a long-standing affection, as we are about to see.

It is least surprising that we should find a reminiscence of Destouches's text in the very plays in which Diderot quotes it: the lackey in *Le Philosophe marié* is anonymous in both the *dramatis personae* and the dialogue, but is revealed in the character headings of some (but not all) editions to share the name of the first of the pair of lackeys, Picard and Flamand, who feature in the opening scenes of *La Pièce et le prologue* and *Est-il bon? Est-il méchant?* The name 'Ariste', as used by Diderot, may also be an allusion to Destouches. Ariste derives from 'best' in Greek, and we have already seen evidence of the tradition of giving it to wise men or philosophers. Diderot adopts it for the character who is most obviously his own alter ego in *La Promenade du sceptique* (*The Walk of the Sceptic*), then returns to it for a similar character introduced in the final pages of *De la poésie dramatique*.

'Mon ami, vous connaissez Ariste ... Il s'était particulièrement livré à l'étude de la philosophie. On l'avait surnommé le Philosophe.'²³ ('My friend, you know Ariste. He had given himself over particularly to the study of philosophy. He had been nicknamed the Philosopher.')

The combination of the name and the appellation *philosophe* provides a striking link with Destouches. Even more striking is the fact that Diderot should have borrowed the less common name of the father of Destouches's central character, with only a variation of spelling, for the father of another of his alter egos: the father in Destouches's play is called Lisimon, whilst the father of Dorval in *Le Fils naturel* is, of course, Lysimond. And that is not all: Damon, the name of the friend of Destouches's Ariste, is used for one of the titular friends in Diderot's undated theatrical plan *Les Deux Amis* (*The Two Friends*).

In the light of these correspondences, it seems unlikely to be purely coincidental that the same line from Racine is alluded to in both *Le Philosophe marié* and *Le Père de famille*. Ariste's monologue that opens Act IV of Destouches's play ends with the line 'Je ne sais où je vais. Je ne sais où je suis.' ('I don't know where I'm going. I don't know where I am.') The substitution of a full stop for the central comma apart, this is a precise quotation of the fourth line of Thésée's speech that opens the equivalent act of *Phèdre* (*Phaedra*). And when Sophie enters in III.2 of *Le Père de famille* she uses an inversion of the same line: 'Je ne sais où je suis ... Je ne sais où je vais.'²⁴

A further link lies in the autobiographical nature of both plays. As we have seen, all the plot elements included in *La Pièce et le prologue* have their roots in real events. In Destouches's play, when the action begins, Ariste has kept his marriage secret for two years, partly because he has previously declared that a *philosophe* should not marry, partly because he is afraid that his marriage will compromise his chances of inheriting money from his uncle. The action leading to the revelation of Ariste's secret includes the confusion caused by a rival for his wife's affections, his fear about his father's reaction if he discovers that he has married in secret, and much nagging from the female characters concerning his secrecy. This action draws, in an approximate way, on Destouches's own marriage, also kept secret for some time. However, it was perhaps less the links with Destouches's life that attracted Diderot, than a more general identification with his own circumstances. For the initial secrecy of his own marriage²⁵ has significant similarities to what we find in *Le Philosophe marié*, even if his subsequent battle against parental opposition does not. Furthermore, the fact that his wife Anne-Toinette turned out to be a difficult woman must have made Diderot feel that he was indeed *le philosophe marié – et très marié* (the *very* married philosopher). Perhaps there is an element of wish fulfilment in the fact that the domestic arrangements of Diderot's alter ego Hardouin suggest that he is not married (see I.8–9).

So what link does the extract from Destouches quoted by Diderot have with his own plays? The speech suggests that the conventional portrait of the *philosophe* as a man whose seriousness makes him immune to female charms is a fallacy – like all men, he will be quickly seduced. As we have noted, Destouches's Ariste is proof of this, as is the play's other philosopher character, who has also, despite earlier protestations, fallen in love (predictably with Ariste's secret wife). The same conventional image of the *philosophe* is repeated in Fagan's *La Pupille*, although his Ariste is wise enough to say from the outset that philosophy does not rule out love. Of course, the implications of the word *philosophe* had changed very significantly between 1727 and the composition of Diderot's plays, and one thing that is clear from our knowledge of the home life of the *philosophes* is that sexual abstinence was not generally one of their priorities. Diderot depicts in Hardouin a man with as much of a roving eye as himself: he agrees to Mme de Chepy's request for a *divertissement* only because asked to by the seductive Mlle Beaulieu (or so he says), and we should remember that its dedicatee Mme de Malves is an alter ego of Diderot's former lover Mme de Maux.[26] Similarly, Hardouin agrees to see and then to help Mme Bertrand only because she is an attractive woman; he tricks the *avocat* (lawyer) Des Renardeaux to oblige a female friend; he assists Mme de Vertillac because they have been lovers in the past. Finally, the reason he helps de Crancey, the only man for whom he instigates an intrigue, is, it is implied, because, as the ex-lover of the mother, he identifies with the man in love with the daughter.

Hence, the quotation from Destouches prefigures to a certain extent the action of Diderot's own plays; but only to a certain extent. For not only is the image of the *philosophe* as the crabbed scholar who thinks himself above the temptations provided by women a cliché; so is the comic reversal that proves him wrong. It is, after all, a standard comic device, particularly in Molièresque *comédie de caractère* (comedy of character), to depict someone unable to live up to his self-image; and having the character fall in love, particularly with someone unsuitable, is the most important device in the playwright's repertoire to extract comedy from this situation. Nevertheless, by the time Diderot wrote his plays the philosophical movement meant that *philosophe* no longer denoted just a comic stereotype, but also a group of real people, including Diderot himself. For this reason, no doubt, rather than being a clichéd figure whose self-image can be subverted, Hardouin has all the contradictions of a real person. Indeed, the stereotypical situation described in the extract from Destouches seems to be deliberately subverted when, on Hardouin's first entry, Mme de Chepy attempts to talk him into providing her with a *divertissement* and fails. The stereotype is then mocked in a different way when Mme de Chepy bad-temperedly decides that Mlle Beaulieu's charms may succeed where hers have not. For Hardouin's decision to change his mind and write the play, although apparently showing his vulnerability to a younger and prettier woman, is really aimed at annoying Mme de Chepy, who has irritated him. After all, he makes the offer before Mlle Beaulieu has even attempted to persuade him, and is not swayed when she insists that he will get her into trouble.

The encounter with Mme Bertrand might seem superficially to conform more closely to the situation described by Destouches, but again there are differences. It is true that Hardouin decides to help her because she is an attractive widow, but the decision has absolutely nothing to do with her powers of seduction, nor is it against his will. Hardouin has already established her attractiveness before agreeing to meet her; this exchange follows the lackey's announcement that one of the people waiting to see Hardouin is a woman:

HARDOUIN (*prenant un visage gai*):   Une femme!
LE LAQUAIS: Enveloppée dans vingt aunes de crêpe. Je gagerais bien que c'est une veuve.
HARDOUIN: Jolie?
LE LAQUAIS: Triste, mais assez bonne à consoler.
HARDOUIN: Quel âge?
LE LAQUAIS: Entre vingt et trente.
HARDOUIN: Faites entrer la veuve.[27]

(HARDOUIN (*with a happy expression*):   A woman!
THE LACKEY: Wrapped up in twenty yards of black. I'd wager she's a widow.
HARDOUIN: Is she pretty?
THE LACKEY: She's sad, but worth comforting.
HARDOUIN: How old?
THE LACKEY: Between twenty and thirty.
HARDOUIN: Show the widow in.)

In other words, whilst it is true that Hardouin takes up a case he has no time for because the supplicant is female, and that this indicates a general vulnerability to the female sex, he is far from being the victim depicted by Destouches. Indeed, his behaviour is not defensive but predatory.

This aspect of his relationship with the female protagonists is also found in the assistance he gives, for, as the second subtitle of the play, *Celui qui les sert tous et qui n'en contente aucun* (*He Who Helps Them All, and Satisfies None of Them*), indicates, he helps them, but not generally in the way they want. Certainly, this is also true of the male protagonists involved in his schemes; but it is significant that the issues relating to the female characters tend to have a sexual dimension. We have noted that Hardouin's thwarting of Mme de Chepy, first by refusing her, then by giving his agreement to Mlle Beaulieu, suggests that she lacks the female skills outlined by Destouches, but then his agreement to Mlle Beaulieu is equally disobliging, for it is clear that the implication that she possesses those powers her mistress lacks will cause trouble for the servant. Hardouin solves the problems of two of the other women by similar means. In the case of Mme Bertrand, he persuades his friend the Premier Commis de la Marine to accede to her demands by leading him to believe, quite wrongly, that her child is not only illegitimate, but that Hardouin is himself the father; and he persuades Mme de Vertillac to allow her daughter to marry de Crancey by convincing her, again wrongly, that her daughter is carrying de Crancey's child. Not only do we see him abusing the power he has over the reputation of these women, we may even see an element of wish fulfilment in his assumption of the paternity of the first of these children – perhaps in both cases if we accept that he feels a sense of identification with de Crancey. And if he does represent an alter ego of Hardouin, de Crancey's reaction when he discovers the stratagem is informative, for whilst the women are horrified, all he can find to say is: 'Je crois qu'il aurait pu mettre un peu plus de délicatesse dans les moyens de m'obliger! mais il est mon ami, mais il voyait ma peine' ('I suppose he could have been more sensitive in the way he helped me! But he's my friend, and he saw my distress'), causing Mme de Vertillac to remark angrily: 'Et cela vous paraît plaisant, à vous monsieur de Crancey?' ('And you think it's funny, M. de Crancey?').[28]

Indeed, as one of the plot lines added for the final version of the play reveals, the true power is not that of women over men, but the power that Hardouin and his ilk have over women. For to Mme de Chepy's comment at the end of her confrontation with Hardouin over his treatment of her daughter: 'Êtes-vous folle? Vous venez pour l'accabler d'injures; et vous lui dites des douceurs' ('Are you mad? You came to give him a good telling off, and you're whispering sweet nothings to him'), Mme de Vertillac replies simply: 'Et voilà comme nous sommes toutes, avec ces monstres-là!'[29] ('That's how we all are with these monsters.') It is also she who, at the end of *Est-il bon?*, provides the justification of Hardouin that Diderot gave to Hardouin himself in *La Pièce et le prologue*:

MADE DE CHEPY: Est-il bon? Est-il méchant?

MADLLE BEAULIEU: L'un après l'autre.

MADE DE VERTILLAC: Comme vous, comme moi, comme tout le monde.[30]

(MME DE CHEPY: Is he good, or is he wicked?

MLLE BEAULIEU: One after the other.

MME DE VERTILLAC: Like you, like me, like everyone.)

Even though Mme de Chepy describes the extract from Destouches's play as 'un certain endroit où Finette fait l'apologie des femmes',[31] it is not entirely unproblematic as an apologia, given the lines: '*Avec tous nos défauts*, nous gouvernons les hommes' and '*Vous avez la raison*, et nous avons les charmes.'[32] And the negative image of women is a continuing feature of Destouches's play: yes, Ariste loves his wife, but he feels himself to be beleaguered by the women around him, who often behave foolishly or illogically (although also a source of annoyance, the male characters are generally more sensible). Hardouin feels similarly beleaguered, and, as in Destouches's play, a high proportion of his persecutors are female. And if Mme Bertrand presents a more serious view of the female sex than any of the characters in *Le Philosophe marié*, and Mlle de Vertillac is similarly sympathetic, her mother's irrationality (she is described as 'une folle' ('a madwoman')[33] by the amiable M. Poultier) and the bad temper of Mme de Chepy mean that we have negative portrayals of female behaviour too. And yet, not only does Mme de Vertillac show affection for Hardouin, despite her obtuseness and volatility, it is with her that Hardouin shares the closest bond. If in real life it was the alter ego of Mme de Malves who had been Diderot's lover, in *Est-il bon?* that role goes to Mme de Vertillac, and the affection persists, despite the fact that she has certain traits that may remind us of Diderot's wife Anne-Toinette. For whilst Destouches's play presents an image of women that is entirely traditional and stereotypical, *Est-il bon? Est-il méchant?* takes delight in the depiction of the great variety of its female characters, who, in general, are much more interestingly drawn than the men. It is very clearly a play about a man who adores women written by a man who shared his enthusiasm. It is also a play by a writer who, despite his aims to make theatre a didactic school for virtue, could not resist the lure of the comic.

NOTES

1. See the Preface to *Le Mariage de Figaro* (*The Marriage of Figaro*) in Pierre-Augustin Caron de Beaumarchais, *Œuvres*, ed. Pierre Larthomas and Jacqueline Larthomas (Paris: Gallimard, 1988), p. 358.

2. See *Corr.*, vol. II, p. 176 (letter of 20 or 21 July).

3. Among other dramatic plans that cannot be decisively dated are two more conventionally comic works, *Le Mari libertin puni* (*The Libertine Husband Punished*) and the *Plan d'un opéra-comique* (*Plan for a Comic Opera*). On the issues of dating all the dramatic plans, see Denis Diderot, *Plans et Canevas*, DPV, vol. x, pp. 453–541 (p. 455, pp. 459–63).

4. See LEW, vol. ix (1971), pp. 14–15, where Roger Lewinter suggests 1770–1 as the most likely period of composition for this play.

5. See Derek Connon, *Innovation and Renewal: A Study of the Theatrical Works of Diderot*, SVEC 258 (Oxford: Voltaire Foundation, 1989), pp. 172–7.

6. See Jack Undank in DPV, vol. xxiii (1981), p. 295.

7. LEW, vol. ix, p. 20.

8. Quoted in DPV, vol. xxiii, p. 295, n. 2.

9. On the issue of sources for these works, see Connon, *Innovation and Renewal*, pp. 172–86.

10. Although the famous remark in the *Paradoxe sur le comédien* (*Paradox on the Actor*) in which Diderot mentions his performance (DPV, vol. xx, p. 74) does not specify which version he is referring to, it is too early to be *Est-il bon?*, and the inclusion of allusions not only to the incident dramatised in the plan, but also to one of those that appears only in the completed plays, means that it cannot be the performance of the plan mentioned above.

11. See DPV, vol. xxiii, pp. 295, n. 1, 297, n. 5.

12. After conventional excuses about how quickly the work was written, he asks his dedicatee's permission to place his offering 'aux pieds de l'amitié qui pardonne beaucoup, et non sur l'autel du goût qui ne pardonne rien' ('at the feet of friendship, which forgives much, and not on the altar of taste, which forgives nothing') (DPV, vol. xxiii, pp. 323, 383). All quotations from the plays follow the text of *Est-il bon? Est-il méchant?*, but, where applicable, the page reference for the comparable passage in *La Pièce et le prologue* is given first.

13. See on this matter Derek Connon, *Diderot's Endgames* (Oxford: Peter Lang, 2002), pp. 20–36.

14. DPV, vol. xxiii, pp. 332, 396.

15. Ibid., p. 470.

16. Ibid., p. 441.

17. DPV, vol. xxiii, pp. 327–8, 391–2.

18. DPV, vol. x, p. 130. The only significant difference between this and the equivalent passage in *La Pièce et le prologue* is the addition in *Est-il bon?* of *Le Philosophe sans le savoir* to the list of plays.

19. See DPV, vol. x, p. 146.

20. See DPV, vol. xx, pp. 74–5.

21. See Connon, *Innovation and Renewal*, p. 124.

22. *Corr.*, vol. ix (1963), p. 119.

23. DPV, vol. x, p. 422.

24. Ibid., p. 250.

25. For details of this, see Arthur M. Wilson, *Diderot* (New York: Oxford University Press, 1972), pp. 44–5.

26. See Connon, *Diderot's Endgames*, pp. 23–6.
27. DPV, vol. XXIII, pp. 339–40, 404.
28. Ibid., p. 455.
29. Ibid., p. 469.
30. Ibid., pp. 380, 479.
31. Ibid., pp. 327, 391.
32. Ibid., pp. 327, 391–2.
33. Ibid., p. 456.

PART V

Music, performance, aesthetics

CHAPTER 14

Diderot's voice(s): music and reform, from the Querelle des Bouffons to Le Neveu de Rameau*

Mark Darlow

> Le titre de musicien ne me va plus. Il y a cinq ou six ans que j'ai perdu le peu de voix que j'avais, pour la raison que nous ne pratiquons pas en France la méthode de la faire durer autant qu'en Italie.[1]
>
> ('The term "musician" no longer suits me. Five or six years ago, I lost what voice I had, because here in France we do not observe the practice which conserves it, as they do in Italy.')

As a topic which straddles the domains of physiology, psychology and linguistic communication, the voice has been recognised in recent decades as an essential matrix for Western thought, partly because it is irreducible to words, whether written or spoken.[2] By necessity, the voice is also central to early modern writings on music, for it is one area where nascent French musicography situated the specificity of music over language, as well as the articulation of the one to the other. Indeed, whilst the famous quip of Fontenelle – 'Sonate, que me veux-tu?' ('Sonata, what do you want of me?') – repudiated purely instrumental music as unintelligible, because it was devoid of verbal language which alone could carry signification, so instrumental music was in turn theorised by analogy with song, itself described and analysed according to characteristics of the voice, such as accent and pitch. It is also true that the intelligibility of vocal music within so-called 'reform' operas by Gluck and others was dependent on the means by which song was conceptualised, because opponents claimed that Gluck's music was noise, since it lacked the melodious contours of song.[3] Voice was also used by defenders of dialogue opera to explain the tension between spoken dialogue and song in lyric theatre, explaining that song sprang from a speaking individual at moments of heightened emotion, in a cry of sheer passion.

---

* I wish to record my gratitude to Marian Hobson, to Kate Tunstall, and to Jacqueline Waeber, for reading this chapter in draft and for making many helpful suggestions.

But our topic has a wider importance than French eighteenth-century vocal music, because *envoicing* is also a central aspect of 'postmodern' musicology, and locates a tension between the semantic (the means by which narrative information is transmitted), and song's sensual resistance to such signification (what the voice betrays in spite of us, or what is irreducible to a verbal code), a distinction crucial to my discussion, and to which I shall return.[4]

Accordingly, this chapter samples some of Diderot's writings on music from the perspective of the singing and speaking voice. In a celebrated discussion, Jean Starobinski has suggested that the adoption of 'la parole des autres' was central both to the early and late phases of Diderot's career, and that writing, for him, was 'parer aux conséquences d'un excès de liberté . . . opposer, à ceux qui jasent, une grande voix étrangère . . . qu'il ne se contente pas de citer, mais dont, sans tarder, il mimera le rôle et les gestes' ('to protect against the consequences of too much freedom, to present, in opposition to those who chatter, a great foreign voice which he will not only cite, but whose gesture and role he will imitate').[5] Indeed, the sheer polyphony of Diderot's writing and his use of envoicing have long been recognised as a noteworthy aspect of his oeuvre as a whole:[6] his use of dialogue for theory and philosophy, for instance, or (conversely) his pioneering of an expressive silent space in the interstices of articulated language in his theory of the stage,[7] go to the heart of a central aspect of Diderot's career: dissonance and variety.

As well as looking at a central aspect of Diderot's thought, focusing on the voice allows us to look again at some common eighteenth-century musicographical problems, such as the respective approaches of 'Italian' and 'French' music to vocal melody, because the voice spans three poles which are aligned and balanced differently according to genre, 'national tradition' and theorist: the body, verbal language and resonating sound. Finally, if it is true that what is original about the way music is conceived in *Le Neveu de Rameau* is the pantomime element more than the discussion, then any means of analysing it needs to be grounded in the corporeal dimension as much as in the verbal.[8] My first section examines the voice as index of individuality, both in Diderot's career and as thematised and theorised in his pamphlets. A second discusses the different approaches to voice of the Italian and French parties during the Querelle des Bouffons. A third examines the implications for the development of musical theatre – reform opera, but also *opéra-comique* and *mélodrame* – of Diderot's consistent call for variety. In this area, he will be seen to be at odds with Jean-Jacques Rousseau, whose own important contributions to music theory called for unity.[9]

MUTE DIDEROT: THE THEORIST AS VENTRILOQUIST; DIGNIFIED SILENCE

On a first and most obvious level, the voice is the medium by which ideas remain identified with particular bodies and is thus the means of giving individuality to expression, and nowhere is this more obvious than in *Le Neveu*, for a voice carries a part of the individual with it in its timbre and inflexions, however paradoxically irrelevant these might be to the strict signification of verbal language itself. Diderot's daughter Angélique reputedly sang with the voice of a nightingale, whereas it was literally impossible to listen to Rameau's nephew, according to Moi's introduction, as he would make you want to stick your fingers in your ears or run away. Striking in this regard is the fact that Diderot remarks upon his own muteness as a musician, both concrete and metaphorical (cited in the epigraph to this chapter), and this in 1754, the crisis year of the end of the so-called Querelle des Bouffons – striking, because music was an important segment of Diderot's career, as has long been recognised:[10] many of his works contain either sustained discussion of, or frequent allusion to, music, and his knowledge and taste in this domain were recognised by his contemporaries.[11] Yet Diderot characterised himself as 'point musicien, mais aimant la musique' ('not a musician but a music-lover'), and tended to tone down his abilities and involvement when talking about himself.[12] On one level, this was simple modesty (or a pose thereof?), for even in an 'interdisciplinary' age, music often induced such discretion in those of its commentators who were devoid of specialist technical training. Diderot's letter of 1754 was speaking of a concrete case of physiological strain, of course; and temporary vocal troubles would not have stopped him signing his texts. But it is probably more than an intellectual pirouette to claim that henceforward his contribution to this art would often be *ventriloquised*, either through his characters, or, as was also often to happen, through his interactions with other living commentators; and this at all stages of his career. Erwin Jacobi cites evidence that Diderot was believed to have been a collaborator in Rameau's *Démonstration du principe de l'harmonie*, lending the theorist some much-needed help with clarity and precision in expression.[13] By Rousseau's own admission, he gave guidance on the second *Discours*. Nor was such tacit help limited to his early career, for he both helped and was helped by Sedaine;[14] and his collaboration with Philidor on *Ernelinde* has been substantially documented,[15] not to mention the most famous example, at least in the field of music, which is his collaboration on the *Leçons de clavecin* by Bemetzrieder.[16] Burney also twice describes a visit to Diderot on 14 December 1770 when he received a pile of manuscripts which Diderot did not intend to use, with an offer that he should publish or otherwise dispose of them as he chose.[17]

'FRENCH' VERSUS 'ITALIAN': THE QUERELLE DES BOUFFONS

A study of the concept of voice in the Querelle des Bouffons remains to be written; yet any discussion of musical thought in eighteenth-century France perforce engages with a comparison between French and Italian vocal music, since this was a constant feature of musical thinking, from Raguenet and Lecerf de la Viéville's skirmish in 1702–4, to the quarrel over Gluck in the 1770s. Beyond a comparison between French and Italian lyric art, each quarrel had specific issues, and to conflate them as episodes in a similar dispute over 'national traditions' robs them of that specificity. But the Querelle des Bouffons, in which Diderot was explicitly involved and on which he retrospectively reflected in *Le Neveu*, indisputably has a national dimension, since it was centred upon a comparison between *opera buffa* performed by visiting artists from Italy, and the *tragédie lyrique* most central to the repertoire of the Paris Opera. Burney claimed, of Diderot's daughter Angélique, that 'not a single French composition was played by her the whole time, all was Italian and German; hence it will not be difficult to form a judgement of M. Diderot's taste in music',[18] a preference apparently borne out by *Le Neveu*. Whatever his personal musical preferences, though, his pamphlets are more nuanced than the simple partiality shown by many of the *philosophes*. The *Lettre sur les sourds et muets* (*Letter on the Deaf and Dumb*) of 1751 had analysed the supposed unmusicality of French syntax in terms of order and reason, making of the contours of spoken language an inappropriate model for song, by comparing the 'hiéroglyphe' ('poetic hieroglyph') with 'harmonie oratoire' ('oratorical harmony'); indeed the pretext of the *Lettre* was a response to Batteux's *Lettre sur la phrase française comparée à la phrase latine* (*Letter on the French Sentence Compared with the Latin Sentence*).[19] The opening conceit of Diderot's 1753 *Arrêt rendu à l'amphithéâtre de l'Opéra* (*Judgement Rendered at the Opera Amphitheatre*) is that the Italian-centred *philosophe* party, or 'Coin de la reine', has not spoken, and here the silent voice seems to be that described in the *Encyclopédie* as having 'beaucoup de grandeur et de sublimité' ('much grandeur and sublimity'). In the same article it is asserted that '[Le silence] consiste à ne pas daigner parler sur un sujet dont on ne pouvoit rien dire sans risquer, ou démontrer quelque apparence de bassesse d'âme, ou de faire voir une élévation capable d'irriter les autres.'[20] ('[Silence] consists in not deigning to speak on a subject where there is a danger of showing spiritual pettiness or irritating arrogance.') This links with material throughout the century which deplores the violence to which artistic quarrels gave rise: indeed, even as early a work as *Les Bijoux indiscrets* (1748) stated that people of taste appreciated both Lully and Rameau, and refrained from participating in the Quarrel: 'Les ignorants et les barbons tenaient tous pour Utmisol; la jeunesse et les virtuoses étaient pour Utremifasolasitutut; et les gens de goût, tant jeunes que barbons, faisaient grand cas de tous les deux.'[21] ('The ignorant and the old were for Utmisol; virtuosi and young people favoured Utremifasolasitutut; and people of taste, whether young or old, esteemed both.') As for Diderot's *Au Petit Prophète de Boehmischbroda* (*To the Little Prophet of Boehmischbroda*), which responds to a prior pamphlet by Grimm, this is all about a classic *dialogue de sourds*:

Si du milieu du parterre, d'où j'élève ma voix, j'étais assez heureux pour être écouté des deux Coins et que la dispute s'engageât avec les armes que je propose, peut-être y prendrais-je quelque part ... Au reste, messieurs, vos brochures étant toutes anonymes, j'ai parlé jusqu'à présent sans avoir personne en vue. Pour inviter à se taire, s'il est possible, ceux d'entre vous qui ignorent les deux langues et qui ont à peine une teinture de musique, il n'était pas nécessaire. [22]

(If I were lucky enough to make myself heard by both camps from the stalls and to impose my choice of weapons in the quarrel, perhaps I would take part. Moreover, gentlemen, since your brochures are all anonymous, I have spoken without singling out any particular individual. To invite those of you who are unfamiliar with both languages and have the barest rudiments of music to be silent, it was hardly necessary.)

These remarks rarely go beyond a rather commonplace metaphor which was to become a cliché of artistic quarrels throughout the century, as Irailh's work demonstrates,[23] but they link muteness with dignity, and seem to characterise the babble of the Querelle as futile, whilst linking personal and individual expression with technical expertise. This is a combination which will become a crucial aspect of the later quarrel over Gluck, as I have elsewhere suggested, because the various pamphlets written for and against Gluck are centred on the fundamental question of who has the knowledge and expertise to judge an art so imbued with technicalities as opera.[24] Diderot's remarks also point to a reconciliation of this rather sterile dispute, since his later theorising of vocal music breaks down the distinction of 'national traditions' by dissociating the accent of spoken language from the contours of musical melody in a manner that foreshadows Michel-Paul Gui de Chabanon, and other theorists of instrumental music at the end of the century.[25]

Part of the problem of discussing *Le Neveu* in the context of musical theory and quarrels is the status of the assertions that it contains, for the written comments on music are allusive, not systematic, and the work crafts an entirely new way of writing and imagining music in the form of Lui's pantomimes. A further difficulty concerns dating, for a difference of ten years would determine whether Lui's comments on the superior musicality of Italian prosody are forward-looking or downright commonplace, and the window for dating *Le Neveu* is greater than that.[26] But *Le Neveu* is often portrayed as discussing and imag(in)ing likely opera reform, and thereby pointing from the 'first stage' of reform (the revelation of Italian *opera buffa*) to a 'second': the experiment of Philidor's *Ernelinde*.[27] The filiation between Italian opera and *Ernelinde* may seem odd; but in the early 1770s Philidor was still glossed as an 'Italianising' composer by Diderot and others, perhaps because no more sophisticated terminology was yet available.[28] Indeed a letter from Burney to Diderot claims that the propensity of the French to think in terms of national traditions was far from defunct in 1771, and attributed the vices of French music to the poor quality of vocal execution: 'La Musique Nationale de votre Pays, il faudra des Siècles pour l'extirper.'[29] ('It will be centuries before your country's national music can be eradicated.') The discussion in *Le Neveu* starts conventionally enough with a claim that *le chant* (song) must be modelled on the speaking line, as an 'autre ligne qui serpenterait sur [celle de la déclamation]'[30] ('another line which would meander around that of speech'). That the singing voice should be modelled on the contours of declamation is commonplace and could be found in Rousseau and a host of other critics besides; but less so is the consequence Lui draws for the 'energy' of song, for he claims: 'la symphonie est au chant, à un peu de libertinage près, inspiré par l'étendue de l'instrument et la mobilité des doigts, ce que le chant est à la déclamation réelle'.[31] ('Instrumental music is to song what song is to declamation, save for a little licence which is due to the extent of the instrument and the agility of the player's fingers.') In this rather problematic sentence, two parallels are seemingly made: on the one hand, *le chant* is modelled upon declamation, whereas instrumental music is modelled on *le chant*; but also the one is a heightened version of the other, so that the symphonic or instrumental would seem paradoxically to be the ultimate point of vocality. By virtue moreover of this double analogy, there is clearly a greater distance between *déclamation* and *symphonie*, and hence a chain of different media, each a version of the preceding, which is why Lui can also claim 'l'air est presque toujours la péroraison de la scène' ('melody is almost always the peroration of the scene'),[32] in that it must grow organically out of preceding recitative, which itself must follow dialogue; for the term implies that song is the last part of a structured discourse in rhetoric, and one led up to by gradated means. In the second pantomime, Lui's performance indeed begins with this kind of gradation:

> Et puis le voilà qui se met à se promener, en murmurant dans son gosier ... Il commençait à entrer en passion, et à chanter tout bas. Il élevait le ton, à mesure qu'il se passionnait davantage; vinrent ensuite, les gestes, les grimaces du visage et les contorsions du corps; et je dis, Bon; voilà la tête qui se perd, et quelque scène nouvelle qui se prépare; en effet, il part d'un éclat de voix, *Je suis un pauvre misérable.*[33]

> (He then began walking about, murmuring *sotto voce*. He began to get excited, and sang quietly, progressively raising his voice; then gesticulated, and made facial grimaces and bodily contortions; I said to myself: ah, here we go, he will lose his mind; thereupon he abruptly began to sing *Je suis un pauvre misérable.*)

Much later, in his review of Cochin's 'Sur la pantomime dramatique' ('On Dramatic Pantomime'), Diderot also calls for such gradation, claiming 'Le bon goût se refuse au passage disparate du ton de la farce au ton pathétique' ('Good taste cannot accept a brusque transition from farce to pathos'),[34] and stating that if one wishes to touch the percipient, 'Il faut que les accents d'une mélodie forte et grande soient employés sur un genre de poésie noble et élevé.'[35] ('The accents of a strident melody must be used with noble, elevated lyrics.')

Elsewhere, in a discussion of the musicality of languages, Lui also says that a duller language needs a more energetic voice: 'Les discours simples, les voix communes de la passion, nous sont d'autant plus nécessaires que la langue sera plus monotone, aura moins d'accent.'[36] ('Simple phrases and the common voices of passion are all the more necessary when language is more monotonous, and has less accent.') D'Alembert had similarly claimed that the superiority of the voice of the Ancients was its variety, derived from natural accentuation: 'Nous savons de plus que les Latins, et surtout les Grecs, élevaient ou abaissaient la voix sur un grand nombre de syllabes; ce qui devait nécessairement contribuer chez eux à la mélodie du discours.'[37] ('We know moreover that the Romans and especially the Greeks, raised or lowered the voice over a series of syllables, which must of necessity have contributed to the melodious nature of their speech.') 'L'accent', as Lui puts it, 'est la pépinière de la mélodie.'[38] ('Accent is the nursery where melody is grown.') And Italian seems to be described as the model in *Le Neveu* because, in a twist to tradition, its prosody makes it more appropriate for dramatic singing, since it is possessed of the kind of variety that favours accent; and 'Sur la pantomime dramatique' has in common with *Le Neveu* the claim that Italian influence stopped French vocal music being 'pauvre, monotone, timide' ('poor, monotonous, timid').[39] What these sources have in common, then, is the idea, first explored in the *Lettre sur les sourds et muets*, that languages can be fit for music to the extent that they are possessed of contours which allow for musical *variety*. Yet, unlike Rousseau, who claims that French is *inherently* unmusical, Diderot will draw the conclusion that it needs to be written with the vocal line in mind. That Rameau's music was *plat* (dull), said *sotto voce* by Lui, does not therefore imply a critique of the French language, but the dullness of his libretti. Indeed, in his letter to Burney of 15 May 1771 Diderot claims that the 'dernier terme de l'art' ('end of art') is 'de faire de la musique très variée, et sans faute, quand on manque de génie; et d'en faire de belle, quand on a du génie'[40] ('to make beautiful music, if one is a genius, and to produce flawless, varied music, if not'), linking with Burney's own critical comments in favour of variety within unity in instrumental music, particularly as concerns Haydn.

Opéra *or* opéra-comique?

If varied and gradated media are the lessons which Diderot's ongoing theory of lyric theatre derives from Italian practice, a central issue rarely discussed in that context is the articulation of language and sound; but this was clearly implicit in any discussion of musical variety – witness Chabanon's own view that gradated variety is central to the independence of music from language.[41] For whereas Rousseau's discussion of Italian recitative claims that the more varied the accentuation of a given language, the more a recitative based upon it will be close to language – will speak – and the less it will be meaningless noise, Chabanon will claim that what makes the recitative expressive is the instrumental ritornello, which prolongs the expressive character of the melody, independently of language; the recitative is the place where the disjunction between the trio composed of music, language and body is first addressed. In fact, as early as *Les Trois Chapitres ou la vision de la nuit du Mardi-Gras au mercredi des Cendres* (*The Three Chapters, or, The Vision of the Night from Shrove Tuesday to Ash Wednesday*) Diderot had problematised this relation, by centring his text upon two instances of vocal dissociation. On the one hand a (disembodied) voice speaks to the 'petit prophète' ('little prophet'), and hence suggests divine inspiration (a key biblical metaphor);[42] and, on the other, the signifying power of mute pantomime and instrumental ritornellos is emphasised, for the superlative quality ascribed to Rousseau's *Devin du village* (*The Village Soothsayer*) in the second 'chapitre' is about 'envoicing', a metaphor for the ways in which instrumental melody carries meaning and emotional expression which will become central to Enlightenment operatic theory and to Diderot's writing alike:

Et il y avait dans un coin un jeune garçon et une jeune fille qui se faisaient des caresses, le Devin les leur montra, et sitôt qu'ils les aperçurent ils s'écrièrent avec surprise, ou plutôt les violons pour eux, car ils ne faisaient tous que des signes, et c'étaient les violons qui parlaient: 'Eh! vraiment oui! et c'est Colin! et c'est Colette!'[43]

(And in one corner I saw a young boy and young girl fondly caressing, the soothsayer pointed them out, and as soon as they saw them, they cried (or rather the violins did so, for they merely gestured, and the violins spoke for them) but yes! It is Colin! And that is Colette!)

This concept of envoicing is also central to the third *Entretien sur Le Fils naturel* (*Conversation on The Natural Son*), which discusses a dramatic ballet in operatic terms, claiming, of the 'programme' for Act I: 'ce récitatif peut être coupé d'une ariette de dépit: c'est à l'orchestre à parler. C'est à lui à rendre les discours, à imiter les actions.'[44] ('This recitative can be cut by an aria expressing pique: the orchestra can speak. It will convey speech, and imitate actions.') And the entry 'Instrumen[t]s' in volume VIII of the *Encyclopédie* describes instruments as 'les voix différentes par lesquelles [un compositeur] parle à nos oreilles' ('the different voices through which the composer speaks to us').[45] The *Lettre sur les sourds et muets* fully recognises the power of the instrumental; and the indisputable source of orchestral envoicing in the opera is the obbligato recitative, itself derived from Italian opera. Much as Diderot approves of the idea that language should be subordinate to music, then, he also does much for the 'emancipation' (to use Neubauer's term) of instrumental melody, and particularly the keyboard, which allows for a simultaneous *plurality* of voices.

Le Neveu's contribution to the theory of lyric theatre has hitherto been seen as pointing to reform opera and particularly *Ernelinde*, as mentioned above. But I would like to conclude by suggesting that the extent to which the work foregrounds the relation between music, language, voice and silence points equally strongly towards those forms of musical drama that either integrate dialogue or mix instrumental music with speech. Indeed, where Didier has described *Le Neveu* as an 'opéra imaginaire',[46] one would be tempted to speak instead of an 'opéra-comique imaginaire', since the one thing it indisputably contains is spoken dialogue interspersed with musical moments at high points of emotional tension. Diderot clearly has nothing against *opéra-comique* which is properly integrated dramatically; in fact he positively approves of it – witness various mentions in his correspondence as well as Lui's citation of Italian-inspired *opéra-comique*[47] – and he was clearly at ease with the coexistence of dialogue and song, as Rebejkow has demonstrated.[48] Indeed, the *pantomime dramatique* (dramatic pantomime) is explicitly described by Diderot as being logically implied by *opéra-comique* and reform opera.[49] And the metaphorical link between colour and sound, first present in Diderot's description of Castel's *clavecin oculaire* (ocular harpsichord), is extended to describe the 'three tones' of the musician's 'palette': speech, recitative and aria.[50] But I wonder whether one could not go beyond *opéra-comique* and suggest that what *Le Neveu* points towards is musical melodrama, by virtue of its problematisation of the relation between music and language, its dramatic integration of pantomime, and its inability to figure song for a reader to whom the verbal language remains inaccessible. A reading of Diderot's review of Garcin's *Traité du mélo-drame* might seem to suggest that Diderot is hostile to melodrama, for he is clearly critical of many of Garcin's ideas.[51] Garcin's work is not, however, primarily a study of melodrama in either of the two senses we would use today: a musical or theatrical work featuring strong emotions of terror akin to the Gothic, as theorised by Peter Brooks; or the more musicological definition of a work combining spoken dialogue, mute pantomime and instrumental music. It is, rather, a study of music drama, and spends much of its time on questions of the inherent musicality of language and on song.

But, more importantly, Diderot writes these remarks on Garcin in response to Burney, who had written on 10 October describing Rousseau's *Pygmalion* as 'plein de pensées ingénieuses et élégantes' ('full of ingenious and elegant thoughts').[52] As Olivier Pot shows, Diderot's response of 28 October 1771, commenting on Garcin, was an indication of how far this type of opera could compete with the Italian musical dramaturgy for expressive purposes; as he demonstrates, 'le dialogue alterné et entrecoupé de la voix et de la symphonie qui se miment réciproquement' ('the alternation of dialogue, speech and instrumental music, each mimicking the other') was a means of going beyond the rather dull question of whether music should be subordinate to words or vice versa.[53] It also allowed the reintegration of accent into instrumental music, which would allow that music to accompany the pantomime, which

Diderot elsewhere theorised in a form of theatre inspired by eighteenth-century debates about Greek drama. We know that the *mélodrame* grows out of Diderot's pronouncements on *style entrecoupé* (broken style) as well as Rousseau's theory of *récitatif obligé*. Jacqueline Waeber comments:

Le mélodrame est né de cette nouvelle sensibilité, mais il est également le fruit d'un sentiment d'impuissance. Ce constat ne vaut pas pour le seul *Pygmalion*: il est aussi et avant tout la marque du mélodrame romantique. Toute entreprise mélodramatique est marquée par le renoncement au chant au profit de la parole et du geste, ce qui peut être perçu comme une forme de méfiance envers les pouvoirs expressifs de la musique. Non pas qu'elle ne soit pas assez expressive, mais bien plus parce qu'elle l'est beaucoup trop.[54]

(Melodrama was born of this new sensibility, but is also due to a feeling of impotence, which goes not just for *Pygmalion*: it is also and above all the hallmark of romantic melodrama. Every melodramatic undertaking is marked by the renunciation of song in favour of speech and gesture, which can also be seen as a form of distrust of the expressive powers of music. Not because music is not expressive enough, but because it is too expressive.)

And maybe one further originality of *Le Neveu* is to have mimed a *mélodrame* itself. Didier has shown how Lui's pantomimes were a particularly original response to the problem of how to 'dire la musique' ('speak music'); and what strikes me about these scenes is how they so often dislocate the trio I mentioned before. Certainly, Lui sings; but we are never given the words to the arias, and the modern reader can at best imagine the qualities of pure music (length, accent, intensity, dynamics, emotion) through the descriptions of his gestures, which Moi provides. For all the apparent immediacy of the pantomime, then, it is an imitation which is filtered by a description concentrating on the physical affect at the expense of the sonic (where are we ever told what the music sounds like?). In fact, for a modern reader (and unlike for Moi, who is watching and listening), this would better be described as a silent opera (or a silent melodrama?), composed alternately of speech, mute gesture, descriptions of disembodied sound but rarely if at all descriptions of embodied song as such: strange for a text that explicitly and repeatedly treats the question of necessary reform in the lyric theatre.

If that is true, then *Le Neveu* needs its passages on music to be read on different levels, whether chronological or enunciative. Although it probably introduces more problems than it solves to talk in terms of a linear progress of musical theorising, the position that claims that the expressive potential of music depends upon the qualities of the accent of language is superseded, historically, by the claim that the vocal qualities of instrumental melody are themselves supremely expressive; and that silence accompanied by gesture is an appropriate medium to employ at a moment of emotional paroxysm. That the latter exists in Diderot's musical thinking as early as *Les Trois Chapitres* suggests that we need to treat the former claim, in *Le Neveu*, with some caution, as ironic and deliberately anachronistic 'theory' immediately superseded by the 'practice' of the pantomimes, and as figuration of the musico-dramatic genre to which *Le Neveu* actually points: the musical melodrama.

To come back to Diderot's unquestionably negative review of Garcin, it is clear that he wants variety to allow for maximal musical expression, and it is the expressive overcharging of song that renders pantomime desirable, and *mélodrame* finally possible. Envoicing is now recognised as one of the means by which musical language could both function and be conceptualised as more than just language: in fact, as a language of its own. Instrumental envoicing grows out of Italian practice (especially the *récitatif obligé*), and so one possibly paradoxical conclusion is that the qualities that commentators perceive in 'Italian' music were precisely the means by which the voice escaped the determinations of verbal language, and which ultimately contribute to the abandonment of exclusive preference for 'through composition', based as it is upon a unity of medium. Another way of putting this would be to say that the qualities that eighteenth-century critics saw in vocality sowed the seeds for the defeat of exclusively vocal music, because it opened the way to an understanding of the instrumental, in a space whose eloquence depends not upon verbal signification but upon physical sensation. This is surely the lesson to be drawn from Moi's citation, in *Le Neveu*, of what sounds suspiciously like Rousseau: 'le silence même se peint par des sons' ('silence itself is depicted by sound').[55] To say that sound can depict silence is the next stage of that same process whereby musical imitation revises the relation between the physical and the *moral* (non-physical), breaking down what one might describe as the *vococentrism* of musical theorising. Amongst other things, this is one reason why it is particularly problematic to see the quarrels of eighteenth-century France as episodes in a long-scale comparison of French and Italian; for Diderot's views, though borrowing qualities from Italian practice, and simultaneously rising above the controversies of the Querelle des Bouffons, indisputably favour variety and dissonance of medium, implicitly pointing away from the rather tame concept of musical periodicity elaborated by Gluck's detractors, the supporters of Piccini such as Marmontel, towards reform opera, *opéra-comique* or *mélodrame*, but also to the nineteenth-century commonplace of an inexpressible music which goes beyond the limitations of the verbal.

NOTES

1. Denis Diderot to Madame de *** (?July–August 1754); see *Corr.*, vol. i, p. 169.
2. For an illuminating introduction to the topic that surveys the central issues and has a useful bibliography, see Mladen Dolar, *A Voice and Nothing More* (Cambridge, MA: MIT Press, 2006).
3. 'Reform opera' sought to replace the complexity of *opera seria* by works of 'noble simplicity'. For an introduction, see Patricia Howard, *C. W. von Gluck, 'Orfeo'* (Cambridge: Cambridge University Press, 1981), pp. 10–26. Michael Evans comments: 'Gluck's new aesthetic responds to three of the principal characteristics of Greek tragedy: its economy, directness, and avoidance of irrelevant display.' See his study, *Opera from the Greek: Studies in the Poetics of Appropriation* (Aldershot: Ashgate, 2007), p. 42.
4. The seminal work is Carolyn Abbate, *Unsung Voices: Opera and Musical Narrative in the Nineteenth Century* (Princeton, NJ: Princeton University Press, 1991). See also Downing Thomas's discussion of voice in Charpentier's *Médée*, in *Aesthetics of Opera in the Ancien Régime, 1647–1785* (Cambridge: Cambridge University Press, 2002), pp. 129–53.
5. LEW, vol. xiii, p. vi.
6. See, for instance, Andrew H. Clark, *Diderot's Part* (Aldershot: Ashgate, 2008), a study centred upon the musical concept of dissonance as a structuring element of Diderot's thought as a whole. Clark shows how Diderot's place in the Querelle des Bouffons, and his approach to that dichotomy, was much more complex than previously thought; and one aim of this chapter is to examine some of the implications for music drama in his later work.
7. See Arnaud Rykner, *L'Envers du théâtre: dramaturgie du silence, de l'âge classique à Maeterlinck* (Paris: Corti, 1996); James Fowler, *Voicing Desire: Family and Sexuality in Diderot's Narrative* (Oxford: Voltaire Foundation, 2000).
8. Although it deals almost exclusively with Roman theatre, Jaucourt's entry for the *Encyclopédie* defines 'pantomime' as the means by which actors 'par des mouvemens, des signes, des gestes, & sans s'aider de discours, exprimoient des passions, des caractères & des événemens' ('by movements, signs, and gestures, and without the aid of speech, expressed passions, characters and events'): *Encyclopédie*, vol. xi (1765), p. 827. It is in this sense, close to 'mime', that the English cognate is used in the present chapter.
9. Rousseau was the author of not only approximately half the articles on music in Diderot and d'Alembert's *Encyclopédie*, but also a revised version of these (*Dictionnaire de musique*) and many other theoretical texts. See his *Œuvres complètes*, ed. Marcel Raymond and Bernard Gagnebin, 5 vols. (Paris: Gallimard, 1959–95), vol. v (1995).
10. For the first systematic treatment of this topic, see Paul Henry Lang, 'Diderot as Musician', *Diderot Studies*, 10 (1968), 95–107. For a review of literature since, see Clark, *Diderot's Part*, which has a full bibliography containing references to the major sources on music.

11. See, for instance, Charles Burney, *Music, Men and Manners in France and Italy 1770* (London: Eulenberg, 1974), p. 225, and, by the same author, *The Present State of Music in France and Italy* (London: Becket, 1773; facsimile edn New York: Boude Brothers, 1968), p. 405.

12. See Lang, 'Diderot as Musician', p. 97. Cf. Diderot's 'Projet d'un nouvel orgue' ('Project for a New Organ'), where he states: 'C'est un ignorant en musique qui le propose' ('suggested by a musical ignorant'). See the *Mercure de France* of October 1747 (p. 104).

13. Jean-Philippe Rameau, *Complete Theoretical Writings*, ed. Erwin Jacobi, 6 vols. (American Institute of Musicology, 1967–72), vol. III, pp. xxxix–xl.

14. See *Corr.*, vol. v, pp. 87–8.

15. See Manuel Couvreur, 'Diderot et Philidor: le philosophe au chevet d'*Ernelinde*', *Recherches sur Diderot et sur l'Encyclopédie*, 11 (October 1991), 83–107.

16. See *Corr.*, vol. XI, pp. 38, 97–9. For a discussion of this topic, see Robert Niklaus, 'Diderot and the *Leçons de clavecin*', in *Modern Miscellany Presented to Eugène Vinaver by Pupils, Colleagues and Friends* (Manchester: Manchester University Press, 1969), pp. 180–94; Jean-Michel Bardez, *Diderot et la musique: valeur de la contribution d'un mélomane* (Paris: Champion, 1975); and Clark, *Diderot's Part*.

17. It seems that Burney indeed used the material, since in a letter of 18 August 1771, acknowledging a gratis copy of *The Present State*, Diderot writes: 'en le publiant, vous y avez mis de l'importance' ('by publishing it, you have given it importance'). See *Corr.*, vol. XI, p. 96. I am indebted, on this point, to Marian Hobson's discussion in her inaugural lecture for the opening of the Besterman Centre for the Enlightenment at Oxford: 'Diderot: The (W)hole of History'. The material given to Burney has not been identified. On Burney's correspondence with Diderot, see R. A. Leigh, 'Les Amitiés françaises du Dr Burney', *Revue de littérature comparée* (April–June 1951), 162–71; and *Corr.*, vol. XI, pp. 37–9, 40–2, 95–9, 196–7, 205–8, 213–17. On the loan, see Burney, *Music, Men and Manners in France and Italy 1770*, p. 225; and Burney, *The Present State*, pp. 405–6.

18. Burney, *The Present State*, p. 405.

19. Claude Jamain, *L'Imaginaire de la musique au siècle des Lumières* (Paris: Champion, 2001), p. 101 (n. 6).

20. 'Silence', *Encyclopédie*, vol. xv (1765), p. 191.

21. DPV, vol. III, p. 69. Examples from the 1760s and 1770s abound. For just one example, see Meister, writing in the midst of the controversy over Gluck: 'De grands philosophes ont prétendu que la vérité ne convenait guère aux hommes, puisqu'elle n'avait jamais été pour eux qu'une source de querelles, de haines et de divisions. On prouverait bien mieux, en suivant le même principe, que la musique ne convient guère à la France, puisque cet art n'a jamais tenté d'y faire le moindre progrès sans soulever contre lui les cabales les plus violentes, les fureurs les plus ridicules.' See *Correspondance littéraire*, May 1777, ed. Maurice Tourneux, 16 vols. (Paris: Garnier, 1877–82), vol. XI, pp. 456–65 (p. 456).

('Great philosophers have claimed that truth did not suit men, because it has only ever been a source of quarrels, hatred and division. Accordingly, it would be that much easier to demonstrate that music did not suit France, because it has never been able to so much as attempt progress without stirring up the most violent cabals and ridiculous furies.') For the editorship of the *Correspondance littéraire*, see Introduction, n. 16.

22. LEW, vol. II, pp. 688–9; DPV, vol. XIX, pp. 14–15.

23. Abbé Simon-Augustin Irailh, *Querelles littéraires: ou Mémoires pour servir à l'histoire des révolutions de la république des lettres, d'Homère à nos jours*, 4 vols. (Paris: Durand, 1761).

24. I put forward this argument in '*Anonymes* and *Ignorants*: Cultural Politics and Knowledge Formation in the Querelle des Gluckistes et des Piccinnistes', a talk delivered at the colloquium 'France, Great Britain and Ireland: Cultural Transfers and the Circulation of Knowledge in the Age of Enlightenment' (University of York, September 2009).

25. On Chabanon's contribution, see Jacqueline Waeber, 'Déconstruire Rousseau: Chabanon annotateur du *Dictionnaire de musique*', *Annales de la société Jean-Jacques Rousseau*, 49 (2010), 241–76. On the problem of instrumental music, see John Neubauer, *The Emancipation of Music from Language: Departure from Mimesis in Eighteenth-Century Aesthetics* (New Haven, CT: Yale University Press, 1986).

26. For Lui's comments, see DPV, vol. XIII, pp. 162–3, 170.

27. See Daniel Heartz, 'Diderot et le théâtre lyrique: "le nouveau stile" proposé par *Le Neveu de Rameau*', *Revue de musicologie*, 64.2 (1978), 229–52; Couvreur, 'Diderot et Philidor'.

28. Diderot, 'Sur la pantomime dramatique', LEW, vol. XII, pp. 750–7 (esp. p. 752). In his first letter to Burney (15 May 1771), recommending Philidor, Diderot also describes him as 'le fondateur de la musique italienne en France' ('the founder of Italian music in France') and compares him with Duni, although ascribing to the former the greater degree of merit because he was not a native Italian composer unlike the latter; see *Corr.*, vol. XI, p. 38. The *Journal de musique* had spoken in similar terms the year before, although more subtly, pointing to the mediating experience of Philidor's study in Germany, albeit of a musical style itself borrowed from Italy. See 'Quelques réflexions sur la musique moderne', *Journal de musique* (May 1770), pp. 3–18 (p. 14).

29. *Corr.*, vol. XI, p. 40 (letter of 27 May 1771).

30. DPV, vol. XII, p. 158.

31. Ibid., p. 162.

32. Ibid., p. 170. It is possible that Diderot's source for this phrase is the theorist of 'reform' opera before Gluck, Francesco Algarotti, whose *Saggio sopra l'opera in musica* (Venice: G. Pasquali, 1755; rev. Livorno: M. Coltellini, 1763) was translated anonymously by Chastellux in 1773 as *Essai sur l'opéra* (Pisa and Paris: Ruault, 1773). Diderot's contacts with Chastellux suggest that he was more than likely aware of the *Essai*. Algarotti applies the term 'péroraison' to the *cadence* as final element of a structured *air* (*Essai*, p. 60). He seems at odds

with Diderot in several respects, including his conception of counterpoint and his rejection of gesture. But he would have agreed that variety within unity is also the guiding principle for the expressive qualities of the singing voice itself: 'C'est un axiome vulgaire que quiconque ne sait pas modérer sa voix, ne sait pas chanter. Le grand secret pour exciter les passions consiste à la soutenir et à la conduire par des nuances imperceptibles' (*Essai*, p. 56; spelling modernised). ('It is a common axiom, that whoever cannot moderate his voice cannot sing. The key to inspiring the passions is supporting the voice and developing it gradually.') The passage reads as follows in the respective Italian editions: 'E la cadenza non dovrebbe esser altro in sostanza, che la perorazione dell'aria medesima' (1755, p. 20); and 'E la cadenza, direm noi, ha pur da nascere dell'aria, ed esserne quasi la perorazione, e l'epilogo' (1763, p. 49). Both may be consulted in the fascimile, ed. Annalisa Bini (Bologna: Libreria Musicale Italiana, 1989). For a study of the complex web of translations of Algarotti's text, see Marion Lafouge, 'De la transposition à l'annotation: Chastellux traducteur du *Saggio sopra l'opera per musica* d'Algarotti', in Francesca Manzari and Fridrun Rinner (eds.), *Traduire le même, l'autre ou le soi* (Aix-en-Provence: Presses de l'Université de Provence, forthcoming).

33. DPV, vol. XII, p. 164. The words 'Je suis un pauvre misérable' ('I am a poor wretch') are from the 1760 *opéra-comique* L'*Île des fous*, with music by Duni; see ibid., p. 158 (n. 254).

34. LEW, vol. XII, p. 752.

35. Ibid. On this passage, see also Jean-Christophe Rebejkow, 'Diderot et l'opéra comique: de la farce au pathétique', *Romanische Forschungen*, 107 (1995), 145–56, which shows that Diderot sought variety of tone with appropriate gradation within a single dramatic work, unless a shock is itself dramatically motivated.

36. DPV, vol. XII, p. 170.

37. 'Sur l'harmonie des langues, et en particulier sur celle qu'on croit sentir dans les langues mortes' ('On the Harmony of Languages, and in Particular the Supposed Harmony of Dead Languages'), in Jean le Rond d'Alembert, *Œuvres*, 5 vols. (Paris: A. Belin, 1821–2), vol. IV, pp. 11–28 (p. 14).

38. DPV, vol. XII, p. 159. In Diderot's striking metaphor there is perhaps an echo of Rousseau's attribution, to Dionysius of Halicarnassus, of the conception of accent as 'la semence de toute musique' ('the seed of all music'). See 'Accent', in Rousseau, *Œuvres complètes*, vol. V, p. 614.

39. DPV, vol. XII, p. 752.

40. *Corr.*, vol. XI, p. 39. Cf. Burney in Rees's *Cyclopaedia*: 'Variety is perhaps more necessary in music than in poetry or painting; but that variety should never amount to wildness, or incoherence, nor should the regularity degenerate into monotony and dullness.' My thanks to Jacqueline Waeber for drawing my attention to this passage.

41. As shown in his 'Sur la musique, à l'occasion de *Castor*', *Mercure de France*, April 1772, pp. 159–79 (p. 161); quoted in Waeber, 'Déconstruire Rousseau'.

42. LEW, vol. II, pp. 692–3; DPV, vol. XIX, pp. 17–18.

43. LEW, vol. II, p. 704; DPV, vol. XIX, p. 28. See David Charlton, "'Envoicing" the *Orchestra*: Enlightenment Metaphors in Theory and Practice', in Charlton, *French Opera 1730–1830: Meaning and Media* (Aldershot: Ashgate, 2000), pp. 1–31.

44. DPV, vol. X, p. 153.

45. *Encyclopédie*, vol. VIII, p. 803; cf. Béatrice Didier, *La Musique des Lumières: Diderot, l'Encyclopédie, Rousseau* (Paris: Presses Universitaires de France, 1985), p. 270.

46. Didier, *La Musique des Lumières*, p. 365.

47. The most important passages outside *Le Neveu* are: a review of Davesne's *Les Jardiniers* in the *Correspondance littéraire* of 1 October 1771 (LEW, vol. IX, pp. 669–73), where Diderot insists upon appropriate unification of tone across dialogue and ariettes; his 'plan d'un opéra-comique', although this contains no discussion of music (LEW, vol. IV, pp. 360–94); and his positive references to Marmontel and Grétry's *Sylvain* in a letter to Grimm dated 19 February 1770 (*Corr.*, vol. X, p. 26).

48. See two articles by Jean-Christophe Rebejkow, 'Diderot et l'opéra-comique', to which we have already referred, and 'Nouvelles recherches sur la musique dans *Le Neveu de Rameau*', *Recherches sur Diderot et sur l'Encyclopédie*, 20 (1996), 57–74.

49. LEW, vol. XII, p. 756.

50. Ibid., p. 753.

51. Laurent Garcin, *Traité du mélo-drame, ou Réflexions sur la musique dramatique* (Paris: Vallat-la-Chapelle, 1772). Diderot's exchange with Burney about Garcin and Chastellux can be found in LEW, vol. IX, pp. 1, 120–8 and *Corr.*, vol. XI, pp. 213–17. As Downing Thomas has remarked, Diderot was aligned with Chastellux in his critique of Garcin's text-centred approach, and this can be seen in their respective approaches to mixture of spoken dialogue and song. See Thomas, *Aesthetics of Opera*, pp. 237–8.

52. Cited in Rousseau, *Œuvres complètes*, Vol. V, p. ccxxvii.

53. Ibid.

54. Jacqueline Waeber, *En musique dans le texte: le mélodrame, de Rousseau à Schoenberg* (Paris: Van Dieren, 2005), p. 40.

55. DPV, vol. XII, p. 167.

CHAPTER 15

Diderot and the aesthetics of the libretto

Béatrice Didier

In his *Essai sur l'opéra* (*Essay on Opera*), translated into French by Chastellux, Algarotti undertakes to defend the librettist, or 'rendre surtout au poète, les droits dont il a été dépouillé très injustement' ('above all give back to the poet the rights of which he has been most unjustly robbed').[1] Therefore he will expand on the key importance of the librettist, whose task goes beyond writing a text to serve as a 'pretext' for the music: 'le poète doit diriger les acteurs, les danseurs, les peintres, les machinistes. Il doit concevoir dans sa tête l'ensemble du drame ... Il doit, en un mot, être l'âme du spectacle.'[2] ('The poet must direct the actors, the dancers, the painters of the decor, the stagehands. He must keep in mind the whole of the dramatic performance ... he must, in a word, be the soul of the spectacle.') This apologia is to be understood in the context of criticisms aimed at libretti throughout the eighteenth century; and Diderot became involved in this protracted debate. We should also remember that the librettist performed some of the functions that would later be assumed by the theatrical director (a role that did not exist in Diderot's time).[3] So we must keep this context in mind if we are to understand the importance, and the occasional bitterness, of the disputes surrounding libretti – disputes that primarily involved Enlightenment authors, many of whom were also librettists.[4] Below we will discuss the following points: first, the extent of Diderot's involvement in the controversy over libretti; second, his conception of the ideal libretto; finally, his own practice as a librettist.

Throughout the eighteenth century, controversies over libretti are linked with discussions of the relative merits of French and Italian music. Such debates become particularly bitter in the infamous 'Querelle des Bouffons', but they have their roots in the seventeenth century. In Diderot's writing we can detect a certain exasperation aroused by the emptiness and the repetitive nature of the arguments put forward on both sides. In *Au Petit Prophète de Boehmischbroda* (*To the Little Prophet of Boehmischbroda*), written in 1753 when the Querelle was at its height, and when certain French voices praised the merits of Lully's *Armide* over those of Terradellas's *Nitocris*, he called on supporters of Italian music to prove 'que le musicien de la France doit tout à son poète; qu'au contraire le poète de l'Italie doit tout à son musicien' ('that the French composer owes everything to his librettist, whilst the Italian librettist owes everything to his composer')[5] – for when it came to opera the Italians were claimed to favour the music, and the French the libretto.

The eighteenth-century debate between supporters of French and Italian music is a complex one. To judge by the statements of the most intransigent on either side of the debate, the issue is quite simple: *prima la parola* ('the words come first') is the French way, whilst *prima la musica* ('the music comes first') is the Italian way. But there are absurd libretti in France, and on the other hand the French *philosophes* never waver in their support of the Italian librettist Metastasio.[6] So there is no clear split on national lines; rather, the debate shifts over time, with disagreements focused on the genre and its evolution. The career of the French playwright and librettist Quinault (1635–88) represents the golden age of the libretto written for operatic tragedy, a genre that becomes unfashionable during the eighteenth century; but a new style of libretto was to appear as a result of the trans-formation of the opera and the coming of *opéra-comique* to France.[7] This situation throws light on the debate, in *Le Neveu de Rameau* (*Rameau's Nephew*), between Lui and Moi, in which Lui asserts that 'La poésie lyrique est encore à naître' ('Lyric poetry is yet to be invented'), in response to which Moi cites Quinault, Lamotte and Fontenelle, but without persuading Lui: 'Il n'y a pas six vers de suite dans tous leurs charmants poèmes qu'on puisse musiquer.'[8] ('There are not six lines together in their charming poems that one might set to music.') Now, the examples of verse which Lui proceeds to cite approvingly might be used in the libretto of an *opera seria* (serious opera), not an *opéra-comique*; and they echo the thoughts on the same subject contained in Diderot's third *Entretien sur Le Fils naturel* (*Conversation on 'The Natural Son'*). So the nephew's ideas concerning the libretto of the future concern *opera seria* at least as much as, if not more than, *opéra-comique*. But we will see below that the libretto which Diderot himself wrote is clearly for an *opéra-comique*, a genre defended more than once by Lui in *Le Neveu de Rameau*.

Here as elsewhere, the dialogic form of *Le Neveu* allows Diderot to give vivid expression to two contradictory impulses. On the one hand, there is his admiration for Quinault, which he shares with many writers of his time. These fellow admirers include Voltaire, who will write to him: 'Tous les philosophes du monde fondus ensemble n'auraient pu parvenir à donner l'*Armide* de

Quinault.'⁹ ('All the *philosophes* in the world combined could not have managed to create Quinault's *Armide*.') On the other hand, there is Diderot's conviction, which he places in Lui's mouth, that a new era has dawned for opera: 'Quel chemin nous avons fait depuis le temps où nous citions la parenthèse d'*Armide*, *Le vainqueur de Renaud, si quelqu'un le peut être*, l'*Obéissons sans balancer* des *Indes galantes*, comme des prodiges de déclamation musicale!'¹⁰ ('What a distance we have come since we used to cite the parenthesis in [Quinault and Lully's] *Armide*, "The conqueror of Renaud, if anyone can defeat him", and that of [Jean-Philippe Rameau's] *Les Indes galantes*, "Let us obey without question", as prodigies of musical declamation!')

If the dialogue form of *Le Neveu de Rameau* lends itself to the expression of contradictory opinions, it also polarises the opinions in question. But we must remember – as it has often been said – that neither Lui nor Moi is the exclusive mouthpiece of the author. And if we consider the whole of Diderot's work, we will conclude that there need be no contradiction between admiring Quinault and believing that librettists of the second half of the eighteenth century should find new styles. Diderot's admiration for Quinault is equalled only by his love of Metastasio. Supporters of French and Italian music, of course, tend to back Quinault and Metastasio respectively (though Quinault raises an awkward problem for the supporters of Italian music who attempt to clinch the argument by citing the Italian poet). However, Diderot refuses to judge the relative merits of the two librettists: 'Il ne s'agit pas de commettre Quinault avec le Métastase. Les transfuges du parti français ne sont déjà que trop persuadés que ce Quinault est leur ennemi le plus redoutable. Il s'agit d'opposer *Lulli* à *Terradellas, Lulli*, le grand *Lulli*.'¹¹ ('I will not set Quinault against Metastasio. The deserters from the French to the Italian cause are already entirely convinced that Quinault is their greatest foe. I propose comparing Lully to Terradellas, Lully, the great Lully.') Diderot is well acquainted with the operas on which Quinault and Lully collaborated, and he spontaneously quotes from them; thus when discussing a painting by Boucher in the *Salon de 1765* he quotes two lines from Quinault which he describes as: 'ces deux vers que Lulli a si bien mis en musique, et qui donnent lieu à toute la bonté d'âme de Roland de se montrer' ('these two lines which Lully set so well to music and which suggest the full extent of Roland's goodness of heart').¹² Diderot is categorical: 'le doux Quinault' ('gentle Quinault') was 'si injustement déprécié par Boileau' ('so unfairly disparaged by Boileau').¹³

The debate had not yet run its course, for it concerned not only the comparison between French and Italian music, but also the relative importance of the librettist and the composer. For instance, the chevalier de

Chastellux, in his *Essai sur l'union de la poésie et de la musique (Essay on the Blending of Poetry and Music)*, published in 1765, crosses swords with Garcin. In a letter of 28 October 1771 to the English musicologist Burney, Diderot resumes this debate in the following terms: 'La grande question entre le chevalier de Chastellux et M. de Garcin, son réfutateur, est, ce me semble, de savoir si le poème doit être fait pour la musique, ou si le poète peut aller à sa fantaisie, et si le musicien n'est que son caudataire.' ('The important question dividing the Chevalier de Chastellux and Monsieur de Garcin, who refutes him, is, I believe, whether the libretto must be written for the music, or if the librettist can do as he pleases, so that the composer is merely his train-bearer.') Diderot certainly felt the debate was rather vain, because in reality libretto and music cannot be dissociated. And so he adds: 'Les poèmes de Quinault sont délicieux à lire, et la musique de Lulli est plate; mais cette plate musique ayant été composée pour ces poèmes, et ces poèmes composés pour cette musique, quiconque a tenté jusqu'à présent de musiquer *Armide* autrement que Lulli a fait de la musique plus plate encore que celle de Lulli.'[14] ('Quinault's verses are delightful to read, and Lully's music is dull; but since this dull music was composed for those verses, and vice versa, whoever has tried to set *Armide* to music differently from Lully has composed music even more dull than Lully's.') Yet later, in 1777, Gluck will rise to this musical challenge.

Once again Diderot calls for an end to hostilities in a review of Garcin's *Traité du mélodrame (Treatise on Drama accompanied by Music)*, where he writes that Marmontel 'n'a commencé à réussir que quand il a pris le parti de lire et d'imiter Métastase, d'être bien convaincu que le poète est fait pour le musicien, et que si le poète tire à lui toute la couverture, ils passeront tous deux une mauvaise nuit' ('only began to succeed when he decided to read and imitate Metastasio, and to be convinced that the poet exists for the convenience of the composer, and that if the poet tries to hog the blanket, they will both spend a restless night'). Naturally 'un grand poète qui serait un grand musicien, ferait beaucoup mieux que celui qui ne sera que l'un ou l'autre' ('a great poet who is also a great musician would produce better work than someone having either talent without the other') concludes Diderot in 'Observations sur le Traité du mélodrame' ('Observations on the *Treatise on Drama accompanied by Music*').[15] Is Diderot thinking of his former friend Jean-Jacques Rousseau, who was both composer and librettist of *Le Devin du village (The Village Soothsayer)*? After all, viewed with the benefit of hindsight, neither the libretto nor the music of Rousseau's opera seems to attain the heights of true genius. Libretti written by composers, even Berlioz or Wagner, seem poor indeed when compared with the corresponding music. But of course they were not written to be read in isolation from the music to which they are matched.

Diderot knew that the reductive quarrel that pitches French fans of libretto against music-loving Italians intersects with other, richer debates: those that centre on the question of declamation, naturalness and the imitation of nature. The development of concepts of the libretto can be linked with changing ideas on declamation, marked by a movement towards greater naturalism in the eighteenth century compared with the seventeenth. Treatises on rhetoric are applicable also to the art of singing, and here too tensions and contradictions surface, with Diderot citing now Racine listening to a performance by La Champmeslé, now Garrick and English acting, as he ponders on how the art of declamation can be renewed.[16] Rameau's nephew asserts: 'n'allez pas croire que le jeu des acteurs de théâtre et leur déclamation puissent nous servir de modèles' ('do not fall into the belief that actors' techniques and their declamation can serve as our models')[17] because he is probably thinking of a rather stiff and solemn style of declamation. But Diderot wanted the delivery of lines in theatre and opera alike to become more 'natural'. In the *Salon de 1767* he asserts: 'C'est nature et nature seule qui dicte la véritable harmonie d'une période entière, d'un certain nombre de vers' ('It is nature and nature alone that dictates the true harmony of an entire period, of a certain number of lines'),[18] but his example is taken from Quinault's *Armide* (ii.4)!

The ultimate model is indeed 'nature', with all the ambiguities of this notion which Diderot does not really question: makers of operas must imitate nature. Theatrical declamation and operatic singing are supposed to do precisely this; but is it 'natural' to sing while dying? Not until the end of the century will the notion of musical imitation be seriously questioned. And when this does happen, it is only in relation to instrumental music, with vocal music continuing to be seen as capable of reproducing the cries of passion, or the deepest and truest expressions of human nature. So there is a distinction to be made between two quite different senses of the word 'nature' in this connection. On the one hand, there is physical nature (storms, thunder, etc.), which instrumental music is not obliged to imitate in a servile manner; and on the other hand there is human nature, expressed in the affects, which are the very foundation of lyric art. The solution which Diderot has already touched upon would consist in using instrumental music, not to achieve a simplistic imitation of sounds, but to emphasise the way individuals respond to the effects of external nature (being frightened in a storm, or happy to see the morning sun).

So what makes a good libretto, according to Diderot? First, the librettist must choose interesting situations.[19] Thus in Fontenelle and Colasse's *Thétis et Pélée*, 'l'effet de cette scène vient de la situation intéressante que le poète a trouvée, mais le bruit de tonnerre n'ajoute rien'.[20] ('The effect of this scene comes from the interesting situation which the poet has hit upon, but the sound of thunder adds nothing.') The interest comes from the psychological tension felt by the characters and not from external effects. Thunder, at least, is a natural phenomenon; but how should the librettist treat *le merveilleux* (the marvellous)? This is a question that runs through all discussions of opera in the eighteenth century. As early as the 'Querelle des anciens et des modernes' ('quarrel of the ancients and moderns'), the fabulous, which was excluded from spoken tragedy, was allowed in the operatic version. This provoked Boileau's contempt, but it aroused the admiration of the 'moderns', who welcomed the fact that the marvellous, like fairy-tale, gave free rein to the imagination. In the third *Entretien sur Le Fils naturel*, the question of the marvellous is one point of disagreement between Dorval and Moi, in spite of their common admiration for Quinault. Moi wishes to allocate it a role in 'higher' forms of the genre: but Dorval insists: 'Le genre burlesque et le genre merveilleux n'ont point de poétique et n'en peuvent avoir.'[21] ('The burlesque and the marvellous genres have no poetics and can have none.') No poetics? What does Dorval mean? That it is impossible to formulate rules for the marvellous because imagination, which Pascal called 'la maîtresse d'erreur et de fausseté' ('the mistress of error and falsehood'), knows no rules? Or does he mean that it is impossible to integrate the fabulous and the marvellous in the poetics of the opera which the Enlightenment endeavours to define?[22]

Readers of the discussion between Dorval and Moi may be surprised to see 'burlesque' and 'marvellous' placed in the same aesthetic category; they may be shocked, even, as Moi is. Yet each of these genres, in its way, loses touch with art's 'proper' object: nature (which is transfigured in the marvellous and caricatured in the burlesque). Still, for Dorval there are degrees of transgression: he totally rejects the burlesque, which 'me déplaît partout' ('I dislike wherever I find it'), whilst he is more nuanced in his judgement of the marvellous. As for Moi, he tries to defend the operatic marvellous by comparing it with the marvellous in Epic. Dorval's answer to this draws on two different arguments. One is historical: marvellous adventures are no longer 'de saison' ('appropriate to our time'). The other – more interesting – concerns the question of staged illusion: 'Et j'ajouterai qu'il y a bien de la différence entre peindre à mon imagination et mettre sous mes yeux.'[23] ('And I will add that there is a great difference between representing something to my imagination and putting it in front of me.')

If the new opera cannot draw on the marvellous, what methods will the librettist use to create interesting situations? The third *Entretien* refers only to operatic tragedy because by now Diderot is considering *opera seria* rather than *opera buffa*, but the problem seems the same: if the aim is to draw cries of passion from great characters (the only kind allowed in tragedy, be it spoken or sung), then in order to 'arracher de ces âmes froides et contraintes l'accent de la nature' ('force the accent of nature from these cold, inhibited souls'),[24] they must be placed in extreme situations. Diderot cites *Iphigénie* and specifically Agamemnon's anguish when he has been persuaded to sacrifice his daughter; and a few pages further on, he proposes a 'récitatif obligé' and an aria for Clytemnestre.[25]

If great characters are to be treated in this way, why not the gods? They appear in the tragedies of the ancients, and in Lully and Rameau's operas. But no one still believes in the gods of mythology. Should we, then, have recourse to our own mythology, Christianity? But it is well known that operas with sacred themes run into difficulties under the *ancien régime*, and if a few little devils are allowed on stage, they are 'de mauvais goût' ('in bad taste').[26] Therefore operatic tragedy will finally have to adopt the same types of situation as spoken tragedy. On another point, too, Diderot proves neo-classical in his thinking: the unities of time, place and action allow for the preservation of unity of character: 'il ne s'agit sur la scène que d'une seule action; que d'une circonstance de la vie; que d'un intervalle très court, pendant lequel il est vraisemblable qu'un homme a conservé son caractère'.[27] ('On stage, there should only be one action; one circumstance; one very brief period of time, during which it is believable that a man should have been consistent in character.')

The imitation of nature remains the fundamental rule, but this rule, which is also the foundation of the neoclassical aesthetic, in fact requires opera to be totally renewed. The genre must abandon the marvellous for new directions: 'Je crains bien que ni les poètes, ni les musiciens, ni les décorateurs, ni les danseurs, n'aient pas encore une idée véritable de leur théâtre.'[28] ('I very much fear that neither the librettists, nor the composers, nor the painters of scenes, nor the dancers have yet attained a true idea of what their theatre might be.') And Dorval proclaims the surprising capacity of opera to surpass all other genres: 'Si le genre lyrique est mauvais, c'est le plus mauvais de tous les genres. S'il est bon, c'est le meilleur. Mais peut-il être bon, si l'on ne s'y propose point l'imitation de la nature, et de la nature la plus forte?'[29] ('If lyric theatre is bad, it is the worst of all genres. If it is good, it is the best. But can it be good, if its creators do not strive to imitate nature, and nature at its most impressive?') Combining all the arts, far from allowing a version of the marvellous, would allow, on the contrary, a truer imitation of nature.

Then there is the problem of dance: the librettist must also choreograph ballets. Dorval hopes that a man of genius will emerge to transform ballet into a kind of mime. Noverre was to do precisely this; but it is important to emphasise that the movement towards dance-as-imitation was begun even before Noverre: for instance by the librettist Cahusac.[30] It is also the librettist's task to give direction to the dancers, as Algarotti asserted. This is a subtle art since all words disappear in performance, yet it is by words alone that the librettist indicates the nature of the dance scenes; he may even have described the dancers' movements quite precisely. Indeed, if the dance becomes truly expressive, it can become independent of the opera, a self-contained spectacle; and the role of the librettist is no less important for that. The third *Entretien* develops into a ballet choreography, which we will examine below; but it is useful to note in advance that the spectacle in question is distinct from *opera seria*, since its characters are humble peasants.

Next, Diderot brings the conversation back to the subject of tragedy: Dorval wishes to establish an operatic version of ancient tragedy, whilst Moi inclines towards domestic tragedy instead.[31] This highlights a puzzling question: how is it that Dorval, a supporter of the *drame* and the mixture of genres in the theatre, remains so attached to the idea of 'pure' operatic tragedy? A few years after the *Entretiens sur Le Fils naturel* but ahead of the great Romantic operas, Da Ponte and Mozart's *Don Giovanni* will provide a magnificent example of tragedy and comedy mixed. Of course, this work cannot be termed a 'domestic tragedy': the action unfolds in an aristocratic world, and the comic elements are supplied by valets and peasants. If one wishes to find the lyric equivalent of the *drame*, it is better to look towards *opéra-comique* which gradually takes on sentimental tones, and is sometimes 'tragic' in the manner of Diderot's bourgeois tragedy.

Is it accurate to claim that Diderot envisages less daring reforms for the opera than the theatre, recommending in particular the use of prose for one but not for the other? Dorval provides the answer, and at the same time emphasises the specificity of the libretto: 'C'est que la tragédie, et en général toute composition destinée pour la scène lyrique, doit être mesurée.'[32] ('Tragedy, and in general any form intended to be sung, must be divided into measures.') So a distinction is proposed between operatic tragedy which remains close to classical tragedy, and *opéra bouffe* which would involve an alternation of spoken prose passages and sung verses. This distinction is fairly conservative. On the face of it, Diderot would indeed seem less bold concerning the reform of libretti and opera than that of spoken theatre.

So Diderot questions neither the division between lyric tragedy and *opéra-comique* nor the dogmatic principle that nature must be imitated.

And he proceeds, with considerable courage, to imagine performances in both genres. At the same time, he restricts himself largely to the text of the libretto and only gives a limited number of musical suggestions. As the basis of a libretto in the genre of operatic tragedy, he chooses two passages from Racine's *Iphigénie*: 'Je ne connais ni dans Quinault ni dans aucun poète des vers plus lyriques, ni de situation plus propre à l'imitation musicale.'[33] ('I know of no verses, nor any situation more suited to musical imitation than these, be they in Quinault or any other poet.') Only when he turns his attention to *opéra-comique* does he produce an original text.

In his treatment of the passage from Racine, he distinguishes three possible styles: straightforward; figurative; and a third, in which the other two would be combined. Clearly, the model for his straightforward style is Lully, whilst behind the combined style we can glimpse the influence of Rameau. The list: 'il n'y a ni *lance*, ni *victoire*, ni *tonnerre*, ni *vol*, ni *gloire*' ('there is neither spear, nor victory, nor thunder, nor flight, nor glory')[34] is virtually identical to the one contained in *Le Neveu de Rameau*.[35] This might seem a mere hangover from the quarrel between the supporters of Lully and those of Rameau, a dispute that Diderot had already caricatured in *Les Bijoux indiscrets* (1748). In that case, we would be returning to the opposition between Lully the melodist and Rameau the harmonist. But the distinction proposed in the third *Entretien* is more subtle, since, as we have seen, Diderot posits not two but three styles. Clytemnestre's aria expresses the deepest passion in the straightforward style. As for the figurative style: 'Ce n'est plus la mère d'Iphigénie que j'entends. C'est la foudre qui gronde; c'est la terre qui tremble; c'est l'air qui retentit de bruits effrayants.'[36] ('I no longer hear Iphigénie's mother. It is the clap of thunder, the earth's trembling, and terrible sounds ringing in the air.') The third style, if possible, would combine these two.

Of interest here is not the music, of which Diderot can only give a vague idea, but rather the libretto itself. The playwright intends to adapt his two passages from Racine's *Iphigénie* (v.4 and iv.4), as follows. First he will select the part that is to become the recitative, then the lines on which the aria will be based – the recitative/aria distinction being standard in the *opera seria*. In both Diderot's examples, the beginning of the aria corresponds to a moment of heightened energy and indignation, and it is easy to imagine a prima donna making the most of this. As for the lines on which the recitative is to be based, they are interrupted after each phrase by a ritornello, i.e. a brief passage for orchestra alone. It should be noted that Diderot adds a response 'par son père' ('by Iphigénie's father'), though there is no such line in Racine; this allows him to emphasise a particularly shocking aspect of the sacrifice. But it is in the libretto for the aria that Diderot takes a certain liberty with Racine's text: using the playwright's exact words, he transforms the passage into broken sentences, as though Clytemnestre were gasping for breath. This involves repeating words which Racine uses only once: 'Barbares, arrêtez' ('Barbaric men, desist') becomes: 'Barbares, barbares, arrêtez, arrêtez' ('Barbaric men, barbaric men, desist, desist').[37] After all, to convey the 'cri animal de la passion' ('the animal cry of passion'), 'il faut que [les] expressions soient pressées les unes sur les autres; il faut que la phrase soit courte; que le sens en soit coupé, suspendu; que le musicien puisse disposer du tout et de chacune de ses parties; en omettre un mot, ou le répéter.'[38] ('Expressions must tumble out pell-mell; each sentence must be short, its meaning truncated, suspended; the composer must be able to do as he wishes with the whole and each of its parts, to miss out a word or to repeat it.') The librettist's freedom with respect to Racine's text will prepare the way for the composer's freedom with respect to the text of the libretto.

Beside these two examples of operatic tragedies, Diderot outlines libretti for an *opéra-comique* and a ballet. The plan for an *opéra-comique* is quite detailed, with the spoken prose passages being written out.[39] The arias are indicated, without the words being completely worked out; in Act I, there is an arietta against marriage and a refrain;[40] in Act II, scene I, the strolling players' song is to be a vaudeville, culminating in a chorus.[41] A burlesque arietta is indicated for scene 2 of the same Act, and 'la chose est difficile' ('the matter is difficult') could well form a sung refrain, but this is not specified; in scene 6 'elle chante un morceau qui peint je ne sais quoi qui se passe en elle' ('she sings a few lines of song that evoke something or other that she is feeling'); in Act III, scene 2 there is 'une chanson d'ironie' ('an ironic song'). There is no detail given for musical passages in Act IV; in Act V, the burlesque trial is sung rather than spoken. Twice there is a suggestion that a 'scène folle' ('crazy scene') could be written in Italian or in the 'langue franque' ('lingua franca'); this would presumably be accompanied by music, though this is not specified.[42]

This text is clearly more than an outline; it is a very detailed scenario, at least as far as the spoken passages and the placing of the singing are concerned. The system of alternate singing and speaking is characteristic of *opéra-comique* as it was becoming established in France; but as Diderot's text is difficult to date with any precision, it is also difficult to know whether his ideas about the genre anticipate or follow prevailing fashion. Either way, his originality is detectable in the verve and dynamism which he brings to his subject. Roger Lewinter sees his contribution as an 'anti-*Devin du village*' ('an anti-*Village*

Soothsayer').[43] In point of fact Diderot's representation of country life is quite different from Rousseau's, being far less idealised: money and wine are clearly referred to, as is Colette's premature pregnancy. The presence of guilds of strolling players and the pseudo-initiation scene certainly belong to a vein of writing in which realism borders on the burlesque – even though the latter was rejected in the third *Entretien* – so that the carnivalesque atmosphere lends itself to Bakhtinian readings.

The description of a ballet is incorporated into the text of the third *Entretien*, as an example of Dorval's suggested reform of theatrical dance. This ballet also has a rustic theme but is less realistic, whilst evoking popular superstitions and belief in ghosts (like the outline for the *opéra-comique* already discussed). Particularly interesting in the planned ballet is the fact that musical terms are used to indicate performers' movements: ('récitatif de la danse' ('dance recitative'), 'ariette de dépit' ('angry arietta'), 'duo' ('duet'), 'quatuor' ('quartet'), 'chœur' ('chorus'), 'ce monologue est un récitatif obligé' ('this monologue is a *récitatif obligé*'), whilst the truly musical passages (which seem to be instrumental, not sung) are also indicated.[44] Thus dance becomes entirely expressive in and of itself, rather than existing simply to render the opera pleasing to watch without being linked to its story. Of course, this new conception of expressive dance still requires the writing of a 'libretto' whose text contains no lines to be spoken or sung, but whose author fully assumes the role of director and choreographer. This kind of reform had already been suggested by Nicolini, who is explicitly named by Diderot; the *théâtres de la Foire* and campaigners for expressive dance had also helped to blaze a trail. But Diderot's contribution is immensely important, and prepares the way for the transformation of the form and function of the libretto as well as of dance itself.

Diderot's theory and practice as a librettist constitute an important part of his work. He does not entirely break with the practices of his time – hence he retains the separation between operatic tragedy in verse and *opéra-comique* in prose (with rhythmic couplets) – a separation that has aesthetic and social ramifications, with comic opera being seen as hierarchically inferior to the tragic version. In this respect, Diderot was less radical than in his theory and practice of the *drame bourgeois*. Had he applied the revolution he had in mind for spoken theatre to its sung equivalent, Romantic opera would have been the result; meanwhile, *opéra-comique*, which was becoming more and more interested in sensibility and in moving situations, was beginning to realise the fusion of genres which Diderot campaigned for more clearly in the *drame bourgeois* than in opera. If Diderot was less radical concerning opera, it is presumably because of the idea so forcibly expressed by Dorval: only rhythmic texts can be successfully set to music. Another factor may have been Diderot's sense of his own limitations as a poet; hence his recourse to Racine for examples of lyric tragedy, and his failure to write the sung passages in his outline of an *opéra-comique* (we can assume that these would have been in verse, as are vaudevilles). Yet prose has rhythms of its own, and soon enough this was to be proved by Romantic opera and by prose poetry. Diderot seems to know this sooner than most when he campaigns for more natural declamation in the theatre; but he remains convinced that 'naturalness' in opera is not the same as elsewhere, that the *opera seria* expresses nature through suffering, as in Clytemnestre's cry of passion which is also the cry of nature. 'All the arts must imitate nature': in the second half of the eighteenth century, this precept appears so complex that it will eventually be abandoned, or at least considerably relaxed, in the musical sphere. This is yet another way in which Diderot proved to be ahead of his time.[45]

NOTES

1. Francesco Algarotti, *Essai sur l'opéra* (*Essay on Opera*), trans. François Jean de Chastellux (Paris: Ruault, 1773), p. 6.
2. Ibid., p. 10.
3. This topic was discussed during a colloquium organised by Pierre Frantz at the Université de Paris IV in December 2008.
4. See Béatrice Didier, *La Musique des Lumières* (Paris: Presses Universitaires de France, 1985).
5. DPV, vol. XIX, p. 13.
6. See my forthcoming article on the myth of Metastasio from Diderot to Stendhal, based on a paper given at the colloquium mentioned above (n. 3).
7. According to Kerry Murphy, '*Opéra-comique* is defined as opera with spoken recitatives in contrast to opera with sung recitatives. It need not have comic subject-matter.' See Peter France (ed.), *The New Oxford Companion to Literature in French* (Oxford: Clarendon Press, 1995), p. 586. *The New Oxford Dictionary of English* gives the following definition of 'recitative': 'musical declamation of the kind usual in the narrative and dialogue parts of opera and oratorio, sung in the rhythm of ordinary speech with many words on the same note' (editor's note).
8. DPV, vol. XII, pp. 168–9.
9. *Corr.*, vol. XII, p. 205. The letter in question is dated 20 April 1773.
10. DPV, vol. XII, pp. 171–2.
11. DPV, vol. XIX, p. 14.
12. DPV, vol. XIV, p. 58.
13. LEW, vol. VIII, p. 268.
14. *Corr.*, vol. XI, pp. 214–15.

15. LEW, vol. ix, p. 941.
16. Marie Desmares Champmeslé (1642–98) was particularly famous for playing roles written by her admirer Racine. David Garrick was the most famous English actor of the eighteenth century (editor's note).
17. DPV, vol. xii, p 170.
18. DPV, vol. xvi, p. 385.
19. In the eighteenth century, 'intéressant' could mean 'moving' as well as 'interesting' (editor's note).
20. LEW, vol. ii, p. 676.
21. DPV, vol. x, pp. 145–6.
22. Dorval proceeds to cite a number of examples, including that of Bluebeard. Picturing Bluebeard's wife at the top of the tower, in desperate hope of rescue, Dorval asks why the scene creates no pathos for an (adult) audience. The answer is: 'C'est qu'il y a une Barbe bleue qui détruit son effet' ('Because there is a Bluebeard that destroys the effect') (DPV, vol. x, pp. 146–7). Whilst there have been successful operatic treatments of Bluebeard – many have been enchanted by Debussy's *Pelléas et Mélisande* (*Pelleas and Melisande*), Paul Dukas' *Ariane et Barbe-Bleue* (*Ariadne and Bluebeard*) or Bartók's *Bluebeard's Castle* – it is also true that opera goers' horizon of expectation has radically changed since Diderot's time.
23. DPV, vol. x, p. 147.
24. Ibid., p. 148.
25. The 1762 edition of the *Dictionnaire de l'Académie française* defines 'récitatif obligé' as follows: 'récitatif avec accompagnement et coupé par des instruments' ('recitative supported by instruments and alternating with purely instrumental passages'). See DPV, vol. x, p. 157 (n. 176) (editor's note).
26. DPV, vol. x, p. 149.
27. Ibid., p. 149.
28. Ibid., p. 150.
29. Ibid.
30. See my forthcoming article, 'Pas de mots' ('No Words'), based on a paper given at the Verona colloquium that took place in December 2008.
31. DPV, vol. x, p. 156.
32. Ibid.
33. Ibid., p. 157.
34. Ibid., p. 159.
35. DPV, vol. xii, p. 73.
36. DPV, vol. x, p. 158.
37. Ibid, pp. 157–8.
38. DPV, vol. xii, p. 169.
39. LEW, vol. iv, pp. 361ff.
40. Ibid., pp. 365, 370.
41. According to S. Beynon John, 'By the eighteenth century, [vaudeville] was used to refer to performances by the strolling players at the Paris fairs.' See France, *The New Oxford Companion*, p. 827 (editor's note).

42. LEW, vol. IV, p. 381 (Act II, scene 5).
43. Ibid., p. 361.
44. DPV, vol. X, pp. 153–60.
45. An article that appeared in *Musica* in March 1911 records an interview of Debussy by Fernand Divoire. In the course of this interview, Debussy addresses himself to a number of questions which have been discussed in this chapter, but his views are markedly different from Diderot's. See Claude Debussy, *Monsieur Croche* (Paris: Gallimard, 1971), pp. 200–1.

CHAPTER 16

Ekphrasis and related issues in Diderot's Salons

Tom Baldwin

Questions of linguistic transparency and opacity have pervaded scholarly discussion about the working of Diderot's ekphrasis. The critical terrain can, broadly speaking, be divided into two approaches. The first consists in a form of detective labour that results in a precise identification of the 'real' work of art described by the text. This work is identified as the source of the ekphrasis, which is construed as a transparent linguistic window. For example, in her impressive two-volume study of Diderot and art, *Diderot critique d'art* (which remains a key reference in Diderot studies), Else Marie Bukdahl writes: 'À des fins de description, d'interprétation, et de caractérisation des différentes œuvres, [Diderot] a élaboré une représentation impartiale et neutre de la totalité artistique mais aussi quelques procédés poétiques qui s'apparentent à une technique de transposition sur le plan de la langue.'[1] ('In order to describe, to interpret and to characterise different works, [Diderot] developed an impartial and neutral representation of the artistic whole as well as certain poetic devices which are similar, at the linguistic level, to a technique of transposition.')

Diderot is presented here as the inventor of 'une technique imparable pour capter les événements du visible' ('a fail-safe technique for capturing events of the visible').[2] The impartiality and neutrality of Diderot's work guarantees its fidelity to its object. Even his more 'poetic' passages, in which attention risks being drawn to the text's literary rather than its mimetic function, are to be understood as a neutral and faithful transposition into language of the painted image. The latter poses little difficulty for the determined art-spotter: 'Diderot entend fournir, sur les œuvres d'art, des descriptions exhaustives et émettre des appréciations précises et impartiales. Il désire que ses comptes rendus se distinguent par l'exactitude des descriptions et l'équité des jugements.'[3] ('Diderot intends to supply exhaustive descriptions and to put forward precise and impartial judgements of works of art. He wants his reviews to stand out on account of their descriptive exactness and fairness of judgement.') In the *Salons*, on this analysis at least,

Diderot produces textual images that are to be understood as faithful transpositions – exact textual imitations – of pictorial images. Insofar as the pictures that are transcribed in Diderot's writing really exist (or existed), 'spotting' them or discovering them amounts to a discovery of the truth, the *fidélité*, of the text.

The second approach understands Diderot's ekphrasis in terms of outright textual 'obliteration' – a radical outdoing – of the painted work. The writing of art criticism is understood as little more than a pretext for an exercise in figurative or poetic language, constituting what David Scott has called a 'flexing of linguistic muscles' which leaves the painted image for dead.[4] The ekphrastic text is particularly brutal in its treatment of the image: a marker of the writer's creativity is his ability to 'virtually obliterate' in writing the painting to which his text might otherwise be taken to refer.[5] This approach is more common in recent work on Diderot and painting. Annie Mavrakis, for example, contends that Diderot merely replaces the painted image 'par son propre tableau' ('with his own painting') which has sprung 'tout entier de son imagination' ('entirely from his imagination').[6]

While these approaches are certainly dominant in the critical literature, the work of some other critics suggests that such extreme models, while instructive in their way, are not supported by Diderot's texts. For example, in *The Object of Art: The Theory of Illusion in Eighteenth-Century France*, Marian Hobson provides a close reading of the well-known 'Promenade Vernet' ('Vernet Promenade') in the *Salon de 1767* and argues that the reader of Diderot's text is engaged in an oscillation between illusion or immersion and awareness.[7] This oscillation is a response to the intricate and playful movement – a careful blurring of the boundaries – between descriptions of nature as art and art as nature in which Diderot is seen to excel. It is in this sense that while he loudly reviles the play of painterly 'papillotage', Diderot's critical practice can in fact be said to represent it.[8] Similarly, in the article on Fragonard's *Corésus et Callirhoé* (an equally well-visited example), art 'refers to nature, to what is beyond itself, and of which it is yet a part'. Diderot's article, in which he describes the painting as part of a dream that takes place in the 'antre de Platon' ('Plato's cave'), is understood by Hobson as a 'doubling back' of the Platonic hierarchy of the arts (with writing firmly rooted at the bottom), in which all is now 'dissimulation' and 'of which art is only one kind'.[9] Fragonard's work is to be viewed, then, merely as a '"grande machine" referring to the non-existent'.[10]

Now, in spite of the undeniable perspicuity of Hobson's account, I would like to try to move the focus away from the appearance of paintings as Diderot describes them and more squarely onto the actual stuff of which his descriptions are made. I would also like to get away from Vernet and Fragonard. In attempting this, I shall comment inter alia upon some recent essays that adopt a similar approach. I will also show that the two extreme approaches to ekphrasis outlined above, which understand the relationship between word and image in terms of linguistic transparency or radical displacement, as either presence or absence, cannot do justice to the shadowy intricacy and instability – the sheer strangeness – of Diderot's words about pictures.

WRITING AND *PAPILLOTAGE*

Shane Agin has argued that Diderot's 'dream' in the 1765 article on Fragonard's *Corésus et Callirhoé* is significant less for what it says about representation in Fragonard's painting than for what it reveals 'about the mimetic relationship in the written account between the art writer, the work of art, and the reader'.[11] While most critics view the 'dream' as another example among many (albeit a highly elaborate one) of Diderot's 'poetic method', by virtue of which the painting is somehow made more 'visible, more tangible in the imagination of the reader', Agin argues that readings of this kind are the victims of a 'powerful artifice of literary representation', since 'what the reader conceives in his/her imagination as Fragonard's painting is, in fact, only tangentially related to the actual object hung on the walls of the Louvre'.[12] The reader is therefore deceived into thinking that he or she has seen Fragonard's painting while all along 'the only work of art they have experienced is Diderot's *conte*'.[13] It might be argued, of course, that this is an effect of all of Diderot's descriptions, not only this one. We never 'see' the work of art in anything like a direct and non-tangential sense. We are, after all, reading Diderot's text. In any case, Agin concludes that such literary deceits are a function of Diderot's realisation that language is simply 'inadequate' to translate 'the beauties of the visual work of art into words'.[14] What Agin calls Diderot's *contes* are to be read, therefore, as a desperate coming to terms with ekphrastic indifference. It is in 1767, Agin argues, that Diderot finally recognises the 'incapacity' of language to represent the visual, calling for images to accompany his texts.[15] This recognition, Agin claims, 'marked the end of the *Salon*-writing project'.[16]

Agin's argument rests above all on the following points: (1) that Diderot intends his reader to conceive of and to experience his articles on Fragonard and Vernet as wholly autonomous literary productions and that none of the articles in the preceding first three *Salons* can be viewed as autonomous in this way; (2) that, consequently, a text which Agin describes as 'tangentially related' to a 'real' painting (Fragonard's *Corésus et Callirhoé*) in fact says almost nothing about that particular painting; (3) that Diderot may have fully believed in the *capacity* of language to represent the visual before 1767 (with the exception of the language of the Fragonard piece, presumably); (4) that Diderot is worn out, his 'art writing' more or less moribund or blind after 1767.[17] Each of these possibilities is problematic. First of all, there is a clear difference between saying that language is fundamentally 'incapable' of representing painting (or of making painting tangible or visible in the imagination of a reader) and arguing that language is not a mere window onto the objects it describes. Diderot does not abandon – at least not absolutely – the idea that language may have the capacity to represent painting. Instead, as we shall see later on, he does nevertheless force his readers to recognise that the language used to describe visual works of art (or any other object) is not transparently mimetic. But this is not to say that a linguistic description is simply powerless to represent the real or to produce a 'reality effect'. As Hobson's analysis of the Vernet article clearly demonstrates, the power of Diderot's text to stimulate an intuition or belief in his readers that he has been successful in describing an object in the world (or in nature) is not at all annihilated by the machinations of a supremely 'autonomous' text. Indeed, one of the important effects of a significant number of Diderot's writings is the subtle *va-et-vient* they impose on their readers' attention, inviting them, much like Diderot himself before a Chardin, to think of referential security *with* incompletion, mimetic transparency *with* material opacity. Second, it is not the case that before 1767 (the article on Fragonard notwithstanding) Diderot believed positively in the powers of texts to conjure up the visual appearance of things. The earlier *Salons* are just as playful and riddled with lures and deceits as the later articles on Fragonard and Vernet. In other words, Diderot *never* makes it easy for his readers to reconstruct mentally the paintings he describes – this is not an effect produced only after 1767.

The 1765 article on Fragonard is understandably a favourite among critics who seek to highlight the teasing play of *papillotage* in Diderot's work. However, to my knowledge, none has drawn attention to the short article that comes immediately after it, in which Diderot describes a *paysage* by the same artist:

On y voit un pâtre debout sur une butte; il joue de la flûte; il a son chien à côté de lui avec une paysanne qui l'écoute. Du même côté une campagne. De l'autre des rochers et des arbres. Les rochers sont beaux; le pâtre est bien éclairé et de bel effet; la femme est faible et floue; le ciel mauvais.[18]

(We see a shepherd standing on a knoll; he plays the flute; his dog is beside him, and a peasant woman who listens to him. On this same side a landscape view. On the other some rocks and trees. The rocks are beautiful; the shepherd is well lit and makes a fine effect; the woman is weak and indistinct; the sky poor.)

This passage provides a written equivalent of the flickering effects of the painting described in the previous article (Fragonard's *Corésus et Callirhoé*). But 'papillotage' is created in this case by the tension between the referential and the more purely literary (some would say self-referential) aspects of the passage. On a referential level, the passage provides the bare minimum in terms of information concerning the painting's content and its *ordonnance*. It represents a shepherd standing on a knoll or hillock, playing the flute. He is accompanied by a dog and a peasant woman. They are in the 'country-side'. The other 'side' of the painting contains representations of rocks and trees. Some effort is being made here to 'represent the visual', even if this is a description (like all descriptions, as Diderot regularly points out) that would 'fit' or could be satisfied by a large number of pictures or even none. However, on a stylistic level, the use of assonance and alliteration in the first and last sentences draws our attention away from the image and towards the text as text. A strong sense of textual artifice disrupts and deflates the reader's sense that he or she can 'visualise' the image in some way, but it cannot be said entirely to destroy it. On a 'generic' level, the passage hints at the familiar conventions of the pastoral through the use of terms such as 'pâtre', 'flûte', 'paysanne', 'chien', 'campagne', 'rochers' and with its basic rhyme structure; but this tendency towards pastoral lyricism is held in check by the use of prosaic terms such as 'butte' (rather than, say, 'colline' ('hill')), which seems only to be there for the sake of the rhyme with 'flûte'. Meanwhile, the sounds of the words used stimulate associations that work against their mimetic function. For while the painting is said to be split into two 'sides', one representing the shepherd and a 'campagne', the other rocks and trees, the sounds of a number of the words used to describe the first 'side' in fact evoke, by association, the content of the second 'side', and vice versa: the dental [t] sounds of 'butte' and 'flûte' evoke the sharp, vertical hardness of rocks rather than the undulations of the countryside, which are suggested in turn by the round sounds ('be*aux*'; 'éclairé'; 'effet'; 'm*auvais*) of most of the final sentence which begins with a description of the rocks. The 'autre' in the middle of it all is the *entre-deux* of this chiasmatic patterning of rhyme. Wherever we look in this description, then, we encounter a form of writerly *papillotage*. The reader is confronted by a form of writing in which 'presence' (principally but not exclusively the presence of the picture) is repeatedly undermined but not entirely absent.

What may appear at first to be comfortably 'present' or identifiable, be it reference (unmediated mimetic transparency), style, or genre, is always accompanied – its univocal 'presence' disrupted – by its 'other' in a spectral movement within the text which guarantees that *nothing* (including the textuality or literarity of the text and not only the painting to which it refers) can be said to be 'there' in a fully stable manner.

THE PAINTING AS PHANTOM

While Norman Bryson may have been the first to write extensively about Diderot's 'phantom *tableaux*', many other critics have augmented the genre.[19] Diderot's description of a composition by Doyen in the *Salon de 1761* is a particularly striking example (to which Bryson and others do not refer). Here is the beginning of the passage in question:

Mais voici une des plus grandes compositions du Salon. C'est le Combat de Diomède et d'Énée, sujet tiré du cinquième livre de l'Iliade d'Homère. J'ai relu à l'occasion du tableau de Doyen cet endroit du poète. Ah, mon ami, il y a là soixante vers à décourager l'homme le mieux appelé à la poésie. C'est un enchantement de situations terribles et délicates, et toujours la couleur et l'harmonie qui conviennent. Voici, si j'avais été peintre, le tableau qu'Homère m'eût inspiré. On aurait vu Énée renversé aux pieds de Diomède. Vénus serait accourue pour le secourir. Elle eût laissé tomber une gaze qui eût dérobé son fils à la fureur du héros grec. Au-dessus de la gaze qu'elle aurait tenue suspendue de ses doigts délicats, se serait montrée la tête divine de la déesse, sa gorge d'albâtre, ses beaux bras, et le reste de son corps mollement balancé dans les airs. J'aurais élevé Diomède sur un amas de cadavres. Le sang eût coulé sous ses pieds. Terrible dans son aspect et son attitude, il eût menacé la déesse de son javelot. Cependant les Grecs et les Troyens se seraient entr'égorgés autour de lui. On aurait vu le char d'Énée fracassé, et l'écuyer de Diomède saisissant ses chevaux fougueux. Pallas aurait plané sur la tête de Diomède. Apollon aurait secoué à ses yeux sa terrible égide. Mars, enveloppé d'une nue obscure, se serait repu de ce spectacle terrible.[20]

(But here is one of the largest compositions in the Salon. It is the Battle between Diomedes and Aeneas, a subject taken from Book Five of Homer's *Iliad*. I re-read this part of the poet's work after seeing Doyen's painting. Ah, my friend, there's enough here to discourage a man with the greatest poetic calling. It's an enchantment of terrible and delicate situations; the colour and the harmony are always exactly as required. If I had been a painter, here is the painting that Homer would have inspired me to do. We would have seen Aeneas, knocked to the ground, at Diomedes' feet. Venus would have rushed over to rescue him. She would have unfurled a gauze that would have shielded her son from the Greek hero's fury. Above the gauze, which she would have held aloft with her delicate fingers, the goddess's divine head, along with her alabaster throat, her beautiful arms, would have been on display, the rest of her body floating gently in the breeze. I would have raised Diomedes up on a pile of corpses. Blood would have run beneath his feet. Terrifying in appearance and attitude, he would have threatened the goddess with his spear. In the meantime, all around him, the Greeks and Trojans would have been slitting each other's throats. We would have seen Aeneas' wrecked chariot with Diomedes' squire seizing his spirited horses. Pallas would have hovered over Diomedes' head and Apollo would have shaken his fearsome shield before his eyes. Mars, shrouded in a dark cloud, would have gorged himself on this fearsome spectacle.)

'Here's what I would have done': statements of this kind occur on numerous occasions in the *Salons*. Annie Mavrakis has argued that, in such cases, Diderot has forgotten that he is not a *painter*: 'celui qui dit "je" ne se souvient plus qu'il n'est pas peintre, il se fantasme tel' ('he who says "I" no longer remembers that he is not a painter; he fantasises himself as such'). For Mavrakis, Diderot's aim here is to 'faire surgir un tableau tout entier de son imagination' ('to make an entire painting spring up from his imagination').[21] While Diderot is keen to modify a great many paintings, it is not clear why such a creative or imaginative act would require him to forget that he is not a painter but a writer. It is surely neither a condition nor a consequence of his imagining himself as a painter that he forget what he is really doing. Surprisingly, Mavrakis does not discuss the third paragraph of the Doyen article, which reads as follows:

[Doyen] a élevé son Diomède sur un tas de cadavres. Il est terrible. Effacé sur un de ses côtés, il porte le fer de javelot en arrière. Il insulte à Vénus qu'on voit au loin renversée entre les bras d'Iris. Le sang coule de sa main blessée le long de son bras. Pallas plane sur la tête de Diomède. Apollon, enveloppé d'une nuée, se jette entre le héros grec et Énée qu'on voit renversé. Le dieu effraye de son regard et de son égide. Cependant on se massacre et le sang coule de tous côtés.[22]

([Doyen] has raised his Diomedes up on a pile of corpses. He is fearsome. Turned to one side, he raises his spear behind him. He is threatening Venus, who can be seen in the distance and has fallen into Iris's arms. Blood drips from his injured hand down the length of his arm. Pallas hovers above Diomedes' head. Apollo, shrouded in a cloud, throws himself between the Greek hero and Aeneas, who, we see, has been knocked to the floor. Both the god's expression and his shield are frightening. Meanwhile, the massacre continues and blood flows on all sides.)

Doyen's picture represents the wrong 'moment' and is consequently 'toute d'effroi' ('all terror').[23] While he has chosen to represent the moment after Venus is injured, Diderot would have shown the moment before the injury occurs. This paragraph – or rather its relation to the preceding one – permits us to highlight a significant problem with the assertion that Diderot merely replaces Doyen's image 'par son propre tableau' ('with his own picture') and which has sprung 'tout entier de son imagination' ('entirely from his imagination').[24] The situation is more complex than that. Mavrakis's assertions do not do justice to the ludic superpositions and manipulations at work in Diderot's text. First, and most importantly, this is a text that, in producing a vivid image of a painting – or two paintings, one virtual and the other actual – will not allow us to forget that it is a text. Its literary effect is to blur the boundaries between the virtual and the actual, the 'real' and the merely 'possible'. It is not the case, as one critic has suggested, that 'cette façon de décrire a ses limites, dans la mesure où elle entraîne l'auteur fort loin des tableaux' ('this method of description has its limits insofar as it greatly distances the author from the paintings') and sees the writer arrogantly 'substituting' the artist's representation with his own.[25] It is mistaken, I think, to view Diderot's phantom *tableau* as a monadic 'idéal littéraire' ('literary ideal') which has lost all contact with Doyen's image. Diderot does not simply 'reinvent' the painting in writing; it is not the case that 'l'ekphrasis du tableau à faire annule aisément le tableau réel, prend sa place et s'impose au lecteur' ('the ekphrasis of the painting-to-be-done readily cancels out the real painting, takes its place and imposes itself on the reader').[26] This view is no less mistaken than that (expressed by Bukdahl, for example) which understands Diderot's work as a neutral and faithful 'transposition' into language of the painted image. If we look closely at the third paragraph, we see that Diderot endeavours to describe what Doyen's composition in fact contains – to represent its visual effect in some way. He also tries to show that the work is not the painting he himself (having re-read Homer) would have made. In the latter regard, we see that, in spite of the clear differences there are also some important similarities, not only in terms of the content of these two items, painting and 'painting' as it were, but also in the language used to describe them. There is no *paryponoian* here, no 'rien de tout cela' ('nothing of the sort') that might help us to separate the virtual from the actual.[27] Where Diderot would have 'élevé Diomède sur un amas de cadavres', Doyen 'a élevé son Diomède sur un tas de cadavres'. Diderot's Diomedes would be 'terrible dans son aspect et son attitude' and Doyen's is 'terrible'. In Diderot's composition, 'Pallas aurait plané sur la tête de Diomède'. In Doyen's, 'Pallas plane sur la tête de Diomède'. Diderot's Apollo would have 'sécoué à ses yeux [Diomedes'] sa terrible égide'. Doyen's god 'l'effraye de son regard et de son égide'. The literary effects of this kind of repetition are difficult to unpack. We might say that the repetitive phrases absorb one another and thus the actual into the virtual and vice versa. Having read the first paragraph, we may wonder what the 'source' of Diderot's ekphrasis in the second paragraph really is. Is it Doyen's painting, the *Iliad*, or a combination of the two? We are subsequently struck by the linguistic similarities between the second paragraph and the first half of the third. Is the 'source' of Diderot's description in the third paragraph Doyen's painting and/or the *Iliad*, then, or is it in fact his own description of that painting and/or text in the second paragraph? While the text may lure the reader into a search for origins (be they in the work of Homer or in Doyen's painting), this search is significantly disrupted by one's awareness of the possibility that this is a self-describing text. Anouchka Vasak suggests that the novelty of Diderot's *Salons* lies in their author's ability to enter 'dans le tableau comme le feront les personnages de *Mary Poppins*' ('into the painting like the characters in *Mary Poppins*').[28] If Diderot is able to behave in this way, we, his readers, are more like the unfortunate – but tireless – Wile E. Coyote of the Warner Bros. cartoon (making Diderot more of a Roadrunner, perhaps) who, while he may see the painted tunnels and holes on the rocky edifices into which his nemesis runs, can never enter them himself. While Diderot can move through the paintings, so to speak, all straightforward readerly 'access' to the paintings he describes in his writing is blocked. Diderot's article is a layered text, composed of a variety of different elements or 'sources': the text of the *Iliad* (even if Diderot does not quote from it directly), his description of the painting by Doyen, and the modification of it. As Michel Delon puts it in his analysis of Diderot's article on Pierre's *Jugement de Pâris* in the *Salon de 1761*, 'il s'agit moins de remplacer une composition ou une expression par une autre que d'instaurer un va-et-vient entre ce qui est et ce qui pourrait être, entre le visible et l'irreprésentable' ('it is less a question of replacing a composition or an expression with another than of setting up a process of coming and going between what is and what could be, between the visible and the unrepresentable').[29] One has the impression of superimposed transparencies rather than a fully present or stable image or text, and this, along with 'tous les subjonctifs et les conditionnels ... du salonnier' ('all of the *salonnier*'s subjunctives and conditionals') creates a sense of oscillation and movement.[30] *Pace* Mavrakis, *phantasia* has not simply 'relayé la mimèsis' ('taken over from mimesis').[31] In the words of Louis Marin (to which Mavrakis's article refers), 'la puissance de l'*ekphrasis* est ici à son comble, à la fois hallucinatoire et identificatrice' ('the power of ekphrasis is at its peak here; it is both hallucinatory and identificatory').[32] We thus encounter the simultaneous work of fixity and flow, of figuration and disfiguration in Diderot's verbal figures – in an image that constitutes what Stéphane Lojkine views as an intermediary or undifferentiated zone, at once grasped by the reader and yet slipping away from him or her.[33]

Diderot wears away the boundaries between *phantasia* and mimesis, adding terms to the *va-et-vient* that Delon describes. Consider, for example, the article on Lagrenée's *La Charité romaine*:

Ce n'est pas là le tableau que j'ai dans l'imagination. Je ne veux pas absolument que ce malheureux vieillard ni cette femme charitable soupçonnent qu'on les observe; ce soupçon arrête l'action et détruit le sujet. J'enchaîne le vieillard; la chaîne attachée aux murs du cachot lui tient les mains sur le dos ... Le luxe de draperie serait ici ridicule; qu'elle soit coiffée pittoresquement, d'humeur; que ses cheveux négligés et longs s'échappent de dessous son linge de tête; que ce linge soit large; qu'elle soit vêtue simplement et d'une étoffe grossière et commune; qu'elle n'ait pas de beaux tétons, bien ronds, mais de bonnes, grosses et larges mamelles, bien pleines de lait, qu'elle soit grande et robuste. Le vieillard, malgré sa souffrance, ne sera pas hideux, si j'ai bien choisi ma nature, qu'on voie à ses muscles, à toute l'habitude de son corps une constitution vigoureuse et athlétique.[34]

(This is not the painting I have in my imagination. I absolutely reject the notion of having this unfortunate old man and this benevolent woman suspect they are being observed; this suspicion impedes the action and destroys the subject. I'd have the old man in chains and the chain, fixed to the dungeon wall, binding his hands behind his back ... Luxurious drapery would be ridiculous here; she should be coiffed rather carelessly, her long, loose hair falling out from beneath her head-scarf, which would be broadly handled; she should be dressed simply, in coarse, workaday fabric; she shouldn't have beautiful, rounded breasts but heavy, large ones that are full of milk; she should be impressive and robust. The old man, despite his suffering, shouldn't be hideous, if I've construed nature correctly; we should see in his muscles, in his entire body a constitution that is vigorous, athletic.)

For Mavrakis, this passage demonstrates 'l'autorité du poète, *celle de la Littérature*' ('the authority of the poet, *of literature*': emphasis in original) more forcefully than any other in Diderot's oeuvre. The painting is condemned, 'covered up' or hidden ('recouvert') by Diderot's text, in which he is thought eagerly to express 'sa propre vision' ('his own vision'). 'La peinture a trahi l'idée' ('painting has betrayed the idea') and is therefore in need of radical modification.[35] There can be no argument that Diderot's article, like those that we have already examined, foregrounds its own textuality, this time in the form of anaphoric enumeration and accumulation (the repetition of 'que'), or that it conceals the paintings to which it refers in some way. But it is arguably not the best example of a text that substitutes its own, fully autonomous, vision for that of a painting it claims to modify. It cannot be said fully to exemplify the 'domination de la littérature sur la peinture' ('the domination of literature over painting').[36] The editors of the Hermann edition make the following observation: 'Ce passage pourrait être considéré comme une description de *Cimon de Pero* de

Rubens, aussi intitulé *Caritas romana*. Un dessin de Greuze, *La Charité romaine*, qui s'inspire de la *Caritas romana* de Rubens, a peut-être attiré l'attention de Diderot sur cette toile de Rubens.'[37] ('This passage could be viewed as a description of Rubens' *Cimon de Pero*, which is also known as *Caritas romana*. A Greuze drawing, entitled *La Charité romaine*, which was inspired by Rubens' *Caritas romana*, may have drawn Diderot's attention to Rubens' canvas.') There is the possibility that Diderot's 'rival' image is, in fact, a description of another work of art (or even of other works of art), forcing us to recognise that the 'phantom *tableau*' is little more than the ekphrasis of another painting or paintings masquerading as the writer's 'propre vision' ('own vision') – that such vision is never 'pure'.[38]

Using concepts and terms adapted from Roland Barthes,[39] Bryson asserts: '[Ekphrasis in the *Salons*] amounts to a form of sign that is "all signified" and "no signifier". . . a sign that has nothing *of itself* that might interfere with the project of transparent communication from one point (Diderot) to another (the visualising reader).'[40] But while Diderot may occasionally desire such transparency for both painting and his writing upon it, my contention is that it is never fully realised. In fact, he regularly does his best to undermine it. This is demonstrated clearly by the examples discussed above. The words on the printed page are never simply 'eliminated' in a miraculous act of readerly 'visualisation' (to use Bryson's terms).[41] In the article on Doyen cited earlier, the sentence 'Pallas aurait plané sur la tête de Diomède', which occurs (like many others) both in Diderot's modification (the phantom picture) and his description of the content of Doyen's composition, does not signify transparently: there is a blurring of the limit that divides the virtual from the actual. The apparently virtual image of Diderot's modification seems to be inflected by the 'actual' content of Doyen's painting, but it is also possible that any purportedly 'actual' content is in fact no more than a palimpsestic rewriting of the virtual merely playing the role of – disguised as – the actual. Whatever the case may be, it is clear that neither the virtual nor the actual is present in a stable or 'complete' sense and that such effects depend on the visibility – albeit a flickering one – of the signifier rather than its obliteration through visualisation.

In this essay, I have suggested that Diderot's writing on art requires a thinking of the relationship between word and image as oscillation, a coming and going, an experimentation on and manipulation of the image in or by the text, and indeed the reader, rather than its outright obliteration. Instead of treating the picture in the text in the manner of either the art-spotter or the reader who sees the painting demolished completely before his or her eyes, Diderot's work can help us to think of ekphrasis in terms of the painting's 'haunting' of the text, of shifting relations of visibility and invisibility, presence and absence, metamorphosis and instability. The painting is neither fully present nor entirely lost: it is a trace, it comes and goes, and changes shape. While there is repeatedly, and perhaps necessarily, the lure of an *hors-texte* in the form of an actual painting which seems to offer a way out (into a visibility of sorts), the art-spotting reader is usually faced with an ineluctable impasse (a nagging invisibility) within the text from which there is no definitive escape. I do not argue here for a mundane (if sometimes correct) understanding of the text as 'open', dynamic, or as the site of several (sometimes conflicting) modes of interpretation, with its mimetic function being of only minor interest. I am suggesting, rather, that Diderot plays with the very stuff of openness and closure, reference and sense, to produce descriptions that actively invite and prey upon the tendency to reach outside the text and that he does so for an exemplary purpose: fictionality is reinforced as the logocentric desire of the reader falls through the fissures of the text.

NOTES

1. Else Marie Bukdahl, *Diderot critique d'art*, 2 vols. (Copenhagen: Rosenkilde et Bagger, 1980), vol. 1, pp. 27–8.
2. Philippe Déan, *Diderot devant l'image* (Paris: Harmattan, 2000), p. 230.
3. Bukdahl, *Diderot critique d'art*, vol. 1, p. 299.
4. David Scott, *Pictorialist Poetics: Poetry and the Visual Arts in Nineteenth-Century France* (Cambridge: Cambridge University Press, 1988), p. 53.
5. Ibid.
6. Annie Mavrakis, 'Ce n'est pas de la poésie; ce n'est que de la peinture', *Poétique* 153 (February 2008), 63–81 (pp. 69–70).
7. Marian Hobson, *The Object of Art: The Theory of Illusion in Eighteenth-Century France* (Cambridge: Cambridge University Press, 1982), p. 59.
8. *Papillotage* is defined in the *Trésor de la langue française informatisé* as follows: 'impression produite par un éparpillement des points lumineux, par une multi-plication des plans, une confusion des détails, qui nuisent à l'unité d'ensemble' ('an impression produced by a scattering of luminous points, by a multiplication of spatial planes, by a confusion of details, which damages the unity of the whole'). Whether of colour or of subject, *papillotage* stimulates rapid changes of reaction – a fragmentation of the spectator's attention, a 'flickering' of illusion and awareness (see Hobson, *The Object of Art*, p. 53).
9. See Hobson, *The Object of Art*, p. 61. One of the best known of all Plato's views is that the weakness of art lies in its deceitful imitative distance from the real. Poetry – or rather 'writing' itself – is in fact presented in the *Republic* and elsewhere as even worse off than painting in this regard. For further discussion

of this Platonic hierarchy, see Jacques Derrida, 'La Pharmacie de Platon', in *La Dissémination* (Paris: Seuil, 1972), pp. 71–197. For Diderot's article on Fragonard, see Denis Diderot, *Salon de 1765*, ed. Else Marie Bukdahl and Annette Lorenceau (Paris: Hermann, 1984), pp. 253–64.

10. Hobson, *The Object of Art*, p. 61.
11. Shane Agin, 'The Development of Diderot's *Salons* and the Shifting Boundary of Representational Language', *Diderot Studies*, 30 (2007), 11–31 (p. 24).
12. Ibid.
13. Ibid.
14. Ibid., p. 25.
15. See Denis Diderot, *Ruines et paysages: Salon de 1767*, ed. Else Marie Bukdahl, Michel Delon and Annette Lorenceau (Paris: Hermann, 1995), p. 56.
16. Agin, 'The Development of Diderot's *Salons*', p. 28.
17. Ibid.
18. Diderot, *Salon de 1765*, pp. 264–5.
19. Norman Bryson, *Word and Image: French Painting of the Ancien Régime* (Cambridge: Cambridge University Press, 1981), p. 185. For more recent examples of the genre, see Stéphane Lojkine, *L'Œil révolté: les 'Salons' de Diderot* (Paris: Actes Sud, Éditions Jacqueline Chambon, 2007), and Mavrakis, 'Ce n'est pas de la poésie'.
20. Denis Diderot, *Essais sur la peinture, Salons de 1759, 1761, 1763*, ed. Gita May and Jacques Chouillet (Paris: Hermann, 1984), p. 152. (I have modernised the French versions of Greek and Roman names by adding accents as appropriate.)
21. Mavrakis, 'Ce n'est pas de la poésie', p. 69.
22. Diderot, *Salon de 1761*, pp. 152–3.
23. Ibid., p. 153.
24. Mavrakis, 'Ce n'est pas de la poésie', pp. 69–70.
25. Florence Boulerie, 'Diderot et le vocabulaire technique de l'art', *Diderot Studies*, 30 (2007), pp. 89–113 (p. 102).
26. Mavrakis, 'Ce n'est pas de la poésie', p. 69.
27. Diderot uses this expression on several occasions in the *Salons*. See, for example, the *Salon de 1761*, p. 123.
28. Anouchka Vasak, 'La Question du genre dans les *Salons*', in *Diderot, l'expérience de l'art*, ed. Geneviève Cammagre and Carole Talon-Hugon (Paris: Presses Universitaires de France, 2007), p. 24.
29. Michel Delon, 'Les *Essais sur la peinture* ou la place de la théorie', *Diderot Studies*, 30 (2007), 31–53 (p. 45).
30. For further analysis of this kind of 'superposition', see Lojkine, *L'Œil révolté*.
31. Mavrakis, 'Ce n'est pas de la poésie', p. 74.
32. Louis Marin, *Des pouvoirs de l'image* (Paris: Seuil, 1993), p. 96 (emphasis in original).
33. See Lojkine, *L'Œil révolté*, p. 135.
34. Diderot, *Salon de 1765*, pp. 90–1.
35. Mavrakis, 'Ce n'est pas de la poésie', p. 70.
36. Ibid., p. 66.

37. Diderot, *Salon de 1765*, p. 91, n. 239.
38. This strategy of 'modification' should not be confused with the procedure identified by Bernadette Fort in her invaluable essay 'Intertextuality and Iconoclasm' as 'textual iconoclasm', which consists in 'eclipsing the works on display by talking about others (by the same or another painter) that were *not* shown at the 1775 exhibition'. See her article 'Intertextuality and Iconoclasm', *Diderot Studies*, 30 (2007), 209–45 (p. 223). Diderot does not mention Rubens (or indeed Greuze) in the 1765 article on Lagrenée.
39. See Roland Barthes, *Mythologies* (Paris: Seuil, 1957), p. 187.
40. Bryson, *Word and Image*, p. 185 (emphasis in original).
41. Ibid.

Select bibliography

WORKS BY DIDEROT

Diderot, Denis, *Contes et romans*, ed. Michel Delon *et al.* (Paris: Gallimard, 2004)
Correspondance, ed. G. Roth and J. Varloot, 16 vols. (Paris: Éditions de Minuit, 1955–70)
Essais sur la peinture, Salons de 1759, 1761, 1763, ed. Gita May and Jacques Chouillet (Paris: Hermann, 1984)
Jacques the Fatalist, ed. Martin Hall, trans. Michael Henry (London: Penguin, 1986)
Lettre sur les aveugles, Lettre sur les sourds et muets, ed. M. Hobson and S. Harvey (Paris: Flammarion, 2000)
Lettres à Sophie Volland, ed. Jean Varloot (Paris: Gallimard, 1984)
The Nun, ed. and trans. Russell Goulbourne (Oxford: Oxford University Press, 2005)
Œuvres, ed. Laurent Versini, 5 vols. (Paris: Laffont, 1994–9)
Œuvres complètes, ed. Herbert Dieckmann, Jean Varloot *et al.* (Paris: Hermann, 1975–)
Œuvres complètes, ed. Roger Lewinter, 15 vols. (Paris: Le Club Français du Livre, 1969–73)
'Rameau's Nephew' and 'D'Alembert's Dream', trans. Leonard Tancock (London: Penguin, 1966)
Le Rêve de d'Alembert, ed. Colas Duflo (Paris: Garnier Flammarion, 2002)
Ruines et paysages: Salon de 1767, ed. Else Marie Bukdahl, Michel Delon and Annette Lorenceau (Paris: Hermann, 1995)
Salon de 1765, ed. Else Marie Bukdahl and Annette Lorenceau (Paris: Hermann, 1984)
and Jean le Rond d'Alembert (eds.), *Encyclopédie, ou Dictionnaire raisonné des sciences, des arts et des métiers, par une société de gens de lettres*, 17 vols. text and 11 vols. plates (Paris: Briasson/David/Le Breton/Durand, 1751–72)

OTHER PRIMARY WORKS

Alembert, Jean le Rond d', *Discours préliminaire de l'Encyclopédie*, ed. Michel Malherbe (Paris: Vrin, 2000)
Œuvres, 5 vols. (Paris: A. Belin, 1821–2)

Algarotti, Francesco, *Essai sur l'opéra*, trans. François Jean de Chastellux (Paris: Ruault, 1773)
Saggio sopra l'opera in musica (Venice: G. Pasquali, 1755; rev. Livorno: M. Coltellini, 1763)
Beaumarchais, Pierre-Augustin Caron de, *Œuvres*, ed. Pierre Larthomas and Jacqueline Larthomas (Paris: Gallimard, 1988)
Berkeley, George, *Works*, ed. A. A. Luce and T. E. Jessop, 9 vols. (London: Nelson, 1964)
Bernardin de Saint-Pierre, Jacques-Henri, *La Vie et les ouvrages de Jean-Jacques Rousseau*, ed. M. Souriau (Paris: Cornélie et Cie, 1907)
Bolts, William, *Considerations on India Affairs; Particularly Respecting the Present State of Bengal*, 3 vols. (London: J. Dodsley, etc., 1772–5)
Bougainville, Louis-Antoine de, *Voyage autour du monde par la frégate du Roi La Boudeuse et la flûte L'Étoile*, ed. Jacques Proust (Paris: Gallimard, 1982)
Buffon, Georges-Louis Leclerc, *Histoire naturelle, générale et particulière avec la description du cabinet du roy* (Paris: Imprimerie royale, 1749)
Burney, Charles, *Music, Men and Manners in France and Italy 1770* (London: Eulenberg, 1974)
The Present State of Music in France and Italy (New York: Boude Brothers, 1968)
Debussy, Claude, *Monsieur Croche* (Paris: Gallimard, 1971)
Descartes, René, *Discours de la méthode*, ed. Geneviève Rodis-Lewis (Paris: Garnier Flammarion, 1966)
'Discourse on Method' and 'The Meditations', ed. and trans. F. E. Sutcliffe (London: Penguin, 1968)
Œuvres, ed. Charles Adam and Paul Tannery, 12 vols. (Paris: Vrin, 1964–74)
Dow, Alexander, *The History of Hindostan*, 3 vols. (London: T. Becket and P. A. De Hondt, 1770–2)
Garcin, Laurent, *Traité du mélo-drame, ou Réflexions sur la musique dramatique* (Paris: Vallat-la-Chapelle, 1772)
Gouges, Olympe de, *Écrits politiques 1788–1791* (Paris: Côté-femmes, 1993)
Œuvres complètes, ed. Félix Castan (Montauban: Cocagne, 1993–)
Grimm, Frédéric-Melchior, baron de, *Correspondance littéraire, philosophique et critique*, ed. M. Tourneux, 16 vols. (Paris: Garnier, 1877–82)
Halhed, Nathaniel Brassey, *A Code of Gentoo Laws, or, Ordinations of the Pundits* (London, 1776)
Holwell, John Zephaniah, *Interesting Historical Events Relative to the Provinces of Bengal and the Empire of Indostan* (London: T. Becket and P. A. De Hondt, 1765)
Horace, *Satires, Epistles and Ars poetica*, ed. H. R. Fairclough (Cambridge, MA: Harvard University Press, 1929)
Leibniz, Gottfried Wilhelm, *Die Philosophischen Schriften*, ed. C. I. Gerhardt, 7 vols. (Berlin 1857–90; reprinted Hildesheim, 1960)
Locke, John, *An Essay Concerning Human Understanding*, ed. Peter Nidditch (Oxford: Clarendon Press, 1975)
An Essay Concerning Human Understanding, ed. Roger Woolhouse (London: Penguin, 1997)

Two Treatises of Government (Cambridge: Cambridge University Press, 1967)

Lucretius, *De rerum natura*, ed. W. H. D. Rouse and M. F. Smith (Cambridge, MA: Harvard University Press, 1982)

Montaigne, Michel de, *The Complete Works*, ed. Stuart Hampshire, trans. Donald Frame (London: Everyman, 2003)

Essais, ed. Albert Thibaudet (Paris: Gallimard, 1950)

Orme, Robert, *A History of the Military Transactions of the British Nation in Indostan* (London: J. Nourse, 1763–78)

Pascal, Blaise, *Entretien avec Sacy sur la philosophie*, ed. Richard Scholar (Arles: Actes Sud, 2003)

Pope, Alexander, *An Essay on Man and Other Poems* (New York: Dover, 1994)

Rameau, Jean-Philippe, *Complete Theoretical Writings*, ed. Erwin Jacobi, 6 vols. (n.p.: American Institute of Musicology, 1967–72)

Raynal, Guillaume, *Histoire philosophique et politique des établissemens et du commerce des Européens dans les Deux Indes* (Geneva: Jean-Leonard Pellet, 1781)

Richardson, Samuel, *Clarissa, or, The History of a Young Lady*, ed. Angus Ross, 2nd edn (London: Penguin, 2004)

Rousseau, Jean-Jacques, *Correspondance complète*, ed. R. H. Leigh, 52 vols. (Oxford: Voltaire Foundation, 1965–98)

Discours sur l'origine et les fondements de l'inégalité parmi les hommes; Discours sur les sciences et les arts, ed. Jacques Roger (Paris: Garnier Flammarion, 1971)

Œuvres complètes, ed. Bernard Gagnebin and Marcel Raymond, 5 vols. (Paris: Gallimard, 1959–95)

Shaftesbury, Anthony Ashley Cooper, Lord, *Characteristicks of Men, Manners, Opinions, Times*, 3 vols. ([London]: [printed by John Darby], 1711)

Sterne, Laurence, *The Life and Opinions of Tristram Shandy, Gentleman*, ed. Melvyn New and Joan New, introductory essay Christopher Ricks (London: Penguin, 2003)

Tristram Shandy (New York: W.W. Norton, 1980)

Virgil, *Eclogues, Georgics, Aeneid 1–6*, ed. H. R. Fairclough and G. P. Goold (Cambridge, MA: Harvard University Press, 1999)

SECONDARY WORKS

Abbate, Carolyn, *Unsung Voices: Opera and Musical Narrative in the Nineteenth Century* (Princeton, NJ: Princeton University Press, 1991)

Agin, Shane, 'The Development of Diderot's *Salons* and the Shifting Boundary of Representational Language', *Diderot Studies*, 30 (2007), 11–31.

Anderson, Wilda, *Diderot's Dream* (Baltimore, MD: Johns Hopkins University Press, 1990)

Aravamudan, Srinivas, *Tropicopolitans: Colonialism and Agency, 1688–1804* (Durham, NC: Duke University Press, 1999)

Audidière, Sophie, Jean-Claude Bourdin and Colas Duflo (eds.), *Encyclopédie du 'Rêve de D'Alembert' de Diderot* (Paris: CNRS, 2006)

Babel, Antoine, *Les Métiers dans l'ancienne Genève: histoire corporative de l'horlogerie, de l'orfèvrerie et des industries anciennes* (Geneva: A. Jullien, Georg et Cie, 1916)

Baczko, Bronislaw, *Rousseau, solitude et communauté* (Paris: Mouton, 1974)

Baker, Eric, 'Lucretius in the European Enlightenment', in S. Gillespie and P. Hardie (eds.), *The Cambridge Companion to Lucretius* (Cambridge: Cambridge University Press, 2007), pp. 274–88

Baker, Keith Michael, 'Epistémologie et politique: pourquoi l'*Encyclopédie* est-elle un dictionnaire?', in Philippe Roger and Robert Morrissey (eds.), *L'Encyclopédie: du réseau au livre et du livre au réseau* (Paris: Champion, 2001), pp. 51–8

Bardez, Jean-Michel, *Diderot et la musique: valeur de la contribution d'un mélomane* (Paris: Champion, 1975)

Barthes, Roland, *Mythologies* (Paris: Seuil, 1957)

Belaval, Yvon, 'Diderot, lecteur de Leibniz?', in *Études leibniziennes: de Leibniz à Hegel* (Paris: Aubier, 1976), pp. 244–63

'Les protagonistes du *Rêve de D'Alembert*', *Diderot Studies*, 3 (1961), 15–32

'Sur le matérialisme de Diderot', in *Europäische Aufklärung: Festschrift für Herbert Dieckmann* (Munich: Fink, 1967), pp. 9–21

Benot, Yves, *Diderot, de l'athéisme à l'anticolonialisme* (Paris: Maspero, 1970)

'Diderot, Pechmeja, Raynal et l'anticolonialisme', in Yves Benot, *Les Lumières, l'esclavage, la colonisation*, ed. Roland Desné and Marcel Dorigny (Paris: La Découverte, 2005), pp. 107–23

'Diderot, Raynal et le mot "colonie"', in Peter France and Anthony Strugnell (eds.), *Diderot. Les dernières années, 1770–1784* (Edinburgh: Edinburgh University Press, 1985), pp. 140–52

Berlin, Isaiah, 'The Counter-Enlightenment', in Henry Hardy and Roger Hausheer (eds.), *The Proper Study of Mankind* (New York: Farrar, Straus and Giroux, 2000), pp. 243–68

Blanc, Olivier, *Marie-Olympe de Gouges, une humaniste à la fin du XVIIIe siècle* (Cahors: René Viénet, 2003)

Boilleau, Anne-Marie, *Liaison et liaisons dans les lettres de Diderot à Sophie Volland* (Paris: Champion, 1999)

Boulerie, Florence, 'Diderot et le vocabulaire technique de l'art', *Diderot Studies*, 30 (2007), 89–113

Bourdin, Jean-Claude, *Diderot. Le matérialisme* (Paris: Presses Universitaires de France, 1998)

'L'Effacement de Diderot par Rousseau dans l'article *Économie politique* et le *Manuscrit de Genève*', in Franck Salaün (ed.), *Diderot–Rousseau: un entretien à distance* (Paris: Desjonquères, 2005), pp. 36–50

'Matérialisme et scepticisme chez Diderot', *Recherches sur Diderot et l'Encyclopédie*, 26 (1999), 85–97

Boury, Dominique, 'Théophile de Bordeu: source et personnage du *Rêve de D'Alembert*', *Recherches sur Diderot et sur l'Encyclopédie*, 34 (2003), 11–34

Bracken, H. M., *The Early Reception of Berkeley's Immaterialism, 1710–1733* (The Hague: Nijhoff, 1959)

Breines, Joseph, "'A Trial Against Myself": Identity and Determinism in Diderot's *Jacques le fataliste*', *The Romanic Review*, 90 (1999), 235–62

Brewer, Daniel, *Enlightenment Past: Reconstructing Eighteenth-Century French Thought* (Cambridge: Cambridge University Press, 2008)

Brown, Stuart, 'Platonic Idealism in Modern Philosophy from Malebranche to Berkeley', in G. A. Rogers, J. M. Vienne and Y. C. Zarka (eds.), *The Cambridge Platonists in Philosophical Context* (Boston: Kluwer, 1997), pp. 197–214

Bryson, Norman, *Word and Image: French Painting of the Ancien Régime* (Cambridge: Cambridge University Press, 1981)

Bukdahl, Else Marie, *Diderot critique d'art*, 2 vols. (Copenhagen: Rosenkilde and Bagger, 1980)

Casini, Paolo, 'Diderot et le portrait du philosophe éclectique', *Revue internationale de philosophie*, 148–9 (1984), 35–45

Castell, Albury, *The Self in Philosophy* (New York: Macmillan, 1965)

Charles, Sébastien, *Berkeley au siècle des Lumières: immatérialisme et scepticisme au xviiie siècle*, ed. Geneviève Brykman (Paris: Vrin, 2003)

Charlton, David, *French Opera 1730–1830: Meaning and Media* (Aldershot: Ashgate, 2000)

Chouillet, Jacques, *Denis Diderot – Sophie Volland. Un dialogue à une voix* (Paris: Champion, 1986)

Clark, Andrew H., *Diderot's Part* (Aldershot: Ashgate, 2008)

Cole, Arthur H. and George B. Watts, *The Handicrafts of France as Recorded in the 'Description des arts et métiers 1771–1788'* (Cambridge, MA: Harvard University Press, 1952)

Connon, Derek, *Innovation and Renewal: A Study of the Theatrical Works of Diderot*, SVEC 258 (Oxford: Voltaire Foundation, 1989)
  Diderot's Endgames (Oxford: Peter Lang, 2002)

Couvreur, Manuel, 'Diderot et Philidor: le philosophe au chevet d'*Ernelinde*', *Recherches sur Diderot et sur l'Encyclopédie*, 11 (October 1991), 83–107

Critchley, Simon, *The Book of Dead Philosophers* (London: Granta, 2008)

Cronk, Nicholas (ed.), *Études sur 'Le Fils naturel' et les 'Entretiens sur Le Fils naturel'* (Oxford: Voltaire Foundation, 2000)

Curran, Andrew, 'Monsters and the Self in the *Rêve de D'Alembert*', *Eighteenth-Century Life*, 21.2 (1997), 48–69
  Sublime Disorder: Physical Monstrosity in Diderot's Universe, SVEC 2001:01 (Oxford: Voltaire Foundation, 2001)

Daniel, Stephen H., 'Berkeley's Pantheistic Discourse', *International Journal for Philosophy of Religion*, 49.3 (2001), 179–94

Déan, Philippe, *Diderot devant l'image* (Paris: Harmattan, 2000)

Deleuze, Gilles, *Kafka. Pour une littérature mineure* (Paris: Minuit, 1975)

Delon, Michel, 'Les *Essais sur la peinture* ou la place de la théorie', *Diderot Studies*, 30 (2007), 31–53

Démoris, René, 'Condillac et la peinture', in Jean Sgard (ed.), *Condillac et les problèmes du langage* (Slatkine, 1982), pp. 379–93

Deneys-Tunney, Anne, 'La Critique de la métaphysique dans *Les Bijoux indiscrets et Jacques le fataliste* de Diderot', *Recherches sur Diderot et sur l'Encyclopédie*, 26 (April 1999), pp. 141–51

Écritures du corps, de Descartes à Laclos (Paris: Presses Universitaires de France, 1992)

Deprun, Jean, 'Diderot devant l'idéalisme', *Revue internationale de philosophie*, 38 (1984), 67–78

Derrida, Jacques, *La Carte postale* (Paris: Flammarion, 1980)

De la grammatologie (Paris: Minuit, 1967)

La Dissémination (Paris: Seuil, 1972)

Of Grammatology, trans. Gayatri Chakravorty Spivak (Baltimore, MD: Johns Hopkins University Press, 1976)

Signéponge/Signsponge, trans. Richard Rand (New York: Columbia University Press, 1984)

Didier, Béatrice, *Diderot, dramaturge du vivant* (Paris: Presses Universitaires de France, 2001)

La Musique des Lumières: Diderot, l'Encyclopédie, Rousseau (Paris: Presses Universitaires de France, 1985)

'Nouvelles recherches sur la musique dans *Le Neveu de Rameau*', *Recherches sur Diderot et sur l'Encyclopédie*, 20 (1996), 57–74

Dieckmann, Herbert, 'Die Künstlerische Form des *Rêve de D'Alembert*', *Arbeitsgemeinschaft für Forschung des Landes Nordrhein-Westfalen*, 127 (1966)

'The *Préface-Annexe* of *La Religieuse*', *Diderot Studies*, 2 (1952), 21–40

Dolar, Mladen, *A Voice and Nothing More* (Cambridge, MA: MIT Press, 2006)

Duchet, Michèle, *Diderot et l'Histoire des deux Indes ou l'Écriture fragmentaire* (Paris: Nizet, 1978)

Duflo, Colas, 'Diderot et Ménuret de Chambaud', *Recherches sur Diderot et sur l'Encyclopédie*, 34 (2003), 25–44

Diderot philosophe (Paris: Champion, 2003)

Dziedzic, Andrzej, 'Liberté, propriété et sexualité dans le *Supplément au voyage de Bougainville*', *Chimères: A Journal of French Literature*, 25.2 (Spring 2001), 45–53

Eaves, T., C. Duncan and Ben D. Kimpel, *Samuel Richardson: A Biography* (Oxford: Clarendon Press, 1971)

Erickson, Lars O., 'Reflection and Projection: Diderot's Theatrical Father' (Unpublished Master's Thesis, University of North Carolina, 1997)

Evans, Michael, *Opera from the Greek: Studies in the Poetics of Appropriation* (Aldershot: Ashgate, 2007)

Fabre, Jean, 'Deux frères ennemis: Diderot et Jean-Jacques', *Diderot Studies*, 3 (1961), 155–213

Fauvergue, Claire, *Diderot, lecteur et interprète de Leibniz* (Paris: Champion, 2006)

Festa, Lynn, 'Life, Liberty, and the Pursuit of Tahitian *Jouissance*', *Romance Quarterly*, 54.4 (2007), 303–25

Feugère, Anatole, *Bibliographie critique de l'abbé Raynal* (Geneva: Slatkine Reprints, 1970)

Fontenay, Élisabeth de, *Diderot ou le matérialisme enchanté* (Paris: Grasset, 1981)

Fort, Bernadette, 'Intertextuality and Iconoclasm', *Diderot Studies*, 30 (2007), 209–45

Foucault, Michel, *Histoire de la sexualité*, vol. 1: *La Volonté de savoir* (Paris: Gallimard, 1976)

Fourny, Diane, 'Ethics and Otherness: An Exploration of Diderot's *conte moral*', *Studies in Eighteenth-Century Culture*, 27 (1998), 283–306

Fowler, James, *Voicing Desire: Family and Sexuality in Diderot's Narrative* (Oxford: Voltaire Foundation, 2000)

France, Peter (ed.), *The New Oxford Companion to Literature in French* (Oxford: Clarendon Press, 1995)

Fredman, Alice Green, *Diderot and Sterne* (New York: Columbia University Press, 1955)

Fremont, Christine, 'Les Contes de la culpabilité', *Stanford French Review*, 12.2–3 (Fall 1998), 245–64

Garrard, Graeme, *Rousseau's Counter-Enlightenment* (Albany: State University of New York Press, 2003)

Garraway, Doris L., 'Nation, Colony, and Enlightenment Universality', in Lynn Festa and Daniel Carey (eds.), *The Postcolonial Enlightenment* (Oxford: Oxford University Press, 2009), pp. 207–39

Genette, Gérard, *Narrative Discourse*, trans. Jane E. Lewin (Ithaca, NY: Cornell University Press, 1980)

Gigandet, Alain, 'Lucrèce vu en songe: Diderot, *Le Rêve de d'Alembert* et le *De rerum natura*', *Revue de métaphysique et de morale*, 3 (2002), 427–39

Gille, Bertrand, 'L'Encyclopédie, dictionnaire technique', in Suzanne Delorme and René Tatou (eds.), *L'"Encyclopédie" et le progrès des sciences et des techniques* (Paris: Presses Universitaires de France, 1952)

Goldberg, Rita, *Sex and Enlightenment: Women in Richardson and Diderot* (Cambridge: Cambridge University Press, 1984)

Goulbourne, Russell, 'Appropriating Horace in Eighteenth-Century France', in L. B. T. Houghton and M. Wyke (eds.), *Perceptions of Horace: A Roman Poet and his Readers* (Cambridge: Cambridge University Press, 2009), pp. 256–70

'Diderot et Horace, ou le paradoxe du théâtre moderne', in N. Cronk (ed.), *Études sur 'Le Fils naturel' et les 'Entretiens sur le Fils naturel' de Diderot* (Oxford: Voltaire Foundation, 2000), pp. 112–22

'Voltaire's Socrates', in M. Trapp (ed.), *Images and Uses of Socrates from Antiquity to the Present* (Aldershot: Ashgate, 2007), pp. 229–47

Gray, John, *Enlightenment's Wake: Politics and Culture at the Close of the Modern Age* (London: Routledge, 1995)

Green, Jeffrey E., 'Two Meanings of Disenchantment', *Philosophy and Theology*, 17.1–2 (2006), 51–84

Greenhalgh, Paul, 'The Progress of Captain Ludd', in Peter Dormer (ed.), *The Culture of Craft* (Manchester: Manchester University Press, 1997), pp. 104–15.

Grell, Chantal, *Le Dix-Huitième Siècle et l'antiquité en France, 1680–1789*, SVEC 330–1 (Oxford: Voltaire Foundation, 1995)

Habermas, Jürgen, *The Structural Transformation of the Public Sphere*, trans. Thomas Bürger (Cambridge: Polity Press, 1989)

Hahn, Roger, *The Anatomy of a Scientific Institution: The Paris Academy of Science, 1666–1803* (Berkeley: University of California Press, 1971)

Heartz, Daniel, 'Diderot et le théâtre lyrique: "le nouveau stile" proposé par *Le Neveu de Rameau*', *Revue de musicologie*, 64.2 (1978), 229–52

Heidegger, Martin, *Discourse on Thinking*, trans. John W. Anderson and E. Hans Freund (London: Harper and Row, 1966)

Hobson, Marian, 'Déictique, dialectique dans *Le Neveu de Rameau*', in Georges Benrekassa, Marc Buffat and Pierre Chartier (eds.), *Études sur Le Neveu de Rameau et Le Paradoxe sur le comédien de Denis Diderot. Actes du Colloque organisé à l'Université Paris VII les 15 et 16 novembre 1991, Cahiers Textuel*, 11 (1992), 11–19

The Object of Art: The Theory of Illusion in Eighteenth-Century France (Cambridge: Cambridge University Press, 1982)

Howard, Patricia, *C.W. von Gluck, 'Orfeo'* (Cambridge: Cambridge University Press, 1981)

Ibrahim, Annie, 'Maupertuis dans Le *Rêve de D'Alembert*: l'essaim d'abeilles et le polype', *Recherches sur Diderot et sur l'Encyclopédie*, 34 (2003), 72–83

Irailh, Simon-Augustin, abbé, *Querelles littéraires: ou Mémoires pour servir à l'histoire des révolutions de la république des lettres, d'Homère à nos jours*, 4 vols. (Paris: Durand, 1761)

Jacob, Margaret C., *The Radical Enlightenment: Pantheists, Freemasons and Republicans* (London: George Allen and Unwin, 1981)

Jamain, Claude, *L'Imaginaire de la musique au siècle des Lumières* (Paris: Champion, 2001)

Kenny, Neil, *Curiosity in Early Modern Europe: Word Histories* (Wiesbaden: Harrassowitz, 1998)

Keymer, Thomas, *Richardson's 'Clarissa' and the Eighteenth-Century Reader* (Cambridge: Cambridge University Press, 2004)

Lang, Paul Henry, 'Diderot as Musician', *Diderot Studies*, 10 (1968), 95–107

Leigh, R. A., 'Les Amitiés françaises du Dr Burney', *Revue de littérature comparée*, April–June 1951, 162–71

Little, Lester K. and Barbara H. Rosenwein, 'Social Meaning in the Monastic and Mendicant Spiritualities', *Past and Present*, 63 (1974), 4–32

Lojkine, Stéphane, *L'Œil révolté: les 'Salons' de Diderot* (Paris: Actes Sud, Éditions Jacqueline Chambon, 2007)

Loomis, Ana, *Colonialism/Postcolonialism* (London: Routledge, 1998)

Lough, John, *The Encyclopédie* (London: Longman, 1971)

Loy, Robert J., *Diderot's Determined Fatalist* (New York: King's Crown Press, 1950)

McGrath, Alister E. (ed.), *The Blackwell Encyclopedia of Modern Christian Thought*, 6th edn (Oxford: Blackwell, 2000)

McMahon, Darrin, *Enemies of Enlightenment* (Oxford: Oxford University Press, 2001)

Mall, Laurence, 'Une autobiolecture: l'*Essai sur les règnes de Claude et de Néron* de Diderot', *Diderot Studies*, 28 (2000), 111–22

'Une œuvre critique: l'*Essai sur les règnes de Claude et de Néron* de Diderot', *Revue d'histoire littéraire de la France*, 106 (2006), 843–57

'Sénèque et Diderot, sujets à caution dans l'*Essai sur les règnes de Claude et de Néron*', *Recherches sur Diderot et sur l'Encyclopédie*, 36 (2004), 43–56

Marchal, France, *La Culture de Diderot* (Paris: Champion, 1999)

Marin, Louis, *Des pouvoirs de l'image* (Paris: Seuil, 1993)

Markovits, Francine, 'L'Antimachiavel-médecin', *Corpus, revue de philosophie*, 31 (1997), pp. 207–36

Marquet, Jean-François, 'La Monadologie de Diderot', *Revue philosophique de la France et de l'étranger*, 3 (1984), 353–70

Matthey-Jeantet, A., *L'Écriture de Jean-Jacques Rousseau (sa pasigraphie, ses abréviations)* (Le Locle: Courvoisier, 1912)

Mavrakis, Annie, 'Ce n'est pas de la poésie; ce n'est que de la peinture', *Poétique*, 153 (February 2008), 63–81

May, Georges, *Diderot et 'La Religieuse': étude historique et littéraire* (Paris: Presses Universitaires de France, 1954)

'Le maître, la chaîne et le chien dans *Jacques le fataliste*', *Cahiers de l'association internationale des études françaises*, 13 (June 1961), 269–82

Quatre visages de Denis Diderot (Paris: Boivin, 1951)

Melançon, Benoît, *Diderot épistolier. Contribution à une poétique de la lettre familière au XVIIIe siècle* (Quebec: Fidès, 1996)

Moreau, Isabelle, 'L'Araignée dans sa toile. Mise en images de l'âme du monde de François Bernier et Pierre Bayle à l'*Encyclopédie*', in Isabelle Moreau (ed.), *Les Lumières en mouvement: la circulation des idées au XVIIIe siècle* (Lyon: École Normale Supérieure, 2009), pp. 199–228

Morrissey, Robert and Philippe Roger (eds.), *L'Encyclopédie: du réseau au livre et du livre au réseau* (Paris: Champion, 2001)

Mortier, Roland, 'À propos du sentiment de l'existence chez Diderot et Rousseau', *Diderot Studies*, 6 (1964), 183–95

Moscovici, Claudia, *From Sex Objects to Sexual Subjects* (London: Routledge, 1996)

Moureaux, José-Michel, 'Un épisode inconnu de la querelle Voltaire–Needham', *SVEC*, 5 (2000), 29–45

Neubauer, John, *The Emancipation of Music from Language: Departure from Mimesis in Eighteenth-Century Aesthetics* (New Haven, CT: Yale University Press, 1986)

Niehues-Pröbsting, Heinrich, 'The Modern Reception of Cynicism: Diogenes in the Enlightenment', in R. B. Branham and Marie-Odile Goulet-Cazé (eds.), *The Cynics: The Cynic Movement in Antiquity and its Legacy* (Berkeley: University of California Press, 1996), pp. 329–65

Niklaus, Robert, 'Diderot and the *Leçons de clavecin*', in *Modern Miscellany presented to Eugène Vinaver by Pupils, Colleagues and Friends* (Manchester: Manchester University Press, 1969), pp. 180–94

'Les *Pensées philosophiques* de Diderot et les *Pensées* de Pascal', *Diderot Studies*, 20 (1981), 201–17

Padgen, Anthony, 'The Savage Critic: Some European Images of the Primitive', *Yearbook of English Studies*, 13 (1983), 32–45

Patey, Douglas Lane, 'Johnson's Refutation of Berkeley: Kicking the Stone Again', *Journal of the History of Ideas*, 47. 1 (1986), 139–45

Pérol, Lucette, 'Diderot, les tragiques grecs et le père Brumoy', *SVEC*, 154 (1976), 1593–1616

Pinker, Aaron, 'A Goat to Go to Azazel', *Journal of Hebrew Scriptures*, 7.8 (2007), 1–25

Proust, Jacques, *Diderot et l'Encyclopédie* (Paris: Colin, 1962)

Quintili, Paolo, 'Les Matérialistes anciens chez Diderot', in M. Benítez *et al.* (eds.), *Materia actuosa: Antiquité, âge classique, lumières. Mélanges en l'honneur d'Olivier Bloch* (Paris: Champion, 2000), pp. 487–512

Rahe, Paul A., 'The Political Needs of a Tool-Making Animal: Madison, Hamilton, Locke, and the Question of Property', *Social Philosophy and Policy*, 22.1 (January 2005), 1–26

Ranum, Orest, 'Les Refuges de l'intimité', in *Histoire de la vie privée*, in Philippe Ariès and Georges Duby (eds.), 5 vols. (Paris: Seuil, 1999), vol. III, pp. 225–8.

Rebejkow, Jean-Christophe, 'Diderot et l'opéra comique: de la farce au pathétique', *Romanische Forschungen*, 107 (1995), 145–56

Richard-Pauchet, Odile, *Diderot dans les 'Lettres à Sophie Volland'. Une esthétique épistolaire* (Paris: Champion, 2007)

  'Sophie Volland et Denis Diderot dans les *Lettres à Sophie Volland* (1759–1774): une amitié particulière', *Recherches sur Diderot et sur l'Encyclopédie*, 39 (2005), 20–1

Roe, Shirley, 'Metaphysics and Materialism: Needham's Response to d'Holbach', *SVEC*, 284 (1991), 309–42

Roger, Jacques, *Les Sciences de la vie dans la pensée française au XVIIIe siècle* (Paris: Vrin, 1963)

Rykner, Arnaud, *L'Envers du théâtre: dramaturgie du silence, de l'âge classique à Maeterlinck* (Paris: Corti, 1996)

Said, Edward W., *Culture and Imperialism* (London: Vintage, 1994)

  Orientalism (London: Routledge, 1978)

Sartre, Jean-Paul, *Being and Nothingness*, trans. Hazel E. Barnes (New York: Philosophical Library, 1970)

Schmidt, Johan W., 'Diderot and Lucretius: The *De rerum natura* and Lucretius's Legacy in Diderot's Scientific, Aesthetic, and Ethical Thought', *SVEC*, 208 (1982), 183–294

Scholar, Richard, 'La Force de l'imagination de Montaigne: Camus, Malebranche, Pascal', *Littératures classiques*, 45 (2002), 127–38

Scott, David, *Pictorialist Poetics: Poetry and the Visual Arts in Nineteenth-Century France* (Cambridge: Cambridge University Press, 1988)

Sennett, Richard, *The Craftsman* (London: Allen Lane, 2008)

Seznec, Jean, *Essais sur Diderot et l'Antiquité* (Oxford: Clarendon Press, 1957)

Sherman, Carol L., *The Family Crucible in Eighteenth-Century Literature* (Aldershot: Ashgate, 2005)

Silver, Bruce, 'Boswell on Johnson's Refutation of Berkeley: Revisiting the Stone', *Journal of the History of Ideas*, 54. 3 (1993), 437–48

Singh, Christine M., 'The *Lettre sur les aveugles*: Its Debt to Lucretius', in J. H. Fox *et al.* (eds.), *Studies in Eighteenth-Century French Literature Presented to Robert Niklaus* (Exeter: University of Exeter Press, 1975), pp. 233–42

Smith, Ian H., '*Le Rêve de d'Alembert* and *De rerum natura*', *Journal of the Australasian Universities Language and Literature Association*, 10 (1959), 128–34

Sollers, Philippe, *Le Cœur absolu* (Paris: Gallimard, 1987)

Starobinski, Jean, 'Diogène dans *Le Neveu de Rameau*', *Stanford French Review*, 8 (1984), 147–65

'L'Incipit du *Neveu de Rameau*', *Nouvelle Revue Française*, 347 (1981), 42–64

'Le Philosophe, le géomètre, l'hybride', *Poétique*, 21 (1975), 8–23

Strugnell, Anthony, 'Mixed Messages: Orientalism and Empire in the Early British Histories of India and their Reception in France', in Hans-Jürgen Lüsebrink (ed.), *Das Europa der Aufklärung, und die außereuropäische koloniale Welt* (Göttingen: Wallstein, 2006), pp. 287–301

Taieb, Nassim Nicholas, *The Black Swan: The Impact of the Highly Improbable* (New York: Random House, 2007)

Thomas, Downing, *Aesthetics of Opera in the Ancien Régime, 1647–1785* (Cambridge: Cambridge University Press, 2002)

Thomson, Ann, 'Diderot, Roubaud, l'Esclavage', *Recherches sur Diderot et sur l'Encyclopédie*, 35 (2003), 69–93

Tilly, Charles, *Contention and Democracy in Europe, 1650–2000* (Cambridge: Cambridge University Press, 2004)

Tonneau, Olivier, '"Ah! Si vous pouviez lire au fond de mon coeur. . .": Diderot et le mythe de l'intériorité', *SVEC*, 12 (2006), 291–8

Trousson, Raymond, *Diderot* (Paris: Gallimard, 2007)

'Diderot et Homère', *Diderot Studies*, 8 (1966), 185–216

'Diderot helléniste', *Diderot Studies*, 12 (1969), 141–326

'Diderot et la leçon du théâtre antique', in Anne-Marie Chouillet (ed.), *Colloque international Diderot (1713–1784): Paris, Sèvres, Reims, Langres, 4–11 juillet 1984* (Paris: Aux Amateurs de livres, 1985), pp. 479–92

'Diderot et l'antiquité grecque', *Diderot Studies*, 6 (1964), 215–45

'Diderot et Térence', in *Mélanges à la mémoire de Franco Simone*, 4 vols. (Geneva: Slatkine, 1980–83), vol. IV, pp. 351–63

Socrate devant Voltaire, Diderot et Rousseau: la conscience en face du mythe (Paris: Minard, 1967)

Tunstall, Kate E., 'Pré-histoire d'un emblème des Lumières: l'aveugle-né de Montaigne à Diderot', in Isabelle Moreau (ed.), *Les Lumières en mouvement: la circulation des idées au XVIIIe siècle* (Lyon: École Normale Supérieure, 2009), pp. 173–97

Undank, Jack, *Diderot: Inside, Outside and In-Between* (Madison, WI: Coda, 1979)

Vaillé, E., *Histoire générale des postes francaises*, 7 vols. (Paris: Presses Universitaires de France, 1953)

Van den Abbeele, Georges, 'Utopian Sexuality and its Discontents: Exoticism and Colonialism in the *Supplément au voyage de Bougainville*', *L'Esprit créateur*, 24.1 (Spring 1984), 43–52

Varloot, Jean, 'Le projet "antique" du *Rêve de d'Alembert*', *Beiträge zur romanischen Philologie*, 2 (1963), 49–61

Vasak, Anouchka, 'La Question du genre dans les *Salons*', in Geneviève Cammagre and Carole Talon-Hugon (eds.), *Diderot, l'expérience de l'art* (Paris: Presses Universitaires de France, 2007)

Venturi, Franco, *Jeunesse de Diderot, 1713–1753* (Paris: Skira, 1939)

Waeber, Jacqueline, *En musique dans le texte: le mélodrame, de Rousseau à Schoenberg* (Paris: Van Dieren, 2005)

Wartofsky, Max W., 'Diderot and the Development of Materialist Monism', *Diderot Studies*, 2 (1952), 279–329

Werner, Stephen, 'Comédie et philosophie: le style du *Rêve de D'Alembert*', *Recherches sur Diderot et sur l'Encyclopédie*, 22 (April 1997), 7–23

Wilson, Arthur M., *Diderot* (New York: Oxford University Press, 1972)

Index